TOASTER'S HANDBOOK

JOKES, STORIES, AND QUOTATIONS

TOASTER'S HANDBOOK

JOKES, STORIES, AND QUOTATIONS

Compiled by
PEGGY EDMUND
and
HAROLD WORKMAN WILLIAMS

Introductions by
MARY KATHERINE REELY

THIRD EDITION
REVISED, WITH NEW MATERIAL

NEW YORK
THE H. W. WILSON COMPANY
1938

Republished by Omnigraphics • Penobscot Building • Detroit • 1998

Library of Congress Cataloging-in-Publication Data

Toaster's handbook : jokes, stories, and quotations / compiled by Peggy
Edmund and Harold Workman Williams : introd. by Mary Katherine
Reely.—3rd ed., rev. with new material.
    p. cm.
Originally published: New York : H. W. Wilson, 1938.
ISBN 0-7808-0270-5 (lib. bdg. : alk. paper)
    1. American wit and humor. 2. Toasts. 3. Quotations, English. I. Edmund,
Peggy. II. Williams, Harold Workman.
PN6161.F2 1997   97-14599
082--dc21   CIP

This book is printed on acid-free paper meeting the ANSI Z39.48
Standard. The infinity symbol that appears above indicates that the paper in
this book meets that standard.

Printed in the United States of America

PREFACE

Nothing so frightens a man as the announcement that he is expected to respond to a toast on some appallingly near-by occasion. All ideas he may ever have had on the subject melt away and like a drowning man he clutches furiously at the nearest solid object. This book is intended for such rescue purpose, buoyant and trustworthy but, it is to be hoped, not heavy.

Let the frightened toaster turn first to the key word of his topic in this dictionary alphabet of selections and perchance he may find toast, story, definition or verse that may felicitously introduce his remarks. Then as he proceeds to outline his talk and to put it into sentences, he may find under one of the many subject headings a bit which will happily and scintillatingly drive home the ideas he is unfolding.

While the larger part of the contents is humorous, there are inserted many quotations of a serious nature which may serve as appropriate literary ballast.

The jokes and quotes gathered for the toaster have been placed under the subject headings where it seemed that they might be most useful, even at the risk of the joke turning on the compilers. To extend the usefulness of such pseudo-cataloging, cross references, similar and dissimilar to those of a library card catalog, have been included.

Should a large number of the inclusions look familiar, let us remark that the friends one likes best are those who have been already tried and trusted and are the most welcome in times of need. However, there are stories of a rising generation, whose acquaintance all may enjoy.

Nearly all these new and old friends have before this made their bow in print and since it rarely was certain where they first appeared, little attempt has been made to credit any source for them. The compilers hereby make a sweeping acknowledgment to the "funny editors" of many books and periodicals.

ON THE POSSESSION OF A SENSE
OF HUMOR

"Man," says Hazlitt, "is the only animal that laughs and weeps, for he is the only animal that is struck with the difference between what things are and what they ought to be." The sources, then, of laughter and tears come very close together. At the difference between things as they are and as they ought to be we laugh, or we weep; it would depend, it seems, on the point of view, or the temperament. And if, as Horace Walpole once said, "Life is a comedy to those who think, a tragedy to those who feel," it is the thinking half of humanity that, at the sight of life's incongruities, is moved to laughter, the feeling half to tears. A sense of humor, then, is the possession of the thinking half, and the humorists must be classified at once with the thinkers.

If one were asked to go further than this and to give offhand a definition of humor, or of that elusive quality, a sense of humor, he might find himself confronted with a difficulty. Yet certain things about it would be patent at the outset: Women haven't it; Englishmen haven't it; it is the chiefest of the virtues, for tho a man speak with the tongues of men and of angels, if he have not humor we will have none of him. Women may continue to laugh over those innocent and innocuous incidents which they find amusing; may continue to write the most delightful of stories and essays—consider Jane Austen and our own Miss Repplier—over which appreciative readers may continue to chuckle; Englishmen may continue, as in the past to produce the most exquisite of the world's humorous literature—think of Charles Lamb—yet the fundamental faith of mankind will remain unshaken: women have no sense of humor, and an Englishman cannot see a joke! And the ability to "see a joke" is the infallible American test of the sense of humor.

But taking the matter seriously, how would one define humor? When in doubt, consult the dictionary, is, as always, an excellent motto, and, following it, we find that our trustworthy friend, Noah Webster, does not fail us. Here is his definition of humor, ready to hand: humor is "the mental faculty of discovering, expressing, or appreciating ludicrous or absurdly incongruous elements in ideas, situations, happenings, or acts," with the added information that it is distinguished from wit as "less purely intellectual and having more kindly sympathy with human nature, and as often blended with pathos." A friendly rival in lexicography defines the same prized human attribute more lightly as "a facetious turn of thought," or more specifically in literature, as "a sportive exercise of the imagination that is apparent in the choice and treatment of an idea or theme." Isn't there something about that word "sportive," on the lips of so learned an authority, that tickles the fancy—appeals to the sense of humor?

Yet if we peruse the dictionary further, especially if we approach that monument to English scholarship, the great Murray, we shall find that the problem of defining humor is not so simple as it might seem; for the word that we use so glibly, with so sure a confidence in its stability, has had a long and varied history and has answered to many aliases. When Shakespeare called a man "humorous" he meant that he was changeable and capricious, not that he was given to a facetious turn of thought or to a "sportive" exercise of the imagination. When he talks in "The Taming of the Shrew" of "her mad and headstrong humor" he doesn't mean to imply that Kate is a practical joker. It is interesting to note in passing that the old meaning of the word still lingers in the verb "to humor." A woman still humors her spoiled child and her cantankerous husband when she yields to their capriciousness. By going back a step further in history, to the late fourteenth century, we met Chaucer's physician who knew "the cause of everye maladye, and where engendered and of what humour" and find that Chaucer is not speaking of a mental state at all, but is referring to those physiological humours of which, according to Hippocrates, the human body contained four: blood, phlegm, bile, and black bile, and by which the disposition was determined. We find, too, that at one time a "humour" meant any animal or plant fluid, and again *any* kind of moisture. "The skie hangs full of humour, and I think we shall haue raine," ran an ancient weather prophet's prediction. Which might give rise to some thoughts on the paradoxical subject of *dry* humor.

Now in part this development is easily traced. Humor, meaning moisture of any kind, came to have a biological significance and was applied only to plant and animal life. It was restricted later within purely physiological boundaries and was applied only to those "humours" of the human body that controlled temperament. From these fluids, determining mental states, the word took on a psychological coloring, but—by what process of evolution did humor reach its present status! After all, the scientific method has its weaknesses!

We can, if we wish, define humor in terms of what it is not. We can draw lines around it and distinguish it from its next of kin, wit. This indeed has been a favorite pastime with the jugglers of words in all ages. And many have been the attempts to define humor, to define wit, to describe and differentiate them, to build high fences to keep them apart.

"Wit is abrupt, darting, scornful; it tosses its analogies in your face; humor is slow and shy, insinuating its fun into your heart," says E. P. Whipple. "Wit is intellectual, humor is emotional; wit is perception of resemblance, humor of contrast— of contrast between ideal and fact, theory and practice, promise and performance," writes another authority. While yet another points out that "Humor is feeling—feelings can always bear repetition, while wit, being intellectual, suffers by repetition." The truth of this is evident when we remember that we repeat a witty saying that we may enjoy the effect on others, while we retell a humorous story largely for our own enjoyment of it.

Yet it is quite possible that humor ought not to be defined. It may be one of those intangible substances, like love and beauty, that are indefinable. It is quite probable that humor should not be explained. It would be distressing, as some one pointed out, to discover that American humor is based on American dyspepsia. Yet the philosophers themselves have endeavored to explain it. Hazlitt held that to understand the ludicrous, we must first know what the serious is. And to apprehend the serious, what better course could be followed than to contemplate the serious—yes and ludicrous—findings of the philosophers in their attempts to define humor and to explain laughter. Consider Hobbes: "The passion of laughter is nothing else but sudden glory arising from the sudden conception of eminency in ourselves by comparison with the inferiority of others, or with our own formerly." According to Professor Bain, "Laughter results from the degradation of some person or interest possessing dignity in circumstances that excite no other strong emotion." Even Kant, desisting for a time from his contemplation of Pure Reason, gave his attention to the human phenomenon of laughter and explained it away as "the result of an expectation which of a sudden ends in nothing." Some modern cynic has compiled a list of the situations on the stage which are always "humorous." One of them, I recall, is the situation in which the clown-acrobat, having made mighty preparations for jumping over a pile of chairs, suddenly changes his mind and walks off without attempting it. The laughter that invariably greets this "funny" maneuver would seem to have philosophical sanction. Bergson, too, the philosopher of creative evolution, has considered laughter to the extent of an entire volume. A reading of it leaves one a little disturbed. Laughter, so we learn, is not the merry-hearted, jovial companion we had thought him. Laughter is a stern mentor, characterized by "an absence of feeling." "Laughter," says M. Bergson, "is above all a corrective, it must make a painful impression on the person against whom it is directed. By laughter society avenges itself for the liberties taken with it. It would fail in its object if it bore the stamp of sympathy or kindness." If this be laughter, grant us occasionally the saving grace of tears, which may be tears of sympathy, and, therefore, kind!

But, after all, since it is true that "one touch of humor makes the whole world grin," what difference does it make what that humor is; what difference why or wherefore we laugh, since somehow or other, in a sorry world, we do laugh?

Of the test for a sense of humor, it has already been said that it is the ability to see a joke. And, as for a joke, the dictionary, again a present help in time of trouble, tells us at once that it is, "something said or done for the purpose of exciting a laugh." But stay! Suppose it does not excite the laugh expected? What of the joke that misses fire? Shall a joke he judged by its intent or by its consequences? Is a joke that does not produce a laugh a joke at all? Pragmatically considered it is not. Agnes Repplier, writing on Humor, speaks of "those beloved writers whom we hold to be humorists because they have made us laugh." We hold them to be so—but there seems to be a suggestion that we may be wrong. Is it possible that the laugh is not the test of the joke? Here is a question over which the philosophers may wrangle. Is there an Absolute in the realm of humor, or must our jokes be judged solely by the pragmatic test? Congreve once told Colly Cibber that there were many witty speeches in one of Colly's plays, and many that looked witty, yet were not really what they seemed at first sight! So a joke is not to be recognized even by its appearance or by the company it keeps. Perhaps there might be established a test of good usage. A joke would be that at which the best people laugh.

Somebody—was it Mark Twain?—once said that there are eleven original jokes in the world—that these were known in prehistoric times, and that all jokes since have been but modifications and adaptations from the originals. Miss Repplier, however, gives to modern times the credit for some inventiveness. Christianity, she says, must be thanked for such contributions as the missionary and cannibal joke, and for the interminable variations of St. Peter at the gate. Max Beerbohm once codified all the English comic papers and found that the following list comprised all the subjects discussed: Mothers-in-law; Hen-pecked husbands; Twins; Old maids; Jews; Frenchmen and Germans; Italians and Niggers; Fatness; Thinness; Long hair (in men); Baldness; Sea sickness; Stuttering; Bloomers; Bad cheese; Red noses. A like examination of American newspapers would perhaps result in a slightly different list. We have, of course, our purely local jokes. Boston will always be a joke to Chicago, the east to the west. The city girl in the country offers a perennial source of amusement, as does the country man in the city. And the foreigner we have always with us, to mix his Y's and J's, distort his H's, and play havoc with the Anglo-Saxon Th. Indeed our great American sense of humor has been explained as an outgrowth from the vast field of incongruities offered by a developing civilization.

It may be that this vaunted national sense has been over-estimated—exaggeration is a characteristic of that humor, anyway—but at least it has one of the Christian virtues—it suffereth long and is kind. Miss Repplier says that it is because we are a "humorous rather than a witty people that we laugh for the most part with, and not at our fellow creatures." This, I think, is something that our fellow creatures from other lands do not always comprehend. I listened once to. a distinguished Frenchman as he addressed the students in a western university chapel. He was evidently astounded and embarrassed by the outbursts of laughter that greeted his mildly humorous remarks. He even stopped to apologize for the deficiencies of his English, deeming them the cause, and was further mystified by the little ripple of laughter that met his explanation—a ripple that came from the hearts of the good-natured students, who meant only to be appreciative and kind. Foreigners, too, unacquainted with American slang often find themselves precipitating a laugh for which they are unprepared. For a bit of current slang, however and whenever used, is always humorous.

The American is not only a humorous person, he is a practical person. So it is only natural that the American humor should be put to practical uses. It was once said that the difference between a man with tact and a man without was that the man with tact, in trying to put a bit in a horse's mouth, would first tell him a funny story, while the man without tact would get an axe. This use of the funny story is the American way of adapting it to practical ends. A collection of funny stories used to be an important part of a drummer's stock in trade. It is by means of the "good story" that the politician makes his way into office; the business man paves the way for a big deal; the after-dinner speaker gets a hearing; the hostess saves her guests from boredom. Such a large place does the "story" hold in our national life that we have invented a social pastime that might be termed a "joke match." "Don't tell a funny story, even if you know one," was the advice of the *Atchison Globe* man, "its narration will only remind your hearers of a bad one." True as this may be, we still persist in telling our funny story. Our hearers are reminded of another, good or bad, which again reminds us—and so on.

A sense of humor, as was intimated before, is the chiefest of the virtues. It is more than this—it is one of the essentials to success. For, as has also been pointed out, we, being a practical people, put our humor to practical uses. It is held up as one of the prerequisites for entrance to any profession. "A lawyer," says a member of that order, must have such and such mental and moral qualities; "but before all else"—and this impressively—"he must possess a sense of humor." Samuel McChord Crothers says that were he on the examining board for the granting of certificates to prospective teachers, he would place a copy of Lamb's *Essay on Schoolmasters* in the hands of each, and if the light of humorous appreciation failed to dawn as the reading progressed, the certificate would be withheld. For, before all else, a teacher must possess a sense of humor! If it be true, then, that the sense of humor is so important in determining the choice of a profession, how wise are those writers who hold it an essential for entrance into that most exacting of professions—matrimony! "Incompatibility in humor," George Eliot held to be the "most serious cause of diversion." And Stevenson, always wise, insists that husband and wife must be able to laugh over the same jokes—have between them many a "grouse in the gun-room" story. But there must always be exceptions if the spice of life is to be preserved, and I recall one couple of my acquaintance, devoted and loyal in spite of this very incompatibility. A man with a highly whimsical sense of humor had married a woman with none. Yet he told his best stories with an eye to their effect on her, and when her response came, peaceful and placid and non-comprehending, he would look about the table with delight, as much as to say, "Isn't she a wonder? Do you know her equal?"

Humor may be the greatest of the virtues, yet it is the one of whose possession we may boast with impunity. "Well, that was too much for my sense of humor," we say. Or, "You know my sense of humor was always my strong point." Imagine thus boasting of one's integrity, or sense of honor! And so is its lack the one vice of which one may not permit himself to be a trifle proud. "I admit that I have a hot temper," and "I know I'm extravagant," are simple enough admissions. But did any one ever openly make the confession, "I know I am lacking in a sense of humor!" However, to recognize the lack one would first have to possess the sense—which is manifestly impossible.

"To explain the nature of laughter and tears is to account for the condition of human life," says Hazlitt, and no philosophy has as yet succeeded in accounting for the condition of human life. "Man is a laughing animal," wrote Meredith, "and at the end of infinite search the philosopher finds himself clinging to laughter as the best of human fruit, purely human, and sane, and comforting." So whether it be the corrective laughter of Bergson, Jove laughing at lovers' vows, Love laughing at locksmiths, or the cheerful laughter of the fool that was like the crackling of thorns to Koheleth, the preacher, we recognize that it is good; that without this saving grace of humor life would be an empty vaunt. I like to recall that ancient usage: "The skie hangs full of humour, and I think we shall haue raine." Blessed humor, no less refreshing today than was the humour of old to a parched and thirsty earth.

TOASTERS, TOASTMASTERS AND TOASTS

Before making any specific suggestions to the prospective toaster or toastmaster, let us advise that he consider well the nature and spirit of the occasion which calls for speeches. The toast, after-dinner talk, or address is always given under conditions that require abounding good humor, and the desire to make everybody pleased and comfortable as well as to furnish entertainment should be uppermost.

Perhaps a consideration of the ancient custom that gave rise to the modern toast will help us to understand the spirit in which a toast should be given. It originated with the pagan custom of drinking to gods and the dead, which in Christian nations was modified, with the accompanying idea of a wish for health and happiness added. In England during the sixteenth century it was customary to put a "toast" in the drink, which was usually served hot. This toast was the ordinary piece of bread scorched on both sides. Shakespeare in "The Merry Wives of Windsor" has Falstaff say, "Fetch me a quart of sack and put a toast in't." Later the term came to be applied to the lady in whose honor the company drank, her name serving to flavor the bumper as the toast flavored the drink. It was in this way that the act of drinking or of proposing a health, or the mere act of expressing good wishes or fellowship at table came to be known as toasting.

Since an occasion, then, at which toasts are in order is one intended to promote good feeling, it should afford no opportunity for the exploitation of any personal or selfish interest or for anything controversial, or antagonistic to any of the company present. The effort of the toastmaster should be to promote the best of feeling among all and especially between speakers. And speakers should cooperate with the toastmaster and with each other to that end. The introductions of the toastmaster may, of course, contain some good-natured bantering, together with compliment, but always without sting. Those taking part may "get back" at the toastmaster, but always in a manner to leave no hard feeling anywhere. The toastmaster should strive to make his speakers feel at ease, to give them good standing with their hearers without overpraising them and making it hard to live up to what is expected of them. In short, let everybody boost good naturedly for everybody else.

The toastmaster, and for that matter everyone taking part, should be carefully prepared. It may be safely said that those who are successful after-dinner speakers have learned the need of careful forethought. A practised speaker may appear to speak extemporaneously by putting together on one occasion thoughts and expressions previously prepared for other occasions, but the neophyte may well consider it necessary to think out carefully the matter of what to say and how to say it. Cicero said of Antonius, "All his speeches were, *in appearance,* the unpremeditated effusion of an honest heart; and yet, in reality, they were *preconceived with so much skill* that the judges were not so well prepared as they should have been to withstand the force of them !"

After considering the nature of the occasion and getting himself in harmony with it, the speaker should next consider the relation of his particular subject to the occasion and to the subjects of the other speakers. He should be careful to hold closely to the subject allotted to him so that he will not encroach upon the ground of other speakers. He should be careful, too, not to appropriate to himself any of their time. And he should consider, without vanity and without humility, his own relative importance and govern himself accordingly. We have all had the painful experience of waiting in impatience for the speech of the evening to begin while some humble citizen made "a fe· introductory remarks."

In planning his speech and in getting it into finished form, the toaster will do well to remember those three essentials to all good composition with which he struggled in school and college days, Unity, Mass and Coherence. The first means that his talk must have a central thought, on which all his stories, anecdotes and jokes will have a bearing; the second that there will be a proper balance between the parts, that it will not be all introduction and conclusion; the third, that it will hang together, without awkward transitions. A toast may consist, as Lowell said, of "a platitude, a quotation and an anecdote," but the toaster must exercise his ingenuity in putting these together.

In delivering the toast, the speaker must of course be natural. The after-dinner speech calls for a conversational tone, not for oratory of voice or manner. Something of an air of detachment on the part of the speaker is advisable. The humorist who can tell a story with a straight face adds to the humorous effect.

A word might be said to those who plan the program. In the number of speakers it is better to err in having too few than too many. Especially is this true if there is one distinguished person who is *the* speaker of the occasion. In such a case the number of lesser lights may well be limited to two or three. The placing of the guest of honor on the program is a matter of importance. Logically he would be expected to come last, as the crowning feature. But if the occasion is a large semi-public affair—a political gathering, for example—where strict etiquet does not require that all remain thru the entire program, there will always be those who will leave early, thus missing the best part of the entertainment. In this case some shifting of speakers, even at the risk of an anti-climax, would be advisable. On ordinary occasions, where the speakers are of much the same rank, order will be determined mainly by subject. And if the topics for discussion are directly related, if they are all component parts of a general subject, so much the better.

Now we are going to add a special paragraph for the absolutely inexperienced person—who has never given, or heard anyone else give, a toast. It would seem hardly possible in this day of banquets to find an individual who has missed these occasions entirely—but he is to be found. Especially is this true in a world where toasting and after-dinner speaking are coming to be more and more in demand at social functions—the college world. Here the young man or woman, coming from a country town where the formal banquet is unknown, who has never heard an after-dinner speech, may be confronted with the necessity of responding to a toast on, say "Needles and Pins." Such a one would like to be told first of all what an after-dinner speech is. It is only a short, informal talk, usually witty, at any rate kindly, with one central idea and a certain amount of illustrative material in the way of anecdotes, quotations and stories. The best advice to such a speaker is: Make your first effort simple. Don't be over ambitious. If, as was suggested in the example cited a moment ago, the subject is fanciful—as it is very apt to be at a college banquet—any interpretation you choose to put upon it is allowable. If the interpretation is ingenious, your case is already half won. Such a subject is in effect a challenge. "Now, let's see what you can make of this," is what it implies. First get an idea; then find something in the way of illustrative material. Speak simply and naturally and sit down and watch how the others do it. Of course the subject on such occasions is often of a more serious nature—Our Class; The Team; Our President—in which case a more serious treatment is called for, with a touch of honest pride and sentiment.

To sum up what has been said, with borrowings from what other have said on the subject, the following general rules have been formulated:

Prepare carefully. Self-confidence is a valuable possession, but beware of being too sure of yourself. Pride goes before a fall, and overconfidence in his ability to improvise has been the downfall of many a would-be speaker. The speaker should strive to give the effect of spontaneity, but this can be done only with practice. The toast calls for the art that conceals art.

Let your speech have unity. As some one has pointed out, the after-dinner speech is a distinct form of expression, just as is the short story. As such it should give a unity of impression. It bears something of the same relation to the oration that the short story does to the novel.

Let it have continuity. James Bryce says: "There is a tendency today to make after-dinner speaking a mere string of anecdotes, most of which have little to do with the subject or with one another. Even the best stories lose their charm when they are dragged in by the head and shoulders, having no connection with the allotted theme. Relevance as well as brevity is the soul of wit."

Do not grow emotional or sentimental. American traditions are largely borrowed from England. We have the Anglo-Saxon reticence. A parade of emotion in public embarrasses us. A simple and sincere expression of feeling is often desirable in a toast—but don't overdo it.

Avoid trite sayings. Don't use quotations that are shopworn, and avoid the set forms for toasts—"Our sweethearts and wives—may they never meet," etc.

Don't apologize. Don't say that you are not prepared; that you speak on very short notice; that you are "no orator as Brutus is." Resolve to do your best and let your effort speak for itself.

Avoid irony and satire. It has already been said that occasions on which toasts are given call for friendliness and good humor. Yet the temptation to use irony and satire may be strong. Especially may this be true at political gatherings where there is a chance to grow witty at the expense of rivals. Irony and satire are keen-edged tools; they have their uses; but they are dangerous. Pope, who knew how to use them said:

> Satire 's my weapon, but I'm too discreet
> To run amuck and tilt at all I meet.

Use personal references sparingly. A certain amount of good-natured chaffing may be indulged in. Yet there may be danger in even the most kindly of fun. One never knows how a jest will be taken. Once in the early part of his career, Mark Twain, at a New England banquet, grew funny at the expense of Longfellow and Emerson, then in their old age and looked upon almost as divinities. His joke fell dead, and to the end of his life he suffered humiliation at the recollection.

Be clear. While you must not draw an obvious moral or explain the point to your jokes, be sure that the point is there and that it is put in such a way that your hearers cannot miss it. Avoid flights of rhetoric and do not lose your anecdotes in a sea of words.

Avoid didacticism. Do not try to instruct. Do not give statistics and figures. They will not be remembered. A historical résumé of your subject from the beginning of time is not called for; neither are well-known facts about the greatness of your city or state or the prominent person in whose honor you may be speaking. Do not tell your hearers things they already know.

Be brief. An after-dinner audience is in a particularly defenceless position. It is so out in the open. There is no opportunity for a quiet nod or two behind a newspaper or the hat of the lady in front. If you bore your hearers by overstepping your time politeness requires that they sit still and look pleased. Spare them. Remember Bacon's advice to the speaker: "Let him be sure to leave other men their turns to speak." But suppose you come late on the program! Suppose the other speakers have not heeded Bacon? What are you going to do about it? Here is a story that James Bryce tells of the most successful after-dinner speech he remembers to have heard. The speaker was a famous engineer, the occasion a dinner of the British Association for the Advancement of Science. "He came last; and midnight had arrived. His toast was Applied Science, and his speech was as follows: 'Ladies and gentlemen, at this late hour I advise you to illustrate the Applications of Science by applying a lucifer match to the wick of your bedroom candle. Let us all go to bed'."

If you are capable of making a similar sacrifice by cutting short your own carefully-prepared, wise, witty and sparkling remarks, your audience will thank you—and they may ask you to speak again.

TOASTERS' HANDBOOK

ABILITY

"Pa," said little Joe, "I bet I can do something you can't."
"Well, what is it?" demanded his pa.
"Grow," replied the youngster triumphantly.—*H. E. Zimmerman.*

ABOLITION

He was a New Yorker visiting in a South Carolina village and he sauntered up to a native sitting in front of the general store, and began a conversation.

"Have you heard about the new manner in which the planters are going to pick their cotton this season?" he inquired.

"Don't believe I have," answered the other.

"Well, they have decided to import a lot of monkeys to do the picking," rejoined the New Yorker. "Monkeys learn readily. They are thorough workers, and obviously they will save their employers a small fortune otherwise expended in wages."

"Yes," ejaculated the native, "and about the time this monkey brigade is beginning to work smoothly, a lot of you fool northerners will come tearing down here and set 'em free."

ABSENT-MINDEDNESS

SHE—"I consider, John, that sheep are the stupidest creatures living."

HE (*absent-mindedly*)—"Yes, my lamb."

ACCIDENTS

The late Dr. Henry Thayer, founder of Thayer's Laboratory in Cambridge, was walking along a street one winter morning. The sidewalk was sheeted with ice and the doctor was making his way carefully, as was also a woman going in the opposite direction. In seeking to avoid each other, both slipped and they came down in a heap. The polite doctor was overwhelmed and his embarrassment paralyzed his speech, but the woman was equal to the occasion.

"Doctor, if you will be kind enough to rise and pick out your legs, I will take what remains," she said cheerfully.

"Help! Help!" cried an Italian laborer near the mud flats of the Harlem river.

"What's the matter there?" came a voice from the construction shanty.

"Queek! Bringa da shov'! Bringa da peek! Giovanni's stuck in da mud."

"How far in?"

"Up to hees knees."

"Oh, let him walk out."

"No, no! He no canna walk! He wronga end up!"

> There once was a lady from Guam,
> Who said, "Now the sea is so calm
> I will swim, for a lark";
> But she met with a shark.
> Let us now sing the ninetieth psalm.

BRICKLAYER (to mate, who had just had a hodful of bricks fall on his feet)—"Dropt 'em on yer toe! That's nothin'. Why, I seen a bloke get killed stone dead, an' 'e never made such a bloomin' fuss as you're doin'."

A preacher had ordered a load of hay from one of his parishioners. About noon, the parishioner's little son came to the house crying lustily. On being asked what the matter was, he said that the load of hay had tipped over in the street. The preacher, a kindly man, assured the little fellow that it was nothing serious, and asked him in to dinner.

"Pa wouldn't like it," said the boy.

But the preacher assured him that he would fix it all right with his father, and urged him to take dinner before going for the hay. After dinner the boy was asked if he were not glad that he had stayed.

"Pa won't like it," he persisted.

The preacher, unable to understand, asked the boy what made him think his father would object.

"Why, you see, pa's under the hay," explained the boy.

There was an old Miss from Antrim,
Who looked for the leak with a glim.
    Alack and alas!
    The cause was the gas.
We will now sing the fifty-fourth hymn.
                —*Gilbert K. Chesterton.*

There was a young lady named Hannah,
Who slipped on a peel of banana.
    More stars she espied
    As she lay on her side
Than are found in the Star Spangled Banner.

A gentleman sprang to assist her;
He picked up her glove and her wrister;
    "Did you fall, Ma'am?" he cried;
    "Did you think," she replied,
"I sat down for the fun of it, Mister?"

At first laying down, as a fact fundamental,
That nothing with God can be accidental.
                —*Longfellow.*

ACTING

Hopkinson Smith tells a characteristic story of a southern friend of his, an actor, who, by the way, was in the dramatization of *Colonel Carter.* On one occasion the actor was appearing in his native town, and remembered an old negro and his wife, who had been body servants in his father's household, with a couple of seats in the theatre. As it happened, he was playing the part of the villain, and was largely concerned with treasons, stratagems and spoils. From time to time he caught a glimpse of the ancient couple in the gallery, and judged from their fearsome countenance and popping eyes that they were being duly impressed.

After the play he asked them to come and see him behind the scenes. They sat together for a while in solemn silence, and then the mammy resolutely nudged her husband. The old man gathered himself together with an effort, and said: "Marse Cha'les, mebbe it ain' for us po' niggers to teach ouh young masser 'portment. But we jes' got to tell yo' dat, in all de time we b'long to de fambly, none o' ouh folks ain' neveh befo' mix up in sechlike dealin's, an' we hope, Marse Cha'les, dat yo' see de erroh of yo' ways befo' yo' done sho' nuff disgrace us."

In a North of England town recently a company of local amateurs produced *Hamlet,* and the following account of the proceedings appeared in the local paper next morning:

"Last night all the fashionables and elite of our town gathered to witness a performance of *Hamlet* at the Town Hall. There has been considerable discussion in the press as to whether the play was written by Shakespeare or Bacon. All doubt can be now set at rest. Let their graves be opened; the one who turned over last night is the author."

Suit the action to the word, the word to the action, with this special observance, that you o'erstep not the modesty of nature.—*Shakespeare.*

> To wake the soul by tender strokes of art,
> To raise the genius, and to mend the heart;
> To make mankind, in conscious virtue bold,
> Live o'er each scene, and be what they behold—
> For this the tragic muse first trod the stage.
> —*Pope.*

ACTORS AND ACTRESSES

An "Uncle Tom's Cabin" company was starting to parade in a small New England town when a big gander, from a farmyard near at hand waddled to the middle of the street and began to hiss.

One of the double-in-brass actors turned toward the fowl and angrily exclaimed:

"Don't be so dern quick to jump at conclusions. Wait till you see the show."—*K. A. Bisbee.*

When William H. Crane was younger and less discreet he had a vaunting ambition to play *Hamlet.* So with his first profits he organized his own company and he went to an inland western town to give vent to his ambition and "try it on."

When he came back to New York a group of friends noticed that the actor appeared to be much downcast.

"What's the matter, Crane? Didn't they appreciate it?" asked one of his friends.

"They didn't seem to," laconically answered the actor.

"Well, didn't they give any encouragement? Didn't they ask you to come before the curtain?" persisted the friend.

"Ask me?" answered Crane. "Man, they dared me!"

LEADING MAN IN TRAVELING COMPANY—"We play *Hamlet* to-night, laddie, do we not?"

SUB-MANAGER—"Yes, Mr. Montgomery."

LEADING MAN—"Then I must borrow the sum of two-pence!"

SUB-MANAGER—"Why?"

LEADING MAN—"I have four days' growth upon my chin. One cannot play *Hamlet* in a beard!"

SUB-MANAGER—"Um—well—we'll put on Macbeth!"

HE—"But what reason have you for refusing to marry me?"

SHE—"Papa objects. He says you are an actor."

HE—"Give my regards to the old boy and tell him I'm sorry he isn't a newspaper critic."

The hero of the play, after putting up a stiff fight with the villain, had died to slow music.

The audience insisted on his coming before the curtain.

He refused to appear.

But the audience still insisted."

Then the manager, a gentleman with a strong accent, came to the front.

"Ladies an' gintlemen," he said, "the carpse thanks ye kindly, but he says he's dead, an' he's goin' to stay dead."

Mrs. Minnie Maddern Fiske, the actress, was having her hair dressed by a young woman at her home. The actress was very tired and quiet, but a chance remark from the dresser made her open her eyes and sit up.

"I should have went on the stage," said the young woman complacently.

"But," returned Mrs. Fiske, "look at me—think how I have had to work and study to gain what success I have, and win such fame as is now mine!"

"Oh, yes," replied the young woman calmly; "but then I have talent."

Orlando Day, a fourth-rate actor in London, was once called, in a sudden emergency, to supply the place of Allen Ainsworth at the Criterion Theatre for a single night.

The call filled him with joy. Here was a chance to show the public how great a histrionic genius had remained unknown for lack of an opportunity. But his joy was suddenly damp-ened by the dreadful thought that, as the play was already in the midst of its run, none of the dramatic critics might be there to watch his triumph.

A bright thought struck him. He would announce the event. Rushing to a telegraph office, he sent to one of the leading critics the following telegram: "Orlando Day presents Allen Ainsworth's part to-night at the Criterion."

Then it occurred to him, "Why not tell them all?" So he repeated the message to a dozen or more important persons.

At a late hour of the same day, in the Garrick Club, a lounging gentleman produced one of the telegrams, and read it to a group of friends. A chorus of exclamations followed the reading: "Why, I got precisely the same message!" "And so did I." "And I, too." "Who is Orlando Day? "What beastly cheek!" "Did the ass fancy that one would pay any attention to his wire?"

J. M. Barrie, the famous author and playwright, who was present, was the only one who said nothing.

"Didn't he wire you too?" asked one of the group.

"Oh, yes."

"But of course you didn't answer."

"Oh, but it was only polite to send an answer after he had taken the trouble to wire me. So, of course, I answered him."

"You did! What did you say?"

"Oh, I just telegraphed him: 'Thanks for timely warning.'"

> Twinkle, twinkle, lovely star!
> How I wonder if you are
> When at home the tender age
> You appear when on the stage.
> —*Mary A. Fairchild.*

Recipe for an actor:

> To one slice of ham add assortment of roles,
> Steep the head in mash notes till it swells,
> Garnish with onions, tomatoes and beets,
> Or with eggs—from afar—in the shells.
> —*Life.*

Recipe for an ingenue:

> A pound and three-quarters of kitten,
> Three ounces of flounces and sighs;
> Add wiggles and giggles and gurgles,
> And ringlets and dimples and eyes.
> —*Life.*

ADAPTATION

"I know a nature-faker," said Mr. Bache, the author, "who claims that a hen of his last month hatched, from a setting of seventeen eggs, seventeen chicks that had, in lieu of feathers, fur.

"He claimed that these fur-coated chicks were a proof of nature's adaptation of all animals to their environment, the seventeen eggs having been of the cold-storage variety."

ADDRESSES

In a large store a child, pointing to a shopper exclaimed, "Oh, mother, that lady lives the same place we do. I just heard her say, 'Send it up C. O. D.' Isn't that where we live?"

An Englishman went into his local library and asked for Frederic Harrison's *George Washington and other American Addresses*. In a little while he brought back the book to the librarian and said:

"This book does not give me what I require; I want to find out the addresses of several American magnates; I know where George Washington has gone to, for he never told a lie."

ADVERTISING

Not long ago a patron of a cafe in Chicago summoned his waiter and delivered himself as follows:

"I want to know the meaning of this. Look at this piece of beef. See its size. Last evening I was served with a portion more than twice the size of this."

"Where did you sit?" asked the waiter.

"What has that to do with it? I believe I sat by the window."

"In that case," smiled the waiter, "the explanation is simple. We always serve customers by the window large portions. It's a good advertisement for the place."

"Advertising costs me a lot of money."

"Why I never saw your goods advertised."

"They aren't. But my wife reads other people's ads."

When Mark Twain, in his early days, was editor of a Missouri paper, a superstitious subscriber wrote to him saying that he had found a spider in his paper, and asking him whether that was a sign of good luck or bad. The humorist wrote him this answer and printed it:

"Old subscriber: Finding a spider in your paper was neither good luck nor bad luck for you. The spider was merely looking over our paper to see which merchant is not advertising, so that he can go to that store, spin his web across the door and lead a life of undisturbed peace ever afterward."

"Good Heavens, man! I saw your obituary in this morning's paper!"

"Yes, I know. I put it in myself. My opera is to be produced to-night, and I want good notices from the critics."

—*C. Hilton Turvey.*

Paderewski arrived in a small western town about noon one day and decided to take a walk in the afternoon. While strolling along he heard a piano, and, following the sound, came to a house on which was a sign reading:

'Miss Jones. Piano lessons 25 cents an hour."

Pausing to listen he heard the young woman trying to play one of Chopin's nocturnes, and not succeeding very well.

Paderewski walked up to the house and knocked. Miss Jones came to the door and recognized him at once. Delighted, she invited him in and he sat down and played the nocturne as only Paderewski can, afterward spending an hour in correcting her mistakes. Miss Jones thanked him and he departed.

Some months afterward he returned to the town, and again took the same walk.

He soon came to the home of Miss Jones, and, looking at the sign, he read:

'Miss Jones. Piano lessons $1.00 an hour. (Pupil of Paderewski.)"

Shortly after Raymond Hitchcock made his first big hit in New York, Eddie Foy, who was also playing in town, happened to be passing Daly's Theatre, and paused to look at the pictures of Hitchcock and his company that adorned the entrance. Near the pictures was a billboard covered with laudatory extracts from newspaper criticisms of the show.

When Foy had moodily read to the bottom of the list, he turned to an unobtrusive young man who had been watching him out of the coner of his eye.

"Say, have you seen this show?" he asked.

'Sure," replied the young man.

"Any good? How's this guy Hitchcock, anyhow?"

"Any good?" repeated the young man pityingly. "Why, say, he's the best in the business. He's got all these other would-be side-ticklers lashed to the mast. He's a scream. Never laughed so much at any one in all my life."

"Is he as good as Foy?" ventured Foy hopefully.

"As good as Foy!" The young man's scorn was superb. "Why, this Hitchcock has got that Foy person looking like a gloom. They're not in the same class. Hitchcock's funny. A man with feelings can't compare them. I'm sorry you asked me, I feel so strongly about it."

Eddie looked at him very sternly and then, in the hollow tones of a tragedian, he said:

"I am Foy."

"I know you are," said the young man cheerfully. "I'm Hitchcock!"

Advertisements are of great use to the vulgar. First of all, as they are instruments of ambition. A man that is by no means big enough for the Gazette, may easily creep into the advertisements; by which means we often see an apothecary in the same paper of news with a plenipotentiary, or a running footman with an ambassador.—*Addison.*

See also Salesmen and Salesmanship.

ADVICE

Her exalted rank did not give Queen Victoria immunity from the trials of a grandmother. One of her grandsons, whose recklessness in spending money provoked her strong disapproval, wrote to the Queen reminding her of his approaching birthday and delicately suggesting that money would be the most acceptable gift. In her own hand she answered, sternly reproving the youth for the sin of extravagance and urging upon him the practice of economy. His reply staggered her:

"Dear Grandma," it ran, "thank you for your kind letter of advice. I have sold the same for five pounds."

Many receive advice, only the wise profit by it.—*Publius Syrus.*

AERONAUTICS

A flea and a fly in a flue,
Were imprisoned; now what could they do?
    Said the fly, "'let us flee."
    "Let us fly," said the flea,
And they flew through a flaw in the flue.

The impression that men will never fly like birds seems to be aeroneous.—*La Touche Hancock.*

AEROPLANES

"Mother, may I go aeroplane?"
"Yes, my darling Mary.
Tie yourself to an anchor chain
And don't go near the airy."

—*Judge.*

Harry N. Atwood, the noted aviator, was the guest of honor at a dinner in New York, and on the occasion his eloquent reply to a toast on aviation terminated neatly with these words:

"The aeroplane has come at last, but it was a long time coming. We can imagine Necessity, the mother of invention, looking up at a sky all criss-cossed with flying machines, and then saying, with a shake of her old head and with a contented smile:

"'Of all my family, the aeroplane has been the hardest to raise.'"

A genius who once did aspire
To invent an aerial flyer,
    When asked, "Does it go?"
    Replied, "I don't know;
I'm awaiting some damphule to try 'er."

AFTER DINNER SPEECHES

A Frenchman once remarked:

"The table is the only place where one is not bored for the first hour."

> Every rose has its thorn
> There's fuzz on all the peaches.
> There never was a dinner yet
> Without some lengthy speeches.

Joseph Chamberlain was the guest of honor at a dinner in an important city. The Mayor presided, and when coffee was being served the Mayor leaned over and touched Mr. Chamberlain, saying, "Shall we let the people enjoy themselves a little longer, or had we better have your speech now?"

"Friend," said one immigrant to another, "this is a grand country to settle in. They don't hang you here for murder."

"What do they do to you?" the other immigrant asked.

"They kill you," was the reply, "with elocution."

When Daniel got into the lions' den and looked around he thought to himself, "Whoever's got to do the after-dinner speaking, it won't be me."

Joseph H. Choate and Chauncey Depew were invited to a dinner. Mr. Choate was to speak, and it fell to the lot of Mr. Depew to introduce him, which he did thus: "Gentlemen, permit me to introduce Ambassador Choate, America's most inveterate after-dinner speaker. All you need to do to get a speech out of Mr. Choate is to open his mouth, drop in a dinner and up comes your speech."

Mr. Choate thanked the Senator for his compliment, and then said: "Mr. Depew says if you open my mouth and drop in a dinner up will come a speech, but I warn you that if you open your mouths and drop in one of Senator Depew's speeches up will come your dinners."

Mr. John C. Hackett recently told the following story:

"I was up in Rockland County last summer, and there was a banquet given at a country hotel. All the farmers were there and all the village characters. I was asked to make a speech.

"'Now,' said I, with the usual apologetic manner, "it is not fair to you that the toastmaster should ask me to speak. I am notorious as the worst public speaker in the State of New York. My reputation extends from one end of the state to the other. I have no rival whatever, when it comes—' I was interrupted by a lanky, ill-clad individual, who had stuck too close to the beer pitcher.

"'Gentlemen,' said he, 'I take 'ception to what this here man says. He ain't the worst public speaker in the state. I am. You all know it, an' I want it made a matter of record that I took 'ception.'

"'Well, my friend,' said I, 'suppose we leave it to the guests. You sit down while I say my piece, and then I'll sit down and let you give a demonstration.' The fellow agreed and I went on. I hadn't gone far when he got up again.

"''S all right,' said he, 'you win; needn't go no farther!'"

Mark Twain and Chauncey M. Depew once went abroad on the same ship. When the ship was a few days out they were both invited to a dinner. Speech-making time came. Mark Twain had the first chance. He spoke twenty minutes and made a great hit. Then it was Mr. Depew's turn.

"Mr. Toastmaster and Ladies and Gentlemen," said the famous raconteur as he arose, "Before this dinner Mark Twain and myself made an agreement to trade speeches. He has just delivered my speech, and I thank you for the pleasant manner in which you received it. I regret to say that I have lost the notes of his speech and cannot remember anything he was to say."

Then he sat down. There was much laughter. Next day an Englishman who had been in the party came across Mark Twain in the smoking-room. "Mr. Clemens," he said, "I consider you were much imposed upon last night. I have always heard that Mr. Depew is a clever man, but, really, that speech of his you made last night struck me as being the most infernal rot."

See also Orators; Politicians; Public Speakers.

AGE

The good die young—Here's hoping that you may live to a ripe old age.

"How old are you, Tommy?" asked a caller.

"Well, when I'm home I'm five, when I'm in school I'm six, and when I'm on the cars I'm four."

"How effusively sweet that Mrs. Blondey is to you, Jonesy," said Witherell. "What's up? Any tender little romance there?"

"No, indeed—why, that woman hates me," said Jonesy.

"She doesn't show it," said Witherell.

"No; but she knows I know how old she is—we were both born on the same day," said Jonesy, "and she's afraid I'll tell somebody."

As every southerner knows, elderly colored people rarely know how old they are, and almost invariably assume an age much greater than belongs to them. In an Atlanta family there is employed an old chap named Joshua Bolton, who has been with that family and the previous generation for more years than they can remember. In view, therefore, of his advanced age, it was with surprise that his employer received one day an application for a few days off, in order that the old fellow might, as he put it, "go up to de ole State of Virginny" to see his aunt.

"Your aunt must be pretty old," was the employer's comment.

"Yassir," said Joshua. "She's pretty ole now. I reckon she's 'bout a hundred an' ten years ole."

"One hundred and ten! But what on earth is she doing up in Virginia?"

"I don't jest know," explained Joshua, "but I understand she's up dere livin' wif her grandmother."

When "Bob" Burdette was addressing the graduating class of a large eastern college for women, he began his remarks with the usual salutation, "Young ladies of '97." Then in a horrified aside he added, "That's an awful age for a girl!"

THE PARSON (about to improve the golden hour)—"When a man reaches your age, Mr. Dodd, he cannot, in the nature of things, expect to live much longer, and I—"

THE NONAGENARIAN—"I dunno, parson. I be stronger on my legs than I were when I started!"

A well-meaning Washington florist was the cause of much embarrassment to a young man who was in love with a rich and beautiful girl.

It appears that one afternoon she informed the young man that the next day would be her birthday, whereupon the suitor remarked that he would the next morning send her some roses, one rose for each year.

That night he wrote a note to his florist, ordering the delivery of twenty roses for the young woman. The florist himself filled the order, and, thinking to improve on it, said to his clerk:

"Here's an order from young Jones for twenty roses. He's one of my best customers, so I'll throw in ten more for good measure."—*Edwin Tarrisse.*

A small boy who had recently passed his fifth birthday was riding in a suburban car with his mother, when they were asked the customary question, "How old is the boy?" After being told the correct age, which did not require a fare, the conductor passed on to the next person.

The boy sat quite still as if pondering over some question, and then, concluding that full information had not been given, called loudly to the conductor, then at the other end of the car: "And mother's thirty-one!"

The late John Bigelow, the patriarch of diplomats and authors, and the no less distinguished physician and author, Dr. S. Weir Mitchell, were together, several years ago, at West Point. Dr. Bigelow was then ninety-two, and Dr. Mitchell eighty.

The conversation turned to the subject of age. "I attribute my many years," said Dr. Bigelow, "to the fact that I have been most abstemious. I have eaten sparingly, and have not used tobacco, and have taken little exercise."

"It is just the reverse in my case," explained Dr. Mitchell. "I have eaten just as much as I wished, if I could get it; I have always used tobacco, immoderately at times; and I have always taken a great deal of exercise."

With that, Ninety-Two-Years shook his head at Eighty-Years and said, "Well, you will never live to be an old man!"—*Sarah Bache Hodge.*

A wise man never puts away childish things.—*Sidney Dark.*

> To the old, long life and treasure;
> To the young, all health and pleasure.
> —*Ben Jonson.*

Youth is a blunder; Manhood a struggle; Old Age a regret.—*Disraeli.*

We do not count a man's years, until he has nothing else to count.—*Emerson.*

To be seventy years young is sometimes far more cheerful and hopeful than to be forty years old.—*O. W. Holmes.*

AGENTS

"John, whatever induced you to buy a house in this forsaken region?"

"One of the best men in the business."—*Life.*

AGRICULTURE

A farmer, according to this definition, is a man who makes his money on the farm and spends it in town. An agriculturist is a man who makes his money in town and spends it on the farm.

In certain parts of the west, where without irrigation the cultivators of the land would be in a bad way indeed, the light rains that during the growing season fall from time to time, are appreciated to a degree that is unknown in the east.

Last summer a fruit grower who owns fifty acres of orchards was rejoicing in one of these precipitations of moisture, when his hired man came into the house.

"Why don't you stay in out of the rain?" asked the fruit-man.

"I don't mind a little dew like this," said the man. "I can work along just the same."

"Oh, I'm not talking about that," exclaimed the fruit-man. "The next time it rains, you can come into the house. I want that water on the land."

> They used to have a farming rule
> Of forty acres and a mule.
> Results were won by later men
> With forty square feet and a hen.
> And nowadays success we see
> With forty inches and a bee.
>
> —*Wasp.*

Blessed be agriculture! if one does not have too much of it.—*Charles Dudley Warner.*

When tillage begins, other arts follow. The farmers, therefore, are the founders of human civilization.—*Daniel Webster.*

ALARM CLOCKS

MIKE (in bed, to alarm-clock as it goes off)—'I fooled yez that time. I was not aslape at all."

ALERTNESS

"Alert?" repeated a congressman, when questioned concerning one of his political opponents. "Why, he's alert as a Providence bridegroom I heard of the other day. You know how bridegrooms starting off on their honeymoons sometimes forget all about their brides, and buy tickets only for themselves? That is what happened to the Providence young man. And when his wife said to him, 'Why, Tom, you bought only one ticket,' he answered without a moment's hesitation, 'By Jove, you're right, dear! I'd forgotten myself entirely!'"

ALIBI

A party of Manila army women were returning in an auto from a suburban excursion when the driver unfortunately collided with another vehicle. While a policeman was taking down the names of those concerned an "English-speaking" Filipino law-student politely asked one of the ladies how the accident had happened.

"I'm sure I don't know," she replied; "I was asleep when it occurred."

Proud of his knowledge of the Anglo-Saxon tongue, the youth replied:

"Ah, madam, then you will be able to prove a lullaby."

ALIMONY

"What is alimony, ma?"
"It is a man's cash surrender value."—*Town Topics.*

The proof of the wedding is in the alimony.

ALLOWANCES

"Why don't you give your wife an allowance?"
"I did once, and she spent it before I could borrow it back."

ALTERNATIVES

See Choices.

ALTRUISM

WILLIE—"Pa!"

PA—"Yes."

WILLIE—"Teacher says we're here to help others."

PA—"Of course we are."

WILLIE—"Well, what are the others here for?"

There was once a remarkably kind boy who was a great angler. There was a trout stream in his neighborhood that ran through a rich man's estate. Permits to fish the stream could now and then be obtained, and the boy was lucky enough to have a permit.

One day he was fishing with another boy when a gamekeeper suddenly darted forth from a thicket. The lad with the permit uttered a cry of fright, dropped his rod, and ran off at top speed. The gamekeeper pursued.

For about half a mile the gamekeeper was led a swift and difficult chase. Then, worn out, the boy halted. The man seized him by the arm and said between pants:

"Have you a permit to fish on this estate?

"Yes to be sure," said the boy, quietly.

"You have? Then show it to me."

The boy drew the permit from his pocket. The man examined it and frowned in perplexity and anger.

"Why did you run when you had this permit?" he asked.

"To let the other boy get away," was the reply. "He didn't have none!"

AMBITION

Oliver Herford sat next to a soulful poetess at dinner one night, and that dreamy one turned her sad eyes upon him. "Have you no other ambition, Mr. Herford," she demanded, "than to force people to degrade themselves by laughter?"

Yes, Herford had an ambition. A whale of an ambition. Some day he hoped to gratify it.

The woman rested her elbows on the table and propped her face in her long, sad hands, and glowed into Mr. Herford's eyes. "Oh, Mr. Herford," she said, "Oliver! Tell me about it."

"I want to throw an egg into an electric fan," said Herford, simply.

"Hubby," said the observant wife, "the janitor of these flats is a bachelor."

"What of it?"

"I really think he is becoming interested in our oldest daughter."

"There you go again with your pipe dreams! Last week it was a duke."

The chief end of a man in New York is dissipation; in Boston conversation.

When you are aspiring to the highest place, it is honorable to reach the second or even the third rank.—*Cicero.*

The man who seeks one thing in life, and but one,
May hope to achieve it before life be done;
But he who seeks all things, wherever he goes,
Only reaps from the hopes which around him he sows
A harvest of barren regrets.

—*Owen Meredith.*

AMERICAN GIRL

Here's to the dearest
  Of all things on earth.
(Dearest precisely—
  And yet of full worth.)
One who lays siege to
  Susceptible hearts.
(Pocket-books also—
  That's one of her arts!)
Drink to her, toast her,
  Your banner unfurl—
Here's to the *priceless*
  American Girl!

—*Walter Pulitzer.*

AMERICANS

Eugene Field was at a dinner in London when the conversation turned to the subject of lynching in the United States.

It was the general opinion that a large percentage of Americans met death at the end of a rope. Finally the hostess turned to Field and asked:

"You, sir, must have often seen these affairs?"

"Yes," replied Field, "hundreds of them."

"Oh, do tell us about a lynching you have seen yourself," broke in half a dozen voices at once.

"Well, the night before I sailed for England," said Field, "I was giving a dinner at a hotel to a party of intimate friends when a colored waiter spilled a plate of soup over the gown of a lady at an adjoining table. The gown was utterly ruined, and the gentlemen of her party at once seized the waiter, tied a rope around his neck, and at a signal from the injured lady swung him into the air."

"Horrible!" said the hostess with a shudder. "And did you actually see this yourself?"

"Well, no," admitted Field apolgetically. "Just at that moment I happened to be downstairs killing the chef for putting mustard in the blanc mange."

> You can always tell the English,
> You can always tell the Dutch,
> You can always tell the Yankees—
> But you can't tell them *much!*

AMUSEMENTS

A newspaper thus defined amusements:

The Friends' picnic this year was not as well attended as it has been for some years. This can be laid to three causes, viz.: the change of place in holding it, deaths in families, and other amusements.

> I wish that my room had a floor;
> I don't so much care for a door;
>   But this crawling around
>   Without touching the ground
> Is getting to be quite a bore.

I am a great friend to public amusements; for they keep people from vice.—*Samuel Johnson.*

ANATOMY

Tommy—"My gran'pa wuz in th' civil war, an' he lost a leg or a arm in every battle he fit it!"

Johnny—"Gee! How many battles was he in?"

Tommy—"About forty."

They thought more of the Legion of Honor in the time of the first Napoleon than they do now. The emperor one day met an old one-armed veteran.

"How did you lose your arm?" He asked.

"Sire, at Austerlitz."

"And were you not decorated?"

"No, sire."

"Then here is my own cross for you; I make you chevalier."

"Your Majesty names me chevalier because I have lost one arm. What would your Majesty have done had I lost both arms?"

"Oh, in that case I should have made you Officer of the Legion."

Whereupon the old soldier immediately drew his sword and cut off his other arm.

There is no particular reason to doubt this story. The only question is, how did he do it?

ANCESTRY

A western buyer is inordinately proud of the fact that one of his ancestors affixed his name to the Declaration of Independence. At the time the salesman called, the buyer was signing a number of checks and affixed his signature with many a curve and flourish. The salesman's patience becoming exhausted in waiting for the buyer to recognize him, he finally observed:

"You have a fine signature, Mr. So-and-So."

"Yes," admitted the buyer, "I should have. One of my forefathers signed the Declaration of Independence."

"So?" said the caller, with rising inflection. And then he added:

"Vell, you aind't got nottings on me. One of my forefathers signed the Ten Commandments."

In a speech in the Senate on Hawaiian affairs, Senator Depew of New York told this story:

When Queen Liliuokalani was in England during the English queen's jubilee, she was received at Buckingham Palace. In the course of the remarks that passed between the two queens, the one from the Sandwich Islands said that she had English blood in her veins.

"How so?" inquired Victoria.

"My ancestors ate Captain Cook."

Signor Marconi, in an interview in Washington, praised American democracy.

"Over here," he said, "you respect a man for what he is himself—not for what his family is—and thus you remind me of the gardener in Bologna who helped me with my first wireless apparatus.

"As my mother's gardener and I were working on my apparatus together a young count joined us one day, and while he watched us work the count boasted of his lineage."

"The gardener, after listening a long while, smiled and said:

"'If you come from an ancient family, it's so much the worse for you sir; for, as we gardeners say, the older the seed the worse the crop.'"

"Gerald," said the young wife, noticing how heartily he was eating, "do I cook as well as your mother did?"

Gerald put up his monocle, and stared at her through it.

"Once and for all, Agatha," he said, "I beg you will remember that although I may seem to be in reduced circumstances now, I come of an old and distinguished family. My mother was not a cook."

"My ancestors came over in the 'Mayflower.' "

"That's nothing; my father descended from an aeroplane."—
Life.

When in England, Governor Foss, of Massachusetts, had
luncheon with a prominent Englishman noted for boasting of
his ancestry. Taking a coin from his pocket, the Englishman
said: "My great-great-grandfather was made a lord by the
king whose picture you see on this shilling." "Indeed!" replied the governor, smiling, as he produced another coin. "What
a coincidence! My great-great-grandfather was made an angel
by the Indian whose picture you see on this cent."

People will not look forward to posterity, who never look
backward to their ancestors.—*Burke.*

> From yon blue heavens above us bent,
> The gardener Adam and his wife
> Smile at the claims of long descent.
> —*Tennyson.*

ANGER

Charlie and Nancy had quarreled. After their supper Mother
tried to re-establish friendly relations. She told them of the
Bible verse, "Let not the sun go down upon your wrath."

"Now, Charlie," she pleaded, "are you going to let the sun go
down on your wrath?"

Charlie squirmed a little. Then:

"Well, how can *I* stop it?"

When a husband loses his temper he usually finds his wife's.

It is easy enough to restrain our wrath when the other fellow
is the bigger.

ANNIVERSARIES

Mrs. Jones—"Does your husband remember your wedding
anniversary?"

Mrs. Smith—"No; so I remind him of it in January and June, and get two presents."

ANTIDOTES

"Suppose," asked the professor in chemistry, "that you were summoned to the side of a patient who had accidentally swallowed a heavy dose of oxalic acid, what would you administer?"

The student who, studying for the ministry, took chemistry because it was obligatory in the course, replied, "I would administer the sacrament."

APPEARANCES

"How fat and well your little boy looks."

"Ah, you should never judge from appearances. He's got a gumboil on one side of his face and he has been stung by a wasp on the other."

APPLAUSE

A certain theatrical troupe, after a dreary and unsuccessful tour, finally arrived in a small New Jersey town. That night, though there was no furore or general uprising of the audience, there was enough hand-clapping to arouse the troupe's dejected spirits. The leading man stepped to the foot-lights after the first act and bowed profoundly. Still clapping continued.

When he went behind the scenes he saw an Irish stagehand laughing heartily. "Well, what do you think of that?" asked the actor, throwing out his chest.

"What d'ye mane?" replied the Irishman.

"Why, the hand-clapping out there," was the reply.

Hand-clapping?

"Yes," said the Thespian, "they are giving me enough applause to show they appreciate me."

"D'ye call thot applause?" inquired the old fellow. "Whoi, thot's not applause. Thot's the audience killin' mosquitoes."

Applause is the spur of noble minds, the end and aim of weak ones.—*Colton.*

O Popular Applause! what heart of man is proof against thy sweet, seducing charms?—*Cowper.*

ARBITRATION, INTERNATIONAL

A war was going on, and one day, the papers being full of the grim details of a bloody battle, a woman said to her husband:

"This slaughter is shocking. It's fiendish. Can nothing be done to stop it?"

"I'm afraid not," her husband answered.

"Why don't both sides come together and arbitrate?" she cried.

"They did," said he. "They did, way back in June. That's how the gol-durned thing started."

ARITHMETIC

"He seems to be very clever."

"Yes, indeed. He can even do the problems that his children have to work out at school."

SONNY—"Aw, pop, I don't wanter study arithmetic."

POP—"What! a son of mine grow up and not be able to figure up baseball scores and batting averages? Never!"

TEACHER—"Now, Johnny, suppose I should borrow $100 from your father and should pay him $10 a month for ten months, how much would I then owe him?"

JOHNNY—"About $3 interest."

"See how I can count, mama," said Kitty. "There's my right foot. That's one. There's my left foot. That's two. Two and one make three. Three feet make a yard, and I want to go out and play in it!"

"Two old salts who had spent most of their lives on fishing smacks had an argument one day as to which was the better mathematician," said George C. Wiedenmayer the other day. "Finally the captain of their ship proposed the following problem which each would try to work out: 'If a fishing crew caught 500 pounds of cod and brought their catch to port and sold it at 6 cents a pound, how much would they receive for the fish?"

"Well, the two old fellows got to work, but neither seemed able to master the intricacies of the deal in fish, and they were unable to get any answer.

"At last old Bill turned to the captain and asked him to repeat the problem. The captain started off: 'If a fishing crew caught 500 ponds of cod and——.'

" 'Wait a moment,' said Bill, 'is it codfish they caught?'

" 'Yep,' said the captain.

" 'Darn it all,' said Bill. 'No wonder I couldn't get an answer. Here I've been figuring on salmon all the time.' "

ARMIES

A new volunteer at a national guard encampment who had not quite learned his business, was on sentry duty, one night, when a friend brought a pie from the canteen.

As he sat on the grass eating pie, the major sauntered up in undress uniform. The sentry, not recognizing him, did not salute, and the major stopped and said:

'What's that you have there?"

"Pie," said the sentry, good-naturedly. "Apple pie. Have a bite?"

The major frowned.

"Do you know who I am?" he asked.

"No," said the sentry, "unless you're the major's groom."

The major shook his head.

"Guess again," he growled.

"The barber from the village?"

"No."

"Maybe"—here the sentry laughed—"maybe you're the major himself?"

"That's right. I am the major," was the stern reply.

The sentry scrambled to his feet.

"Good gracious!" he exclaimed. "Hold the pie. will you, while I present arms!"

The battle was going against him. The commander-in-chief, himself ruler of the South American republic, sent an aide to the rear, ordering General Blanco to bring up his regiment at once. Ten minutes passed; but it didn't come. Twenty, thirty, and an hour—still no regiment. The aide came tearing back hatless, breathless.

"My regiment! My regiment! Where is it? Where it is?" shrieked the commander.

"General," answered the excited aide, "Blanco started it all right, but there are a couple of drunken Americans down the road and they won't let it go by."

An army officer decided to see for himself how his sentries were doing their duty. He was somewhat surprised at overhearing the following:

"Halt! Who goes there?"

"Friend—with a bottle."

"Pass, friend. Halt, bottle."

"A war is a fearful thing," said Mr. Dolan.

"It is," replied Mr. Rafferty. "When you see the fierceness of members of the army toward one another, the fate of a common enemy must be horrible."

See also Military Discipline.

ARMY RATIONS

The colonel of a volunteer regiment camping in Virginia came across a private on the outskirts of the camp, painfully munching on something. His face was wry and his lips seemed to move only with the greatest effort.

"What are you eating?" demanded the colonel.

"Persimmons, sir."

"Good Heavens! Haven't you got any more sense than to eat persimmons at this time of the year? They'll pucker the very stomach out of you."

"I know, sir. That's why I'm eatin' 'em. I'm tryin' to shrink me stomach to fit me rations."

On the occasion of the annual encampment of a western militia, one of the soldiers, a clerk who lived well at home, was experiencing much difficulty in disposing of his rations.

A fellow-sufferer nearby was watching with no little amusement the first soldier's attempts to Fletcherize a piece of meat. "Any trouble, Tom?" asked the second soldier sarcastically.

"None in particular," was the response. Then after a sullen survey of the bit of beef he held in his hand, the amateur fighter observed:

"Bill, I now fully realize what people mean when they speak of the sinews of war."—*Howard Morse.*

ART

There was an old sculptor named Phidias,
Whose knowledge of Art was invidious.
  He carved Aphrodite
  Without any nightie—
Which startled the purely fastidious.
        —*Gilbert K. Chesterton.*

The friend had dropped in to see D'Auber, the great animal painter, put the finishing touches on his latest painting. He was mystified, however, when D'Auber took some raw meat and rubbed it vigorously over the painted rabbit in the foreground.

"Why on earth did you do that?" he asked.

"Why you see," explained D'Auber, "Mrs Millions is coming to see this picture today. When she sees her pet poodle smell that rabbit, and get excited over it, she'll buy it on the spot."

A young artist once persuaded Whistler to come and view his latest effort. The two stood before the canvas for some moments in silence. Finally the young man asked timidly, "Don't you think, sir, that this painting of mine is—well—er—tolerable?"

Whistler's eyes twinkled dangerously.

"What is your opinion of a tolerable egg?" he asked.

The amateur artist was painting—sunset, red with blue streaks and green dots.

The old rustic, at a respectful distance, was watching.

"Ah," said the artist looking up suddenly, "perhaps to you, too, Nature has opened her sky picture page by page! Have you seen the lambent flame of dawn leaping across the livid east; the red-stained, sulphurous islets floating in the lake of fire in the west; the ragged clouds at midnight, black as a raven's wing, blotting out the shuddering moon?"

"No," replied the rustic, "not since I give up drink."

Art is indeed not the bread but the wine of life.—*Jean Paul Richter.*

Now nature is not at variance with art, nor art with nature; they being both the servants of His providence. Art is the perfection of nature. Were the world now as it was the sixth day, there were yet a chaos. Nature hath made one world, and art another. In brief, all things are artificial; for nature is the art of God.—*Sir Thomas Browne.*

ARTISTS

ARTIST—"I'd like to devote my last picture to a charitable purpose."

CRITIC—"Why not give it to an institution for the blind?"

"Wealth has its penalties," said the ready-made philosopher.

"Yes," replied Mr. Cumrox. "I'd rather be back at the dear old factory than learning to pronounce the names of the old masters in my picture-gallery."

CRITIC—"By George, old chap, when I look at one of your paintings I stand and wonder—"

ARTIST—"How I do it?"

CRITIC—"No; why you do it."

He that seeks popularity in art closes the door on his own genius: as he must needs paint for other minds, and not for his own.—*Mrs. Jameson.*

ATHLETES

The caller's eye had caught the photograph of Tommie Billups, standing on the desk of Mr. Billups.

"That your boy, Billups?" he asked.

"Yes," said Billups, "he's a sophomore up at Binkton College."

"Looks intellectual rather than athletic," said the caller.

"Oh, he's an athlete all right," said Billups. "When it comes to running up accounts, and jumping his board-bill, and lifting his voice, and throwing a thirty-two pound bluff, there isn't a gladiator in creation that can give my boy Tommie any kind of a handicap. He's just written for an extra check."

"And as a pround father you are sending it, I don't doubt,' smiled the caller.

"Yes," grinned Billups; "I am sending him a rain-check I got at the ball-game yesterday. As an athlete, he'll appreciate its value."—*J. K. B.*

ATTENTION

The supervisor of a school was trying to prove that children are lacking in observation.

To the children he said, "Now, children, tell me a number to put on the board."

Some child said, "Thirty-six." The supervisor wrote sixty-three.

He asked for another number, and seventy-six was given. He wrote sixty-seven.

When a third number was asked, a child who apparently had paid no attention called out:

Theventy-theven. Change *that* you thucker!"

AUTHORS

The following is a recipe for an author:
Take the usual number of fingers,
Add paper, manila or white,
A typewriter, plenty of postage—
And something or other to write.

—*Life.*

Oscar Wilde, upon hearing one of Whistler's *bon mots* exclaimed: "Oh, Jimmy; I wish I had said that!" "Never mind, dear Oscar," was the rejoinder, "you will!"

THE AUTHOR—"Would you advise me to get out a small edition?"

THE PUBLISHER—"Yes, the smaller the better. The more scarce a book is at the end of four or five centuries the more money your realize from it."

AMBITIOUS AUTHOR—"Hurray! Five dollars for my latest story, 'The Call of the Lure!'"

FAST FRIEND—"Who from?"

AMBITIOUS AUTHOR—"The express company. They lost it."

A lady who had arranged an authors' reading at her house succeeded in persuading her reluctant husband to stay home that evening to assist in receiving the guests. He stood the entertainment as long as he could—three authors, to be exact— and then made an excuse that he was going to open the front door to let in some fresh air. In the hall he found one of the servants asleep on a settee.

"Wake up!" he commanded, shaking the fellow roughly. "What does this mean, your being asleep out here? You must have been listening at the keyhole."

An ambitious young man called upon a publisher and stated that he had decided to write a book.

"May I venture to inquire as to the nature of the book you propose to write?" asked the publisher, very politely.

"Oh," came in an offhand way from the aspirant to literary fame, "I think of doing something on the line of 'Les Miserables,' only livelier, you know."

"So you have had a long siege of nervous prostration?" we say to the haggard author. "What cause it? Overwork?"

"In a way, yes," he answers weakly. "I tried to do a novel with a Robert W. Chambers hero and a Mary E. Wilkins heroine."—*Life.*

Mark Twain at a dinner at the Authors' Club said: "Speaking of fresh eggs, I am reminded of the town of Squash. In my early lecturing days I went to Squash to lecture in Temperance Hall, arriving in the afternoon. The town seemed very poorly billed. I thought I'd find out if the people knew anything at all about what was in store for them. So I turned in at the general store. 'Good afternoon, friend,' I said to the general storekeeper. 'Any entertainment here tonight to help a stranger while away his evening?' The general storekeeper, who was sorting mackerels, straightened up, wiped his briny hands on his apron, and said: 'I expect there's goin' to be a lecture. I've been sellin' eggs all day."

An American friend of Edmond Rostand says that the great dramatist once told him of a curious encounter he had had with a local magistrate in a town not far from his own.

It appears that Rostand had been asked to register the birth of a friend's newly arrived son. The clerk at the registry office was an officious little chap, bent on carrying out the letter of the law. The following dialogue ensued:

"Your name, sir?"

"Edmond Rostand."

"Vocation?"

"Man of letters, and member of the French Academy."

"Very well, sir. You must sign your name. Can you write? If not, you may make a cross."—*Howard Morse.*

George W. Cable, the southern writer, was visiting a western city where he was invited to inspect the new free library. The librarian conducted the famous writer through the building until they finally reached the department of books devoted to fiction.

"We have all your books, Mr. Cable," proudly said the librarian. "You see there they are—all of them on the shelves there: not one missing."

And Mr. Cable's hearty laugh was not for the reason that the librarian thought!

Brief History of a Successful Author: From ink-spots to fleshpots.—*R. R. Kirk.*

"It took me nearly ten years to learn that I couldn't write stories."

"I suppose you gave it up then?"

"No, no. By that time I had a reputation."

"I dream my stories," said Hicks, the author.

"How you must dread going to bed!" exclaimed Cynicus.

The five-year-old son of James Oppenheim, author of "The Olympian," was recently asked what work he was going to do when he became a man. "Oh," Ralph replied, "'I'm not going to work at all." "Well, what are you going to do, then?" he was asked. "Why," he said seriously, "I'm just going to write stories, like daddy."

William Dean Howells is the kindliest of critics, but now and then some popular novelist's conceit will cause him to bristle up a little.

"You know," said one, fishing for compliments, "I get richer and richer, but all the same I think my work is falling off. My new work is not so good as my old."

"Oh, nonsense!" said Mr. Howells. "You write just as well as you ever did. Your taste is improving, that's all."

James Oliver Curwood, a novelist, tells of a recent encounter with the law. The value of a short story he was writing depended upon a certain legal situation which he found difficult to manage. Going to a lawyer of his acquaintance he told him the plot and was shown a way to the desired end. "You've saved me just $100," he exclaimed, "for that's what I am going to get for this story."

A week later he received a bill from the lawyer as follows: "For literary advice, $100." He says he paid.

"Tried to skin me, that scribbler did!"

"What did he want?"

"Wanted to get out a book jointly, he to write the book and I to write the advertisements. I turned him down. I wasn't going to do all the literary work."

At a London dinner recently the conversation turned to the various methods of working employed by literary geniuses. Among the examples cited was that of a well-known poet, who, it is said, was wont to arouse his wife about four o'clock in the morning and exclaim, "Maria, get up; I've thought of a good word!" Whereupon the poet's obedient helpmate would crawl out of bed and make a note of the thought-of word.

About an hour later, like as not, a new inspiration would seize the bard, whereupon he would again arouse his wife, saying, "Maria, Maria, get up! I've thought of a better word!"

The company in general listened to the story with admiration, but a merry-eyed American girl remarked: "Well, if he'd been my husband I should have replied, 'Alpheus, get up yourself; I've thought of a bad word!'"

"There is probably no hell for authors in the next world—they suffer so much from critics and publishers in this."—*Bovee.*

> A thought upon my forehead,
>   My hand up to my face;
> I want to be an author,
>   An air of studied grace!
> I want to be an author,
>   With genius on my brow;
> I want to be an author,
>   And I want to be it now!
>   *Ella Hutchison Ellwanger.*

That writer does the most, who gives his reader the *most* knowledge, and takes from him the *least time.*——*C. C. Colton.*

> Habits of close attention, thinking heads,
> Become more rare as dissipation spreads,
> Till authors hear at length one general cry
> Tickle and entertain us, or we die!
>   *—Cowper*

The author who speaks about his own books is almost as bad as a mother who talks about her own children.—*Disraeli.*

AUTOMOBILES

TEACHER—"If a man saves $2 a week, how long will it take him to save a thousand?"

BOY—"He never would, ma'am. After he got $900 he'd buy a car."

"How fast is your car, Jimpson?" asked Harkaway.

"Well," said Jimpson, "it keeps about six months ahead of my income generally."

"What is the name of your automobile?"

"I don't know."

"You don't know? What do your folks call it?"

"Oh, as to that, father always says 'The Mortgage'; brother Tom calls it 'The Fake'; mother, 'My Limousine'; sister, 'Our Car'; grandma, 'That Peril'; the chauffeur, 'Some Freak,' and our neighbors, 'The Limit.' "—*Life.*

"What little boy can tell me the difference between the 'quick' and the 'dead?' " asked the Sunday-school teacher.

Willie waved his hand frantically.

"Well, Willie?"

"Please, ma'am, the 'quick' are the ones that get out of the way of automobiles; the ones that don't are the 'dead.' "

"Do you have much trouble with your automobile?"

"Trouble! Say, I couldn't have more if I was married to the blamed machine."

A little "Brush" chugged painfully up to the gate of a race track.

The gate-keeper, demanding the usual fee for automobiles, called:

"A dollar for the car!"

The owner looked up with a pathetic smile of relief and said:

"Sold!"

Autos rush in where mortgages have dared to tread.

See also Fords; Profanity.

AUTOMOBILING

"Sorry, gentlemen," said the new constable, "but I'll hev to run ye in. We been keepin' tabs on ye sence ye left Huckleberry Corners."

"Why, that's nonsense!" said Dubbleigh. "It's taken us four hours to come twenty miles, thanks to a flabby tire. That's only five miles an hour."

"Sure!" said the new constable, "but the speed law round these here parts is ten mile an hour, and by Jehosophat I'm goin' to make you ottermobile fellers live up to it."

Two street pedlers in Bradford, England, bought a horse for $11.25. It was killed by a motor-car one day and the owner of the car paid them $115 for the loss. Thereupon a new industry sprang up on the roads of England.

"It was very romantic," says the friend. "He proposed to her in the automobile."

"Yes?" we murmur, encouragingly.

"And she accepted him in the hospital."

"What you want to do is to have that mudhole in the road fixed," said the visitor.

"That goes to show," replied Farmer Corntassel, "how little you reformers understand local conditions. I've purty nigh paid off a mortgage with the money I made haulin' automobiles out o' that mud-hole."

The old lady from the country and her small son were driving to town when a huge automobile bore down upon them. The horse was badly frightened and began to prance, whereupon the old lady leaped down and waved wildly to the chauffeur, screaming at the top of her voice.

The chauffeur stopped the car and offered to help get the horse past.

"That's all right," said the boy, who remained composedly in the carriage, "I can manage the horse. You just lead Mother past."

"What makes you carry that horrible shriek machine for an automobile signal?"

"For humane reasons," replied Mr. Chuggins. "If I can paralyze a person with fear he will keep still and I can run to one side of him."

In certain sections of West Virginia there is no liking for automobilists, as was evidenced in the case of a Washingtonian who was motoring in a sparsely settled region of the State.

This gentleman was haled before a local magistrate upon the complaint of a constable. The magistrate, a good-natured man, was not, however, absolutely certain that the Washingtonian's car had been driven too fast; and the owner stoutly insisted that he had been progressing at the rate of only six miles an hour.

"Why, your Honor," he said, "my engine was out of order, and I was going very slowly because I was afraid it would break down completely. I give you my word, sir, you could have walked as fast as I was running."

"Well," said the magistrate, after due reflection, "you don't appear to have been exceeding the speed limit, but at the same time you must have been guilty of something, or you wouldn't be here. I fine you ten dollars for loitering."—*Fenimore Martin.*

AVIATION

The aviator's wife was taking her first trip with her husband in his airship. "Wait a minute, George," she said. "I'm afraid we will have to go down again."

"What's wrong?" asked her husband.

"I believe I have dropped one of the pearl buttons off my jacket. I think I can see it glistening on the ground."

"Keep your seat, my dear," said the aviator, "that's Lake Erie."

AVIATOR (to young assistant, who has begun to be frightened)—"Well, what do you want now?"

ASSISTANT (whimpering)—"I want the earth."—*Abbie C. Dixon.*

When Claude Grahame-White the famous aviator, author of "The Aeroplane in War," was in this country not long ago, he was spending a week-end at a country home. He tells the following story of an incident that was very amusing to him.

"The first night that I arrived, a dinner party was given. Feeling very enthusiastic over the recent flights, I began to tell the young woman who was my partner at the table of some of the details of the aviation sport.

"It was not until the dessert was brought on that I realized that I had been doing all the talking; indeed, the young woman seated next me had not uttered a single word since I first began talking about aviation. Perhaps she was not interested in the subject, I thought, although to an enthusiast like me it seemed quite incredible.

"'I am afraid I have been boring you with this shop talk,' I said, feeling as if I should apologize.

"'Oh, not at all,' she murmured, in very polite tones; 'but would you mind telling me, what is aviation?'"—*M. A. Hitchcock.*

AVIATORS

Little drops in water—
Little drops on land—
Make the aviator,
Join the heavenly band.

—*Satire.*

"Are you an experienced aviator?"

"Well, sir, I have been at it six weeks and I am all here."

—*Life.*

BABIES

See Children.

BACCALAUREATE SERMONS

Proud Father—"Rick, my boy, if you live up to your oration you'll be an honor to the family."

Valedictorian—"I expect to do better than that, father. I am going to try to live up to the baccalaureate sermon."

BACTERIA

There once were some learned M. D.'s,
Who captured some germs of disease,
And infected a train
Which, without causing pain,
Allowed one to catch it with ease.

Two doctors met in the hall of the hospital.

"Well," said the first, "what's new this morning?"

"I've got a most curious case. Woman, cross-eyed; in fact, so cross-eyed that when she cries the tears run down her back."

"What are you doing for her?"

"Just now," was the answer, "we're treating her for bacteria."

BADGES

Mrs. Philpots came panting downstairs on her way to the temperance society meeting. She was a short, plump woman. "Addie, run up to my room and get my blue ribbon rosette, the temperance badge," she directed her maid. "I have forgotten it. You will know it, Addie—blue ribbon and gold lettering."

"Yas'm, I knows it right well." Addie could not read, but she knew a blue ribbon with gold lettering when she saw it, and therefore had not trouble in finding it and fastening it properly on the dress of her mistress.

At the meeting Mrs. Philpots was too busy greeting her friends to note that they smiled when they shook hands with her. When she reached home supper was served, so she went directly to the dining-room, where the other members of the family were seated.

"Gracious me, Mother!" exclaimed her son: "that blue ribbon—you haven't been wearing that at the temperance meeting?"

A loud laugh went up on all sides.

"Why, what is it, Harry?" asked the good woman, clutching at the ribbon in surprise.

"Why, Mother dear, didn't you know that was the ribbon I won at the show?"

The gold lettering on the ribbon read:

INTERSTATE POULTRY SHOW

First Prize   Bantam

BAGGAGE

An Aberdonian went to spend a few days in London with his son, who had done exceptionally well in the great metropolis. After their first greetings at King's Cross Station, the young fellow remarked: "Feyther, you are not lookin' weel. Is there anything the matter?" The old man replied, "Aye, lad, I have had quite an accident." "What was that, feyther?" "Mon," he said, "on this journey frae bonnie Scotland I lost my luggage." "Dear, dear, that's too bad; 'oo did it happen?" "Aweel" replied the Aberdonian, "the cork cam' oot."

Johnnie Poe, one of the famous Princeton football family, and incidentally a great-nephew of Edgar Allan Poe, was a general in the army of Honduras in one of their recent wars. Finally, when things began to look black with peace and the American general discovered that his princely pay when translated into United States money was about sixty cents a day, he struck for the coast. There he found a United States warship and asked transportation home.

"Sure," the commander told him. "We'll be glad to have you. Come aboard whenever you like and bring your luggage."

"Thanks," said Poe warmly. "I'll sure do that. I only have fifty-four pieces."

"What!" exclaimed the commander. "What do you think I'm running? A freighter?"

"Oh, well, you needn't get excited about it," purred Poe. "My fifty-four pieces consist of one pair of socks and a pack of playing cards."

BALDNESS

One mother who still considers Marcel waves as the most fashionable way of dressing the hair was at work on the job.

Her little eight-year-old girl was crouched on her father's lap, watching her mother. Every once in a while the baby fingers would slide over the smooth and glossy pate which is Father's.

"No waves for you, Father," remarked the little one. "You're all beach."

"Were any of your boyish ambitions ever realized?" asked the sentimentalist.

"Yes," replied the practical person. "When my mother used to cut my hair I often wished I might be bald-headed."

Congressman Longworth is not gifted with much hair, his head being about as shiny as a billiard ball.

One day ex-president Taft, then Secretary of War, and Congressman Longworth sallied into a barbershop.

"Hair cut?" asked the barber of Longworth.

"Yes," answered the Congressman.

"Oh, no, Nick," commented the Secretary of War from the next chair, "you don't want a hair cut; you want a shine."

"O, Mother, why are the men in the front baldheaded?"

"They bought their tickets from scalpers, my child."

The costumer came forward to attend to the nervous old beau who was mopping his bald and shining poll with a big silk handkerchief.

"And what can I do for you?" he asked.

"I want a little help in the way of a suggestion," said the old fellow. "I intend going to the French Students' masquerade ball to-night, and I want a distinctly original costume—something I may be sure no one else will wear. What would you suggest?"

The costumer looked him over attentively, bestowing special notice on the gleaming knob.

"Well, I'll tell you," he said then, thoughtfully: "why don't you sugar your head and go as a pill?"—*Frank X. Finnegan.*

United States Senator Ollie James, of Kentucky, is bald.
"Does being bald bother you much?" a candid friend asked
him once.

"Yes, a little," answered the truthful James.

"I suppose you feel the cold severely in winter," went on the
friend.

"No; it's not that so much," said the Senator. "The main
bother is when I'm washing myself—unless I keep my hat on I
don't know where my face stops."

A near-sighted old lady at a dinner-party, one evening, had
for her companion on the left a very bald-headed old gentleman.
While talking to the gentleman at her right she dropped her
napkin unconsciously. The bald-headed gentleman, in stooping
to pick it up, touched her arm. The old lady turned around,
shook her head, and very politely said: "No melon, thank
you."

BANKS AND BANKING

During a financial panic, a German farmer went to a bank
for some money. He was told that the bank was not paying out
money, but was using cashier's checks. He could not understand this, and insisted on money.

The officers took him in hand, one after another, with little
effect. At last the president tried his hand, and after long and
minute explanation, some inkling of the situation seemed to be
dawning on the farmer's mind. Much encouraged, the president
said: "You understand now how it is, don't you, Mr. Schmidt?"

"I t'ink I do," admitted Mr. Schmidt. "It's like dis, aindt it?
Ven my baby vakes up at night and vants some milk, I gif
him a milk ticket."

She advanced to the paying teller's window and, handing in
a check for fifty dollars, stated that it was a birthday present
from her husband and asked for payment. The teller informed
her that she must first endorse it.

"I don't know what you mean," she said hesitatingly.

"Why, you see," he explained, "you must write your name on the back, so that when we return the check to your husband, he will know we have paid you the money."

"Oh, is that all?" she said, relieved. . . . One minute elapses.

Thus the "endorsement": "Many thanks, dear, I've got the money. Your loving wife, Evelyn."

FRIEND—"So you're going to make it hot for that fellow who held up the bank, shot the cashier, and got away with the ten thousand?"

BANKER—"Yes, indeed. He was entirely too fresh. There's a decent way to do that, you know. If he wanted to get the money, why didn't he come into the bank and work his way up the way the rest of us did?"—*Puck.*

BAPTISM

A revival was being held at a small colored Baptist church in southern Georgia. At one of the meetings the evangelist, after an earnest but fruitless exhortation, requested all of the congregation who wanted their souls washed white as snow to stand up. One old darky remained sitting.

"Don' yo' want y' soul washed w'ite as snow, Brudder Jones?"

"Mah soul done been washed w'ite as snow, pahson."

"Whah wuz yo' soul washed w'ite as snow, Brudder Jones?"

"Over yander to the Methodis' chu'ch acrost de railroad."

"Brudder Jones, yo' soul wa'nt washed—hit were dry-cleaned."—*Life.*

BAPTISTS

An old colored man first joined the Episcopal Church, then the Methodist and next the Baptist, where he remained. Questioned as to the reason for his church travels he responded:

"Well, suh, hit's this way: de 'Piscopals is gemmen, suh, but I couldn't keep up wid de answerin' back in dey church. De Methodis', dey always holdin' inquiry meetin', and I don't like too much inquirin' into. But de Baptis', suh, dey jes' dip and are done wid hit."

A Methodist Negro exhorter shouted: "Come up en jine de army ob de Lohd." "I'se done jined," replied one of the congregation. "Whar'd yoh jine?" asked the exhorter. "In de Baptis' Chu'ch." "Why, chile," said the exhorter, "yoh ain't in the army; yoh's in de navy."

BARGAINS

MANAGER (five-and-ten-cent-store)—"What did the lady who just went out want?"

SHOPGIRL—"She inquired if we had a shoe department."

"Hades," said the lady who loves to shop, "would be a magnificent and endless bargain counter and I looking on without a cent."

Newell Dwight Hillis, the now famous New York preacher and author, some years ago took charge of the First Presbyterian Church of Evanston, Illinois. Shortly after going there he required the services of a physician, and on the advice of one of his parishioners called in a doctor noted for his ability properly to emphasize a good story, but who attended church very rarely. He proved very satisfactory to the young preacher, but for some reason could not be induced to render a bill. Finally Dr. Hillis, becoming alarmed at the inroads the bill might make in his modest stipend, went to the physician and said, "See here, Doctor, I must know how much I owe you."

After some urging, the physician replied: "Well, I'll tell you what I'll do with you, Hillis. They say you're a pretty good preacher, and you seem to think I am a fair doctor, so I'll make this bargain with you. I'll do all I can to keep you out of heaven if you do all you can to keep me out of hell, and it won't cost either of us a cent. Is it a go?"

"My wife and I are trying to get up a list of club magazines. By taking three you get a discount."

"How are you making out?"

"Well, we can get one that I don't want, and one that she doesn't want, and one that neither wants for $2.25."

BASEBALL

A run in time saves the nine.

Knowin' all 'bout baseball is jist 'bout as profitable as bein' a good whittler.—*Abe Martin.*

"Plague take that girl!"
"My friend, that is the most beautiful girl in this town."
"That may be. But she obstructs my view of second base."

When Miss Cheney, one of the popular teachers in the Swarthmore schools, had to deal with a boy who played "hookey," she failed to impress him with the evil of his ways.

"Don't you know what becomes of little boys who stay away from school to play baseball?" asked Miss Cheney.

"Yessum," replied the lad promptly. "Some of 'em gets to be good players and pitch in the big leagues."

BATHS AND BATHING

The only unoccupied room in the hotel—one with a private bath in connection with it—was given to the stranger from Kansas. The next morning the clerk was approached by the guest when the latter was ready to check out.

"Well, did you have a good night's rest?" the clerk asked.

"No, I didn't," replied the Kansan. "The room was all right, and the bed was pretty good, but I couldn't sleep very much for I was afraid some one would want to take a bath, and the only door to it was through my room."

Rural Constable—"Now then, come out o' that. Bathing's not allowed 'ere after 8 a. m."

The Face in the Water—"Excuse me, Sergeant, I'm not bathing; I'm only drowning."—*Punch.*

A woman and her brother lived alone in the Scotch Highlands. She knitted gloves and garments to sell in the Lowland towns. Once when she was starting out to market her wares, her brother said he would go with her and take a dip in the ocean. While the woman was in the town selling her work, Sandy was sporting in the waves. When his sister came down to join him, however, he met her with a wry face. "Oh, Kirstie," he said, "I've lost me weskit." They hunted high and low, but finally as night settled down decided that the waves must have carried it out to sea.

The next year, at about the same season, the two again visited the town. And while Kirstie sold her wool in the town, Sandy splashed about in the brine. When Kirstie joined her brother she found him with a radiant face, and he cried out to her, "Oh, Kirstie, I've found me weskit. 'Twas under me shirt."

In one of the lesser Indian hill wars an English detachment took an Afghan prisoner. The Afghan was very dirty. Accordingly two privates were deputed to strip and wash him.

The privates dragged the man to a stream of running water, undressed him, plunged him in, and set upon him lustily with stiff brushes and large cakes of white soap.

After a long time one of the privates came back to make a report. He saluted his officer and said disconsolately:

"It's no use, sir. It's no use."

"No use?" said the officer. "What do you mean? Haven't you washed that Afghan yet?"

"It's no use, sir," the private repeated. "We've washed him for two hours, but it's no use."

"How do you mean it's no use?" said the officer angrily.

"Why, sir," said the private, "after rubbin' him and scrubbin' him till our arms ached I'll be hanged if we didn't come to another suit of clothes."

BAZARS

Once upon a time a deacon who did not favor church bazars was going along a dark street when a footpad suddenly appeared, and, pointing his pistol, began to relieve his victim of his money.

The thief, however, apparently suffered some pangs of remorse. "It's pretty rough to be gone through like this, ain't it, sir?" he inquired.

"Oh, that's all right, my man," the "held-up" one answered cheerfully. "I was on my way to a bazar. You're first, and there's an end of it."

BEARDS

There was an old man with a beard,
Who said, "It is just as I feared!—
    Two owls and a hen,
    Four larks and a wren,
Have all built their nests in my beard."

BEAUTY

If eyes were made for seeing,
Then beauty is its own excuse for being.

—Emerson.

A thing of beauty is a joy forever;
Its loveliness increases; it will never
Pass into nothingness; but still will keep
A bower quiet for us, and a sleep
Full of sweet dreams, and health, and quiet breathing.

BEAUTY, PERSONAL

In good looks I am not a star.
There are others more lovely by far.
    But my face—I don't mind it,
    Because I'm behind it—
It's the people in front that I jar.

"Shine yer boots, sir?"

"No," snapped the man.

"Shine 'em so's yer can see yer face in 'em?" urged the bootblack.

"No, I tell you!"

"Coward," hissed the bootblack.

A farmer returning home late at night, found a man standing beside the house with a lighted lantern in his hand. "What are you doing here?" he asked, savagely, suspecting he had caught a criminal. For answer came a chuckle, and—"It's only mee, zur."

The farmer recognized John, his shepherd.

"It's you, John, is it? What on earth are you doing here this time o' night?"

Another chuckle. "I'm a-coortin' Ann, zur."

"And so you've come courting with a lantern, you fool. Why I never took a lantern when I courted your mistress."

"No, zur, you didn't, zur," John chuckled. "We can all zee you didn't, zur."

The senator and the major were walking up the avenue. The senator was more than middle-aged and considerably more than fat, and dearly as the major loved him, he also loved his joke.

The senator turned with a pleased expression on his benign countenance and said, "Major, did you see that pretty girl smile at me?

"Oh, that's nothing," replied his friend. "The first time I saw you I laughed out loud!"—*Harper's Magazine.*

Pat, thinking to enliven the party, stated, with watch in hand: "I'll present a box of candy to the loidy that makes the homeliest face within the next three minutes."

The time expired, Pat announced: "Ah, Mrs. McGuire, you get the prize."

"But," protested Mrs. McGuire, "go way wid ye! I wasn't playin' at all."

ARTHUR—"They say dear, that people who live together get to look alike."

KATE—"Then you must consider my refusal as final."

In the Negro car of a railway train in one of the gulf states a bridal couple were riding—a very light, rather good looking colored girl and a typical full blooded Negro of possibly a reverted type, with receding forehead, protruding eyes, broad, flat nose, very thick lips and almost no chin. He was positively and aggressively ugly.

They had been married just before boarding the train and, like a good many of their white brothers and sisters, were very much interested in each other, regardless of the amusement of their neighbors. After various "billings and cooings" the man sank down in the seat and, resting his head on the lady's shoulder, looked soulfully up into her eyes.

She looked fondly down upon him and after a few minutes murmured gently, "Laws, honey, ain't yo' shamed to be so han'some?"

> Little dabs of powder,
> 　Little specks of paint,
> Make my lady's freckles
> 　Look as if they ain't.
>
> 　　　　　—*Mary A. Fairchild.*

> He kissed her on the cheek,
> 　It seemed a harmless frolic;
> He's been laid up a week
> 　They say, with painter's colic.
>
> 　　　　　—*The Christian Register.*

MOTHER (to inquisitive child)—"Stand aside. Don't you see the gentleman wants to take the lady's picture?"

"Why does he want to?"—*Life.*

One day, while walking with a friend in San Francisco, a professor and his companion became involved in an argument as to which was the handsomer man of the two. Not being able to arrive at a settlement of the question, they agreed, in a spirit of fun, to leave it to the decision of a Chinaman who was seen approaching them. The matter being laid before him, the Oriental considered long and carefully; then he announced in a tone of finality, "Both are worse."

"What a homely woman!"

"Sir, that is my wife. I'll have you understand it is a woman's privilege to be homely."

"Gee, then she abused the privilege."

Beauty is worse than wine; it intoxicates both the holder and the beholder.—*Zimmermann.*

BEDS

A western politician tells the following story as illustrating the inconveniences attached to campaigning in certain sections of the country.

Upon his arrival at one of the small towns in South Dakota, where he was to make a speech the following day, he found that the so-called hotel was crowded to the doors. Not having telegraphed for accommodations, the politician discovered that he would have to make shift as best he could. Accordingly, he was obliged for that night to sleep on a wire cot which had only some blankets and a sheet on it. As the politician is an extremely fat man, he found his improvised bed anything but comfortable.

"How did you sleep?" asked a friend in the morning.

"Fairly well," answered the fat man, "but I looked like a waffle when I got up."

BEER

A man to whom illness was chronic,
When told that he needed a tonic,
  Said, "O Doctor dear,
  Won't you please make it beer?"
"No, no," said the Doc., "that's Teutonic."

BEES

TEACHER—"Tommy, do you know 'How Doth the Little Busy Bee'?"

TOMMY—"No; I only know he doth it!"

BEETLES

Now doth the frisky June Bug
　Bring forth his aeroplane,
And try to make a record,
　And busticate his brain!
He bings against the mirror,
　He bangs against the door,
He caroms on the ceiling,
　And turtles on the floor!
He soars aloft, erratic,
　He lands upon my neck,
And makes me creep and shiver,
　A neurasthenic wreck!

—*Charles Irvin Junkin.*

BEGGING

THE "ANGEL" (about to give a beggar a dime)—"Poor man! And are you married?"

BEGGAR—"Pardon me, madam! D'ye think I'd be relyin' on total strangers for support if I had a wife?"

MAN—"Is there any reason why I should give you five cents?"

BOY—"Well, if I had a nice high hat like yours I wouldn't want it soaked with snowballs."

MILLIONAIRE (to ragged beggar)—"You ask alms and do not even take your hat off. Is that the proper way to beg?"

BEGGAR—"Pardon me, sir. A policeman is looking at us from across the street. If I take my hat off he'll arrest me for begging; as it is, he naturally takes us for old friends."

Once, while Bishop Talbot, the giant "cowboy bishop," was attending a meeting of church dignitaries in St. Paul, a tramp accosted a group of churchmen in the hotel porch and asked for aid.

"No," one of them told him, "I'm afraid we can't help you. But you see that big man over there?" pointing to Bishop Talbot.

"Well, he's the youngest bishop of us all, and he's a very generous man. You might try him."

The tramp approached Bishop Talbot confidently. The others watched with interest. They saw a look of surprise come over the tramp's face. The bishop was talking eagerly. The tramp looked troubled. And then, finally, they saw something pass from one hand to the other. The tramp tried to slink past the group without speaking, but one of them called to him:

"Well, did you get something from our young brother?"

The tramp grinned sheepishly. "No," he admitted, "I gave him a dollar for his damned new cathedral at Laramie!"

> To get thine ends, lay bashfulnesse aside;
> Who feares to aske, doth teach to be deny'd.
> —*Herrick.*

> Well, whiles I am a beggar I will rail
> And say, there is no sin but to be rich;
> And being rich, my virtue then shall be
> To say, there is no vice but beggary.
> —*Shakespeare.*

See also Flattery; Millionaires.

BETTING

The officers' mess was discussing rifle shooting.

"I'll bet anyone here," said one young lieutenant, "that I can fire twenty shots at two hundred yards and call each shot correctly without waiting for the marker. I'll stake a box of cigars that I can."

"Done!" cried a major.

The whole mess was on hand early next morning to see the experiment tried.

The lieutenant fired.

"Miss," he calmly announced.

A second shot.

"Miss," he repeated.

A third shot.

"Miss."

"Here, there! Hold on!" protested the major. "What are you trying to do? You're not shooting for the target at all."

"Of course not," admitted the lieutenant. "I'm firing for those cigars." And he got them.

Two old cronies went into a drug store in the downtown part of New York City, and, addressing the proprietor by his first name, one of them said:

"Dr. Charley, we have made a bet of the ice-cream sodas. We will have them now and when the bet is decided the loser will drop in and pay for them."

As the two old fellows were departing after enjoying their temperance beverage, the druggist asked them what the wager was.

"Well," said one of them, "our friend George bets that when the tower of the Singer Building falls, it will topple over toward the North River, and I bet that it won't."

BIBLE INTERPRETATION

"Miss Jane, did Moses have the same after-dinner complaint my papa's got?" asked Percy of his governess.

"Gracious me, Percy! Whatever do you mean, my dear?"

"Well, it says here that the Lord gave Moses two tablets."

"Mr. Preacher," said a white man to a colored minister who was addressing his congregation, "you are talking about Cain, and you say he got married in the land of Nod, after he killed Abel. But the Bible mentions only Adam and Eve as being on earth at that time. Who, then, did Cain marry?"

The colored preacher snorted with unfeigned contempt. "Huh!" he said, "you hear dat, brederen an' sisters? You hear dat fool question I am axed? Cain, he went to de land o' Nod just as de Good Book tells us, an' in de land o' Nod Cain gits so lazy an' so shif'less dat he up an' marries a gal o' one o' dem no' count pore white trash families dat de inspired apostle didn't consider fittin' to mention in de Holy Word.

BIGAMY

There once was an old man of Lyme.
Who married three wives at a time:
    When asked, "Why a third?"
    He replied, "One's absurd!
And bigamy, sir, is a crime."

BILLS

The proverb, "Where there's a will there's a way" is now revised to "When there's a bill we're away."

Young Doctor—"Why do you always ask your patients what they have for dinner?"

Old Doctor—"It's a most important question, for according to their ménus I make out my bills."

Farmer Gray kept summer boarders. One of these, a school-teacher, hired him to drive her to the various points of interest around the country. He pointed out this one and that, at the same time giving such items of information as he possessed.

The school-teacher, pursing her lips, remarked, "It will not be necessary for you to talk."

When her bill was presented, there was a five-dollar charge marked "Extra."

"What is this?" she asked, pointing to the item.

"That," replied the farmer, "is for sass. I don't often take it, but when I do I charge for it."—*E. Egbert.*

Patient (*angrily*)—"The size of your bill makes my blood boil."

Doctor—"Then that will be $20 more for sterilizing your system."

At the bedside of a patient who was a noted humorist, five doctors were in consultation as to the best means of producing a perspiration.

The sick man overheard the discussion, and, after listening for a few moments, he turned his head toward the group and whispered with a dry chuckle:

"Just send in your bills, gentlemen; that will bring it on at once."

"Thank Heaven, those bills are got rid of," said Bilkins, fervently, as he tore up a bundle of statements of account dated October 1st.

"All paid, eh?" said Mrs. Bilkins.

"Oh, no," said Bilkins. "The duplicates dated November 1st have come in and I don't have to keep these any longer."

BIRTHDAYS

When a man has a birthday he takes a day off, but when a woman has a birthday she takes a year off.

BLUFFING

Francis Wilson, the comedian, says that many years ago when he was a member of a company playing "She Stoops to Conquer," a man without any money, wishing to see the show, stepped up to the box-office in a small town and said:

"Pass me in, please."

The box-office man gave a loud, harsh laugh.

"Pass you in? What for?" he asked.

The applicant drew himself up and answered haughtily:

"What for? Why, because I am Oliver Goldsmith, author of the play."

"Oh, I beg your pardon, sir," replied the box-office man, as he hurriedly wrote out an order for a box.

BLUNDERS

An early morning customer in an optician's shop was a young woman with a determined air. She addressed the first salesman she saw. "I want to look at a pair of eyeglasses, sir, of extra magnifying power."

"Yes, ma'am," replied the salesman; "something very strong?"

"Yes, sir. While visiting in the country I made a very painful blunder which I never want to repeat."

"Indeed! Mistook a stranger for an acquaintance?"

"No, not exactly that; I mistook a bumblebee for a blackberry."

The ship doctor of an English liner notified the death watch steward, an Irishman, that a man had died in stateroom 45. The usual instructions to bury the body were given. Some hours later the doctor peeked into the room and found that the body was still there. He called the Irishman's attention to the matter and the latter replied:

"I thought you said room 46. I wint to that room and noticed wan of thim in a bunk. 'Are ye dead?' says I. 'No,' says he, 'but I'm pretty near dead.'

"So I buried him."

Telephone girls sometimes glory in their mistakes if there is a joke in consequence. The story is told by a telephone operator in one of the Boston exchanges about a man who asked her for the number of a local theater.

He got the wrong number and, without asking to whom he was talking, he said, "Can I get a box for two to-night?"

A startled voice answered him at the other end of the line, "We don't have boxes for two."

"Isn't this the —— Theater?" he called crossly.

"Why, no," was the answer, "this is an undertaking shop."

He canceled his order for a "box for two."

A good Samaritan, passing an apartment house in the small hours of the morning, noticed a man leaning limply against the doorway.

"What's the matter?" he asked, "Drunk?"

"Yep."

"Do you live in this house?"

"Yep."

"Do you want me to help you upstairs?"

"Yep."

With much difficulty he half dragged, half carried the drooping figure up the stairway to the second floor.

"What floor do you live on?" he asked. "Is this it?"

"Yep."

Rather than face an irate wife who might, perhaps, take him for a companion more at fault than her spouse, he opened the first door he came to and pushed the limp figure in.

The good Samaritan groped his way downstairs again. As he was passing through the vestibule he was able to make out the dim outlines of another man, apparently in worse condition than the first one.

"What's the matter?" he asked. "Are you drunk, too?"

"Yep," was the feeble reply.

"Do you live in this house, too?"

"Yep."

"Shall I help you upstairs?"

"Yep."

The good Samaritan pushed, pulled, and carried him to the second floor, where this man also said he lived. He opened the same door and pushed him in.

As he reached the front door he discerned the shadow of a third man, evidently worse off than either of the other two. He was about to approach him when the object of his solicitude lurched out into the street and threw himself into the arms of a passing policeman.

"For Heaven's sake, off'cer," he gasped, "protect me from that man. He's done nothin' all night long but carry me upstairs 'n throw me down th' elevator shaf'."

> There was a young man from the city,
> Who met what he thought was a kitty;
>   He gave it a pat,
>   And said, "Nice little cat!"
> And they buried his clothes out of pity.

BOASTING

Maybe the man who boasts that he doesn't owe a dollar in the world couldn't if he tried.

"What sort of chap is he?"

"Well, after a beggar has touched him for a dime he'll tell you he 'gave a little dinner to an acquaintance of his.' "—*R. R. Kirk.*

WILLIE—"All the stores closed on the day my uncle died."

TOMMY—"That's nothing. All the banks closed for three weeks the day after my pa left town."—*Puck.*

Two men were boasting about their rich kin. Said one:

"My father has a big farm in Connecticut. It is so big that when he goes to the barn on Monday morning to milk the cows he kisses us all good-by, and he doesn't get back till the following Saturday."

"Why does it take him so long?" the other man asked.

"Because the barn is so far away from the house."

"Well, that may be a pretty big farm, but compared to my father's farm in Pennsylvania your father's farm ain't no bigger than a city lot!"

"Why, how big is your father's farm?"

"Well, it's so big that my father sends young married couples out to the barn to milk the cows, and the milk is brought back by their grandchildren."

BONANZAS

A certain Congressman had disastrous experience in gold-mine speculations. One day a number of colleagues were discussing the subject of his speculation, when one of them said to this Western member:

"Old chap, as an expert, give us a definition of the term, 'bonanza.' "

"A 'bonanza,' " replied the Western man with emphasis, "is a hole in the ground owned by a champion liar!"

BOOKKEEPING

Tommy, fourteen years old, arrived home for the holidays, and at his father's request produced his account book, duly kept at school. Among the items "S. P. G." figured largely and frequently. "Darling boy," fondly exclaimed his doting mamma: "see how good he is—always giving to the missionaries." But Tommy's sister knew him better than even his mother did, and took the first opportunity of privately inquiring what those mystic letters stood for. Nor was she surprised ultimately to find that they represented, not the venerable Society for the Propagation of the Gospel, but "Sundries, Probably Grub."

BOOKS AND READING

Lady President—"What book has helped you most?"
New Member—"My husband's check-book."
                                          —*Martha Young.*

"You may send me up the complete works of Shakespeare, Goethe and Emerson—also something to read."

There are three classes of bookbuyers: Collectors, women and readers.

The owner of a large library solemnly warned a friend against the practice of lending books. To punctuate his advice he showed his friend the well-stocked shelves. "There!" said he. "Every one of those books was lent me."

In science, read, by preference, the newest works; in literature, the oldest.—*Bulwer-Lytton.*

Learning hath gained most by those books by which the Printers have lost.—*Fuller.*

> Books should to one of these four ends conduce,
> For wisdom, piety, delight, or use.
>   —*Sir John Denham.*

A darky meeting another coming from the library with a book accosted him as follows:
"What book you done got there, Rastus?"
"'Last Days of Pompeii.'"

"Last days of Pompey? Is Pompey dead? I never heard about it. Now what did Pompey die of?"

"I don't 'xactly know, but it must hab been some kind of 'ruption."

"I don't know what to give Lizzie for a Christmas present," one chorus girl is reported to have said to her mate while discussing the gift to be made to a third.

"Give her a book," suggested the other.

And the first one replied meditatively, "No, she's got a book."
—*Literary Digest.*

BOOKSELLERS AND BOOKSELLING

A bookseller reports these mistakes of customers in sending orders:

AS ORDERED	CORRECT TITLE
Lame as a Roble	*Les Misérables*
God's Image in Mud	*God's Image in Man*
Pair of Saucers	*Paracelsus*
Pierre and His Poodle	*Pierre and His People*

When a customer in a Boston department store asked a clerk for Hichens's *Bella Donna,* the reply was, "Drug counter, third aisle over."

It was a few days before Christmas in one of New York's large book-stores.

CLERK—"What is it, please?"

CUSTOMER—"I would like Ibsen's *A Doll's House.*"

CLERK—"To cut out?"

BOOKWORMS

"A book-worm," said papa, "is a person who would rather read than eat, or it is a worm that would rather eat than read."

BOOMERANGS

See Repartee; Retaliation.

BORES

"What kind of a looking man is that chap Gabbleton you just mentioned? I don't believe I have met him."

"Well, if you see two men off in a corner anywhere and one of them looks bored to death, the other is Gabbleton."—*Puck.*

A man who was a well known killjoy was described as a great athlete. He could throw a wet blanket two hundred yards in any gathering.

See also Conversation; Husbands; Preaching; Public speakers; Reformers.

BORROWERS

A well-known but broken-down Detroit newspaper man, who had been a power in his day, approached an old friend the other day in the Pontchartrain Hotel and said:

"What do you think? I have just received the prize insult of my life. A paper down in Muncie, Ind., offered me a job."

"Do you call that an insult?"

"Not the job, but the salary. They offered me twelve dollars a week."

"Well," said the friend, "twelve dollars a week is better than nothing."

"Twelve a week—thunder!" exclaimed the old scribe. "I can borrow more than that right here in Detroit."—*Detroit Free Press.*

One winter morning Henry Clay, finding himself in need of money, went to the Riggs Bank and asked for the loan of $250 on his personal note. He was told that while his credit was perfectly good, it was the inflexible rule of the bank to require an indorser. The great statesman hunted up Daniel Webster and asked him to indorse the note.

"With pleasure," said Webster. "But I need some money myself. Why not make your note for five hundred, and you and I will split it?"

This they did. And to-day the note is in the Riggs Bank—unpaid.

BOSSES

The insurance agent climbed the steps and rang the bell.

"Whom do you wish to see?" asked the careworn person who came to the door.

"I want to see the boss of the house," replied the insurance agent. "Are you the boss?"

"No," meekly returned the man who came to the door; "I'm only the husband of the boss. Step in, I'll call the boss."

The insurance agent took a seat in the hall, and in a short time a tall dignified woman appeared.

"So you want to see the boss?" repeated the woman. "Well, just step into the kitchen. This way, please. Bridget, this gentleman desires to see you."

"Me th' boss!" exclaimed Bridget, when the insurance agent asked her the question. "Indade Oi'm not! Sure here comes th' boss now."

She pointed to a small boy of ten years who was coming toward the house.

"Tell me," pleaded the insurance agent, when the lad came into the kitchen, "are you the boss of the house?"

"Want to see the boss?" asked the boy. "Well, you just come with me."

Wearily the insurance agent climbed up the stairs. He was ushered into a room on the second floor and guided to the crib of a sleeping baby.

"There!" exclaimed the boy, "that's the real boss of this house."

BOSTON

A tourist from the east, visiting an old prospector in his lonely cabin in the hills, commented: "And yet you seem so cheerful and happy." "Yes," replied the one of the pick and shovel. "I spent a week in Boston once, and no matter what happens to me now, it seems good luck in comparison."

A little Boston girl with exquisitely long golden curls and quite an angelic appearance in general, came in from an afternoon walk with her nurse and said to her mother, "Oh, Mamma, a strange woman on the street said to me, 'My, but ain't you got beautiful hair!'"

The mother smiled, for the compliment was well merited, but she gasped as the child innocently continued her account:

"I said to her, 'I am *very* glad to have you like my hair, but I am sorry to hear you use the word "ain't"!"—*E. R. Bickford.*

NAN—"That young man from Boston is an interesting talker, so far as you can understand what he says; but what a queer dialect he uses."

FAN—"That isn't dialect; it's vocabulary. Can't you tell the difference?"

A Bostonian died, and when he arrived at St. Peter's gate he was asked the usual questions:

"What is your name, and where are you from?"

The answer was, "Mr. So-and-So, from Boston."

"You may come in," said Peter, "but I know you won't like it."

> There was a young lady from Boston,
> A two-horned dilemma was tossed on,
>   As to which was the best,
>   To be rich in the west
> Or poor and peculiar in Boston.

BOXING

John L. Sullivan was asked why he had never taken to giving boxing lessons.

"Well, son, I tried it once," replied Mr. Sullivan. "A husky young man took one lesson from me and went home a little the worse for wear. When he came around for his second lesson he said: 'Mr. Sullivan, it was my idea to learn enough about boxing from you to be able to lick a certain young gentleman what I've got it in for. But I've changed my mind,' says he. 'If it's all the same to you, Mr. Sullivan, I'll send this young gentleman down here to take the rest of my lessons for me.'"

BOYS

A certain island in the West Indies is liable to the periodical advent of earthquakes. One year before the season of these terrestrial disturbances, Mr. X., who lived in the danger zone, sent his two sons to the home of a brother in England, to secure them from the impending havoc.

Evidently the quiet of the staid English household was disturbed by the irruption of the two West Indians, for the returning mail steamer carried a message to Mr. X., brief but emphatic:

"Take back your boys; send me the earthquake."

Aunt Eliza came up the walk and said to her small nephew: "Good morning, Willie. Is your mother in?"

"Sure she's in," replied Willie truculently. "D'you s'pose I'd be workin' in the garden on Saturday morning if she wasn't?"

An iron hoop bounded through the area railings of a suburban house and played havoc with the kitchen window. The woman waited, anger in her eyes, for the appearance of the hoop's owner. Presently he came.

"Please, I've broken your window," he said, "and here's Father to mend it."

And, sure enough, he was followed by a stolid-looking workman, who at once started to work, while the small boy took his hoop and ran off.

"That'll be four bits, ma'am," announced the glazier when the window was whole once more.

"Four bits!" gasped the woman. "But your little boy broke it—the little fellow with the hoop, you know. You're his father, aren't you?"

The stolid man shook his head.

"Don't know him from Adam," he said. "He came around to my place and told me his mother wanted her winder fixed. You're his mother, aren't you?"

And the woman shook her head also.—*Ray Trum Nathan.*

See also Egotism; Employers and employees; Office boys.

BREAKFAST FOODS

Pharaoh had just dreamed of the seven full and the seven blasted ears of corn.

"You are going to invent a new kind of breakfast food," interpreted Joseph.—*Judge.*

BREATH

One day a teacher was having a first-grade class in physiology. She asked them if they knew that there was a burning fire in the body all of the time. One little girl spoke up and said:

"Yes'm, when it is a cold day I can see the smoke."

Said the bibulous gentleman who had been reading birth and death statistics: "Do you know, James, every time I breathe a man dies?"

"Then," said James, "why don't you chew cloves?"

BREVITY

An after-dinner speaker was called on to speak on "The Antiquity of the Microbe." He arose and said, "Adam had 'em," and then sat down.

A negro servant, on being ordered to announce visitors to a dinner party, was directed to call out in a loud, distinct voice their names. The first to arrive was the Fitzgerald family, numbering eight persons. The negro announced Major Fitzgerald, Miss Fitzgerald, Master Fitzgerald, and so on.

This so annoyed the master that he went to the negro and said, "Don't announce each person like that; say something shorter."

The next to arrive were Mr. and Mrs. Penny and their daughter. The negro solemnly opened the door and called out, "Thrupence!"

Dr. Abernethy, the famous Scotch surgeon, was a man of few words, but he once met his match—in a woman. She called at his office in Edinburgh, one day, with a hand badly inflamed and swollen. The following dialogue, opened by the doctor, took place.

"Burn?"

"Bruise."

"Poultice."

The next day the woman called, and the dialogue was as follows:

"Better?"

"Worse."

"More poultice."

Two days later the woman made another call.

"Better?"

"Well. Fee?"

"Nothing. Most sensible woman I ever saw."

BRIBERY

A judge, disgusted with a jury that seemed unable to reach an agreement in a perfectly evident case, rose and said, "I discharge this jury."

One sensitive talesman, indignant at what he considered a rebuke, obstinately faced the judge.

"You can't discharge me," he said in tones of one standing upon his rights.

"And why not?" asked the surprised judge.

"Because," announced the juror, pointing to the lawyer for the defense, "I'm being hired by that man there!"

BRIDES

"My dear," said the young husband as he took the bottle of milk from the dumb-waiter and held it up to the light, "have you noticed that there's never cream on this milk?"

"I spoke to the milkman about it," she replied, "and he explained that the company always fill their bottles so full that there's no room for cream on top."

"Do you think only of me?" murmured the bride. "Tell me that you think only of me."

"It's this way," explained the groom gently. "Now and then I have to think of the furnace, my dear."

BRIDGE WHIST

"How about the sermon?"

"The minister preached on the sinfulness of cheating at bridge."

"You don't say! Did he mention any names?"

BROOKLYN

At the Brooklyn Bridge.—"Madam, do you want to go to Brooklyn?"

"No, I have to."—*Life.*

BRYAN, WILLIAM JENNINGS

Some time after the presidential election of 1908, one of Champ Clark's friends noticed that he still wore one of the Bryan watch fobs so popular during the election. On being asked the reason for this, Champ replied: "Oh, that's to keep my watch running."

BUILDINGS

Pat had gone back home to Ireland and was telling about New York.

"Have they such tall buildings in America as they say, Pat?" asked the parish priest.

"Tall buildings ye ask, sur?" replied Pat. "Faith, sur, the last one I worked on we had to lay on our stomachs to let the moon pass."

BURGLARS

A burglar was one night engaged in the pleasing occupation of stowing a good haul of swag in his bag when he was startled by a touch on the shoulder, and, turning his head, he beheld a venerable, mild-eyed clergyman gazing sadly at him.

"Oh, my brother," groaned the reverend gentleman, "wouldst thou rob me? Turn, I beseech thee—turn from they evil ways. Return those stolen goods and depart in peace, for I am merciful and forgive. Begone!"

And the burglar, only too thankful at not being given into custody of the police, obeyed and slunk swiftly off.

Then the good old man carefully and quietly packed the swag into another bag and walked softly (so as not to disturb the slumber of the inmates) out of the house and away into the silent night.

BUSINESS

A Boston lawyer, who brought his wit from his native Dublin, while cross-examining the plaintiff in a divorce trial, brought forth the following:

"You wish to divorce this woman because she drinks?"

"Yes, sir."

"Do you drink yourself?"

"That's *my* business!" angrily.

Whereupon the unmoved lawyer asked: "Have you any other business?"

At the Boston Immigration Station one blank was recently filled out as follows:

Name—Abraham Cherkowsky.

Born—Yes.

Business—Rotten.

BUSINESS ENTERPRISE

It happened in Topeka. Three clothing stores were on the same block. One morning the middle proprietor saw to the right of him a big sign—"Bankrupt Sale," and to the left— "Closing Out at Cost." Twenty minutes later there appeared over his own door, in larger letters, "Main Entrance."

In a section of Washington where there are a number of hotels and cheap restaurants, one enterprising concern has displayed in great illuminated letters, "Open All Night." Next to it was a restaurant bearing with equal prominence the legend: "We Never Close."

Third in order was a Chinese laundry in a little, low-framed, tumbledown hovel, and upon the front of this building was the sign, in great, scrawling letters:

"Me wakee, too."

A boy looking for something to do saw the sign "Boy Wanted" hanging outside of a store in New York. He picked up the sign and entered the store.

The proprietor met him. "What did you bring that sign in here for?" asked the storekeeper.

"You won't need it any more," said the boy cheerfully. "I'm going to take the job."

A Chinaman found his wife lying dead in a field one morning; a tiger had killed her.

The Chinaman went home, procured some arsenic, and, returning to the field, sprinkled it over the corpse.

The next day the tiger's dead body lay beside the woman's. The Chinaman sold the tiger's skin to a mandarin, and its body to a physician to make fear-cure powders, and with the proceeds he was able to buy a younger wife.

A rather simple-looking lad halted before a blacksmith's shop on his way home from school and eyed the doings of the proprietor with much interest.

The brawny smith, dissatisfied with the boy's curiosity, held a piece of red-hot iron suddenly under the youngster's nose, hoping to make him beat a hasty retreat.

"If you'll give me half a dollar I'll lick it," said the lad.

The smith took from his pocket half a dollar and held it out.

The simple-looking youngster took the coin, licked it, dropped it in his pocket and slowly walked away whistling.

"Do you know where Johnny Locke lives, my little boy?" asked a gentle-voiced old lady.

"He ain't home, but if you give me a penny I'll find him for you right off," replied the lad.

"All right, you're a nice little boy. Now where is he?"

"Thanks—I'm him."

"From each according to his ability, to each according to his need," would seem to be the principle of the Chinese storekeeper whom a traveler tells about. The Chinaman asked $2.50 for five pounds of tea, while he demanded $7.50 for ten pounds of the same brand. His business philosophy was expressed in these words of explanation: "More buy, more rich—more rich, more can pay!"

In a New York street a wagon loaded with lamp globes collided with a truck and many of the globes were smashed. Considerable sympathy was felt for the driver as he gazed ruefully at the shattered fragments. A benevolent-looking old gentleman eyed him compassionately.

"My poor man," he said, "I suppose you will have to make good this loss out of your own pocket?"

"Yep," was the melancholy reply.

"Well, well," said the philanthropic old gentleman, "hold out your hat—here's a quarter for you; and I dare say some of these other people will give you a helping hand too."

The driver held out his hat and several persons hastened to drop coins in it. At last, when the contributions had ceased, he emptied the contents of his hat into his pocket. Then, pointing to the retreating figure of the philanthropist who had started the collection, he observed: "Say, maybe he ain't the wise guy! That's me boss!"

BUSINESS ETHICS

"Johnny," said his teacher, "if coal is selling at $6 a ton and you pay your dealer $24 how many tons will he bring you?"

"A little over three tons, ma'am," said Johnny promptly.

"Why, Johnny, that isn't right," said the teacher.

"No, ma'am, I know it ain't," said Johnny, "but they all do it."

BUSINESS WOMEN

Wanted—A housekeeping man by a business woman. Object matrimony.

CAMPAIGNS

See Candidates; Public speakers.

CAMPING

Camp life is just one canned thing after another.

CANDIDATES

"When I first decided to allow the people of Tupelo to use my name as a candidate for Congress, I went out to a neighboring parish to speak," said Private John Allen recently to some friends at the old Metropolitan Hotel in Washington.

"An old darky came up to greet me after the meeting. 'Marse Allen,' he said, 'I's powerful glad to see you. I's known ob you sense you was a babby. Knew yoh pappy long befo' you-all wuz bohn, too. He used to hold de same office you got now. I 'members how he held dat same office fo' years an' years.'

" 'What office do you mean, uncle?' I asked, as I never knew pop held any office.

" 'Why, de office ob candidate, Marse John; yoh pappy was candidate fo' many years.' "

A good story is told on the later Senator Vance. He was traveling down in North Carolina, when he met an old darky one Sunday morning. He had known the old man for many years, so he took the liberty of inquiring where he was going.

"I am, sah, pedestrianin' my appointed way to de tabernacle of de Lord."

"Are you an Episcopalian?" inquired Vance.

"No, sah, I can't say dat I am an Epispokapillian."

"Maybe you are a Baptist?"

"No, sah, I can't say dat I's ever been buried wid de Lord in de waters of baptism."

"Oh, I see you are a Methodist."

"No, sah, I can't say dat I's one of dose who hold to argy-ments of de faith of de Medodists."

"What are you, then, uncle?"

"I's a Presbyterian, Marse Zeb, just de same as you is."

"Oh nonsense, uncle, you don't mean to say that you subscribe to all the articles of the Presbyterian faith?"

"'Deed I do sah."

"Do you believe in the doctrine of election to be saved?"

"Yas, sah, I b'lieve in the doctrine of 'lection most firmly and un'quivactin'ly."

"Well then tell me do you believe that I am elected to be saved?"

The old darky hesitated. There was undoubtedly a terrific struggle going on in his mind between his veracity and his desire to be polite to the Senator. Finally he compromised by saying:

"Well, I'll tell you how it is, Marse Zeb. You see I's never heard of anybody bein' 'lected to anything for what they wasn't a candidate. Has you, sah?"

A political office in a small town was vacant. The office paid $250 a year and there was keen competition for it. One of the candidates, Ezekiel Hicks, was a shrewd old fellow, and a neat campaign fund was turned over to him. To the astonishment of all, however, he was defeated.

"I can't account for it," said one of the leaders of Hicks' party, gloomily.

"With that money we should have won. How did you lay it out, Ezekiel."

"Well," said Ezekiel, slowly pulling his whiskers, "yer see that office only pays $250 a year salary, an' I didn't see no sense in paying $900 out to get the office, so I bought a little truck farm instead."

The little daughter of a Democratic candidate for a local office in Saratoga County, New York, when told that her father had got the nomination, cried out, "Oh, mama, do they ever die of it?"

"I am willing," said the candidate, after he had hit the table a terrible blow with his fist, "to trust the people."

"Gee!" yelled a little man in the audience. "I wish you'd open a grocery."

"Now, Mr. Blank," said a temperance advocate to a candidate for municipal honors, "I want to ask you a question. Do you ever take alcoholic drinks?"

"Before I answer the question," responded the wary candidate, "I want to know whether it is put as an inquiry or as an invitation!"

See also Politicians.

CANNING AND PRESERVING

A canner, exceedingly canny,
One morning remarked to his granny,
    "A canner can can
    Anything that he can;
But a canner can't can a can, can he?"

—*Carolyn Wells.*

CAPITALISTS

Of the late Bishop Charles G. Grafton a Fond du Lac man said: "Bishop Grafton was remarkable for the neatness and point of his pulpit utterances. Once, during a disastrous strike, a capitalist of Fond du Lac arose in a church meeting and asked leave to speak. The bishop gave him the floor, and the man delivered himself of a long panegyric upon captains of industry, upon the good they do by giving men work, by booming the country, by reducing the cost of production, and so forth. When the capitalist had finished his self-praise and, flushed and satisfied, had sat down again, Bishop Grafton rose and said with quiet significance: 'Is there any other sinner that would like to say a word?'"

CAREFULNESS

Michael Dugan, a journeyman plumber, was sent by his employer to the Hightower mansion to repair a gas-leak in the drawing-room. When the butler admitted him he said to Dugan:

"You are requested to be careful of the floors. They have just been polished."

"They's no danger iv me slippin' on thim," replied Dugan "I hov spikes in me shoes."—*Lippincott's.*

CARPENTERS

While building a house, Senator Platt of Connecticut had occasion to employ a carpenter. One of the applicants was a plain Connecticut Yankee, without any frills.

"You thoroughly understand carpentry?" asked the senator.

"Yes, sir."

"You can make doors, windows, and blinds?"

"Oh, yes sir!"

"How would you make a Venetian blind?"

The man scratched his head and thought deeply for a few seconds. "I should think, sir," he said finally, "about the best way would be to punch him in the eye."

CARVING

To Our National Birds—the Eagle and the Turkey—(while the host is carving):

May one give us peace in all our States,
And the other a piece for all our plates.

CASTE

In some parts of the South the darkies are still addicted to the old style country dance in a big hall, with the fiddlers, banjoists, and other musicians on a platform at one end.

At one such dance held not long ago in an Alabama town, when the fiddlers had duly resined their bows and taken their places on the platform, the floor manager rose.

"Git yo' partners fo' de nex' dance!" he yelled. "All you ladies an' gennulmens dat wears shoes an' stockin's, take yo' places in de middle of de room. All you ladies an' gennulmens dat wears shoes an' no stockin's, take yo' places immejitly behin' dem. An' yo' barfooted crowd, you jes' jig it roun' in de corners."—*Taylor Edwards.*

CATS

There was a young lady whose dream
Was to feed a black cat on whipt cream,
But the cat with a bound
Spilt the milk on the ground,
So she fed a whipt cat on black cream.

There once were two cats in Kilkenny,
And each cat thought that there was one cat too many,
And they scratched and they fit and they tore and they bit,
'Til instead of two cats—there weren't any.

CAUSE AND EFFECT

Archbishop Whately was one day asked if he rose early. He replied that once he did, but he was so proud all the morning and so sleepy all the afternoon that he determined never to do it again.

A man who has an office downtown called his wife by telephone the other morning and during the conversation asked what the baby was doing.

"She was crying her eyes out," replied the mother.

"What about?"

"I don't know whether it is because she has eaten too many strawberries or because she wants more," replied the discouraged mother.

BANKS—"I had a new experience yesterday, one you might call unaccountable. I ate a hearty dinner, finishing up with a Welsh rabbit, a mince pie and some lobster à la Newburgh. Then I went to a place of amusement. I had hardly entered the building before everything swam before me."

BINKS—"The Welsh rabbit did it."

BUNKS—"No; it was the lobster."

BONKS—"I think it was the mince pie."

BANKS—"No; I have a simpler explanation than that. I never felt better in my life; I was at the Aquarium."—*Judge*.

Among a party of Bostonians who spent some time in a hunting-camp in Maine were two college professors. No sooner had the learned gentlemen arrived than their attention was attracted by the unusual position of the stove, which was set on posts about four feet high.

This circumstance afforded one of the professors immediate opportunity to comment upon the knowledge that woodsmen gain by observation.

"Now," said he, "this man has discovered that heat emanating from a stove strikes the roof, and that the circulation is so quickened that the camp is warmed in much less time than would be required were the stove in its regular place on the floor."

But the other professor ventured the opinion that the stove was elevated to be above the window in order that cool and pure air could be had at night.

The host, being of a practical turn, thought that the stove was set high in order that a good supply of green wood could be placed under it.

After much argument, they called the guide and asked why the stove was in such a position.

The man grinned. "Well, gents," he explained, "when I brought the stove up the river I lost most of the stove-pipe overboard; so we had to set the stove up that way so as to have the pipe reach through the roof."

Jack Barrymore, son of Maurice Barrymore, and himself an actor of some ability, is not over-particular about his personal appearance and is a little lazy.

He was in San Francisco on the morning of the earthquake. He was thrown out of bed by one of the shocks, spun around on the floor and left gasping in a corner. Finally, he got to his feet and rushed for a bathtub, where he stayed all that day. Next day he ventured out. A soldier, with a bayonet on his gun, captured Barrymore and compelled him to pile bricks for two days.

Barrymore was telling his terrible experience in the Lambs' Club in New York.

"Extraordinary," commented Augustus Thomas, the playwright. "It took a convulsion of nature to make Jack take a bath, and the United States Army to make him go to work."

CAUTION

Marshall Field, 3rd, according to a story that was going the rounds several years ago, bids fair to become a very cautious business man when he grows up. Approaching an old lady in a Lakewood hotel, he said:

"Can you crack nuts?"

"No, dear," the old lady replied. "I lost all my teeth ages ago."

"Then," requested Master Field, extending two hands full of pecans, "please hold these while I go and get some more."

CHAMPAGNE

MR. HILTON—"Have you opened that bottle of champagne, Bridget?"

BRIDGET—"Faith, I started to open it, an' it began to open itself. Sure, the mon that filled that bottle must 'av' put in two quarts instead of wan."

Sir Andrew Clark was Mr. Gladstone's physician, and was known to the great statesman as a "temperance doctor" who very rarely prescribed alcohol for his patients. On one occasion he surprised Mr. Gladstone by recommending him to take some wine. In answer to his illustrious patient's surprise he said:

"Oh, wine does sometimes help you get through work! For instance, I have often twenty letters to answer after dinner, and a pint of champagne is a great help."

"Indeed!" remarked Mr. Gladstone; "does a pint of champagne really help you to answer the twenty letters?"

"No," Sir Andrew explained; "but when I've had a pint of champagne I don't care a rap whether I answer them or not."

CHARACTER

The Rev. Charles H. Spurgeon was fond of a joke and his keen wit was, moreover, based on sterling common sense. One day he remarked to one of his sons:

"Can you tell me the reason why the lions didn't eat Daniel?"

"No sir. Why was it?"

"Because the most of him was backbone and the rest was grit."

They were trying an Irishman, charged with a petty offense, in an Oklahoma town, when the judge asked: "Have you any one in court who will vouch for your good character?"

"Yis, your honor," quickly responded the Celt, "there's the sheriff there."

Whereupon the sheriff evinced signs of great amazement.

"Why, your honor," declared he, "I don't even know the man."

"Observe, your honor," said the Irishman, triumphantly, "observe that I've lived in the country for over twelve years an' the sheriff doesn't know me yit! Ain't that a character for ye?"

We must have a weak spot or two in a character before we can love it much. People that do not laugh or cry, or take more of anything than is good for them, or use anything but dictionary-words, are admirable subjects for biographies. But we don't care most for those flat pattern flowers that press best in the herbarium.—*O. W. Holmes.*

CHARITY

"Charity," said Rev. B., "is a sentiment common to human nature. A never sees B in distress without wishing C to relieve him."

Dr. C. H. Parkhurst, the eloquent New York clergyman, at a recent banquet said of charity:

"Too many of us, perhaps, misinterpret the meaning of charity as the master misinterpreted the Scriptural text. This master, a pillar of a western church, entered in his journal:

"'The Scripture ordains that, "if a man take away thy coat, let him have thy cloak also." To-day, having caught the hostler stealing my potatoes, I have given him the sack.'"

THE LADY—"Well, I'll give you a dime; not because you deserve it, mind, but because it pleases me."

THE TRAMP—"Thank you, mum. Couldn't yer make it a quarter an' thoroly enjoy yourself?"

Porter Emerson came into the office yesterday. He had been out in the country for a week and was very cheerful. Just as he was leaving, he said: "Did you hear about that man who died the other day and left all he had to the orphanage?"

"No," some one answered. "How much did he leave?"

"Twelve children."

"I made a mistake," said Plodding Pete. "I told that man up the road I needed a little help 'cause I was lookin' for me family from whom I had been separated fur years."

"Didn't that make him come across?"

"He couldn't see it. He said dat he didn't know my family, but he wasn't goin' to help in bringing any such trouble on 'em."

"It requires a vast deal of courage and charity to be philanthropic," remarked Sir Thomas Lipton, apropos of Andrew Carnegie's giving. "I remember when I was just starting in business. I was very poor and making every sacrifice to enlarge my little shop. My only assistant was a boy of fourteen, faithful and willing and honest. One day I heard him complaining, and with justice, that his clothes were so shabby that he was ashamed to go to chapel.

"'There's no chance of my getting a new suit this year,' he told me. 'Dad's out of work, and it takes all of my wages to pay the rent.'

"I thought the matter over, and then took a sovereign from my carefully hoarded savings and bought the boy a stout warm suit of blue cloth. He was so grateful that I felt repaid for my sacrifice. But the next day he didn't come to work. I met his mother on the street and asked her the reason.

"'Why, Mr. Lipton,' she said, curtsying, 'Jimmie looks so respectable, thanks to you, sir, that I thought I would send him around town today to see if he couldn't get a better job.'"

"Good morning, ma'am," began the temperance worker. "I'm collecting for the Inebriates' Home and——"

"Why, me husband's out," replied Mrs. McGuire, "but if ye can find him anywhere's ye're welcome to him."

Charity is a virtue of the heart, and not of the hands.—*Addison.*

You find people ready enough to do the Samaritan, without the oil and twopence.—*Sydney Smith.*

CHICAGO

A western bookseller wrote to a house in Chicago asking that a dozen copies of Canon Farrar's "Seekers after God" be shipped to him at once.

Within two days he received this reply by telegraph:

"No seekers after God in Chicago or New York. Try Philadelphia."

CHICKEN STEALING

Senator Money of Mississippi asked an old colored man what breed of chickens he considered best, and he replied:

"All kinds has merits. De w'ite ones is de easiest to find; but de black ones is de easiest to hide aftah you gits 'em."

Ida Black had retired from the most select colored circles for a brief space, on account of a slight difficulty connected with a gentleman's poultry-yard. Her mother was being consoled by a white friend.

"Why, Aunt Easter, I was mighty sorry to hear about Ida——'

"Marse John, Ida ain't nuvver tuk dem chickens. Ida wouldn't do sich a thing! Ida wouldn't demeange herse'f to rob nobody's hen-roost—and, any way, dem old chickens warn't nothing 't all but feathers when we picked 'em."

"Does de white folks in youah neighborhood keep eny chickens, Br'er Rastus?"

"Well, Br'er Johnsing, mebbe dey does keep a few."

Henry E. Dixey met a friend one afternoon on Broadway.

"Well, Henry," exclaimed the friend, "you are looking fine! What do they feed you on?"

"Chicken mostly," replied Dixey. "You see, I am rehearsing in a play where I am to be a thief, so, just by way of getting into training for the part I steal one of my own chickens every morning and have the cook broil it for me. I have accomplished the remarkable feat of eating thirty chickens in thirty consecutive days."

"Great Scott!" exclaimed the friend. "Do you still like them?"

"Yes, I do," replied Dixey; "and, what is better still, the chickens like me. Why they have got so when I sneak into the hen-house they all begin to cackle, 'I wish I was in Dixey.'"

—*A. S. Hitchcock.*

A southerner, hearing a great commotion in his chicken-house one dark night, took his revolver and went to investigate.

"Who's there?" he sternly demanded, opening the door.

No answer.

"Who's there? Answer, or I'll shoot!"

A trembling voice from the farthest corner:

"'Deed, sah, dey ain't nobody hyah ceptin' us chickens."

A colored parson, calling upon one of his flock, found the object of his visit out in the back yard working among his hencoops. He noticed with surprise that there were no chickens.

"Why, Brudder Brown," he asked, "whar'r all yo' chickens?"

"Huh," grunted Brother Brown without looking up, "some fool niggah lef' de do' open an' dey all went home."

CHILD LABOR

"What's up old man; you look as happy as a lark!"

"Happy? Why shouldn't I look happy? No more hard, weary work by yours truly. I've got eight kids and I'm going to move to Alabama."—*Life.*

CHILDREN

Two weary parents once advertised:

WANTED, AT ONCE—Two fluent and well-learned persons, male or female, to answer the questions of a little girl of three and a boy of four; each to take four hours per day and rest the parents of said children."

Another couple advertised:

"WANTED: A governess who is good stenographer, to take down the clever sayings of our child."

A boy twelve years old with an air of melancholy resignation, went to his teacher and handed in the following note from his mother before taking his seat:

"Dear Sir: Please excuse James for not being present yesterday.

"He played truant, but you needn't whip him for it, as the boy he played truant with and him fell out, and he licked James; and a man they threw stones at caught him and licked him; and the driver of a cart they hung onto licked him; and the owner of a cat they chased licked him. Then I licked him when he came home, after which his father licked him; and I had to give him another for being impudent to me for telling his father. So you need not lick him until next time.

"He thinks he will attend regular in future."

Mrs. Post—"But why adopt a baby when you have three children of your own under five years old?"

Mrs. Parker—"My own are being brought up properly. The adopted one is to enjoy."

The neighbors of a certain woman in a New England town maintain that this lady entertains some very peculiar notions touching the training of children. Local opinion ascribes these oddities on her part to the fact that she attended normal school for one year just before her marriage.

Said one neighbor: "She does a lot of funny things. What do you suppose I heard her say to that boy of hers this afternoon?"

"I dunno. What was it?"

"Well, you know her husband cut his finger badly yesterday with a hay-cutter; and this afternoon as I was goin' by the house I heard her say:

"'Now, William, you must be a very good boy, for your father has injured his hand, and if you are naughty he won't be able to whip you.'"—*Edwin Tarrisse.*

Childhood has no forebodings; but then, it is soothed by no memories of outlived sorrow.—*George Eliot.*

Better to be driven out from among men than to be disliked of children.—*R. H. Dana.*

See also Boys; Families.

CHOICES

William Phillips, our secretary of embassy at London, tells of an American officer who, by the kind permission of the British Government, was once enabled to make a week's cruise on one of His Majesty's battleships. Among other things that impressed the American was the vessel's Sunday morning service. It was very well attended, every sailor not on duty being there. At the conclusion of the service the American chanced to ask one of the jackies:

"Are you obliged to attend these Sunday morning services?"

"Not exactly obliged to, sir," replied the sailor-man, "but our grog would be stopped if we didn't, sir."—*Edwin Tarrisse.*

A well-known furniture dealer of a Virginia town wanted to give his faithful negro driver something for Christmas in recognition of his unfailing good humor in toting out stoves, beds, pianos, etc.

"Dobson," he said, "you have helped me through some pretty tight places in the last ten years, and I want to give you something as a Christmas present that will be useful to you and that you will enjoy. Which do you prefer, a ton of coal or a gallon of good whiskey?"

"Boss," Dobson replied, "Ah burns wood."

A man hurried into a quick-lunch restaurant recently and called to the waiter: "Give me a ham sandwich."

"Yes, sir," said the waiter, reaching for the sandwich; "will you eat it or take it with you?"

"Both," was the unexpected but obvious reply.

CHOIRS

See Singers.

CHRISTIAN SCIENTISTS

While waiting for the speaker at a public meeting a pale little man in the audience seemed very nervous. He glanced over his shoulder from time to time and squirmed and shifted about in his seat. At last, unable to stand it longer, he arose and demanded, in a high, penetrating voice, "Is there a Christian Scientist in this room?"

A woman at the other side of the hall got up and said, "I am a Christian Scientist."

"Well, then, madam," requested the little man, "would you mind changing seats with me? I'm sitting in a draft."

CHRISTIANS

At a dinner, when the gentlemen retired to the smoking room and one of the guests, a Japanese, remained with the ladies, one asked him:

"Aren't you going to join the gentlemen, Mr. Nagasaki?"

"No. I do not smoke, I do not swear, I do not drink. But then, I am not a Christian."

A traveler who believed himself to be sole survivor of a shipwreck upon a cannibal isle hid for three days, in terror of his life. Driven out by hunger, he discovered a thin wisp of smoke rising from a clump of bushes inland, and crawled carefully to study the type of savages about it. Just as he reached the clump he heard a voice say: "Why in hell did you play that card?" He dropped on his knees and, devoutly raising his hands, cried: "Thank God they are Christians!"

CHRISTMAS GIFTS

"As you don't seem to know what you'd like for Christmas, Freddie," said his mother, "here's a printed list of presents for a good little boy."

Freddie read over the list, and then said:

"Mother, haven't you a list for a bad little boy?"

'Twas the month after Christmas,
And Santa had flit;
Came there tidings for father
Which read: "Please remit!"

—*R. L. F.*

Little six-year-old Harry was asked by his Sunday-school teacher:

"And, Harry, what are you going to give your darling little brother for Christmas this year?"

"I dunno," said Harry; "I gave him the measles last year."

For little children everywhere
A joyous season still we make;
We bring our precious gifts to them,
Even for the dear child Jesus' sake.
—*Phoebe Cary.*

I will, if you will,
devote my Christmas giving to the children and the needy,
reserving only the privilege of, once in a while,
giving to a dear friend a gift which then will have
the old charm of being a genuine surprise.
I will, if you will,
keep the spirit of Christmas in my heart, and,
barring out hurry, worry, and competition,
will consecrate the blessed season, in joy and love.
to the One whose birth we celebrate.
—*Jane Porter Williams.*

CHRONOLOGY

Tourist—"They have just dug up the corner-stone of an ancient library in Greece, on which is inscribed '4000 B. C.'"
Englishman—"Before Carnegie, I presume."

CHURCH ATTENDANCE

"Tremendous crowd up at our church last night."
"New minister?"
"No it was burned down."

"I understand," said a young woman to another, "that at your church you are having such small congregations. Is that so?"

"Yes," answered the other girl, "so small that every time our rector says 'Dearly Beloved' you feel as if you had received a proposal!"

"Are you a pillar of the church?"
"No, I'm a flying buttress—I support it from the outside."

CHURCH DISCIPLINE

Pius the Ninth was not without a certain sense of humor. One day, while sitting for his portrait to Healy, the painter, speaking of a monk who had left the church and married, he observed, not without malice: "He has taken his punishment into his own hands."

CIRCUS

A well-known theatrical manager repeats an instance of what the late W. C. Coup, of circus fame, once told him was one of the most amusing features of the show-business; the faking in the "side-show."

Coup was the owner of a small circus that boasted among its principal attractions a man-eating ape, alleged to be the largest in captivity. This ferocious beast was exhibited chained to the dead trunk of a tree in the side-show. Early in the day of the first performance of Coup's enterprise at a certain Ohio town, a countryman handed the man-eating ape a piece of tobacco, in the chewing of which the beast evinced the greatest satisfaction.

The word was soon passed around that the ape would chew tobacco; and the result was that several plugs were thrown at him. Unhappily, however, one of these had been filled with cayenne pepper. The man-eating ape bit it; then, howling with indignation, snapped the chain that bound him to the tree, and made straight for the practical joker who had so cruelly deceived him.

"Lave me at 'im!" yelled the ape. "Lave me at 'im, the dirty villain! I'll have the rube's loife, or me name ain't Magillicuddy!"

Fortunately for the countryman and for Magillicuddy, too, the man-eating ape was restrained by the bystanders in time to prevent a killing.

> Willie to the circus went,
> He thought it was immense;
> His little heart went pitter-pat,
> For the excitement was in tents.
> —*Harvard Lampoon.*

A child of strict parents, whose greatest joy had hitherto been the weekly prayer-meeting, was taken by its nurse to the circus for the first time. When he came home he exclaimd:

"Oh, Mama, if you once went to the circus you'd never, never go to a prayer-meeting again in all your life."

Johnny, who had been to the circus, was telling his teacher about the wonderful things he had seen.

"An' teacher," he cried, "they had one big animal they called the hip—hip—

"Hippopotamus, dear," prompted the teacher.

"I can't just say its name," exclaimed Johnny, "but it looks just like 9,000 pounds of liver."

CIVILIZATION

An officer of the Indian Office at Washington tells of the patronizing airs frequently assumed by visitors to the government schools for the redskins.

On one occasion a pompous little man was being shown through one institution when he came upon an Indian lad of seventeen years. The worker was engaged in a bit of carpentry, which the visitor observed in silence for some minutes. Then, with the utmost gravity, he asked the boy:

"Are you civilized?"

The youthful redskin lifted his eyes from his work, calmly surveyed his questioner, and then replied:

"No, are you?"—*Taylor Edwards.*

"My dear, listen to this," exclaimed the elderly English lady to her husband, on her first visit to the States. She held the hotel menu almost at arm's length, and spoke in a tone of horror: " 'Baked Indian pudding!' Can it be possible in a civilized country?"

"The path of civilization is paved with tin cans."—*The Philistine.*

CLEANLINESS

"Among the tenements that lay within my jurisdiction when I first took up mission work on the East Side," says a New York young woman, "was one to clean out which would have called for the best efforts of the renovator of the Augean stables. And the families in this tenement were almost as hopeless as the tenement itself.

"On one occasion I felt distinctly encouraged, however, since I observed that the face of one youngster was actually clean.

" 'William,' said I, 'your face is fairly clean, but how did you get such dirty hands?'

" 'Washin' me face,' said William."

A woman in one of the factory towns of Massachusetts recently agreed to take charge of a little girl while her mother, a seamstress, went to another town for a day's work.

The woman with whom the child had been left endeavored to keep her contented, and among other things gave her a candy dog, with which she played happily all day.

At night the dog had disappeared, and the woman inquired whether it had been lost.

"No, it ain't lost," answered the little girl. "I kept it 'most all day, but it got so dirty that I was ashamed to look at it; so I et it."—*Fenimore Martin.*

"How old are you?" once asked Whistler of a London newsboy. "Seven," was the reply. Whistler insisted that he must be older than that, and turning to his friend he remarked: "I don't think he could get as dirty as that in seven years, do you?"

If dirt was trumps, what hands you would hold!—*Charles Lamb.*

CLERGY

"Now, children," said the visiting minister who had been asked to question the Sunday-school, "with what did Samson arm himself to fight against the Philistines?"

None of the children could tell him.

"Oh, yes, you know!" he said, and to help them he tapped his jaw with one finger. "What is this?" he asked.

This jogged their memories, and the class cried in chorus: "The jawbone of an ass."

All work and no plagiarism makes a dull parson.

Bishop Doane of Albany was at one time rector of an Episcopal church in Hartford, and Mark Twain, who occasionally attended his services, played a joke upon him, one Sunday.

"Dr. Doane," he said at the end of the service, "I enjoyed your sermon this morning. I welcomed it like on old friend. I have, you know, a book at home containing every word of it."

"You have not," said Dr. Doane.

"I have so."

"Well, send that book to me. I'd like to see it."

"I'll send it," the humorist replied. Next morning he sent an unabridged dictionary to the rector.

The four-year-old daughter of a clergyman was ailing one night and was put to bed early. As her mother was about to leave her she called her back.

"Mamma," she said, "I want to see my papa."

"No, dear," her mother replied, "your papa is busy and must not be disturbed."

"But, mamma," the child persisted, "I want to see my papa."

As before, the mother replied: "No, your papa must not be disturbed."

But the little one came back with a clincher:

"Mamma," she declared solemnly, "I am a sick woman, and I want to see my minister."

Professor—"Now, Mr. Jones, assuming you were called to attend a patient who had swallowed a coin, what would be your method of procedure?"

Young Medico—"I'd send for a preacher, sir. They'll get money out of anyone."

Archbishop Ryan was once accosted on the streets of Baltimore by a man who knew the archbishop's face, but could not quite place it.

"Now, where in hell have I seen you?" he asked perplexedly.

"From where in hell do you come, sir?"

A Duluth pastor makes it a point to welcome any strangers cordially, and one evening, after the completion of the service, he hurried down the aisle to station himself at the door.

He noticed a Swedish girl, evidently a servant, so he welcomed her to the church. and expressed the hope that she would be a regular attendant. Finally he said if she would be at home some evening during the week he would call.

"T'ank you," she murmured bashfully, "but ay have a fella.'

A minister of a fashionable church in Newark had always left the greeting of strangers to be attended to by the ushers, until he read the newspaper articles in reference to the matter.

"Suppose a reporter should visit our church?" said his wife. "Wouldn't it be awful?"

"It would," the minister admitted.

The following Sunday evening he noticed a plainly dressed woman in one of the free pews. She sat alone and was clearly not a member of the flock. After the benediction the minister hastened and intercepted her at the door.

"How do you do?" he said, offering his hand, "I am very glad to have you with us."

"Thank you," replied the young woman.

"I hope we may see you often in our church home," he went on. "We are always glad to welcome new faces."

"Yes, sir."

"Do you live in this parish?" he asked.

The girl looked blank.

"If you will give me your address my wife and I will call on you some evening."

"You wouldn't need to go far, sir," said the young woman, "I'm your cook!"

Bishop Goodsell, of the Methodist Episcopal church, weighs over two hundred pounds. It was with mingled emotions, therefore that he read the following *Zion's Herald* some time ago:

"The announcement that our New England bishop, Daniel A. Goodsell, has promised to preach at the Willimantic camp meeting, will give great pleasure to the hosts of Israel who are looking forward to that feast of fat things."

It is a standing rule of a company whose boats ply the Great Lakes that clergymen and Indians may travel on its boats for half-fare. A short time ago an agent of the company was approached by an Indian preacher from Canada, who asked for free transportation on the ground that he was entitled to one-half rebate because he was an Indian, and the other half because he was a clergyman.—*Elgin Burroughs.*

Booker Washington, as all the world knows, believes that the salvation of his race lies in industry. Thus, if a young man wants to be a clergyman, he will meet with but little encouragement from the head of Tuskegee; but if he wants to be a blacksmith or a bricklayer, his welcome is warm and hearty.

Dr. Washington, in a recent address in Chicago, said:

"The world is overfull of preachers and when an aspirant for the pulpit comes to me, I am inclined to tell him about the old uncle working in the cotton field who said:

"'De cotton am so grassy, de work am so hard, and de sun am so hot, Ah 'clare to goodness Ah believe dis darkey am called to preach.'"

On one occasion the minister delivered a sermon of but ten minutes' duration—a most unusual thing for him.

Upon the conclusion of his remarks he added: "I regret to inform you, brethren, that my dog, who appears to be peculiarly fond of paper, this morning ate that portion of my sermon that I have not delivered. Let us pray."

After the service the clergyman was met at the door by a man who as a rule, attended divine service in another parish. Shaking the good man by the hand he said:

"Doctor, I should like to know whether that dog of yours has any pups. If so I want to get one to give to my minister."

Recipe for a parson:
> To a cupful of negative goodness
> Add the pleasure of giving advice.
> Sift in a peck of dry sermons,
> And flavor with brimstone or ice.

—Life

A pompous Bishop of Oxford was once stopped on a London street by a ragged urchin.

"Well, my little man, and what can I do for you?" inquired the churchman.

"The time o' day, please, your lordship."

With considerable difficulty the portly bishop extracted his timepiece.

"It is exactly half past five, my lad."

"Well," said the boy, setting his feet for a good start, "at 'alf past six you go to 'ell!"—and he was off like a flash and around the corner. The bishop, flushed and furious, his watch dangling from its chain, floundered wildly after him. But as he rounded the corner he ran plump into the outstretched arms of the venerable Bishop of London.

"Oxford, Oxford," remonstrated that surprised dignitary, "why this unseemly haste?"

Puffing, blowing, spluttering, the outraged Bishop gasped out:

"That young ragamuffin—I told him it was half past five—he—er—told me to go to hell at half past six."

"Yes, yes," said the Bishop of London with the suspicion of a twinkle in his kindly old eyes, "but why such haste? You've got almost an hour."

> Skilful alike with tongue and pen,
> He preached to all men everywhere
> The Gospel of the Golden Rule,
> The New Commandment given to men,
> Thinking the deed, and not the creed,
> Would help us in our utmost need.

—Longfellow.

See also Burglars; Contribution box; Preaching; Resignation.

CLIMATE

In a certain town the local forecaster of the weather was so often wrong that his predictions became a standing joke, to his no small annoyance, for he was very sensitive. At length, in despair of living down his reputation, he asked headquarters to transfer him to another station.

A brief correspondence ensued.

"Why," asked headquarters, "do you wish to be transferred?"

"Because," the forecaster promptly replied, "the climate doesn't agree with me."

CLOTHING

One morning as Mark Twain returned from a neighborhood morning call, sans necktie, his wife met him at the door with the exclamation: "There, Sam, you have been over to the Stowes's again without a necktie! It's really disgraceful the way you neglect your dress!"

Her husband said nothing, but went up to his room.

A few minutes later his neighbor—Mrs. S.—was summoned to the door by a messenger, who presented her with a small box neatly done up. She opened it and found a black silk necktie, accompanied by the following note: "Here is a necktie. Take it out and look at it. I think I stayed half an hour this morning. At the end of that time will you kindly return it as it is the only one I have?—Mark Twain."

A man whose trousers bagged badly at the knees was standing on a corner waiting for a car. A passing Irishman stopped and watched him with great interest for two or three minutes; at last he said:

"Well, why don't ye jump?"

"The evening wore on," continued the man who was telling the story.

"Excuse me," interrupted the would-be-wit; "but can you tell us what the evening wore on that occasion?"

"I don't know that it is important," replied the story-teller. "But if you must know, I believe it was the close of a summer day."

"See that measuring worm crawling up my skirt!" cried Mrs. Bjenks. "That's a sign I'm going to have a new dress."

"Well, let him make it for you," growled Mr. Bjenks. "And while he's about it, have him send a hookworm to do you up the back. I'm tired of the job."

Dwellers in huts and in marble halls—
    From Shepherdess up to Queen—
Cared little for bonnets, and less for shawls,
    And nothing for crinoline.
But now simplicity's *not* the rage,
    And it's funny to think how cold
The dress they wore in the Golden Age
    Would seem in the Age of Gold.
                            —*Henry S. Leigh.*

Costly thy habit as thy purse can buy,
But not express'd in fancy; rich, not gaudy;
For the apparel oft proclaims the man.
                            —*Shakespeare.*

CLUBS

Belle and Ben had just announced their engagement.

"When we are married," said Belle, "I shall expect you to shave every morning. It's one of the rules of the club I belong to that none of its members shall marry a man who won't shave every morning."

"Oh, that's all right," replied Ben; "but what about the mornings I don't get home in time? I belong to a club, too."
                            —*M. A. Hitchcock.*

The guest landing at the yacht club float with his host, both of them wearing oilskins and sou'-westers to protect them from the drenching rain, inquired:

"And who are those gentlemen seated on the veranda, looking so spick and span in their white duck yachting caps and trousers, and keeping the waiters running all the time?"

"They're the rocking-chair members. They never go outside, and they're waterproof inside."

One afternoon thirty ladies met at the home of Mrs. Lyons to form a woman's club. The hostess was unanimously elected president. The next day the following ad appeared in the newspaper:

"Wanted—a reliable woman to take care of a baby. Apply to Mrs. J. W. Lyons."

COAL DEALERS

In a Kansas town where two brothers are engaged in the retail coal business a revival was recently held and the elder of the brothers was converted. For weeks he tried to persuade his brother to join the church. One day he asked:

"Why can't you join the church like I did?"

"It's a fine thing for you to belong to the church," replied the younger brother, "If I join the church who'll weigh the coal?"

COEDUCATION

The speaker was waxing eloquent, and after his peroration on woman's rights he said: "When they take our girls, as they threaten, away from the coeducational colleges, what will follow? What will follow, I repeat?"

And a loud, masculine voice in the audience replied: "I will!"

COFFEE

Among the coffee-drinkers a high place must be given to Bismarck. He liked coffee unadulterated. While with the Prussian Army in France he one day entered a country inn and asked the host if he had any chicory in the house. He had. Bismarck said—"Well, bring it to me; all you have." The man obeyed and handed Bismarck a canister full of chicory. "Are you sure this is all you have?" demanded the Chancellor. Yes, my lord, every grain." "Then," said Bismarck, keeping the canister by him, "go now and make me a pot of coffee."

COINS

He had just returned from Paris and said to his old aunt in the country: "Here, Aunt, is a silver franc piece I brought you from Paris as a souvenir."

"Thanks, Herman," said the old lady. "I wish you'd thought to have brought me home one of them Latin quarters I read so much about."

COLLECTING OF ACCOUNTS

An enterprising firm advertised: "All persons indebted to our store are requested to call and settle. All those indebted to our store and not knowing it are requested to call and find out. Those knowing themselves indebted and not wishing to call, are requested to stay in one place long enough for us to catch them."

"Sir," said the haughty American to his adhesive tailor, "I object to this boorish dunning. I would have you know that my great-great-grandfather was one of the early settlers."

"And yet," sighed the anxious tradesman, "there are people who believe in heredity."

A retail dealer in buggies doing business in one of the large towns in northern Indiana wrote to a firm in the east ordering a carload of buggies. The firm wired him:

"Cannot ship buggies until you pay for your last consignment."

"Unable to wait so long," wired back the buggy dealer, "cancel order."

> The saddest words of tongue or pen
> May be perhaps, "It might have been,"
> The sweetest word we know, by heck,
> Are only these "Enclosed find check!"
>
> *Minne-Ha-Ha.*

COLLECTORS AND COLLECTING

Sir Walter Raleigh had called to take a cup of tea with Queen Elizabeth.

"It was very good of you, Sir Walter," said her Majesty, smiling sweetly upon the gallant Knight, "to ruin your cloak the other day so that my feet should not be wet by that horrid puddle. May I not instruct my Lord High Treasurer to reimburse you for it?"

"Don't mention it, your Majesty," replied Raleigh. "It only cost two and six, and I have already sold it to an American collector for eight thousand pounds."

COLLEGE GRADUATES

"Can't I take your order for one of our encyclopedias!" asked the dapper agent.

"No I guess not," said the busy man. "I might be able to use it a few times, but my son will be home from college in June."

COLLEGE STUDENTS

"Say, dad, remember that story you told me about when you were expelled from college?"

"Yes."

"Well, I was just thinking, dad, how true it is that history re-repeats itself."

WANTED: Burly beauty-proof individual to read meters in sorority houses. We haven't made a nickel in two years. The Gas Co.—*Michigan Gargoyle.*

FRESHMAN—"I have a sliver in my finger."
SOPH—"Been scratching your head?"

STUDE—"Do you smoke, professor?"
PROF.—"Why, yes, I'm very fond of a good cigar.
STUDE—"Do you drink, sir?"
PROF.—"Yes, indeed, I enjoy nothing better than a bottle of wine."
STUDE—"Gee, it's going to cost me something to pass this course."—*Cornell Widow.*

Three boys from Yale, Princeton and Harvard were in a room when a lady entered. The Yale boy asked languidly if some fellow ought not to give a chair to the lady; the Princeton boy slowly brought one, and the Harvard boy deliberately sat down in it.—*Life.*

A college professor was one day nearing the close of a history lecture and was indulging in one of those rhetorical climaxes in which he delighted when the hour struck. The students immediately began to slam down the movable arms of their lecture chairs and to prepare to leave.

The professor, annoyed at the interruption of his flow of eloquence, held up his hand:

"Wait just one minute, gentlemen. I have a few more pearls to cast."

When Rutherford B. Hayes was a student at college it was his custom to take a walk before breakfast.

One morning two of his student friends went with him After walking a short distance they met an old man with a long white beard. Thinking that they would have a little fun at the old man's expense, the first one bowed to him very gracefully and said: "Good morning, Father Abraham."

The next one made a low bow and said: "Good morning, Father Isaac."

Young Hayes then made his bow and said: "Good morning Father Jacob."

The old man looked at them a moment and then said: "Young men, I am neither Abraham, Isaac nor Jacob. I am Saul, the son of Kish, and I am out looking for my father's asses, and lo, I have found them."

A western college boy amused himself by writing stories and giving them to papers for nothing. His father objected and wrote to the boy that he was wasting his time. In answer the college lad wrote:

"So, dad, you think I am wasting my time in writing for the local papers and cite Johnson's saying that the man who writes, except for money, is a fool. I shall act upon Doctor Johnson's suggestion and write for money. Send me fifty dollars."

The president of an eastern university had just announced in chapel that the freshman class was the largest enrolled in the history of the institution. Immediately he followed the announcement by reading the text for the morning: "Lord, how are they increased that trouble me!"

STUDE—"Is it possible to confide a secret to you?"
FRIEND—"Certainly. I will be as silent as the grave."
STUDE—"Well, then, I have a pressing need for two bucks."
FRIEND—"Do not worry. It is as if I had heard nothing.
                                        —*Michigan Gargoyle.*

"Why did you come to college, anyway? You are not studying," said the Professor.

"Well," said Willie, "I don't know exactly myself. Mother says it is to fit me for the Presidency; Uncle Bill, to sow my wild oats; Sis, to get a chum for her to marry, and Pa, to bankrupt the family."

A young Irishman at college in want of twenty-five dollars wrote to his uncle as follows:

"Dear Uncle—If you could see how I blush for shame while I am writing, you would pity me. Do you know why? Because I have to ask you for a few dollars, and do not know how to express myself. It is impossible for me to tell you. I prefer to die. I send you this by messenger, who will wait for an answer. Believe me, my dearest uncle, your most obedient and affectionate nephew.

"P.S.—Overcome with shame for what I have written, I have been running after the messenger in order to take the letter from him, but I cannot catch him. Heaven grant that something may happen to stop him, or that this letter may get lost."

The uncle was naturally touched, but was equal to the emergency. He replied as follows:

"My Dear Jack—Console yourself and blush no more. Providence has heard your prayers. The messenger lost your letter. Your affectionate uncle."

The professor was delivering the final lecture of the term. He dwelt with much emphasis on the fact that each student should devote all the intervening time preparing for the final examinations.

"The examination papers are now in the hand of the printer. Are there any questions to be asked?"

Silence prevailed. Suddenly a voice from the rear inquired: "Who's the printer?"

It was Commencement Day at a well-known woman's college, and the father of one of the young women came to attend the graduation exercises. He was presented to the president, who said, "I congratulate you, sir, upon your extremely large and affectionate family."

"Large and affectionate?" he stammered and looking very much surprised.

"Yes, indeed," said the president. "Not less than twelve of your daughter's brothers have called frequently during the winter to take her driving and sleighing, while your eldest son escorted her to the theater at least twice a week. Unusually nice brothers they are."

The world's great men have not commonly been great scholars, nor its great scholars great men.—*O. W. Holmes.*

See also Harvard university; Scholarship.

COLLEGES AND UNIVERSITIES

The college is a coy maid—
    She has a habit quaint
Of making eyes at millionaires
    And winking at the taint.—*Judge.*

"What is a 'faculty'?"
"A 'faculty' is a body of men surrounded by red tape."
                                        —*Cornell Widow.*

Yale University is to have a ton of fossils. Whether for the faculty or for the museums is not announced.
                                        —*The Atlanta Journal.*

FIRST TRUSTEE—"But this ancient institution of learning will fail unless something is done."

SECOND TRUSTEE—"True; but what can we do? We have already raised the tuition until it is almost 1 per cent of the fraternity fees."—*Puck.*

The president of the university had dark circles under his eyes. His cheek was pallid; his lips were trembling; he wore a hunted expression.

"You look ill," said his wife. "What is wrong, dear?"

"Nothing much," he replied. "But—I—I had a fearful dream last night, and I feel this morning as if I—as if I—" It was evident that his nervous system was shattered.

"What was the dream?" asked his wife.

"I—I—dreamed the trustees required that—that I should—that I should pass the freshman examination for—admission!" sighed the president.

COMMON SENSE

A mysterious building had been erected on the outskirts of a small town. It was shrouded in mystery. All that was known about it was that it was a chemical laboratory. An old farmer, driving past the place after work had been started, and seeing a man in the doorway, called to him:

"What be ye doin' in this place?"

"We are searching for a universal solvent—something that will dissolve all things," said the chemist.

"What good will thet be?"

"Imagine, sir! It will dissolve all things. If we want a solution of iron, glass, gold—anything, all that we have to do is to drop it in this solution."

"Fine," said the farmer, "fine! What be ye goin' to keep it in?"

COMMUTERS

BRIGGS—"Is it true that you have broken off your engagement to that girl who lives in the suburbs?"

GRIGGS—"Yes; they raised the commutation rates on me and I have transferred to a town girl."

"I see you carrying home a new kind of breakfast food," remarked the first commuter.

"Yes," said the second commuter, "I was missing too many trains. The old brand required three seconds to prepare. You can fix this new brand in a second and a half."

After the sermon on Sunday morning the rector welcomed and shook hands with a young German.

"And are you a regular communicant?" said the rector.

"Yes," said the German: "I take the 7:45 every morning."
                                                —*M. L. Hayward.*

A suburban train was slowly working its way through one of the blizzards of 1894. Finally it came to a dead stop and all efforts to start it again were futile.

In the wee, small hours of the morning a weary commuter, numb from the cold and the cramped position in which he had tried to sleep, crawled out of the train and floundered through the heavy snow-drifts to the nearest telegraph station. This is the message he handed to the operator:

"Will not be at office to-day. Not home yesterday yet."

A nervous commuter on his dark, lonely way home from the railroad station heard footsteps behind him. He had an uncomfortable feeling that he was being followed. He increased his speed. The footsteps quickened accordingly. The commuter darted down a lane. The footsteps still pursued him. In desperation he vaulted over a fence and, rushing into a churchyard, threw himself panting on one of the graves.

"If he follows me here," he thought fearfully, "there can be not doubt as to his intentions."

The man behind was following. He could hear him scrambling over the fence. Visions of highwaymen, maniacs, garroters and the like flashed through his brain. Quivering with fear, the nervous one arose and faced his pursuer.

"What do you want?" he demanded. "Wh-why are you following me?"

"Say," asked the stranger, mopping his brow, "do you always go home like this? I'm going up to Mr. Brown's and the man at the station told me to follow you, as you lived next door. Excuse my asking you, but is there much more to do before we get there?"

COMPARISONS

A milliner endeavored to sell a colored woman one of the last season's hats at a very moderate price. It was a big white picture-hat.

"Law, no, honey!" exclaimed the woman. "I could nevah wear that. I'd look jes' like a blueberry in a pan of milk."

A well-known author tells of an English spinster who said, as she watched a great actress writhing about the floor as Cleopatra:

"How different from the home life of our late dear queen!"

"Darling," whispered the ardent suitor, "I lay my fortune at your feet."

"Your fortune?" she replied in surprise. "I didn't know you had one."

"Well, it isn't much of a fortune, but it will look large besides those tiny feet."

"Girls make me tired," said the fresh young man. "They are always going to palmists to have their hands read."

"Indeed!" said she sweetly; "is that any worse than men going into saloons to get their noses red?"

A friend once wrote Mark Twain a letter saying that he was in very bad health, and concluding: "Is there anything worse than having toothache and earache at the same time?"

The humorist wrote back: "Yes, rheumatism and Saint Vitus's dance."

The Rev. Dr. William Emerson, of Boston, son of Ralph Waldo Emerson, recently made a trip through the South, and one Sunday attended a meeting in a colored church. The preacher was a white man, however, a white man whose first name was George, and evidently a prime favorite with the colored brethren. When the service was over Dr. Emerson walked home behind two members of the congregation, and overheard this conversation: "Massa George am a mos' pow'-ful preacher." "He am dat." "He's mos's pow'ful as Abraham Lincoln." "Huh! He's mo' pow'ful dan Lincoln." "He's mos' 's pow'ful as George Washin'ton." "Huh! He's mo' pow'ful dan Washin'ton." "Massa George ain't quite as pow'ful as God." "N-n-o, not quite. But he's a young man yet."

Is it possible your pragmatical worship should not know that the comparisons made between wit and wit, courage and cour-age, beauty and beauty, birth and birth, are always odious and ill taken?—*Cervantes.*

COMPENSATION

"Speakin' of de law of compensation," said Uncle Eben, "an automobile goes faster dan a mule, but at de same time it hits harder and balks longer."

COMPETITION

A new baby arrived at a house. A little girl—now fifteen—had been the pet of the family. Every one made much of her, but when there was a new baby she felt rather neglected.

"How are you, Mary?" a visitor asked of her one afternoon.

"Oh, I'm all right," she said, "except that I think there is too much competition in this world."

A farmer during a long-continued drought invented a ma-chine for watering his fields. The very first day while he was trying it there suddenly came a downpour of rain. He put away his machine.

"It's no use," he said; "you can do nothing nowadays without competition."

COMPLIMENTS

Supper was in progress, and the father was telling about a row which took place in front of his store that morning: "The first thing I saw was one man deal the other a sounding blow, and then a crowd gathered. The man who was struck ran and grabbed a large shovel he had been using on the street, and rushed back, his eyes blazing fiercely. I thought he'd surely knock the other man's brains out, and I stepped right in between them."

The young son of the family had become so hugely interested in the narrative as it proceeded that he had stopped eating his pudding. So proud was he of his father's valor, his eyes fairly shone, and he cried:

"He couldn't knock any brains out of you, could he, Father?"

Father looked at him long and earnestly, but the lad's countenance was frank and open.

Father gasped slightly, and resumed his supper.

See also Tact.

COMPOSERS

Recipe for the musical comedy composer:
　　Librettos of all the operas,
　　　Some shears and a bottle of paste,
　　Curry the hits of last season,
　　　Add tumpty-tee tra la to taste.

—Life.

COMPROMISES

Boss—"There's $10 gone from my cash drawer, Johnny; you and I were the only people who had keys to that drawer."

Office Boy—"Well, s'pose we each pay $5 and say no more about it."

CONFESSIONS

"You say Garston made a complete confession? What did he get—five years?"

"No, fifty dollars. He confessed to the magazines."—*Puck.*

Little Ethel had been brought up with a firm hand and was always taught to report misdeeds promptly. One afternoon she came sobbing penitently to her mother.

"Mother, I—I broke a brick in the fireplace."

"Well, it might be worse. But how on earth did you do it, Ethel?"

"I pounded it with your watch."

"Confession is good for the soul."

"Yes, but it's bad for the reputation."

CONGRESS

Congress is a national inquisitorial body for the purpose of acquiring valuable information and then doing nothing about it.—*Life*.

"Judging from the stuff printed in the newspapers," says a congressman, "we are a pretty bad lot. Almost in the class a certain miss whom I know unconsciously puts us in. It was at a recent examination at her school that the question was put, 'Who makes the laws of our government?'

" 'Congress,' was the united reply.

" 'How is Congress divided?' was the next query.

"My young friend raised her hand.

" 'Well,' said the teacher, 'what do you say the answer is?'

"Instantly, with an air of confidence as well as triumph, the Miss replied, 'Civilized, half civilized, and savage.' "

CONGRESSMEN

It was at a banquet in Washington given to a large body of congressmen, mostly from the rural districts. The tables were elegant, and it was a scene of fairy splendor; but on one table there were no decorations but plain leaves.

"Here," said a congressman to the head waiter, "why don't you put them things on our table too?" pointing to the plants.

The head waiter didn't know he was a congressman.

"We cain't do it boss," he whispered confidentially; "dey's mostly congressmen at 'dis table, an' if we put pa'ms on de table dey take um for celery an' eat um all up sho. 'Deed dey would, boss. We knows 'em."

Representative X, from North Carolina, was one night awakened by his wife, who whispered, "John, John, get up! There are robbers in the house."

"Robbers?" he said. "There may be robbers in the Senate, Mary; but not in the House! It's preposterous!"

—*John N. Cole, Jr.*

Champ Clark loves to tell of how in the heat of a debate Congressman Johnson of Indiana called an Illinois representative a jackass. The expression was unparliamentary, and in retraction Johnson said:

"While I withdraw the unfortunate word, Mr. Speaker, I must insist that the gentleman from Illinois is out of order."

"How am I out of order?" yelled the man from Illinois.

"Probably a veterinary surgeon could tell you," answered Johnson, and that was parliamentary enough to stay on the record.

A Georgia Congressman had put up at an American-plan hotel in New York. When, upon sitting down at dinner the first evening of his stay, the waiter obsequiously handed him a bill of fare, the Congressman tossed it aside, slipped the waiter a dollar bill, and said, "Bring me a good dinner."

The dinner proving satisfactory, the Southern member pursued this plan during his entire stay in New York. As the last tip was given, he mentioned that he was about to return to Washington.

Whereupon, the waiter, with an expression of great earnestness, said:

"Well, sir, when you or any of your friends that can't read come to New York, just ask for Dick."

CONSCIENCE

The moral of this story may be that it is better to heed the warnings of the "still small voice" before it is driven to the use of the telephone.

A New York lawyer, gazing idly out of his window, saw a sight in an office across the street that made him rub his eyes and look again. Yes, there was no doubt about it. The pretty stenographer was sitting upon the gentleman's lap. The lawyer noticed the name that was lettered on the window and then searched in the telephone book. Still keeping his eye upon the scene across the street, he called the gentleman up. In a few moments he saw him start violently and take down the receiver.

"Yes," said the lawyer through the telephone, "I should think you would start."

The victim whisked his arm from its former position and began to stammer something.

"Yes," continued the lawyer severely, "I think you'd better take that arm away. And while you're about it, as long as there seems to be plenty of chairs in the room—"

The victim brushed the lady from his lap, rather roughly, it is to be feared. "Who—who the devil is this, anyhow?" he managed to splutter.

"I," answered the lawyer in deep, impressive tones, "am your conscience!"

> A quiet conscience makes one so serene!
> Christians have burnt each other, quite persuaded
> That all the Apostles would have done as they did.
> —*Byron.*

> Oh, Conscience! Conscience! man's most faithful friend,
> Him canst thou comfort, ease, relieve, defend;
> But if he will thy friendly checks forego,
> Thou art, oh! woe for me his deadliest foe!
> —*Crabbe.*

CONSEQUENCES

A teacher asked her class in spelling to state the difference between the words "results" and "consequences."

A bright girl replied, "Results are what you expect, and consequences are what you get."

Consequences are unpitying. Our deeds carry their terrible consequences, quite apart from any fluctuations that went before —consequences that are hardly ever confined to ourselves.
—*George Eliot.*

CONSIDERATION

The goose had been carved at the Christmas dinner and everybody had tasted it. It was excellent. The negro minister, who was the guest of honor, could not restrain his enthusiasm.

"Dat's as fine a goose as I evah see, Bruddah Williams," he said to his host. "Whar did you git such a fine goose?"

"Well, now, Pahson," replied the carver of the goose, exhibiting great dignity and reticence, "when you preaches a speshul good sermon I never axes you whar you got it. I hopes you will show me da same considerashion."

A clergyman, who was summoned in haste by a woman who had been taken suddenly ill, answered the call though somewhat puzzled by it, for he knew that she was not of his parish, and was, moreover, known to be a devoted worker in another church. While he was waiting to be shown to the sick-room he fell to talking to the little girl of the house.

"It is very gratifying to know that your mother thought of me in her illness," said he, "Is your minister out of town?"

"Oh, no," answered the child, in a matter-of-fact tone. "He's home; only we thought it might be something contagious, and we didn't want to take any risks."

CONSTANCY

A soldier belonging to a brigade in command of a General who believed in a celibate army asked permission to marry, as he had two good-conduct badges and money in the savings-bank.

"Well, go-away," said the General, "and if you come back to me a year from today in the same frame of mind you shall marry. I'll keep the vacancy."

On the anniversary the soldier repeated his request.

"But do you really, after a year, want to marry?" inquired the General in a surprised tone.

"Yes, sir; very much."

"Sergeant-Major, take his name down. Yes, you may marry. I never believed there was so much constancy in man or woman. Right face; quick march!"

As the man left the room, turning his head, he said, "Thank you, sir; but it isn't the same woman"

CONTRIBUTION BOX

> The parson looks it o'er and frets.
> It puts him out of sorts
> To see how many times he gets
> A penny for his thoughts.
>
> —*J. J. O'Connell.*

There were introductions all around. The big man stared in a puzzled way at the club guest. "You look like a man I've seen somewhere, Mr. Blinker," he said. "Your face seems familiar. I fancy you have a double. And a funny thing about it is that I remember I formed a strong prejudice against the man who looks like you—although, I'm quite sure, we never met."

The little guest softly laughed. "I'm the man," he answered, "and I know why you formed the prejudice. I passed the contribution plate for two years in the church you attended."

The collections had fallen off badly in the colored church and the pastor made a short address before the box was passed.

"I don' want any man to gib mo' dan his share, bredern," he said gently, "but we mus' all gib ercordin' to what we rightly hab. I say 'rightly hab,' bredern, because we don't want no tainted money in dis box. Squire Jones tol' me dat he done miss some chickens dis week. Now if any of our bredern hab fallen by de wayside in connection wif dose chickens let him stay his hand from de box.

"Now, Deacon Smiff, please pass de box while I watch de signs an' see if dere's any one in dis congregation dat needs me ter wrastle in prayer fer him."

A newly appointed Scotch minister on his first Sunday of office had reason to complain of the poorness of the collection. "Mon," replied one of the elders, "they are close—vera close.

But," confidentially, "the auld meenister he put three or four saxpenses into the plate hissel', just to gie them a start. Of course he took the saxpenses awa' with him afterward." The new minister tried the same plan, but the next Sunday he again had to report a dismal failure. The total collection was not only small, but he was grieved to find that his own sixpenses were missing. "Ye may be a better preacher than the auld meenister," exclaimed the elder, "but if ye had half the knowledge o' the world, an' o' yer ain flock in particular, ye'd ha' done what he did an' glued the saxpenses to the plate."

POLICE COMMISSIONER—"If you were ordered to disperse a mob, what would you do?"

APPLICANT—"Pass around the hat, sir."

POLICE COMMISSIONER—"That'll do; you're engaged."

"I advertised that the poor were made welcome in this church," said the vicar to his congregation, "and as the offertory amounts to ninety-five cents, I see that they have come."

See also **Salvation.**

CONUNDRUMS

"Mose, what is the difference between a bucket of milk in a rain storm and a conversation between two confidence men?"

"Say, boss, dat nut am too hard to crack; I'se gwine to give it up."

"Well, Mose, one is a thinning scheme and the other is a skinning theme."

CONVERSATION

"My dog understands every word I say."

"Um."

"Do you doubt it?"

"No, I do not doubt the brute's intelligence. The scant attention he bestows upon your conversation would indicate that he understands it perfectly."

THE TALL AND AGGRESSIVE ONE—"Excuse me, but I'm in a hurry! You've had that phone twenty minutes and not said a word!"

THE SHORT AND MEEK ONE—"Sir, I'm talking to my wife."
—*Puck.*

HUB (during a quarrel)—"You talk like an idiot."
WIFE—"I've got to talk so you can understand me."

Irving Bacheller, it appears, was on a tramping tour through New England. He discovered a chin-bearded patriarch on a roadside rock.

"Fine corn," said Mr. Bacheller, tentatively, using a hillside filled with straggling stalks as a means of breaking the conversational ice.

"Best in Massachusetts," said the sitter.

"How do you plow that field?" asked Mr. Bacheller. "It is so very steep."

"Don't plow it," said the sitter. "When the spring thaws come, the rocks rolling down hill tear it up so that we can plant corn."

"And how do you plant it?" asked Mr. Bacheller. The sitter said that he didn't plant it, really. He stood in his back door and shot the seed in with a shotgun.

"Is that the truth?" asked Bacheller.

"H—ll no," said the sitter, disgusted. "That's conversation."

Conversation is the laboratory and workshop of the student. —*Emerson.*

A single conversation across the table with a wise man is better than ten years' study of books.—*Longfellow.*

COOKERY

"John, John," whispered an alarmed wife, poking her sleeping husband in the ribs. "Wake up, John; there are burglars in the pantry and they're eating all my pies."

"Well, what do we care," mumbled John, rolling over, "so long as they don't die in the house?"

"This is certainly a modern cook-book in every way."

"How so?"

"It says: 'After mixing your bread, you can watch two reels at the movies before putting it in the oven.'"—*Puck.*

There was recently presented to a newly-married young woman in Baltimore such a unique domestic proposition that she felt called upon to seek expert advice from another woman, whom she knew to possess considerable experience in the cooking line.

"Mrs. Jones," said the first mentioned young woman, as she breathlessly entered the apartment of the latter, "I'm sorry to trouble you, but I *must* have your advice."

"What is the trouble, my dear?"

"Why, I've just had a 'phone message from Harry, saying that he is going out this afternoon to shoot clay pigeons. Now, he's bound to bring a lot home, and I haven't the remotest idea how to cook them. Won't you please tell me?"—*Taylor Edwards.*

Heaven sends us good meat, but the devil sends us cooks.—*David Garrick.*

COOKS

See Servants.

CORNETS

Spurgeon was once asked if the man who learned to play a cornet on Sunday would go to heaven.

The great preacher's reply was characteristic. Said he: "I don't see why he should not, but"—after a pause—"I doubt whether the man next door will."

CORNS

Great aches from little toe-corns grow.

CORPULENCE

The wife of a prominent Judge was making arrangements with the colored laundress of the village to take charge of their washing for the summer. Now, the Judge was pompous and extremely fat. He tipped the scales at some three hundred pounds.

"Missus," said the woman, "I'll do your washing, but I'se gwine ter charge you double for your husband's shirts."

"Why, what is your reason for that Nancy," questioned the mistress.

"Well," said the laundress, "I don't mind washing fur an ordinary man, but I draws de line on circus tents, I sho' do."

An employee of a rolling mill was on his vacation when he fell in love with a handsome German girl. Upon his return to the works, he went to Mr. Carnegie and announced that as he wanted to get married he would like a little further time off. Mr. Carnegie appeared much interested. "Tell me about her," he said. "Is she short or is she tall, slender, willowy?"

"Well, Mr. Carnegie," was the answer, "all I can say is that if I'd had the rolling of her, I should have given her two or three more passes."

A very stout old lady, bustling through the park on a sweltering hot day, became aware that she was being closely followed by a rough-looking tramp.

"What do you mean by following me in this manner?" she indignantly demanded. The tramp slunk back a little. But when the stout lady resumed her walk he again took up his position directly behind her.

"See here," she exclaimed, wheeling angrily, "if you don't go away at once I shall call a policeman!"

The unfortunate man looked up at her appealingly.

"For Heaven's sake, kind lady, have mercy an' don't call a policeman; ye're the only shady spot in the whole park."

A jolly steamboat captain with more girth than height was asked if he had ever had any very narrow escapes.

"Yes," he replied, his eyes twinkling; "once I fell off my boat at the mouth of Bear Creek, and, although I'm an expert swimmer, I guess I'd be there now if it hadn't been for my crew. You see the water was just deep enough so's to be over my head when I tried to wade out, and just shallow enough"—he gave his body an explanatory pat—"so that whenever I tried to swim out I dragged bottom."

A very large lady entered a street car and a young man near the door rose and said: "I will be one of three to give the lady a seat."

To our Fat Friends: May their shadows never grow less.

See also Dancing.

COSMOPOLITANISM

Secretary of State Lazansky refused to incorporate the Hell Cafe of New York.

"New York's cafes are singular enough," said Mr. Lazansky, "without the addition of such a queerly named institution as the Hell."

He smiled and added:

"Is there anything quite so queerly cosmopolitan as a New York cafe? In the last one I visited, I saw a Portuguese, a German and an Italian, dressed in English clothes and seated at a table of Spanish walnut, lunching on Russian caviar, French rolls, Scotch salmon, Welsh rabbit, Swiss cheese, Dutch cake and Malaga raisins. They drank China tea and Irish whisky."

COST OF LIVING

"Did you punish our son for throwing a lump of coal at Willie Smiggs?" asked the careful mother.

"I did," replied the busy father. "I don't care so much for the Smiggs boy, but I can't have anybody in this family throwing coal around like that."

"Live within your income," was a maxim uttered by Mr. Carnegie on his seventy-sixth birthday. This is easy; the difficulty is to live without it.—*Satire.*

"You say your jewels were stolen while the family was at dinner?"

"No, no! This is an important robbery. Our dinner was stolen while we were putting on our jewels."

A grouchy butcher, who had watched the price of porterhouse steak climb the ladder of fame, was deep in the throes of an unusually bad grouch when a would-be customer, eight years old, approached him and handed him a penny.

"Please, mister, I want a cent's worth of sausage."

Turning on the youngster with a growl, he let forth this burst of good salesmanship:

"Go smell o' the hook!"

TOM—"My pa is very religious. He always bows his head and says something before meals."

DICK—"Mine always says something when he sits down to eat, but he don't bow his head."

TOM—"What does he say?"

DICK—"Go easy on the butter, kids, it's forty cents a pound."

COUNTRY LIFE

BILTER (at servants' agency)—"Have you got a cook who will go to the country?"

MANAGER (calling out to girls in next room)—"Is there any one here who would like to spend a day in the country?"—*Life.*

VISITOR—"You have a fine road leading from the station."

SUBUBS—"That's the path worn by servant-girls."

See also Commuters; Servants.

COURAGE

AUNT ETHEL—"Well, Beatrice, were you very brave at the dentist's?"

BEATRICE—"Yes, auntie, I was."

AUNT ETHEL—"Then, there's the half crown I promised you. And now tell me what he did to you."

BEATRICE—"He pulled out two of Willie's teeth!"—*Punch.*

He was the small son of a bishop, and his mother was teaching him the meaning of courage.

"Supposing," she said, "there were twelve boys in one bedroom, and eleven got into bed at once, while the other knelt down to say his prayers, that boy would show true courage."

"Oh!" said the young hopeful. "I know something that would be more courageous than that! Supposing there were twelve bishops in one bedroom, and one got into bed without saying his prayers!"

Courage, the highest gift, that scorns to bend
To mean devices for a sordid end.
Courage—an independent spark from Heaven's bright throne,
By which the soul stands raised, triumphant, high, alone.
Great in itself, not praises of the crowd.
Above all vice, it stoops not to be proud.
Courage, the mighty attribute of powers above,
By which those great in war, are great in love.
The spring of all brave acts is seated here,
As falsehoods draw their sordid birth from fear.

—*Farquhar.*

COURTESY

The mayor of a French town had, in accordance with the regulations, to make out a passport for a rich and highly respectable lady of his acquaintance, who, in spite of a slight disfigurement, was very vain of her personal appearance. His native politeness prompted him to gloss over the defect, and, after a moment's reflection, he wrote among the items of personal description: "Eyes dark, beautiful, tender, expressive, but one of them missing."

Mrs. Taft, at a diplomatic dinner, had for a neighbor a distinguished French traveler who boasted a little unduly of his nation's politeness.

"We French," the traveler declared, "are the politest people in the world. Every one acknowledges it. You Americans are a remarkable nation, but the French excel you in politeness. You admit it yourself, don't you?"

Mrs. Taft smiled delicately.

"Yes," she said. "That is our politeness."

Justice Moody was once riding on the platform of a Boston street car standing next to the gate that protected passengers from cars coming on the other track. A Boston lady came to the door of the car and, as it stopped, started toward the gate, which was hidden from her by the man standing before it.

"Other side, lady," said the conductor.

He was ignored as only a born-and-bred Bostonian can ignore a man. The lady took another step toward the gate.

"You must get off the other side," said the conductor.

"I wish to get off on this side," came the answer, in tones that congealed that official. Before he could explain or expostulate Mr. Moody came to his assistance.

"Stand to one side, gentlemen," he remarked quietly. "The lady wishes to climb over the gate."

COURTS

One day when old Thaddeus Stevens was practicing in the courts he didn't like the ruling of the presiding Judge. A second time when the Judge ruled against "old Thad," the old man got up with scarlet face and quivering lips and commenced tying up his papers as if to quit the courtroom.

"Do I understand, Mr. Stevens," asked the Judge, eying "old Thad" indignantly, "that you wish to show your contempt for this court?"

"No, sir; no, sir," replied "old Thad." "I don't want to show my contempt, sir; I'm trying to conceal it."

"It's all right to fine me, Judge," laughed Barrowdale, after the proceedings were over, "but just the same you were ahead of me in your car, and if I was guilty you were too."

"Ya'as, I know," said the judge with a chuckle, "I found myself guilty and hev jest paid my fine into the treasury same ez you."

"Bully for you!" said Barrowdale. "By the way, do you put these fines back into the roads?"

"No," said the judge. "They go to the trial jestice in loo o' sal'ry."

A stranger came into an Augusta bank the other day and presented a check for which he wanted the equivalent in cash.

"Have to be indentified," said the clerk.

The stranger took a bunch of letters from his pocket all addressed to the same name as that on the check.

The clerk shook his head.

The man thought a minute and pulled out his watch, which bore the name on its inside cover.

Clerk hardly glanced at it.

The man dug into his pockets and found one of those "If-I-should-die-tonight-please-notify-my-wife" cards, and called the clerk's attention to the description, which fitted to a T.

But the clerk was still obdurate.

"Those things don't prove anything," he said. "We've got to have the word of a man that we know."

"But, man, I've given you an identification that would convict me of murder in any court in the land."

"That's probably very true," responded the clerk, patiently, "but in matters connected with the bank we have to be more careful."

See also Jury; Witnesses.

COURTSHIP

"Do you think a woman believes you when you tell her she is the first girl you ever loved?"

"Yes, if you're the first liar she has ever met."

Augustus Fitzgibbons Moran
Fell in love with Maria McCann.
   With a yell and a whoop
   He cleared the front stoop
Just ahead of her papa's brogan.

SPOONLEIGH—"Does your sister always look under the bed?"
HER LITTLE BROTHER—"Yes, and when you come to see her
she always looks under the sofa."—*J. J. O'Connell.*

There was a young man from the West,
Who loved a young lady with zest;
   So hard did he press her
   To make her say, "Yes, sir,"
That he broke three cigars in his vest.

"I hope your father does not object to my staying so late,"
said Mr. Stayput as the clock struck twelve.
"Oh, dear, no," replied Miss Dabbs, with difficulty suppressing
a yawn, "He says you save him the expense of a night-watch-
man."

There was an old monk of Siberia,
Whose existence grew drearier and drearier;
   He burst from his cell
   With a hell of a yell,
And eloped with the Mother Superior.

It was scarcely half-past nine when the rather fierce-looking
father of the girl entered the parlor where the timid lover was
courting her. The father had his watch in his hand.
"Young man," he said brusquely, "do you know what time
it is?"
"Y-y-yes sir," stuttered the frightened lover, as he scrambled out into the hall; "I—I was just going to leave!"
After the beau had made a rapid exit, the father turned to
the girl and said in astonishment:
"What was the matter with that fellow? My watch has run
down, and I simply wanted to know the time."

"What were you and Mr. Smith talking about in the parlor?" asked her mother. "Oh, we were discussing our kith and kin," replied the young lady.

The mother look dubiously at her daughter, whereupon her little brother, wishing to help his sister, said:

"Yeth they wath, Mother. I heard 'em. Mr. Thmith asked her for a kith and she thaid, 'You kin.'"

During a discussion of the fitness of things in general some one asked: "If a young man takes his best girl to the grand opera, spends $8 on a supper after the performance, and then takes her home in a taxicab, should he kiss her goodnight?"

An old bachelor who was present growled: "I don't think she ought to expect it. Seems to me he has done enough for her."

A young woman who was about to wed decided at the last moment to test her sweetheart. So, selecting the prettiest girl she knew, she said to her, though she knew it was a great risk.

"I'll arrange for Jack to take you out tonight—a walk on the beach in the moonlight, a lobster supper and all that sort of thing—and I want you, in order to put his fidelity to the proof, to ask him for a kiss."

The other girl laughed, blushed and assented. The dangerous plot was carried out. Then the next day the girl in love visited the pretty one and said anxiously:

"Well, did you ask him?"

"No, dear."

"No? Why not?"

"I didn't get a chance. He asked me first."

Uncle Nehemiah, the proprietor of a ramshackle little hotel in Mobile, was aghast at finding a newly arrived guest with his arm around his daughter's waist.

"Mandy, tell that niggah to take his arm from around yo' wais'," he indignantly commanded.

"Tell him you'self," said Amanda. "He's a puffect stranger to me."

"Jack and I have parted forever."

"Good gracious! What does that mean?"

"Means that I'll get a five-pound box of candy in about an hour."

Here's to solitaire with a partner.

The only game in which one pair beats three of a kind.

See also Love; Proposals.

COWARDS

Mrs. Hicks was telling some ladies about the burglar scare in her house the night before.

"Yes," she said, "I heard a noise and got up, and there, from under the bed, I saw a man's legs sticking out."

"Mercy!" exclaimed a woman. "The burglar's legs?"

"No, my dear; my husband's legs. He heard the noise, too."

Mrs. Peck—"Henry, what would you do if burglars broke into our house some night?"

Mr. Peck (*valiantly*)—"Humph! I should keep perfectly cool, my dear."

And when, a few nights later, burglars *did* break in, Henry kept his promise: he hid in the ice-box.

Johnny hasn't been to school long, but he already holds some peculiar views regarding the administration of his particular room.

The other day he came home with a singularly morose look on his usually smiling face.

"Why, Johnny," said his mother, "what's the matter?"

"I ain't going to that old school no more," he fiercely announced.

"Why, Johnny," said his mother reproachfully, "you mustn't talk like that. What's wrong with the school?"

"I ain't goin' there no more," Johnny replied; "an' it's because all th' boys in my room is blamed old cowards!"

"Why, Johnny, Johnny!'

"Yes, they are. There was a boy whisperin' this mornin', an' teacher saw him an' bumped his head on th' desk ever an' ever so many times. An' those big cowards sat there an' didn't say quit nor nothin'. They let that old teacher bang th' head off th' poor little boy, an' they just sat there an' seen her do it!"

"And what did you do, Johnny?"

"I didn't do nothin'—I was the boy!"—*Cleveland Plain Dealer.*

A negro came running down the lane as though the Old Boy were after him.

"What are you running for, Mose?" called the colonel from the barn.

"I ain't a-runnin' fo'," shouted back Mose. "I'se a-runnin' from!"

COWS

Little Willie, being a city boy, had never seen a cow. While on a visit to his grandmother he walked out across the fields with his cousin John. A cow was grazing there, and Willie's curiosity was greatly excited.

"Oh, Cousin John, what is that?" he asked.

"Why, that is only a cow," John replied.

"And what are those things on her head?"

"Horns," answered John.

Before they had gone far the cow mooed long and loud.

Willie was astounded. Looking back, he demanded, in a very fever of interest:

"Which horn did she blow?"

There was an old man who said, "How
Shall I flee from this horrible cow?
    I will sit on this stile
    And continue to smile,
Which may soften the heart of that cow."

CRITICISM

First Music Critic—"I wasted a whole evening by going to that new pianist's concert last night!"

Second Music Critic—"Why?"

First Music Critic—"His playing was above criticism!"

As soon
Seek roses in December—ice in June,
    Hope, constancy in wind, or corn in chaff;
Believe a woman or an epitaph,
Or any other thing that's false, before
You trust in critics.

—Byron.

It is much easier to be critical than to be correct.—*Disraeli.*

See also Dramatic criticism.

CRUELTY

"Why do you beat your little son? It was the cat that upset the vase of flowers."

"I can't beat the cat. I belong to the S. P. C. A."

CUCUMBERS

Consider the ways of the little green cucumber, which never does its best fighting till it's down.—*Stanford Chaparral.*

CULTURE

See Kultur.

CURFEW

A former resident of Marshall, Mo., was asking about the old town.

"I understand they have a curfew law out there now," he said.

"No," his informant answered, "they did have one, but they abandoned it."

"What was the matter?"

"Well, the bell rang at 9 o'clock, and almost everyone complained that it woke them up."

CURIOSITY

The Christmas church services were proceeding very successfully when a woman in the gallery got so interested that she leaned out too far and fell over the railing. Her dress caught in a chandelier, and she was suspended in mid-air. The minister noticed her undignified position and thundered at the congregation:

"Any person in this congregation who turns around will be struck stone-blind."

A man, whose curiosity was getting the better of him, but who dreaded the clergyman's warning, finally turned to his companion and said:

"I'm going to risk one eye."

A one-armed man entered a restaurant at noon and seated himself next to a dapper little other-people's-business man. The latter at once noticed his neighbor's left sleeve hanging loose and kept eying it in a how-did-it-happen sort of a way. The one-armed man paid no attention to him but kept on eating with his one hand. Finally the inquisitive one could stand it no longer. He changed his position a little, cleared his throat, and said: "I beg pardon, sir, but I see you have lost an arm."

The one-armed man picked up his sleeve with his right hand and peered anxiously into it. "Bless my soul!" he exclaimed, looking up with great surprise. "I do believe you're right."

See also Wives.

CYCLONES

See Windfalls.

DACHSHUNDS

A little boy was entertaining the minister the other day until his mother could complete her toilet. The minister, to make congenial conversation, inquired: "Have you a dog?"

"Yes, sir; a dachshund," responded the lad.

"Where is he?" questioned the dominie, knowing the way to a boy's heart.

"Father sends him away for the winter. He says it takes him so long to go in and out of the door he cools the whole house off."

DAMAGES

A Chicago lawyer tells of a visit he received from a Mrs. Delehanty, accompanied by Mr. Delehanty, the day after Mrs. Delehanty and a Mrs. Cassidy had indulged in a little difference of opinion.

When he had listened to the recital of Mrs. Delehanty's troubles, the lawyer said:

"You want to get damages, I suppose?"

"Damages! Damages!" came in shrill tones from Mrs. Delehanty. "Haven't I got damages enough already, man? What I'm after is satisfaction."

A Chicago man who was a passenger on a train that met with an accident not far from that city tells of a curious incident that he witnessed in the car wherein he was sitting.

Just ahead of him were a man and his wife. Suddenly the train was derailed, and went bumping down a steep hill. The man evinced signs of the greatest terror; and when the car came to a stop he carefully examined himself to learn whether he had received any injury. After ascertaining that he was unhurt, he thought of his wife and damages.

"Are you hurt, dear?" he asked.

"No, thank Heaven!" was the grateful response.

"Look here, then," continued hubby, "I'll tell you what we'll do. You let me black your eye, and we'll soak the company good for damages! It won't hurt you much. I'll give you just one good punch."—*Howard Morse.*

Up in Minnesota Mr. Olsen had a cow killed by a railroad train. In due season the claim agent for the railroad called.

"We understand, of course, that the deceased was a very docile and valuable animal," said the claim agent in his most persuasive claim-agentlemanly manner "and we sympathize with you and your family in your loss. But, Mr. Olsen, you must remember this: Your cow had no business being upon our tracks. Those tracks are our private property and when she invaded them, she became a trespasser. Technically speaking, you, as her owner, became a trespasser also. But we have no desire to carry the issue into court and possibly give you trouble. Now then, what would you regard as a fair settlement between you and the railroad company?"

"Vall," said Mr. Olsen slowly, "Ay bane poor Swede farmer, but Ay shall give you two dollars."

DANCING

He was a remarkably stout gentleman, excessively fond of dancing, so his friends asked him why he had stopped, and was it final?

"Oh, no, I hope not," sighed the old fellow. "I still love it, and I've merely stopped until I can find a concave lady for a partner."

George Bernard Shaw was recently entertained at a house party. While the other guests were dancing, one of the onlookers called Mr. Shaw's attention to the awkward dancing of a German professor.

"Really horrid dancing, isn't it, Mr. Shaw?"

G. B. S. was not at a loss for the true Shavian response. "Oh that's not dancing" he answered. "That's the New Ethical Movement!"

On a journey through the South not long ago, Wu Ting Fang was impressed by the preponderance of negro labor in one of the cities he visited. Wherever the entertainment committee led him, whether to factory, store or suburban plantation, all the hard work seemed to be borne by the black men.

Minister Wu made no comment at the time, but in the evening when he was a spectator at a ball given in his honor, after watching the waltzing and two-stepping for half an hour, he remarked to his host:

"Why don't you make the negroes do that for you, too?"

If they had danced the tango and the trot
  In days of old, there is no doubt we'd find
The poet would have written—would he not?—
  "On with the dance, let joy be unrefined!"
                                    —*J. J. O'Connell*

DEAD BEATS

See Bills; Collecting of accounts.

DEBTS

A train traveling through the West was held up by masked bandits. Two friends, who were on their way to California, were among the passengers.

"Here's where we lose all our money," one said, as a robber entered the car.

"You don't think they'll take everything, do you?" the other asked nervously.

"Certainly," the first replied. "These fellows never miss anything."

"That will be terrible," the second friend said. "Are you quite sure they won't leave us any money?" he persisted.

"Of course," was the reply. "Why do you ask?"

The other was silent for a minute. Then, taking a fifty dollar note from his pocket, he handed it to his friend.

"What is this for?" the first asked, taking the money.

"That's the fifty dollars I owe you," the other answered. "Now we're square."—*W. Dayton Wegefarth.*

WILLIS—"He calls himself a dynamo."

GILLIS—"No wonder; everything he has on is charged."
                                    —*Judge.*

Anticipated rents, and bills unpaid,
Force many a shining youth into the shade,
Not to redeem his time, but his estate,
And play the fool, but at the cheaper rate.
—*Cowper.*

I hold every man a debtor to his profession.—*Bacon.*

DEER

"The deer's a mighty useful beast
From Petersburg to Tennyson
"For while he lives he lopes around
And when he's dead he's venison."
—*Ellis Parker Butler.*

DEGREES

A young theologian named Fiddle
Refused to accept his degree;
"For," said he, "'tis enough to be Fiddle,
Without being Fiddle D. D."

DEMOCRACY

"Why are you so vexed, Irma?"
"I am so exasperated! I attended the meeting of the Social
Equality League, and my parlor-maid presided, and she had the
audacity to call me to order three times."—*M. L. Hayward.*

See also Ancestry

DEMOCRATIC PARTY

Hospital Physician—"Which ward do you wish to be taken
to? A pay ward or a—"
Maloney—"Iny of thim, Doc, thot's safely Dimocratic."

DENTISTRY

Our young hopeful came running into the house. His suit was dusty, and there was a bump on his small brow. But a gleam was in his eye, and he held out a baby tooth.

"How did you pull it?" demanded his mother.

"Oh," he said bravely, "it was easy enough. I just fell down, and the whole world came up and pushed it out."

DENTISTS

The dentist is one who pulls out the teeth of others to obtain employment for his own.

One day little Flora was taken to have an aching tooth removed. That night, while she was saying her prayers, her mother was surprised to hear her say: "And forgive us our debts as we forgive our dentists."—*Everybody's.*

One said a tooth drawer was a kind of unconscionable trade, because his trade was nothing else but to take away those things whereby every man gets his living.—*Hazlitt.*

DESCRIPTION

A popular soprano is said to have a voice of fine timbre, a willowy figure, cherry lips, chestnut hair, and hazel eyes. She must have been raised in the lumber regions.—*Ella Hutchison Ellwanger.*

DESIGN, DECORATIVE

Harold watched his mother as she folded up an intricate piece of lace she had just crocheted.

"Where did you get the pattern, Mamma?" he questioned.

"Out of my head," she answered lightly.

"Does your head feel better now, Mamma?" he asked anxiously.—*C. Hilton Turvey.*

DESTINATION

A Washington car conductor, born in London and still a cockney, has succeeded in extracting thrills from the alphabet—imparting excitement to the names of the national capitol's streets. On a recent Sunday morning he was calling the streets thus

"Haitch!"

"High!"

"Jay!"

"Kay!"

"Hell!"

At this point three prim ladies picked up their prayer-books and left the car.—*Lippincott's Magazine.*

Andrew Lang once invited a friend to dinner when he was staying in Marlow's road, Earl's Court, a street away at the end of that long Cromwell road, which seems to go on forever. The guest was not very sure how to get there, so Lang explained:

"Walk right along Cromwell road," he said, "till you drop dead and my house is just opposite!"

DETAILS

Charles Frohman was talking to a Philadelphia reporter about the importance of detail.

"Those who work for me," he said, "follow my directions down to the very smallest item. To go wrong in detail, you know, is often to go altogether wrong—like the dissipated husband.

"A dissipated husband as he stood before his house in the small hours searching for his latchkey, muttered to himself:

" 'Now which did my wife say—hic—have two whishkies an' get home by 12, or—hic—have twelve whishkies an' get home by 2?' "

DETECTIVES

When Conan Doyle arrived for the first time in Boston he was instantly recognized by the cabman whose vehicle he had engaged. When the great literary man offered to pay his fare the cabman said quite respectfully:

"If you please, sir, I should much prefer a ticket to your lecture. If you should have none with you a visiting-card penciled by yourself would do."

Conan Doyle laughed.

"Tell me," he said, "how did you know who I was, and I will give you tickets for your family."

"Thank you sir," was the reply. "Why, we all knew—that is, all the members of the Cabmen's Literary Guild knew—that you were coming by this train. I happen to be the only member on duty at the station this morning. If you will excuse personal remarks your coat lapels are badly twisted downward where they have been grasped by the pertinacious New York reporters. Your hair has the Quakerish cut of a Philadelphia barber, and your hat, battered at the brim in front, shows where you have tightly grasped it in the struggle to stand your ground at a Chicago literary luncheon. Your right overshoe has a large block of Buffalo mud just under the instep, the odor of a Utica cigar hangs about your clothing, and the overcoat itself shows the slovenly brushing of the porters of the through sleepers from Albany, and stenciled upon the very end of the 'Wellington' in fairly plain lettering is your name, 'Conan Doyle.'"

DETERMINATION

After the death of Andrew Jackson the following conversation is said to have occurred between an Anti-Jackson broker and a Democratic merchant:

MERCHANT (*with a sigh*)—"Well, the old General is dead."

BROKER (*with a shrug*)—"Yes, he's gone at last."

MERCHANT (*not appreciating the shrug*)—"Well, sir, he was a good man."

BROKER (*with shrug more pronounced*)—"I don't know about that."

MERCHANT (*energetically*)—"He was a good man, sir. If

any man has gone to heaven, General Jackson has gone to heaven."

BROKER (*doggedly*)—"I don't know about that."

MERCHANT—"Well, sir, I tell you that if Andrew Jackson had made up his mind to go to heaven, you may depend upon it he's there."

DIAGNOSIS

An epileptic dropped in a fit on the streets of Boston not long ago, and was taken to a hospital. Upon removing his coat there was found pinned to his waistcoat a slip of paper on which was written:

"This is to inform the house-surgeon that this is just a case of plain fit: not appendicitis. My appendix has already been removed twice."

DIET

Eat, drink, and be merry, for to-morrow ye diet.—*William Gilmore Beymer.*

> There was a young lady named Perkins,
> Who had a great fondness for gherkins;
>   She went to a tea
>   And ate twenty-three,
> Which pickled her internal workin's.

"Mother," asked the little one, on the occasion of a number of guests being present at dinner, "will the dessert hurt me, or is there enough to go round?"

The doctor told him he needed carbohydrates, proteids, and above all, something nitrogenous. The doctor mentioned a long list of foods for him to eat. He staggered out and wabbled into a Penn avenue restaurant.

"How about beefsteak?" he asked the waiter. "Is that nitrogenous?"

The waiter didn't know.

"Are fried potatoes rich in carbohydrates or not?"

The waiter couldn't say.

"Well, I'll fix it," declared the poor man in despair. "Bring me a large plate of hash."

A Colonel, who used to assert
That naught his digestion could hurt,
  Was forced to admit
  That his weak point was hit
When they gave him hot shot for desert.

To abstain that we may enjoy is the epicurianism of reason.
—*Rousseau.*

They are as sick that surfeit with too much, as they that starve with nothing.—*Shakespeare.*

DILEMMAS

A story that has done service in political campaigns to illustrate supposed dilemmas of the opposition will likely be revived in every political "heated term."

Away back, when herds of buffalo grazed along the foothills of the western mountains, two hardy prospectors fell in with a bull bison that seemed to have separated from his kind and run amuck. One of the prospectors took to the branches of a tree and the other dived into a cave. The buffalo bellowed at the entrance to the cavern and then turned toward the tree. Out came the man from the cave, and the buffalo took after him again. The man made another dive for the hole. After this had been repeated several times, the man in the tree called to his comrade, who was trembling at the mouth of the cavern:

"Stay in the cave, you idiot!"

"You don't know nothing about this hole," bawled the other. "There's a bear it in!"

DINING

A twelve course dinner might be described as a gastronomic marathon.—*John E. Rosser.*

"That was the spirit of your uncle that made that table stand, turn over, and do such queer stunts."

"I am not surprised; he never did have good table manners."

"Chakey, Chakey," called the big sister as she stood in the doorway and looked down the street toward the group of small boys: "Chakey, come in already and eat youseself. Maw she's on the table and Paw he's half et."

> There was a young lady of Cork,
> Whose Pa made a fortune in pork;
> He bought for his daughter
> A tutor who taught her
> To balance green peas on her fork.

An anecdote about Dr. Randall Davidson, bishop of Winchester, is that after an ecclesiastical function, as the clergy were trooping in to luncheon, an unctuous archdeacon observed: "This is the time to put a bridle on our appetites!"

"Yes," replied the bishop, "this is the time to put a bit in our mouths!"—*Christian Life.*

> There was a young lady named Maud,
> A very deceptive young fraud;
> She never was able
> To eat at the table,
> But out in the pantry—O Lord!

"Father's trip abroad did him so much good," said the self-made man's daughter. "He looks better, feels better, and as for appetite—honestly, it would just do your heart good to hear him eat!"

Whistler, the artist, was one day invited to dinner at a friend's house and arrived at his destination two hours late.

"How extraordinary!" he exclaimed, as he walked into the dining-room where the company was seated at the table; "really, I should think you might have waited a bit—why, you're just like a lot of pigs with your eating!"

A macaroon,
  A cup of tea,
An afternoon,
  Is all that she
Will eat;
  She's in society.
But let me take
  This maiden fair
To some café,
  And, then and there,
She'll eat the whole
  Blame bill of fare.

—*The Mystic Times.*

The small daughter of the house was busily setting the table for expected company when her mother called to her: "Put down three forks at each place, dear."

Having made some observations on her own account when the expected guests had dined with her mother before, she inquired thoughtfully:

"Shall I give Uncle John three knives?"

For a man seldom thinks with more earnestness of anything than he does of his dinner—*Samuel Johnson.*

DIPLOMACY

WIFE—"Please match this piece of silk for me before you come home."

HUSBAND—"At the counter where the sweet little blond works? The one with the soulful eyes and—"

WIFE—"No. You're too tired to shop for me when your day's work is done, dear. On second thought, I won't bother you."

Scripture tells us that a soft answer turneth away wrath A witty repartee sometimes helps one immensely also.

When Richard Olney was secretary of state he frequently gave expression to the opinion that appointees to the consular service should speak the language of the countries to which they were respectively accredited. It is said that when a certain breezy and enterprising western politician who was desirous of serving the Cleveland administration in the capacity of consul of the Chinese ports presented his papers to Mr. Olney, the secretary remarked:

"Are you aware, Mr. Blank, that I never recommend to the President the appointment of a consul unless he speaks the language of the country to which he desires to go? Now, I suppose you do not speak Chinese?"

Whereupon the westerner grinned broadly. "If, Mr. Secretary," said he, "you will ask me a question in Chinese, I shall be happy to answer it." He got the appointment.

"Miss de Simpson," said the young secretary of legation, "I have opened negotiations with your father upon the subject of—er—coming to see you oftener, with a view ultimately to forming an alliance, and he has responded favorably. May I ask if you will ratify the arrangement, as a *modus vivendi?*"

"Mr. von Harris," answered the daughter of the eminent diplomat, "don't you think it would have been a more graceful recognition of my administrative entity if you had asked me first?"

> I call'd the devil and he came,
>   And with wonder his form did I closely scan;
> He is not ugly, and is not lame,
>   But really a handsome and charming man.
> A man in the prime of life is the devil,
> Obliging, a man of the world, and civil;
> A diplomatist too, well skill'd in debate,
> He talks quite glibly of church and state.
>
> —*Heine.*

DISCIPLINE

See Military discipline; Parents.

DISCOUNTS

A train in Arizona was boarded by robbers, who went through the pockets of the luckless passengers. One of them happened to be a traveling salesman from New York, who, when his turn came, fished out $200, but rapidly took $4 from the pile and placed it in his vest pocket.

"What do you mean by that?" asked the robber, as he toyed with his revolver. Hurriedly came the answer: "Mine frent, you surely vould not refuse me two per zent discount on a strictly cash transaction like dis?"

DISCRETION

When you can, use discretion; when you can't, use a club.

DISPOSITION

One eastern railroad has a regular form for reporting accidents to animals on its right of way. Recently a track foreman had the killing of a cow to report. In answer to the question, "Disposition of carcass?" he wrote: "Kind and gentle."

There was one man who had a reputation for being even tempered. He was always cross.

DISTANCES

A regiment of regulars was making a long, dusty march across the rolling prairie land of Montana last summer. It was a hot, blistering day and the men, longing for water and rest, were impatient to reach the next town.

A rancher rode past.

"Say, friend," called out one of the men, "how far is it to the next town?"

"Oh, a matter of two miles or so, I reckon," called back the rancher. Another long hour dragged by, and another rancher was encountered.

"How far to the next town?" the men asked him eagerly.

"Oh, a good two miles."

A weary half-hour longer of marching, and then a third rancher.

"Hey, how far's the next town?"

"Not far," was the encouraging answer. "Only about two miles."

"Well," sighed an optimistic sergeant, "thank God, we're holdin' our own, anyhow!"

DIVORCE

"When a woman marries and then divorces her husband inside of a week what would you call it?"

"Taking his name in vain."—*Princeton Tiger.*

DOGS

LADY (to tramp who had been commissioned to find her lost poodle)—"The poor little darling, where did you find him?"

TRAMP—"Oh, a man 'ad 'im, miss, tied to a pole, and was cleaning the windows wiv 'im!"

A family moved from the city to a suburban locality and were told that they should get a watchdog to guard the premises at night. So they bought the largest dog that was for sale in the kennels of a neighboring dog fancier, who was a German. Shortly afterward the house was entered by burglars who made a good haul, while the big dog slept. The man went to the dog fancier and told him about it.

"Vell, vat you need now," said the dog merchant, "is a leedle dog to vake up the big dog."

"Dogs is mighty useful beasts
 They might seem bad at first
They might seem worser right along
 But when they're dead
  They're wurst."

—*Ellis Parker Butler.*

"My dog took first prize at the cat show."

"How was that?"

"He took the cat."—*Judge.*

Fair Visitor—"Why are you giving Fido's teeth such a thorough brushing?"

Fond Mistress—"Oh! The poor darling's just bitten some horrid person, and, really, you know, one can't be too careful."
—*Life.*

"Do you know that that bulldog of yours killed my wife's little harmless, affectionate poodle?"

"Well, what are you going to do about it?"

"Would you be offended if I was to present him with a nice brass collar?"

> Fleshy Miss Muffet
> Sat down on Tuffet,
>   A very good dog in his way;
> When she saw what she'd done,
> She started to run—
>   And Tuffet was buried next day.
>
> —*L. T. H.*

William J. Stevens, for several years local station agent at Swansea, R. I., was peacefully promenading his platform one morning when a rash dog ventured to snap at one of William's plump legs. Stevens promptly kicked the animal halfway across the tracks, and was immediately confronted by the owner, who demanded an explanation in language more forcible than courteous.

"Why," said Stevens when the other paused for breath, "your dog's mad."

"Mad! Mad! You double-dyed blankety-blank fool, he ain't mad!"

"Oh, ain't he?" cut in Stevens. "Gosh! I should be if any one kicked me like that!"

One would have it that a collie is the most sagacious of dogs, while the other stood up for the setter.

"I once owned a setter," declared the latter, "which was very intelligent. I had him on the street one day, and he acted so queerly about a certain man we met that I asked the man his name, and——"

"Oh, that's an old story!" the collie's advocate broke in sneeringly. "The man's name was Partridge, of course, and because of that the dog came to a set. Ho, ho! Come again!"

"You're mistaken," rejoined the other suavely. "The dog didn't come quite to a set, though almost. As a matter of fact, the man's name was Quayle, and the dog hesitated on account of the spelling!"—*P. R. Benson.*

The more one sees of men the more one likes dogs.

See also Dachshunds.

DOMESTIC FINANCE

"Talk about Napoleon! That fellow Wombat is something of a strategist himself."

"As to how?"

"Got his salary raised six months ago, and his wife hasn't found it out yet."—*Washington Herald.*

A Lakewood woman was recently reading to her little boy the story of a young lad whose father was taken ill and died, after which he set himself diligently to work to support himself and his mother. When she had finished her story she said:

"Dear Billy, if your papa were to die, would you work to support your dear mama?"

"Naw!" said Billy unexpectedly.

"But why not?"

"Ain't we got a good house to live in?"

"Yes, dearie, but we can't eat the house, you know."

"Ain't there a lot o' stuff in the pantry?"

"Yes, but that won't last forever."

"It'll last till you get another husband, won't it? You're a pretty good looker, ma!"

Mamma gave up right there.

"I am sending you a thousand kisses," he wrote to his fair young wife who was spending her first month away from him. Two days later he received the following telegram: "Kisses received. Landlord refuses to accept any of them on account." Then he woke up and forwarded a check.

See also Trouble.

DOMESTIC RELATIONS

There was a young man of Dunbar,
Who playfully poisoned his Ma;
    When he'd finished his work,
    He remarked with a smirk,
"This will cause quite a family jar."

See also Families; Marriage.

DRAMA

The average modern play calls in the first act for all our faith, in the second for all our hope, and in the last for all our charity.—*Eugene Walter.*

The young man in the third row of seats looked bored. He wasn't having a good time. He cared nothing for the Shakespearean drama.

"What's the greatest play you ever saw?" the young woman asked, observing his abstraction.

Instantly he brightened.

"Tinker touching a man out between second and third and getting the ball over to Chance in time to nab the runner to first!" he said.

LARRY—"I like Professor Whatishisname in Shakespeare. He brings things home to you that you never saw before."

HARRY—"Huh! I've got a laundryman as good as that."

I think I love and reverence all arts equally, only putting my own just above the others. . . . To me it seems as if when

God conceived the world, that was Poetry: He formed it, and that was Sculpture; He colored it, and that was Painting; He peopled it with living beings, and that was the grand, divine, eternal Drama.—*Charlotte Cushman.*

Two women were leaving the theater after a performance of "The Doll's House."

"Oh, don't you *love* Ibsen?" asked one, ecstatically. "Doesn't he just take all the hope out of life?"

DRAMATIC CRITICISM

Theodore Dreiser, the novelist, was talking about criticism.

"I like pointed criticism," he said, "criticism such as I heard in the lobby of a theater the other night at the end of the play."

"The critic was an old gentleman. His criticism, which was for his wife's ears alone, consisted of these words:

" 'Well, you would come!' "

Nat Goodwin, the American comedian, when at the Shaftesbury Theatre, London, told of an experience he once had with a juvenile deadhead in a town in America. Standing outside the theater a little time before the performance was due to begin he observed a small boy with an anxious, forlorn look on his face and a weedy-looking pup in his arms.

Goodwin inquired what was the matter, and was told that the boy wished to sell the dog so as to raise the price of a seat in the gallery. The actor suspected at once a dodge to secure a pass on the "sympathy racket," but allowing himself to be taken in he gave the boy a pass. The dog was deposited in a safe place and the boy was able to watch Goodwin as the Gilded Fool from a good seat in the gallery. Next day Goodwin saw the boy again near the theater, so he asked:

"Well, sonny, how did you like the show?"

"I'm glad I didn't sell my dog," was the reply.

DRAMATISTS

"I hear Scribbler finally got one of his plays on the boards."
"Yes, the property man tore up his manuscript and used it in the snow storm scene."

"So you think the author of this play will live, do you?" remarked the tourist.
"Yes," replied the manager of the Frozen Dog Opera House. "He's got a five-mile start and I don't think the boys kin ketch him."—*Life.*

We all know the troubles of a dramatist are many and varied.
Here's an advertisement taken from a morning paper that shows to what a pass a genius may come in a great city:
"Wanted—A collaborator, by a young playwright. The play is already written; collaborator to furnish board and bed until play is produced."

DRESSMAKERS

WIFE—"Wretch! Show me that letter."
HUSBAND—"What letter?"
WIFE—"That one in your hand. It's from a woman, I can see by the writing, and you turned pale when you saw it."
HUSBAND—"Yes. Here it is. It's your dressmaker's bill."

DRINKING

He who goes to bed, and goes to bed sober,
Falls as the leaves do, and dies in October;
But he who goes to bed, and does so mellow,
Lives as he ought to, and dies a good fellow.
                    —*Parody on Fletcher.*

I drink when I have occasion, and sometimes when I have no occasion.—*Cervantes.*

I have very poor and unhappy brains for drinking. I could wish courtesy would invent some other custom of entertainment.
—*Shakespeare.*

The Frenchman loves his native wine;
　The German loves his beer;
The Englishman loves his 'alf and 'alf,
　Because it brings good cheer;
The Irishman loves his "whiskey straight,"
　Because it gives him dizziness;
The American has no choice at all,
　So he drinks the whole blamed business.

A young Englishman came to Washington and devoted his days and nights to an earnest endeavor to drink all the Scotch whiskey there was. He couldn't do it, and presently went to a doctor, complaining of a disordered stomach.

"Quit drinking!" ordered the doctor.

"But, my dear sir, I cawn't. I get so thirsty."

"Well," said the doctor, "whenever you are thirsty eat an apple instead of taking a drink."

The Englishman paid his fee and left. He met a friend to whom he told his experience.

"Bally rot!" he protested. "Fawncy eating forty apples a day!"

If you are invited to drink at any man's house more than you think is wholesome, you may say "you wish you could, but so little makes you both drunk and sick; that you should only be bad company by doing so."—*Lord Chesterfield.*

There is many a cup 'twixt the lip and the slip.—*Judge*

One swallow doesn't make a summer, but it breaks a New Year's resolution.—*Life.*

Doctor (feeling Sandy's pulse in bed)—"What do you drink."

Sandy (with brightening face)—"Oh, I'm nae particular, doctor! Anything you've got with ye."

Here's to the girls of the American shore,
I love but one, I love no more,
Since she's not here to drink her part,
I'll drink her share with all my heart.

A well-known Scottish architect was traveling in Palestine recently, when news reached him of an addition to his family circle. The happy father immediately provided himself with some water from the Jordan to carry home for the christening of the infant, and returned to Scotland.

On the Sunday appointed for the ceremony he duly presented himself at the church, and sought out the beadle in order to hand over the precious water to his care. He pulled the flask from his pocket, but the beadle held up a warning hand, and came nearer to whisper:

"No the noo, sir; no the noo! Maybe after the kirk's oot!"

When President Eliot of Harvard was in active service as head of the university, reports came to him that one of his young charges was in the habit of absorbing more liquor than was good for him, and President Eliot determined to do his duty and look into the matter.

Meeting the young man under suspicion in the yard shortly after breakfast one day the president marched up to him and demanded, "Young man, do you drink?"

"Why, why, why," stammered the young man, "why President Eliot, not so early in the morning, thank you."

WIFE (on auto tour)—"That fellow back there said there is a road-house a few miles down the road. Shall we stop there?"

HUSBAND—"Did he whisper it or say it out loud?"

A priest went to a barber shop conducted by one of his Irish parishioners to get a shave. He observed the barber was suffering from a recent celebration, but decided to take a chance. In a few moments the barber's razor had nicked the father's cheek. "There, Pat, you have cut me," said the priest as he raised his hand and caressed the wound. "Yis, y'r riv'rance," answered the barber. "That shows you," continued the priest, in a tone of censure, "what the use of liquor will do." "Yis, y'r riv'rance," replied the barber, humbly, "it makes the skin tender."

Ex-congressman Asher G. Garuth, of Kentucky, tells this story of an experience he once had on a visit to a little Ohio town.

"I went up there on legal business," he says, "and, knowing that I should have to stay all night, I proceeded directly to the only hotel. The landlord stood behind the desk and regarded me with a kindly air as I registered. It seems that he was a little hard of hearing, a fact of which I was not aware. As I jabbed the pen back into the dish of bird shot, I said:

"'Can you direct me to the bank?'

"He looked at me blankly for a second, then swinging the register around, he glanced down swiftly, caught the 'Louisville' after my name, and an expression of complete understanding lighting up his countenance, he said:

"'Certainly, sir. You will find the bar right through that door at the left.'"

See also Drunkards; Good fellowship; Temperance; Wine.

DROUGHTS

Governor Glasscock of West Virginia, while traveling through Arizona, noticed the dry, dusty appearance of the country.

"Doesn't it ever rain around here?" he asked one of the natives.

"Rain?" The native spat. "Rain? Why say pardner, there's bullfrogs in this yere town over five years old that hain't learned to swim yet!"

DRUNKARDS

Sing a song of sick gents,
Pockets full of rye,
Four and twenty highballs,
We wish that we might die.

Two booze-fiends were ambling homeward at an early hour, after being out nearly all night.

"Don't your wife miss you on these occasions" asked one.

"Not often," replied the other; "she throws pretty straight."

"Where's old Four-Fingered Pete?" asked Alkali Ike. "I ain't seen him around here since I got back."

"Pete?" said the bartender. "Oh, he went up to Hyena Tongue and got jagged. Went up to a hotel winder, stuck his head in and hollered 'Fire!' and everybody did."

The Irish talent for repartee has an amusing illustration in Lord Rossmore's recent book "Things I Can Tell." While acting as magistrate at an Irish village, Lord Rossmore said to an old offender brought before him: "You here again?" "Yes, your honor." "What's brought you here?" "Two policemen, your honor." "Come, come, I know that—drunk again, I suppose?" "Yes, your honor, both of them."

The colonel came down to breakfast New Year's morning with a bandaged hand.

"Why, colonel, what's the matter?" they asked.

"Confound it all!" the colonel answered, "we had a little party last night, and one of the younger men got intoxicated and stepped on my hand."

MAGISTRATE—"And what was the prisoner doing?"

CONSTABLE—"E were 'avin' a very 'eated argument with a cab driver, yer worship."

MAGISTRATE—"But that doesn't prove he was drunk."

CONSTABLE—"Ah, but there worn't no cab driver there, yer worship."

A Scotch minister and his servant, who were coming home from a wedding, began to consider the state into which their potations at the wedding feast had left them.

"Sandy," said the minister, "just stop a minute here till I go ahead. Maybe I don't walk very steady and the good wife might remark something not just right."

He walked ahead of the servant for a short distance and then asked:

"How is it? Am I walking straight?"

"Oh, ay," answered Sandy thickly, "ye're a' recht—but who's that who's with ye?"

A man in a very deep state of intoxication was shouting and kicking most vigorously at a lamp post, when the noise attracted a near-by policeman.

"What's the matter?" he asked the energetic one.

"Oh, never mind, mishter. Thash all right," was the reply; "I know she'sh home all right—I shee a light upshtairs."

A pompous little man with gold-rimmed spectacles and a thoughtful brow boarded a New York elevated train and took the only unoccupied seat. The man next him had evidently been drinking. For a while the little man contented himself with merely sniffing contemptuously at his neighbor, but finally he summoned the guard.

"Conductor," he demanded indignantly, "do you permit drunken people to ride upon this train?"

"No, sir," replied the guard in a confidential whisper. "But don't say a word and stay where you are, sir. If ye hadn't told me I'd never have noticed ye."

A noisy bunch tacked out of their club late one night, and up the street. They stopped in front of an imposing residence. After considerable discussion one of them advanced and pounded on the door. A woman stuck her head out of a second-story window and demanded, none too sweetly: "What do you want?"

"Ish thish the residence of Mr. Smith?" inquired the man on the steps, with an elaborate bow.

"It is. What do you want?"

"Ish it possible I have the honor of speakin' to Misshus Smith?"

"Yes. What do you want?"

"Dear Misshus Smith! Good Misshus Smith! Will you—hic—come down an' pick out Mr. Smith? The resh of us want to go home."

That clever and brilliant genius, McDougall, who represented California in the United States Senate, was like many others of his class somewhat addicted to fiery stimulants, and unable to battle long with them without showing the effect of the struggle. Even in his most exhausted condition he was, however, brilliant at repartee; but one night, at a supper of journalists given to the late George D. Prentice, a genius of the same mold and the same unfortunate habit, he found a foeman worthy of his steel in General John Cochrane. McDougall had taken offense at some anti-slavery sentiments which had been uttered—it was in war times—and late in the evening got on his legs for the tenth time to make a reply. The spirit did not move him to utterance, however; on the contrary, it quite deprived him of the power of speech; and after an ineffectual attempt at speech he suddenly concluded:

"Those are my sentiments, sir, and my name's McDougall."

"I beg the gentleman's pardon," said General Cochrane, springing to his feet; "but what was that last remark?"

McDougall pronounced it again: "My name's McDougall."

"There must be some error," said Cochrane, gravely. "I have known Mr. McDougall many years, and there never was a time when as late as twelve o'clock at night he knew what his name was."

On a pleasant Sunday afternoon an old German and his youngest son were seated in the village inn. The father had partaken liberally of the home-brewed beer, and was warning his son against the evils of intemperance. "Never drink too much, my son. A gentleman stops when he has enough. To be drunk is a disgrace."

"Yes, Father, but how can I tell when I have enough or am drunk?"

The old man pointed with his finger. "Do you see those two men sitting in the corner? If you see four men there, you would be drunk."

The boy looked long and earnestly. "Yes, Father, but— but— there is only one man in that corner."—*W. Karl Hilbrich.*

William R. Hearst, who never touches liquor, had several men in important positions on his newspapers who were not strangers to intoxicants. Mr. Hearst has a habit of appearing at his office at unexpected times and summoning his chiefs of departments for instructions. One afternoon he sent for Mr. Blank.

"He hasn't come down yet, sir," reported the office boy.

"Please tell Mr. Dash I want to see him."

"He hasn't come down yet either."

"Well, find Mr. Star or Mr. Sun or Mr. Moon—anybody; I want to see one of them at once."

"Ain't none of 'em here yet, sir. You see there was a celebration last night and——"

Mr. Hearst sank back in his chair and remarked in his quiet way:

"For a man who don't drink I think I suffer more from the effects of it than anybody in the world."

"What is a drunken man like, Fool?"

"Like a drowned man, a fool and a madman: one draught above heat makes him a fool; the second mads him; and a third drowns him."—*Shakespeare.*

DYSPEPSIA

"Ah," she sighed "for many years I've suffered from dyspepsia."

"And don't you take anything for it?" her friend asked. "You look healthy enough."

"Oh," she replied, "I haven't indigestion: my husband has."

ECHOES

An American and a Scotsman were walking one day near the foot of one of the Scotch mountains. The Scotsman, wishing to impress the visitor, produced a famous echo to be heard in that place. When the echo returned clearly after nearly four monutes, the proud Scotsman, turning to the Yankee exclaimed:

"There, mon, ye canna show anything like that in your country."

"Oh, I don't know," said the American, "I guess we can better that. Why in my camp in the Rockies, when I go to bed

I just lean out of my window and call out, "Time to get up: wake up !' and eight hours afterward the echo comes back and wakes me."

ECONOMY

An economist is usually a man who can save money by cutting down some other person's expenses.

Economy is going without something you do want in case you should, some day, want something which you probably won't want.—*Anthony Hope.*

Economy is a way of spending money without getting any fun out of it.

Ther's lots o' difference between thrift an' tryin' t' revive a last year's straw hat.—*Abe Martin.*

Economy is a great revenue.—*Cicero.*

See also Domestic finance; Saving; Thrift.

EDITORS

Recipe for an editor:
Take a personal hatred of authors,
Mix this with a fiendish delight
In refusing all efforts of genius
And maiming all poets on sight.

—*Life.*

The city editor of a great New York daily was known in the newspaper world as a martinet and severe disciplinarian. Some of his caustic and biting criticisms are classics. Once, however, the tables were turned upon him in a way that left him speechless for days.

A reporter on the paper wrote an article that the city editor did not approve of. The morning of publication this reporter drifted into the office and encountered his chief, who was in a white heat of anger. Carefully suppressing the explosion, however, the boss started in with ominous and icy words:

"Mr. Blank, I am not going to criticize you for what you

have written. On the other hand, I am profoundly sorry for you. I have watched your work recently, and it is my opinion, reached after calm and dispassionate observation, that you are mentally unbalanced. You are insane. Your mind is a wreck. Your friends should take you in hand. The very kindest suggestion I can make is that you visit an alienist and place yourself under treatment. So far you have shown no sign of violence, but what the future holds for you no one can tell. I say this in all kindness and frankness. You are discharged."

The reporter walked out of the office and wandered up to Bellevue Hospital. He visited the insane pavilion, and told the resident surgeon that there was a suspicion that he was not all right mentally and asked to be examined. The doctor put him through the regular routine and then said,

"Right as a top."

"Sure?" asked the reporter. "Will you give me a certificate to that effect?" The doctor said he would and did. Clutching the certificate tightly in his hand the reporter entered the office an hour later, walked up to the city editor, handed it to him silently, and then blurted out,

"Now you go get one."

EDUCATION

Along in the sixties Pat Casey pushed a wheelbarrow across the plains from St. Joseph, Mo., to Georgetown, Colo., and shortly after that he "struck it rich"; in fact, he was credited with having more wealth than any one else in Colorado. A man of great shrewdness and ability, he was exceedingly sensitive over his inability to read or write. One day an old-timer met him with:

"How are you getting along, Pat?"

"Go 'way from me now," said Pat genially, "me head's bustin' wid business. It takes two lid-pincils a day to do me wurruk."

A catalog of farming implements sent out by the manufacturer finally found its way to a distant mountain village where it was evidently welcomed with interest. The firm received a carefully written, if somewhat clumsily expressed letter from a southern "cracker" asking further particulars about one of the listed articles.

To this, in the usual course of business, was sent a type-written answer. Almost by return mail came a reply:

"You fellows need not think you are so all-fired smart, and you need not print your letters to me. I can read writing."

EFFICIENCY

An American motorist went to Germany in his car to the army maneuvers. He was especially impressed with the German motor ambulances. As the tourist watched the maneuvers from a seat under a tree, the axle of one of the motor ambulances broke. Instantly the man leaped out, ran into the village, returned in a jiffy with a new axle, fixed it in place with wonderful skill, and teuffed-teuffed off again almost as good as new.

"There's efficiency for you," said the American admirably. "There's German efficiency for you. No matter what breaks, there's always a stock at hand from which to supply the needed part."

And praising the remarkable instance of German efficiency he had just witnessed, the tourist returned to the village and ordered up his car. But he couldn't use it. The axle was missing.

A curious little man sat next an elderly, prosperous looking man in a smoking car.

"How many people work in your office?" he asked.

"Oh," responded the elderly man, getting up and throwing away his cigar, "I should say, at a rough guess, about two-thirds of them."

EGOTISM

In the Chicago schools a boy refused to sew, thinking it below the dignity of a man of ten years.

"Why," said the teacher, "George Washington did his own sewing in the wars, and do you think you are better than George Washington?"

"I don't know," replied the boy seriously. "Only time can tell that."

John D. Rockefeller tells this story on himself:

"Golfing one bright winter day I had for caddie a boy who didn't know me.

"An unfortunate stroke landed me in clump of high grass.

" 'My, my,' I said, 'what am I to do now?'

" 'See that there tree?' said the boy, pointing to a tall tree a mile away. 'Well, drive straight for that.'

"I lofted vigorously, and, fortunately, my ball soared up into the air; it landed, and it rolled right on to the putting green.

" 'How's that, my boy?' I cried.

"The caddie stared at me with envious eyes.

" 'Gee, boss,' he said, 'if I had your strength and you had my brains what a pair we'd make!' "

The late Marshall Field had a very small office-boy who came to the great merchant one day with a request for an increase in wages.

"Huh!" said Mr. Field, looking at him as if through a magnifying-glass. "Want a raise, do you? How much are you getting?"

"Three dollars a week," chirped the little chap.

"Three dollars a week!" exclaimed his employer. "Why, when I was your age I only got two dollars."

"Oh, well, that's different," piped the youngster. "I guess you weren't worth any more."

> Here's to the man who is wisest and best,
> Here's to the man who with judgment is blest.
> Here's to the man who's as smart as can be—
> I mean the man who agrees with me.

ELECTIONS

In St. Louis there is one ward that is full of breweries and Germans. In a recent election a local option question was up.

After the election some Germans were counting the votes. One German was calling off and another taking down the option votes. The first German, running rapidly through the ballots, said: "Vet, vet, vet, vet, . . ." Suddenly he stopped. *"Mein Gott!"* he cried: *"Dry!"*

Then he went on—"Vet, vet, vet, vet, . . ."

Presently he stopped again and mopped his brow. *"Himmel!"* he said. "Der son of a gun repeated!"

WILLIS—"What's the election today for? Anybody happen to know?"

GILLIS—"It is to determine whether we shall have a convention to nominate delegates who will be voted on as to whether they will attend a caucus which will decide whether we shall have a primary to determine whether the people want to vote on this same question again next year."—*Puck.*

One year, when the youngsters of a certain Illinois village met for the purpose of electing a captain of their baseball team for the coming season, it appeared that there were an excessive number of candidates for the post, with more than the usual wrangling.

Youngster after youngster presented his qualifications for the post; and the matter was still undecided when the son of the owner of the ball-field stood up. He was a small, snub-nosed lad, with a plentiful supply of freckles, but he glanced about him with a dignified air of controlling the situation.

"I'm going to be captain this year," he announced convincingly, "or else Father's old bull is going to be turned into the field."

He was elected unanimously.—*Fenimore Martin.*

I consider biennial elections as a security that the sober second thought of the people shall be law.—*Fisher Ames.*

ELECTRICITY

In school a boy was asked this question in physics: "What is the difference between lightning and electricity?"

And he answered: "Well, you don't have to pay for lightning."

EMBARRASSING SITUATIONS

A young gentleman was spending the week-end at little Willie's cottage at Atlantic City, and on Sunday evening after dinner, there being a scarcity of chairs on the crowded piazza, the young gentleman took Willie on his lap.

Then, during a pause in the conversation, little Willie looked up at the young gentleman and piped:

"Am I as heavy as sister Mabel?"

The late Charles Coghlan was a man of great wit and resource. When he was living in London, his wife started for an out-of-town visit. For some reason she found it necessary to return home, and on her way thither she saw her husband step out of a cab and hand a lady from it. Mrs. Coghlan confronted the pair. The actor was equal to the situation.

"My dear," he said to his wife, "allow me to present Miss Blank. Mrs. Coghlan, Miss Blank."

The two bowed coldly while Coghlan quickly added:

"I know you ladies have ever so many things you want to say to each other, so I will ask to be excused."

He lifted his hat, stepped into the cab, and was whirled away.

The evening callers were chatting gaily with the Kinterbys when a patter of little feet was heard from the head of the stairs. Mrs. Kinterby raised her hand, warning the others to silence.

"Hush!" she said, softly. "The children are going to deliver their 'good-night' message. It always gives me a feeling of reverence to hear them—they are so much nearer the Creator than we are, and they speak the love that is in their little hearts never so fully as when the dark has come. Listen!"

There was a moment of tense silence. Then—"Mama," came the message in a shrill whisper, "Willy found a bedbug!"

"I was in an awkward predicament yesterday morning," said a husband to another.

"How was that?"

"Why, I came home late, and my wife heard me and said, 'John, what time is it?' and I said, 'Only twelve, my dear,' and just then that cuckoo clock of ours sang out three times."

"What did you do?"

"Why, I just had to stand there and cuckoo nine times more."

"Your husband will be all right now," said an English doctor to a woman whose husband was dangerously ill.

"What do you mean?" demanded the wife. "You told me 'e couldn't live a fortnight."

"Well, I'm going to cure him, after all," said the doctor. "Surely you are glad?"

The woman wrinkled her brows.

"Puts me in a bit of an 'ole," she said. "I've bin an' sold all 'is clothes to pay for 'is funeral."

EMPLOYERS AND EMPLOYEES

"You want more money? Why, my boy, I worked three years for $11 a month right in this establishment, and now I'm owner of it."

"Well, you see what happened to your boss. No man who treats his help that way can hang on to his business."

EARNEST YOUNG MAN—"Have you any advice to a struggling young employee?"

FRANK OLD GENTLEMAN—"Yes. Don't work."

EARNEST YOUNG MAN—"Don't work?"

FRANK OLD GENTLEMAN—"No. Become an employer."

General Benjamin F. Butler built a house in Washington on the same plans as his home in Lowell, Mass., and his studies were furnished in exactly the same way. He and his secretary, M. W. Clancy, afterward City Clerk of Washington for many years, were constantly traveling between the two places.

One day a senator called upon General Butler in Lowell and the next day in Washington to find him and his secretary engaged upon the same work that had occupied them in Massachusetts.

"Heavens, Clancy, don't you ever stop?"

"No," interposed General Butler,

" 'Satan finds some mischief still

For idle hand to do.' "

Clancy arose and bowed, saying:

"General, I never was sure until now what my employer was. I had heard the rumor, but I always discredited it."

W. J. ("Fingy") Conners, the New York politician, who is not precisely a Chesterfield, secured his first great freight-handling contract when he was a roustabout on the Buffalo docks. When the job was about to begin he called a thousand burly "dock-wallopers" to order, as narrated by one of his business friends:

"Now," roared Conners, "yez are to worruk for me, and I want ivery man here to understand what's what. I kin lick anny man in the gang."

Nine hundred and ninety-nine swallowed the insult, but one huge, double-fisted warrior moved uneasily and stepping from the line he said "You can't lick me, Jim Conners."

"I can't, can't I?" bellowed "Fingy."

"No, you can't," was the determined response.

"Oh, well, thin, go to the office and git your money," said "Fingy." "I'll have no man in me gang that I can't lick."

Outside his own cleverness there is nothing that so delights Mr. Wiggins as a game of baseball, and when he gets a chance to exploit the two, both at the same time, he may be said to be the happiest man in the world. Hence it was that the other day, when little red headed Willie Mulligan, his office boy, came sniffing into his presence to ask for the afternoon off that he might attend his grandfather's funeral, Wiggins deemed it a masterly stroke to answer:

"Why, certainly, Willie. What's more, my boy, if you'll wait for me I'll go with you."

"All right, sir," sniffed Willie as he returned to his desk and waited patiently.

And, lo and behold, poor little Willie had told the truth, and when he and Wiggins started out together the latter not only lost one of the best games of the season, but had to attend the obsequies of an old lady in whom he had no interest whatever as well.

CHIEF CLERK (to office boy)—"Why on earth don't you laugh when the boss tells a joke?"

OFFICE BOY—"I don't have to; I quit on Saturday."—*Satire.*

James J. Hill, the Railway King, told the following amusing incident that happened on one of his roads:

"One of our division superintendents had received numerous complaints that freight trains were in the habit of stopping on a grade crossing in a certain small town, thereby blocking travel for long periods. He issued orders, but still the complaints came in. Finally he decided to investigate personally.

"A short man in size and very excitable, he went down to the crossing, and, sure enough, there stood, in defiance of his orders, a long freight train, anchored squarely across it. A brakeman who didn't know him by sight sat complacently on the top of the car.

" 'Move that train on!' sputtered the little 'super.' 'Get it off the crossing so people can pass. Move on, I say!'

"The brakeman surveyed the tempestuous little man from head to foot. 'You go to the deuce, you little shrimp,' he replied. 'You're small enough to crawl under.' "

ENEMIES

An old man who had led a sinful life was dying, and his wife sent for a near-by preacher to pray with him.

The preacher spent some time praying and talking, and finally the old man said: "What do you want me to do, Parson?"

"Renounce the Devil, renounce the Devil," replied the preacher.

"Well, but, Parson," protested the dying man, "I ain't in position to make any enemies."

It is better to decide a difference between enemies than friends, for one of our friends will certainly become an enemy and one of our enemies a friend.—*Bias.*

> The world is large when its weary leagues
> two loving hearts divide;
> But the world is small when your enemy is
> loose on the other side.
> —*John Boyle O'Reilly.*

ENGLAND

See Great Britain.

ENGLISH LANGUAGE

A popular hotel in Rome has a sign in the elevator reading: "Please do not touch the Lift at your own risk."

The class at Heidelberg was studying English conjugations, and each verb considered was used in a model sentence, so that the students would gain the benefit of pronouncing the connected series of words, as well as learning the varying forms of the verb. This morning it was the verb "to have" in the sentence, "I have a gold mine."

Herr Schmitz was called to his feet by Professor Wulff.

"Gonjugate 'do haff' in der sentence, 'I haff a golt mine,'" the professor ordered.

"I haff a golt mine, du hast a golt dein, he hass a golt hiss. Ve, you or dey haff a golt ours, yours or deirs, as de case may be."

Language is the expression of ideas, and if the people of one country cannot preserve an identity of ideas, they cannot retain an identity of language.—*Noah Webster.*

ENGLISHMEN

He who laughs last is an Englishman.—*Princeton Tiger.*

Nat Goodwin was at the club with an English friend and became the center of an appreciative group. A cigar man offered the comedian a cigar, saying that it was a new production.

"With each cigar, you understand," the promoter said, "I will give a coupon, and when you have smoked three thousand of them you may bring the coupons to me and exchange them for a grand piano."

Nat sniffed the cigar, pinched it gently, and then replied: "If I smoked three thousand of these cigars, I think I would need a harp instead of a grand piano."

There was a burst of laughter in which the Englishman did not join, but presently he exploded with merriment. "I see the point," he exclaimed. "Being an actor, you have to travel around the country a great deal and a harp would be so much more convenient to carry."

ENTHUSIASM

Theodore Watts, says Charles Rowley in his book *Fifty Years of Work Without Wages,* tells a good story against himself. A nature enthusiast, he was climbing Snowdon, and overtook on old gypsy woman. He began to dilate upon the sublimity of the scenery, in somewhat gushing phrases. The woman paid no attention to him. Provoked by her irresponsiveness, he said, "You don't seem to care for this magnificent scenery?" She took the pipe from her mouth and delivered this settler: "I enjies it; I don't jabber."

EPITAPHS

LITTLE CLARENCE—"Pa!"

HIS FATHER—"Well, my son?"

LITTLE CLARENCE—"I took a walk through the cemetery to-day and read the inscriptions on the tombstones."

HIS FATHER—"And what were your thoughts after you had done so?"

LITTLE CLARENCE—"Why, pa, I wondered where all the wicked people were buried."—*Judge.*

The widower had just taken his fourth wife and was showing her around the village. Among the places visited was the churchyard, and the bride paused before a very elaborate tombstone that had been erected by the bridegroom. Being a little nearsighted she asked him to read the inscription, and in reverent tones he read:

"Here lies Susan, beloved wife of John Smith; also Jane, beloved wife of John Smith; also Mary, beloved wife of John Smith——"

He paused abruptly, and the bride, leaning forward to see the bottom line, read, to her horror:

"Be Ye Also Ready."

A man wished to have something original on his wife's headstone and hit upon, "Lord, she was Thine." He had his own ideas of the size of the letters and the space between words, and gave instructions to the stonemason. The latter carried them out all right, except that he could not get in the "E" in Thine.

In a cemetery at Middlebury, Vt., is a stone, erected by a widow to her loving husband, bearing this inscription:

"Rest in peace—until we meet again."

An epitaph in an old Moravian cemetery reads thus:

Remember, friend, as you pass by,
As you are now, so once was I;
As I am now thus you must be,
So be prepared to follow me.

There had been written underneath in pencil, presumably by some wag:

To follow you I'm not content
Till I find out which way you went.

I expected it, but I didn't expect it quite so soon.—*Life*.

After Life's scarlet fever
I sleep well.

Here lies the body of Sarah Sexton,
Who never did aught to vex one.
(Not like the woman under the next stone.)

As a general thing, the writer of epitaphs is a monumental liar.—*John E. Rosser.*

Maria Brown,
Wife of Timothy Brown,
aged 80 years.
She lived with her husband fifty years, and died
in the confident hope of a better life.

Here lies the body of Enoch Holden, who died suddenly and unexpectedly by being kicked to death by a cow. Well done, good and faithful servant!

A bereaved husband feeling his loss very keenly found it desirable to divert his mind by traveling abroad. Before his departure, however, he left orders for a tombstone with the inscription:

"The light of my life has gone out."

Travel brought unexpected and speedy relief, and before the time for his return he had taken another wife. It was then that he remembered the inscription, and thinking it would not be pleasing to his new wife, he wrote to the stone-cutter, asking that he exercise his ingenuity in adapting it to the new conditions. After his return he took his new wife to see the tombstone and found that the inscription had been made to read:

"The light of my life has gone out,
But I have struck another match."

Here lies Bernard Lightfoot,
Who was accidentally killed in the forty-fifth year
of his age.
This monument was erected by his grateful family.

I thought it mushroom when I found
It in the woods, forsaken;
But since I sleep beneath this mound,
I must have been mistaken.

On the tombstone of a Mr. Box appears this inscription:
Here lies one Box within another.
The one of wood was very good,
We cannot say so much for t'other.

Nobles and heralds by your leave,
Here lies what once was Matthew Prior;
The son of Adam and of Eve;
Can Bourbon or Nassau claim higher?

—Prior.

Kind reader! take your choice to cry or laugh;
Here Harold lies—but where's his Epitaph?
If such you seek, try Westminster, and view
Ten thousand, just as fit for him as you.

—Byron.

I conceive disgust at these impertinent and misbecoming familiarities inscribed upon your ordinary tombstone.—*Charles Lamb.*

EPITHETS

John Fiske, the historian, was once interrupted by his wife, who complained that their son had been very disrespectful to some neighbors. Mr. Fiske called the youngster into his study.

"My boy, is it true that you called Mrs. Jones a fool?"

The boy hung his head. "Yes, father."

"And did you call Mr. Jones a worse fool?"

"Yes, father."

Mr. Fiske frowned and pondered for a minute. Then he said:

"Well, my son, that is just about the distinction I should make."

"See that man over there. He is a bombastic mutt, a windjammer nonentity, a false alarm, and an encumberer of the earth!"

"Would you mind writing all that down for me?"

"Why in the world——"

"He's my husband, and I should like to use it on him some time."

EQUALITY

As one of the White Star steamships came up New York harbor the other day, a grimy coal barge floated immediately in front of her. "Clear out of the way with that old mud scow!" shouted an officer on the bridge.

A round, sun-browned face appeared over the cabin hatchway. "Are ye the captain of that vessel?"

"No," answered the officer.

"Then spake to yer equals. I'm the captain o' this!" came from the barge.

ERMINE

Said an envious, erudite ermine:
"There's one thing I cannot determine:
  When a man wears my coat,
  He's a person of note,
While I'm but a species of vermin!"

ESCAPES

There was once a chap who went skating too early and all of a sudden that afternoon loud cries for help began to echo among the bleak hills that surrounded the skating pond.

A farmer, cobbling his boots before his kitchen fire heard the shouts and yells, and ran to the pond at break-neck speed. He saw a large black hole in the ice, and a pale young fellow stood with chattering teeth shoulder-deep in the cold water.

The farmer laid a board on the thin ice and crawled out on it to the edge of the hole. Then, extending his hand, he said:

"Here, come over this way, and I'll lift you out."

"No, I can't swim," was the impatient reply. "Throw a rope to me. Hurry up. It's cold in here."

"I ain't got no rope," said the farmer; and he added angrily. "What if you can't swim—you can wade, I guess! The water's only up to your shoulders."

"Up to my shoulders?" said the young fellow. "It's eight feet deep if it's an inch. I'm standing on the blasted fat man who broke the ice!"

ETHICS

My ethical state,
Were I wealthy and great,
Is a subject you wish I'd reply on.
Now who can foresee
What his morals *might* be?
What would yours be if you were a lion?

Martial; tr. by Paul Nixon.

ETIQUET

A Boston girl the other day said to a southern friend who was visiting her, as two men rose in a car to give them seats: "Oh, I wish they would not do it." "Why not? I think it is very nice of them," said her friend, settling herself comfortably. 'Yes, but one can't thank them, you know, and it is so awkward." "Can't thank them! Why not?" "Why, you would not speak to a strange man, would you?" said the Boston maiden, to the astonishment of her southern friend.

A little girl on the train to Pittsburgh was chewing gum. Not only that, but she insisted on pulling it out in long strings and letting it fall back into her mouth again.

"Mabel!" said her mother in a horrified whisper. "Mabel, don't do that. Chew your gum like a little lady."

LITTLE BROTHER—"What's etiquet?"

LITTLE BIGGER BROTHER—"It's saying 'No, thank you,' when you want to holler 'Gimme!' "—*Judge.*

> A Lady there was of Antigua,
> Who said to her spouse, "What a pig you are!"
>   He answered, "My queen,
>   Is it manners you mean,
> Or do you refer to my figure?"
> —*Gilbert K. Chesterton.*

They were at dinner and the dainties were on the table.

"Will you take tart or pudding?" asked Papa of Tommy.

"Tart," said Tommy promptly.

His father sighed as he recalled the many lessons on manners he had given the boy.

"Tart, what?" he queried kindly.

But Tommy's eyes were glued on the pastry.

"Tart, what?" asked the father again, sharply this time.

"Tart, first," answered Tommy triumphantly.

TOMMY'S AUNT—"Won't you have another piece of cake, Tommy?"

TOMMY (on a visit)—"No, I thank you."

TOMMY'S AUNT—"You seem to be suffering from loss of appetite."

TOMMY—"That ain't loss of appetite. What I'm sufferin' from is politeness."

> There was a young man so benighted,
> He never knew when he was slighted;
>   He would go to a party,
>   And eat just as hearty,
> As if he'd been really invited.

EUROPEAN WAR

OFFICER (as Private Atkins worms his way toward the enemy)—"You fool! Come back at once!"

TOMMY—"No bally fear, sir! There's a hornet in the trench."—*Punch.*

"You can tell an Englishman nowadays by the way he holds his head up."

"Pride, eh?"

"No, Zeppelin neck."

LITTLE GIRL (who has been sitting very still with a seraphic expression)—"I wish I was an angel, mother!"

MOTHER—"What makes you say that, darling?"

LITTLE GIRL—"Because then I could drop bombs on the Germans!"—*Punch.*

From a sailor's letter to his wife:

"Dear Jane,—I am sending you a postal order for 10s., which I hope you may get—but you may not—as this letter has to pass the Censor."—*Punch.*

Two country darkies listened, awe-struck, while some planters discussed the tremendous range of the new German guns.

"Dar now," exclaimed one negro, when his master had finished expatiating on the hideous havoc wrought by a forty-two-centimeter shell, "jes' lak I bin tellin' yo' niggehs all de time! Don' le's have no guns lak dem roun' heah! Why, us niggehs could start runnin' erway—run all day, git almos' home free, an' den git kilt jus' befo' suppeh!"

"Dat's de trufe," assented his companion, "an' lemme tell yo' sumpin' else, Bo. All dem guns needs is jus' yo' *ad*-dress, dat's all; jes' giv' em de *ad*-dress an' they'll git yo'."

See also War.

EVIDENCE

From a crowd of rah-rah college boys celebrating a crew victory, a policeman had managed to extract two prisoners.

"What is the charge against these young men?" asked the magistrate before whom they were arraigned.

"Disturbin' the peace, yer honor," said the policeman. "They were givin' their college yells in the street an' makin' trouble generally."

"What is your name?" the judge asked one of the prisoners.

"Ro-ro-robert Ro-ro-rollins," stuttered the youth.

"I asked for your name, sir,—not the evidence."

Maud Muller, on a summer night,
Turned down the only parlor light.
The judge, beside her, whispered things
Of wedding bells and diamond rings.
He spoke his love in burning phrase,
And acted foolish forty ways.
When he had gone Maud gave a laugh
And then turned off the dictagraph.

—*Milwaukee Sentinel.*

One day a hostess asked a well known Parisian judge:

"Your Honor, which do you prefer, Burgundy or Bordeaux?"

"Madame, that is a case in which I have so much pleasure in taking the evidence that I always postpone judgment," was the wily jurist's reply.

See also Courts; Witnesses.

EXAMINATIONS

An instructor in a church school where much attention was paid to sacred history, dwelt particularly on the phrase "And Enoch was not, for God took him." So many times was this repeated in connection with the death of Enoch that he thought even the dullest pupil would answer correctly when asked in examination: State in the exact language of the Bible what is said of Enoch's death.

But this was the answer he got:

"Enoch was not what God took him for."

A member of the faculty of the University of Wisconsin tells of some amusing replies made by a pupil undergoing an examination in English. The candidate had been instructed to write out examples of the indicative, the subjunctive, the potential and the exclamatory moods. His efforts resulted as follows:

"I am endeavoring to pass an English examination. If I answer twenty questions I shall pass. If I answer twelve questions I may pass. God help me!"

The following selection of mistakes in examinations may convince almost any one that there are some peaks of ignorance which he has yet to climb:

Magna Charta said that the King had no right to bring soldiers into a lady's house and tell her to mind them.

Panama is a town of Colombo, where they are trying to make an isthmus.

The three highest mountains in Scotland are Ben Nevis, Ben Lomond and Ben Jonson.

Wolsey saved his life by dying on the way from York to London.

Bigamy is when a man tries to serve two masters.

"Those melodious bursts that fill the spacious days of great Elizabeth" refers to the songs that Queen Elizabeth used to write in her spare time.

Tennyson wrote a poem called Grave's Energy.

The Rump Parliament consisted entirely of Cromwell's stalactites.

The plural of spouse is spice.

Queen Elizabeth rode a white horse from Kenilworth through Coventry with nothing on, and Raleigh offered her his cloak.

The law allowing only one wife is called monotony.

When England was placed under an Interdict the Pope stopped all births, marriages and deaths for a year.

The Pyramids are a range of mountains between France and Spain.

The gods of the Indians are chiefly Mahommed and Buddha, and in their spare time they do lots of carving.

Every one needs a holiday from one year's end to another.

The Seven Great Powers of Europe are gravity, electricity, steam, gas, fly-wheels, and motors, and Mr. Lloyd George.

The hydra was married to Henry VIII. When he cut off her head another sprung up.

Liberty of conscience means doing wrong and not worrying about it afterward.

The Habeas Corpus act was that no one need stay in prison longer than he liked.

Becket put on a camel-air shirt and his life at once became dangerous.

The two races living in the north of Europe are Esquimaux and Archangels.

Skeleton is what you have left when you take a man's insides out and his outsides off.

Ellipsis is when you forget to kiss.

A bishop without a diocese is called a suffragette.

Artificial perspiration is the way to make a person alive when they are only just dead.

A night watchman is a man employed to sleep in the open air.

The tides are caused by the sun drawing the water out and the moon drawing it in again.

The liver is an infernal organ of the body.

A circle is a line which meets its other end without ending.

Triangles are of three kinds, the equilateral or three-sided, the quadrilateral or four-sided, and the multilateral or polyglot.

General Braddock was killed in the Revolutionary War. He had three horses shot under him and a fourth went through his clothes.

A buttress is the wife of a butler.

The young Pretender was co called because it was pretended that he was born in a frying-pan.

A verb is a word which is used in order to make an exertion.

A Passive Verb is when the subject is the sufferer, *e.g.*, I am loved.

Lord Raleigh was the first man to see the invisible Armada.

A schoolmaster is called a pedigree.

The South of the U. S. A. grows oranges, figs, melons and a great quantity of preserved fruits, especially tinned meats.

The wife of a Prime Minister is called a Primate.

The Greeks were too thickly populated to be comfortable.

The American war was started because the people would persist in sending their parcels thru the post without stamps.

Prince William was drowned in a butt of Malmsey wine; he never laughed again.

The heart is located on the west side of the body.

Richard II is said to have been murdered by some historians; his real fate is uncertain.

Subjects have a right to partition the king.

A kaiser is a stream of hot water springin' up an' disturbin' the earth.

He had nothing left to live for but to die.

Franklin's education was got by himself. He worked himself up to be a great literal man. He was also able to invent electricity. Franklin's father was a tallow chandelier.

Monastry is the place for monsters.

Sir Walter Raleigh was put out once when his servant found him with fire in his head. And one day after there had been a lot of rain, he threw his cloak in a puddle and the queen stepped dryly over.

The Greeks planted colonists for their food supplies.

Nicotine is so deadly a poison that a drop on the end of a dog's tail will kill a man.

A mosquito is the child of black and white parents.

An author is a queer animal because his tales (tails) come from his head.

Wind is air in a hurry.

The people that come to America found Indians, but no people.

Shadows are rays of darkness.

Lincoln wrote the address while riding from Washington to Gettysburg on an envelope.

Queen Elizabeth was tall and thin, but she was a stout protestant.

An equinox is a man who lives near the north pole.

An abstract noun is something we can think of but cannot feel—as a red hot poker.

The population of New England is too dry for farming.

Anatomy is the human body, which consists of three parts, the head, the chist, and the stummick. The head contains the eyes and brains, if any. The chist contains the lungs and a piece of the liver. The stummick is devoted to the bowels, of which there are five, a, e, i, o, u, and sometimes w and y.

Filigree means a list of your descendants.

"The Complete Angler" was written by Euclid because he knew all about angles.

The imperfect tense in French is used to express a future action in past time which does not take place at all.

Arabia has many syphoons and very bad ones; It gets into your hair even with your mouth shut.

The modern name for Gaul is vinegar.

Some of the West India Islands are subject to torpedoes.

The Crusaders were a wild and savage people until Peter the Hermit preached to them.

On the low coast plains of Mexico yellow fever is very popular.

Louis XVI was gelatined during the French Revolution.

Gender shows whether a man is masculine, feminine, or neuter.

An angle is a triangle with only two sides.

Geometry teaches us how to bisex angels.

Gravitation is that which if there were none we should all fly away.

A vacuum is a large empty space where the Pope lives.

A deacon is the lowest kind of Christian.

Vapor is dried water.

The Salic law is that you must take everything with a grain of salt.

The Zodiac is the Zoo of the sky, where lions, goats and other animals go after they are dead.

The Pharisees were people who like to show off their goodness by praying in synonyms.

An abstract noun is something you can't see when you are looking at it.

EXCUSES

The children had been reminded that they must not appear at school the following week without their application blanks properly filled out as to names of parents, addresses, dates and place of birth. On Monday morning Katie Barnes arrived, the tears streaming down her cheeks. "What is the trouble?" Miss Green inquired, seeking to comfort her. "Oh," sobbed the little girl, "I forgot my excuse for being born."

O. Henry always retained the whimsical sense of humor which made him quickly famous. Shortly before his death he called on the cashier of a New York publishing house, after vainly writing several times for a check which had been promised as an advance on his royalties.

"I'm sorry," explained the cashier, "but Mr. Blank, who signs the checks, is laid up with a sprained ankle."

"But, my dear sir," expostulated the author, "does he sign them with his feet?"

Strolling along the boardwalk at Atlantic City, Mr. Mulligan, the wealthy retired contractor, dropped a quarter through a crack in the planking. A friend came along a minute later and found him squatted down, industriously poking a two dollar bill through the treacherous cranny with his forefinger.

"Mulligan, what the divvil ar're ye doin'?" inquired the friend.

"Sh-h," said Mr. Mulligan, "I'm tryin' to make it wort' me while to tear up this board."

A captain, inspecting his company one morning, came to an Irishman who evidently had not shaved for several days.

"Doyle," he asked, "how is it that you haven't shaved this morning?"

"But Oi did, sor."

"How dare you tell me that with the beard you have on your face?"

"Well, ye see, sor," stammered Doyle, "there wus nine of us to one small bit uv a lookin'-glass, an' it must be thot in th' gineral confusion Oi shaved some other man's face."

"Is that you, dear?" said a young husband over the telephone. "I just called up to say that I'm afraid I won't be able to get home to dinner to-night, as I am detained at the office."

"You poor dear," answered the wife sympathetically. "I don't wonder. I don't see how you manage to get anything done at all with that orchestra playing in your office. Good-by."

What is the matter, dearest?" asked the mother of a small girl who had been discovered crying in the hall.

Somfing awful's happened, Mother."

"Well, what is it, sweetheart?"

"My d'doll-baby got away from me and broked a plate in the pantry."

A poor casual laborer, working on a scaffolding, fell five stories to the ground. As his horrified mates rushed down pell-mell to his aid, he picked himself up, uninjured, from a great, soft pile of sand.

"Say, fellers," he murmured anxiously, "is the boss mad? Tell him I had to come down anyway for a ball of twine."

Cephas is a darky come up from Maryland to a border town in Pennsylvania, where he has established himself as a handy man to do odd jobs. He is a good worker, and sober, but there are certain proclivities of his which necessitate a pretty close watch on him. Not long ago he was caught with a chicken under his coat, and was haled to court to explain its presence there.

"Now, Cephas," said the judge very kindly, "you have got into a new place, and you ought to have new habits. We have been good to you and helped you, and while we like you as a sober and industrious worker, this other business cannot be tolerated. Why did you take Mrs. Gilkie's chicken?"

Cephas was stumped, and he stood before the majesty of the law, rubbing his head and looking ashamed of himself. Finally he answered:

"Deed, I dunno, Jedge," he explained, "ceptin' 't is dat chickens is chickens and niggers is niggers."

GRANDMA—"Johnny, I have discovered that you have taken more maple-sugar than I gave you."

JOHNNY—"Yes, Grandma, I've been making believe there was another little boy spending the day with me."

Mr. X was a prominent member of the B. P. O. E. At the breakfast table the other morning he was relating to his wife an incident that occurred at the lodge the previous night. The president of the order offered a silk hat to the brother who could stand up and truthfully say that during his married life he had never kissed any woman but his own wife. "And, would you believe it, Mary?—not a one stood up." "George," his wife said, "why didn't you stand up?" "Well," he replied, "I was going to, but I know I look like hell in a silk hat."

> And oftentimes excusing of a fault
> Doth make the fault the worse by the excuse,
> As patches set upon a little breach,
> Discredit more in hiding of the fault
> Than did the fault before it was so patched.
> —*Shakespeare.*

EXPOSURE

TRAMP—"Lady, I'm dying from exposure."

WOMAN—"Are you a tramp, politician or financier?"—*Judge.*

EXTORTION

See Dressmakers.

EXTRAVAGANCE

> There was a young girl named O'Neill,
> Who went up in the great Ferris wheel;
>   But when half way around
>   She looked at the ground,
> And it cost her an eighty-cent meal.

Everybody knew that John Polkinhorn was the carelessest man in town, but nobody ever thought he was careless enough to marry Susan Rankin, seeing that he had known her for years. For awhile they got along fairly well but one day after five years of it John hung himself in the attic, where Susan used to dry the wash on rainy days, and a carpenter, who went up to the roof to do some repairs, found him there. He told Susan, and Susan hurried up to see about it, and, sure enough, the carpenter was right. She stood looking at her late husband for about a minute—kind of dazed, the carpenter thought—then she spoke.

"Well, I declare!" she exclaimed. "If he hasn't used my new clothes-line, and the old would have done every bit as well! But, of course, that's just like John Polkinhorn."

"The editor of my paper," declared the newspaper business manager to a little coterie of friends, "is a peculiar genius. Why, would you believe it, when he draws his weekly salary he keeps out only one dollar for spending money and sends the rest to his wife in Indianapolis!"

His listeners—with one exception, who sat silent and reflective—gave vent to loud murmurs of wonder and admiration.

'Now, it may sound thin," added the speaker, "but it is true, nevertheless."

"Oh, I don't doubt it at all!" quickly rejoined the quiet one; "I was only wondering what he does with the dollar!"

An Irish soldier was recently given leave of absence the morning after pay day. When his leave expired he didn't appear. He was brought at last before the commandant for sentence, and the following dialogue is recorded:

"Well, Murphy, you look as if you had had a severe engagement."

"Yes, sur."

"Have you any money left?"

"No, sur."

"You had $35 when you left the fort, didn't you?"

"Yes, sur."

"What did you do with it?"

"Well, sur, I was walking along and I met a friend and we went into a place and spint $8. Thin we came out and I met another friend and we spint $8 more, and thin I come out and we met another friend and we spint $8 more, and thin we come out and we met another bunch of friends, and I spint $8 more—and thin I come home."

'But, Murphy, that makes only $32. What did you do with the other $3?" Murphy thought. Then he shook his head slowly and said:

"I dunno, colonel, I recken I must have squandered that money foolishly."

FAILURES

Little Ikey came up to his father with a very solemn face. "Is it true, father," he asked, "that marriage is a failure?"

His father surveyed him thoughtfully for a moment. "Well, Ikey," he finally replied, "If you get a rich wife, it's almost as good as a failure."

FAITH

Faith is that quality which leads a man to expect that his flowers and garden will resemble the views shown on the seed packets.—*Country Life in America.*

"What is faith, Johnny?" asked the Sunday school teacher.

"Pa says," answers Johnny, "that it's readin' in the papers that the price o' things has come down, an expectin' to find it true when the bills comes in."

Faith is believing the dentist when he says it isn't going to hurt.

"As I understand it, Doctor, if I believe I'm well, I'll be well. Is that the idea?"

"It is."

"Then, if you believe you are paid, I suppose you'll be paid."

"Not necessarily."

"But why shouldn't faith work as well in one case as in the other?"

"Why, you see, there is considerable difference between having faith in Providence and having faith in you."—*Horace Zimmerman.*

Mother had been having considerable argument with her infant daughter as to whether the latter was going to be left alone in a dark room to go to sleep. As a clincher, the mother said: "There is no reason at all why you should be afraid. Remember that God is here all the time, and, besides, you have your dolly. Now go to sleep like a good little girl." Twenty minutes later a wail came from upstairs, and mother went to the foot of the stairs to pacify her daughter. "Don't cry," she said; "remember what I told you—God is there with you and you have your dolly." "But I don't want them," wailed the baby; "I want you, muvver; I want somebody here that has got a skin face on them."

> Faith is a fine invention
>   For gentlemen who see;
> But Microscopes are prudent
>   In an emergency
>
> —*Emily Dickinson.*

FAITHFULNESS

A wizened little Irishman applied for a job loading a ship. At first they said he was too small, but he finally persuaded them to give him a trial. He seemed to be making good, and they gradually increased the size of his load until on the last trip he was carrying a 300-pound anvil under each are. When he was half-way across the gangplank it broke and the Irishman fell in. With a great splashing and spluttering he came to the surface.

"T'row me a rope, I say!" he shouted again. Once more he sank. A third time he rose struggling.

"Say!" he spluttered angrily, 'if one uv you shpalpeens don't hurry up an' t'row me a rope I'm goin' to drop one uv these damn t'ings!"

FAME

Fame is the feeling that you are the constant subject of admiration on the part of people who are not thinking of you.

Many a man thinks he has become famous when he has merely happened to meet an editor who was hard up for material.

Were not this desire of fame very strong, the difficulty of obtaining it, and the danger of losing it when obtained, would be sufficient to deter a man from so vain a pursuit.—*Addison.*

FAMILIES

"Yes, sir, our household represents the United Kingdom of Great Britain," said the proud father of number one to the rector. "I am English, my wife's Irish, the nurse is Scotch and the baby wails."

Mrs. O'Flarity is a scrub lady, and she had been absent from her duties for several days. Upon her return her employer asked her the reason for her absence.

"Sure, I've been carin' for wan of me sick children," she replied.

"And how many children have you, Mrs. O'Flarity?" he asked.

"Siven in all," she replied. "Four by the third wife of me second husband; three by the second wife of me furst."

A man descended from an excursion train and was wearily making his way to the street-car, followed by his wife and fourteen children, when a policeman touched him on the shoulder and said:

"Come along wid me."

"What for?"

"Blamed if I know; but when ye're locked up I'll go back and find out why that crowd was following ye."

FAREWELLS

Happy are we met, Happy have we been,
Happy may we part, and Happy meet again.

A dear old citizen went to the cars the other day to see his daughter off on a journey. Securing her a seat he passed out

of the car and went around to the car window to say a last parting word. While he was leaving the car the daughter crossed
the aisle to speak to a friend, and at the same time a grim old
maid took the seat and moved up to the window.

Unaware of the change the old gentleman hurriedly put his
head up to the window and said: "One more kiss, pet."

In another instant the point of a cotton umbrella was thrust
from the window, followed by the wrathful injunction: "Scat,
you gray-headed wretch!"

"I am going to make my farewell tour in Shakespeare. What
shall be the play? Hamlet? Macbeth?"

"This is your sixth farewell tour, I believe."

"Well, yes."

"I would suggest "Much Adieu About Nothing."

> "Farewell!"
> For in that word—that fatal word—howe'er
> We promise—hope—believe—there breathes despair.
>
> —*Byron.*

FASHION

There are two kinds of women: The fashionable ones and
those who are comfortable.—*Tom P. Morgan.*

There had been a dressmaker in the house and Minnie had
listened to long discussions about the very latest fashions. That
night when she said her prayers, she added a new petition, uttered with unwonted fervency:

"And, dear Lord, please make us all very stylish."

> Nothing is thought rare
> Which is not new, and follow'd; yet we know
> That what was worn some twenty years ago
> Comes into grace again.
>
> —*Beaumont and Fletcher.*

As good be out of the World as out of the Fashion.—*Colley
Cibber.*

FATE

Fate hit me very hard one day.
I cried: "What is my fault?
What have I done? What causes, pray,
This unprovoked assault?"
She paused, then said: "Darned if I know;
I really can't explain."
Then just before she turned to go
She whacked me once again!

—*La Houche Hancock.*

So in the Libyan fable it is told
That once an eagle stricken with a dart,
Said, when he saw the fashion of the shaft,
"With our own feathers, not by others' hands,
Are we now smitten."

Æschylus.

FATHERS

A director of one of the great transcontinental railroads was showing his three-year-old daughter the pictures in a work on natural history. Pointing to a picture of a zebra, he asked the baby to tell him what it represented. Baby answered "Coty."

Pointing to a picture of a tiger in the same way, she answered "Kitty." Then a lion, and she answered "Doggy." Elated with her seeming quick perception, he then turned to the picture of a chimpanzee and said:

"Baby, what is this?"

"Papa."

FAULTS

Women's faults are many,
Men have only two—
Everything they say,
And everything they do.

—*Le Crabbe.*

FEES

See Tips.

FEET

BIG MAN (with a grouch)—"Will you be so kind as to get off my feet?"

LITTLE MAN (with a bundle)—"I'll try, sir. Is it much of a walk?"

FIGHTING

"Who gave ye th' black eye, Jim?"

"Nobody give it t' me; I had t' fight fer it."—*Life.*

"There! You have a black eye, and your nose is bruised, and your coat is torn to bits," said Mamma, as her youngest appeared at the door. "How many times have I told you not to play with that bad Jenkins boy?"

"Now, look here, Mother," said Bobby, "do I look as if we'd been playing?"

Two of the leading attorneys of Memphis, who had been warm friends for years, happened to be opposing counsel in a case some time ago. The older of the two was a man of magnificent physique, almost six feet four, and built in proportion, while the younger was barely five feet and weighed not more than ninety pounds.

In the course of his argument the big man unwittingly made some remark that aroused the ire of his small adversary. A moment later he felt a great pulling and tugging at his coat tails. Looking down, he was greatly astonished to see his opponent wildly gesticulating and dancing around him.

"What on earth are you trying to do there, Dudley" he asked.

"By Gawd, suh, I'm fightin', suh!"

An Irishman boasted that he could lick any man in Boston, yes, Massachusetts, and finally he added New England. When he came to, he said: "I tried to cover too much territory."

"Dose Irish make me sick, alvays talking about vat gread fighders dey are," said a Teutonic resident of Hoboken, with great contempt. "Vhy, at Minna's vedding der odder night dot drunken Mike O'Hooligan butted in, und me und mein bruder, und mein cousin Fritz und mein frient Louie Hartmann—vhy, ve pretty near kicked him oudt of der house!"

VILLAGE GROCER—"What are you running for, sonny?"
BOY—"I'm tryin' to keep two fellers from fightin'."
VILLAGE GROCER—"Who are the fellows?"
BOY—"Bill Perkins and me!"—*Puck.*

An aged, gray-haired and very wrinkled old woman, arrayed in the outlandish calico costume of the mountains, was summoned as a witness in court to tell what she knew about a fight in her house. She took the witness-stand with evidences of backwardness and proverbial Bourbon verdancy. The Judge asked her in a kindly voice what took place. She insisted it did not amount to much, but the Judge by his persistency finally got her to tell the story of the bloody fracas.

"Now, I tell ye, Jedge, it didn't amount to nuthin'. The fust I knowed about it was when Bill Saunder called Tom Smith a liar, en Tom knocked him down with a stick o' wood. One o' Bill's friends then cut Tom with a knife, slicin' a big chunck out o' him. Then Sam Jones, who was a friend of Tom's, shot the other feller and two more shot him, en three or four others got cut right smart by somebody. That nachly caused some excitement, Jedge, en then they commenced fightin'."

"Do you mean to say such a physical wreck as he gave you that black eye?" asked the magistrate.

"Sure, your honor, he wasn't a physical wreck till after he gave me the black eye," replied the complaining wife.—*London Telegraph.*

A pessimistic young man dining alone in a restaurant ordered broiled live lobster. When the waiter put it on the table it was obviously minus one claw. The pessimistic young man promptly kicked. The waiter said it was unavoidable—there had been a fight in the kitchen between two lobsters. The other one had torn off one of the claws of this lobster and had eaten it. The young man pushed the lobster over toward the waiter. "Take it away," he said wearily, "and bring me the winner."

There never was a good war or a bad peace.—*Benjamin Franklin.*

The master-secret in fighting is to strike once, but in the right place.—*John C. Snaith.*

FINANCE

Willie had a savings bank;
'Twas made of painted tin.
He passed it 'round among the boys,
Who put their pennies in.

Then Willie wrecked that bank and bought
Sweetmeats and chewing gum.
And to the other envious lads
He never offered some.

"What will we de?" his mother said:
"It is a sad mischance."
His father said: "We'll cultivate
His gift for high finance."

—*Washington Star.*

Hicks—"I've got to borrow $200 somewhere."

Wicks—"Take my advice and borrow $300 while you are about it."

"But I only need $200."

"That doesn't make any difference. Borrow $300 and pay back $100 of it in two installments at intervals of a month or so. Then the man that you borrow from will think he is going to get the rest of it."

It is said J. P. Morgan could raise $10,000,000 on his check any minute; but the man who is raising a large family on $9 a week is a greater financier than Morgan.

To modernize an old prophecy, "out of the mouths of babes shall come much worldly wisdom." Mr. K. has two boys whom he dearly loves. One day he gave each a dollar to spend. After much bargaining, they brought home a wonderful four-wheeled steamboat and a beautiful train of cars. For awhile the transportation business flourished, and all was well, but one day Craig explained to his father that while business had been good, he could do much better if he only had the capital to buy a train of cars like Joe's. His arguments must have been good, for the money was forthcoming. Soon after, little Joe, with probably less logic but more loving, became possessed of a dollar to buy a steamboat like Craig's. But Mr. K., who had furnished the additional capital, looked in vain for the improved service. The new rolling stock was not in evidence, and explanations were vague and unsatisfactory, as is often the case in the railroad game at which men play. It took a stern court of inquiry to develop the fact that the railroad and steamship had simply changed hands—and at a mutual profit of one hundred per cent. And Mr. K., as he told his neighbor, said it was worth that much to know that his boys would not need much of a legacy from him.—*P. A. Kershaw.*

An old artisan who prided himself on his ability to drive a close bargain contracted to paint a huge barn in the neighborhood for the small sum of twelve dollars.

"Why on earth did you agree to do it for so little?" his brother inquired.

"Well," said the old painter, "you see, the owner is a mighty onreliable man. If I'd said I'd charge him twenty-five dollars, likely he'd only paid me nineteen. And if I charge him twelve dollars, he may not pay me but nine. So I thought it over, and decided to paint it for twelve dollars, so I wouldn't lose so much."

FINGER-BOWLS

MISTRESS (to new servant)—"Why, Bridget, this is the third time I've had to tell you about the finger-bowls. Didn't the lady you last worked for have them on the table?"

BRIDGET—"No, mum; her friends always washed their hands before they came."

FIRE DEPARTMENTS

Clang, clatter, bang! Down the street came the fire engines.

Driving along ahead, oblivious of any danger, was a farmer in a ramshackle old buggy. A policeman yelled at him: "Hi there, look out! The fire department's coming."

Turning in by the curb the farmer watched the hose cart, salvage wagon and engine whiz past. Then he turned out into the street again and drove on. Barely had he started when the hook and ladder came tearing along. The rear wheel of the big truck slewed into the farmer's buggy, smashing it to smithereens and sending the farmer sprawling into the gutter. The policeman ran to his assistance.

"Didn't I tell you to keep out of the way?" he demanded crossly. "Didn't I tell ye the fire department was comin'?"

"Wall, consarn ye," said the peeved farmer, "I *did* git outer the way for th' fire department. But what in tarnation was them drunken painters in sech an all-fired hurry fer?

Two Irishmen fresh from Ireland had just landed in New York and engaged a room in the top story of a hotel. Mike, being very sleepy, threw himself on the bed and was soon fast asleep. The sights were so new and strange to Pat that he sat at the window looking out. Soon an alarm of fire was rung in and a fire-engine rushed by throwing up sparks of fire and clouds of smoke. This greatly excited Pat, who called to his comrade to get up and come to the window, but Mike was fast asleep. Another engine soon followed the first, spouting smoke and file like the former. This was too much for poor Pat, who rushed excitedly to the bedside, and shaking his friend called loudly:

"Mike, Mike, wake up! They are moving Hell, and two loads have gone by already."

FIRE ESCAPES

Fire escape: A steel stairway on the exterior of a building, erected after a FIRE to ESCAPE the law.

FIRES

"Ikey, I hear you had a fire last Thursday."

"Sh! Next Thursday."

FIRST AID IN ILLNESS AND INJURY

The father of the family hurried to the telephone and called up the family physician. "Our little boy is sick, Doctor," he said, "so please come at once."

"I can't get over much under an hour," said the doctor.

"Oh please do, Doctor. You see, my wife has a book on 'What to Do Before the Doctor Comes,' and I'm so afraid she'll do it before you get here!"

NURSE GIRL—"Oh, ma'am, what shall I do? The twins have fallen down the well!"

FOND PARENT—"Dear me! how annoying! Just go into the library and get the last number of *The Modern Mother's Magazine*; it contains an article on 'How to Bring Up Children.'"

SURGEON AT NEW YORK HOSPITAL—"What brought you to this dreadful condition? Were you run over by a street-car?"

PATIENT—"No, sir; I fainted, and was brought to by a member of the Society of First Aid to the Injured."—*Life*.

A prominent physician was recently called to his telephone by a colored woman formerly in the service of his wife. In great agitation the woman advised the physician that her youngest child was in a bad way.

"What seems to be the trouble?" asked the doctor

"Doc, she done swallered a bottle of ink!"

"I'll be over in a short while to see her," said the doctor. "Have you done anything for her?"

"I done give her three pieces o' blottin'-paper, Doc," said the colored woman doubtfully.

FISH

A man went into a restaurant recently and said, "Give me a half dozen fried oysters."

"Sorry, sah!" answered the waiter, "but we's all out o' shell fish, sah, 'ceptin' eggs."

Little Elizabeth and her mother were having luncheon together, and the mother, who always tried to impress facts upon her young daughter, said:

"These little sardines, Elizabeth, are sometimes eaten by the larger fish."

Elizabeth gazed at the sardines in wonder, and then asked: "But, mother, how do the large fish get the cans open?"

FISHERMEN

At the birth of President Cleveland's second child no scales could be found to weigh the baby. Finally the scales that the President always used to weigh the fish he caught on his trips were brought up from the cellar, and the child was found to weigh twenty-five pounds.

"Doin' any good?" asked the curious individual on the bridge."

"Any good?" answered the fisherman, in the creek below. "Why I caught forty bass out o' here yesterday."

"Say, do you know who I am?" asked the man on the bridge.

The fisherman replied that he did not.

"Well, I am the county fish and game warden."

The angler, after a moment's thought, exclaimed, "Say, do you know who I am?"

"No," the officer replied.

"Well, I'm the biggest liar in eastern Indiana," said the crafty angler, with a grin.

A young lady who had returned from a tour through Italy with her father informed a friend that he liked all the Italian cities, but most of all he loved Venice.

"Ah, Venice, to be sure!" said the friend. "I can readily understand that your father would like Venice, with its gondolas, and St. Markses and Michelangelos."

"Oh, no," the young lady interrupted, "it wasn't that. He liked it because he could sit in the hotel and fish from the window."

Smith the other day went fishing. He caught nothing, so on his way back home he telephoned to his provision dealer to send a dozen of bass around to his house.

He got home late himself. His wife said to him on his arrival:

"Well, what luck?"

"Why, splendid luck, of course," he replied. "Didn't the boy bring that dozen bass I gave him?"

Mrs. Smith started. Then she smiled.

"Well, yes, I suppose he did," she said. "There they are."

And she showed poor Smith a dozen bottles of Bass's ale.

"You'll be a man like one of us some day," said the patronizing sportsman to a lad who was throwing his line into the same stream.

"Yes, sir," he answered, "I s'pose I will some day, but I b'lieve I'd rather stay small and ketch a few fish."

The more worthless a man, the more fish he can catch.

As no man is born an artist, so no man is born an angler.
—*Izaak Walton.*

FISHING

A man was telling some friends about a proposed fishing trip to a lake in Colorado which he had in contemplation.

"Are there any trout out there?" asked one friend.

"Thousands of 'em," replied Mr. Wharry.

"Will they bite easily?" asked another friend.

"Will they?" said Mr. Wharry. "Why they're absolutely vicious. A man has to hide behind a tree to bait a hook."

"I got a bite—I got a bite!" sang out a tiny girl member of a fishing party. But when an older brother hurriedly drew in the line there was only a bare hook. "Where's the fish?" he asked. "He unbit and div," said the child.

The late Justice Brewer was with a party of New York friends on a fishing trip in the Adirondacks, and around the camp fire one evening the talk naturally ran on big fish. When it came his turn the jurist began, uncertain as to how he was going to come out:

"We were fishing one time on the Grand Banks for—er—for—"

"Whales," somebody suggested.

"No," said the Justice, "we were baiting with whales."

"Lo, Jim! Fishin'?"

"Naw; drowning worms."

We may say of angling as Dr. Boteler said of strawberries: "Doubtless God could have made a better berry, but doubtless God never did"; and so (if I might be judge), God never did make a more calm, quiet, innocent recreation than angling. —*Izaak Walton.*

FLATS

"Hello, Tom, old man, got your new flat fitted up yet?"

"Not quite," answered the friend. "Say, do you know where I can buy a folding toothbrush?"

She hadn't told her mother yet of their first quarrel, but she took refuge in a flood of tears.

"Before we were married you said you'd lay down your life for me," she sobbed.

"I know it," he returnd solemnly; "but this confounded flat is so tiny that there's no place to lay anything down."

FLATTERY

With a sigh she laid down the magazine article upon Daniel O'Connell. "The day of great men," she said, "is gone forever."

"But the day of beautiful women is not," he responded.

She smiled and blushed. "I was only joking," she explained, hurriedly.

MAGISTRATE (about to commit for trial)—"You certainly effected the robbery in a remarkably ingenius way; in fact, with quite exceptional cunning."

PRISONER—"Now, yer honor, no flattery, please; no flattery, I begs yer."

OLD MAID—"But why should a great strong man like you be found begging?"

WAYFARER—"Dear lady, it is the only profession I know in which a gentleman can address a beautiful woman without an introduction."

William——was said to be the ugliest, though the most lovable, man in Louisiana. On returning to the plantation after a short absence, his brother said:

"Willie, I met in New Orleans a Mrs. Forrester who is a great admirer of yours. She said, though, that it wasn't so much the brillancy of your mental attainments as your marvelous physical and facial beauty which charmed and delighted her."

"Edmund," cried William earnestly, "that is a wicked lie, but tell it to me again!"

"You seem to be an able-bodied man. You ought to be strong enough to work."

"I know, mum. And you seem to be beautiful enough to go on the stage, but evidently you prefer the simple life."

After that speech he got a square meal and no reference to the woodpile.

> O, that men's ears should be
> To counsel deaf, but not to flattery!
> —*Shakespeare.*

FLIES

See Pure food.

FLIRTATION

It sometimes takes a girl a long time to learn that a flirtation is attention without intention.

"There's a belief that summer girls are always fickle."
"Yes, I got engaged on that theory, but it looks as if I'm in for a wedding or a breach of promise suit."

A teacher in one of the primary grades of the public school had noticed a striking platonic friendship that existed between Tommy and little Mary, two of her pupils.

Tommy was a bright enough youngster, but he wasn't disposed to prosecute his studies with much energy, and his teacher said that unless he stirred himself before the end of the year he wouldn't be promoted.

"You must study harder," she told him, "or you won't pass. How would you like to stay back in this class another year and have little Mary go ahead of you?"

"Ah," said Tommy. "I guess there'll be other little Marys."

FLOWERS

Lulu was watching her mother working among the flowers. "Mama, I know why flowers grow," she said; "they want to get out of the dirt."

FOOD

A man went into a southern restaurant not long ago and asked for a piece of old-fashioned Washington pie. The waiter, not understanding and yet unwilling to concede his lack of knowledge, brought the customer a piece of chocolate cake.

"No, no, my friend," said the smiling man. "I meant *George* Washington, not *Booker* Washington."

One day a pastor was calling upon a dear old lady, one of the "pillars" of the church to which they both belonged. As he thought of her long and useful life, and looked upon her sweet, placid countenance bearing but few tokens of her ninety-two years of earthly pilgrimage, he was moved to ask her, "My dear Mrs. S., what has been the chief source of your strength and sustenance during all these years? What has appealed to you as the real basis of your unusual vigor of mind and body, and has been to you an unfailing comfort through joy and sorrow? Tell me, that I may pass the secret on to others, and, if possible, profit by it myself."

The old lady thought a moment, then lifting her eyes, dim with age, yet kindling with sweet memories of the past, answered briefly, "Victuals."—*Sarah L. Tenney.*

A girl reading in a paper that fish was excellent brain-food wrote to the editor:

Dear Sir: Seeing as you say how fish is good for the brains, what kind of fish shall I eat?

To this the editor replied:

Dear Miss: Judging from the composition of your letter I should advise you to eat a whale.

A hungry customer seated himself at a table in a quick-lunch restaurant and ordered a chicken pie. When it arrived he raised the lid and sat gazing at the contents intently for a while. Finally he called the waiter.

"Look here, Sam," he said, "what did I order?"

"Chicken pie, sah."

"And what have you brought me?"

"Chicken pie, sah."

"Chicken pie, you black rascal!" the customer replied. "Chicken pie? Why, there's not a piece of chiken in it, and never was."

"Dat's right, boss—dey ain't no chicken in it."

"Then why do you call it chicken pie? I never heard of such a thing."

"Dat's all right, boss. Dey don't have to be no chicken in a chicken pie. Dey ain't no dog in a dog biscuit, is dey?"

See also Dining.

FOOTBALL

His Sister—"His nose seems broken."
His Fiancee—"And he's lost his front teeth."
His Mother—"But he didn't drop the ball!"—*Life.*

FORDS

A boy stood with one foot on the sidewalk and the other on the step of a Ford automobile. A playmate passed him, looked at his position, then sang out: "Hey, Bobbie, have you lost your other skate?"

A farmer noticing a man in automobile garb standing in the road and gazing upward, asked him if he were watching the birds.

"No," he answered, "I was cranking my Ford car and my hand slipped off and the thing got away and went straight up in the air."

FORECASTING

A lady in a southern town was approached by her colored maid.

"Well, Jenny?" she asked, seeing that something was in the air.

"Please, Mis' Mary, might I have the aft'noon off three weeks frum Wednesday?" Then, noticing an undecided look in her mistress's face, she added hastily—"I want to go to my fiance's fun'ral."

"Goodness me," answered the lady—"Your fiancé's funeral! Why, you don't know that he's even going to die, let alone the date of his funeral. That is something we can't any of us be sure about—when we are going to die."

"Yes'm," said the girl doubtfully. Then, with a triumphant note in her voice—"I'se sure about him, Mis', 'cos he's goin' to be hung!"

FORESIGHT

"They tell me you're working 'ard night an' day, Sarah?" her bosom friend Ann said.

"Yes," returned Sarah. "I'm under bonds to keep the peace for pullin' the whiskers out of that old scoundrel of a husban' of mine, and the Magistrate said that if I come afore 'im ag'in, or laid me 'ands on the old man, he'd fine me forty shillin's!"

"And so you're working 'ard to keep out of mischief?"

"Not much; I'm workin' 'ard to save up the fine!"

"Mike, I wish I knew where I was goin' to die. I'd give a thousand dollars to know the place where I'm going to die."

"Well, Pat, what good would it do if yez knew?"

"Lots," said Pat. "Shure I'd never go near that place."

There once was a pious young priest,
Who lived almost wholly on yeast;
  "For," he said, "it is plain
  We must all rise again,
And I want to get started, at least."

FORGETFULNESS

See Memory.

FORTUNE HUNTERS

HER FATHER—"So my daughter has consented to become your wife. Have you fixed the day of the wedding?"

SUITOR—"I will leave that to my fiancée."

H. F.—"Will you have a church or a private wedding?"

S.—"Her mother can decide that, sir."

H. F.—"What have you to live on?"

S.—"I will leave that entirely to you, sir."

The London consul of a continental kingdom was informed by his government that one of his countrywomen, supposed to be living in Great Britain, had been left a large fortune. After advertising without result, he applied to the police, and a smart young detective was set to work. A few weeks later his chief asked how he was getting on.

"I've found the lady, sir."

"Good! Where is she?"

"At my place. I married her yesterday."

"I would die for you," said the rich suitor.

"How soon?" asked the practical girl.

He—"I'd like to meet Miss Bond."

She—"Why?"

"I hear she has thirty thousand a year and no incumbrance."

"Is she looking for one?"—*Life*.

Maude—"I've just heard of a case where a man married a girl on his deathbed so she could have his millions when he was gone. Could you love a girl like that?"

Jack—"That's just the kind of a girl I could love. What's her address?"

"Yes," said the old man to his young visitor, "I am proud of my girls, and would like to see them comfortably married, and as I have made a little money they will not go penniless to their husbands. There is Mary, twenty-five years old, and a really good girl. I shall give her $1,000 when she marries. Then comes Bet, who won't see thirty-five again, and I shall give her $3,000, and the man who takes Eliza, who is forty, will have $5,000 with her."

The young man reflected for a moment and then inquired: "You haven't one about fifty, have you?"

FOUNTAIN PENS

"Fust time you've ever milked a cow, is it?" said Uncle Josh to his visiting nephed. "Wal, y' do it a durn sight better'n most city fellers do."

"It seems to come natural somehow," said the youth, flushing with pleasure. "I've had a good deal of practice with a fountain pen."

"Percy" asks if we know anything which will change the color of the fingers when they have become yellow from cigarette smoking.

He might try using one of the inferior makes of fountain pens.

FOURTH OF JULY

"You are in favor of a safe and sane Fourth of July?"

"Yes," replied Mr. Growcher. "We ought to have that kind of a day at least once a year."

One Fourth of July night in London, the Empire Music Hall advertised special attractions to American visitors. All over the auditorium the Union Jack and Stars and Stripes enfolded one another, and at the interludes were heard "Yankee Doodle" and "Hail Columbia," while a quartette sang "Down upon the Swanee River." It was an occasion to swell the heart of an exiled patriot. Finally came the turn of the Human Encyclopedia, who advanced to the front of the stage and announced himself ready to answer, sight unseen, all questions the audience might propound. A volley of queries was fired at him, and the Encyclopedia breathlessly told the distance of the earth from Mars, the number of bones in the human skeleton, of square miles in the British Empire, and other equally important facts. There was a brief pause, in which an American stood up.

"What great event took place July 4, 1776?" he propounded in a loud glad voice.

The Human Encyclopedia glared at him. "Th' hincident you speak of, sir was a hinfamous houtrage!"

FREAKS

See Husbands.

FREE THOUGHT

TOMMY—"Pop, what is a freethinker?"

POP—"A freethinker, my son, is any man who isn't married."

FRENCH LANGUAGE

"I understand you speak French like a native."

"No," replied the student; "I've got the grammar and the accent down pretty fine. But it's hard to learn the gestures."

In Paris last summer a southern girl was heard to drawl between the acts of "Chantecler": "I think it's mo' fun when you don't understand French. It sounds mo' like chickens!"

—*Life.*

FRESHMEN

See College Students.

FRIENDS

The Lord gives our relatives,
Thank God we can choose our friends.

"Father."
"Well, what is it?"
"It says here, 'A man is known by the company he keeps.' Is that so, Father?"
"Yes, yes, yes."
"Well, Father, if a good man keeps company with a bad man, is the good man bad because he keeps company with the bad man, and is the bad man good because he keeps company with the good man?"—*Punch.*

Here's champagne to our real friends.
And real pain to our sham friends.

It's better to make friends fast
Than to make fast friends.

Some friends are a habit—some a luxury.

A friend is one who overlooks your virtues and appreciates your faults.

FRIENDS, SOCIETY OF

A visitor to Philadelphia, unfamiliar with the garb of the Society of Friends, was much interested in two demure and placid Quakeresses who took seats directly behind her in the

Broad Street Station. After a few minutes' silence she was somewhat startled to hear a gentle voice inquire: "Sister Kate, will thee go to the counter and have a milk punch on me?" —*Carolina Lockhart.*

FRIENDSHIP

Friendly may we part and quickly meet again.

> There's fellowship
> In every sip
> Of friendship's brew.

May we all travel through the world and sow it thick with friendship.

> Here's to the four hinges of Friendship—
> Swearing, Lying, Stealing and Drinking.
> When you swear, swear by your country;
> When you lie, lie for a pretty woman,
> When you steal, steal away from bad company
> And when you drink, drink with me.

The trouble with having friends is the upkeep.

"Brown volunteered to lend me money."

"Did you take it?"

"No. That sort of friendship is too good to lose."

"I let my house furnished, and they've had measles there. Of course we've had the place disinfected; so I suppose it's quite safe. What do you think?"

"I fancy it would be all right, dear; but I think, perhaps, it would be safer to lend it to a friend first."—*Punch.*

"Hoo is it, Jeemes, that you mak' sic an enairmous profit aff yer potatoes? Yer price is lower than ony ither in the toon and ye mak' extra reduction for yer friends."

"Weel, ye see, I knock aff twa shillin's a ton because a customer is a freend o' mine, an' then I jist tak' twa hundertweight aff the ton because I'm a friend o' his."—*Punch.*

The conductor of a western freight train saw a tramp stealing a ride on one of the forward cars. He told the brakeman in the caboose to go up and put the man off at the next stop. When the brakeman approached the tramp, the latter waved a big revolver and told him to keep away.

"Did you get rid of him?" the conductor asked the brakeman when the train was under motion again.

"I hadn't the heart," was the reply. "He turned out to be an old school friend of mine."

"I'll take care of him," said the conductor, as he started over the tops of the cars.

After the train had made another stop and gone on, the brakeman came into the caboose and said to the conductor:

"Well, in he off?"

"No; he turned out to be an old school friend of mine, too."

If a man does not make new acquaintances, as he advances through life, he will soon find himself left alone. A man, Sir, should keep his friendship in constant repair.

—*Samuel Johnson.*

They say, and I am glad they say,
  It is so; and it may be so;
It may be just the other way,
  I cannot tell, but this I know—
From quiet homes and first beginnings
  Out to the undiscovered ends
There's nothing worth the wear of winning
  Save laughter and the love of friends.

—*Hilaire Belloc.*

FUN

Fun is like life insurance, th' older you git th' more it costs.
—*Abe Martin.*

See also Amusements.

FUNERALS

There was an old man in a hearse,
Who murmured, "This might have been worse;
  Of course the expense
  Is simply immense,
But it doesn't come out of my purse."

FURNITURE

GUEST—"That's a beautiful rug. May I ask how much it cost you?"

HOST—"Five hundred dollars. A hundred and fifty for it and the rest for furniture to match."

FUTURE LIFE

A certain young man's friends thought he was dead, but he was only in a state of coma. When, in ample time to avoid being buried, he showed signs of life, he was asked how it seemed to be dead.

"Dead?" he exclaimed. "I wasn't dead. I knew all that was going on. And I knew I wasn't dead, too, because my feet were cold and I was hungry."

"But how did that fact make you think you were still alive?" asked one of the curious.

"Well, this way; I knew that if I were in heaven I wouldn't be hungry. And if I was in the other place my feet wouldn't be cold."

FATHER (impressively)—"Suppose I should be taken away suddenly, what would become of you, my boy?"

IRREVERENT SON—I'd stay here. The question is, What would become of you?"

"Look here, now, Harold," said a father to his little son, who was naughty, "if you don't say your prayers you won't go to Heaven."

"I don't want to go to Heaven," sobbed the boy; "I want to go with you and mother."

On a voyage across the ocean an Irishman died and was about to be buried at sea. His friend Mike was the chief mourner at the burial service, at the conclusion of which those in charge wrapped the body in canvas preparatory to dropping it overboard. It is customary to place heavy shot with a body to insure its immediate sinking, but in this instance, nothing else being available, a large lump of coal was substituted. Mike's cup of sorrow overflowed his eyes, and he tearfully exclaimed,

"Oh, Pat, I knew you'd never get to heaven, but, begorry, I didn't think you'd have to furnish your own fuel."

An Irishman told a man that he had fallen so low in this life that in the next he would have to climb up hill to get into hell.

When P. T. Barnum was at the head of his "great moral show," it was his rule to send complimentary tickets to clergymen, and the custom is continued to this day. Not long ago, after the Reverend Doctor Walker succeeded to the pastorate of the Reverend Doctor Hawks, in Hartford, there came to the parsonage, addressed to Doctor Hawks, tickets for the circus, with the compliments of the famous showman. Doctor Walker studied the tickets for a moment, and then remarked:

"Doctor Hawks is dead and Mr. Barnum is dead; evidently they haven't met."

Archbishop Ryan once attended a dinner given him by the citizens of Philadelphia and a brilliant company of men was present. Among others were the president of the Pennsylvania Railroad; ex-Attorney-General MacVeagh, counsel for the road, and other prominent railroad men.

Mr. MacVeagh, in talking to the guest of the evening, said: "Your Grace, among others you see here a great many railroad men. There is a peculiarity of railroad men that even on social occasions you will find that they always take their lawyer with them. That is why I am here. They never go anywhere without their counsel. Now they have nearly everything that men want, but I have a suggestion to make to you for an exchange with us. We can give free passes on all the railroads of the country. Now if you would only give us—say a free pass to Paradise by way of exchange."

"Ah, no," said His Grace, with a merry twinkle in his eye, "that would never do. I would not like to separate them from their counsel."

GARDENING

Th' only time some fellers ever dig in th' gardens is just before they go a fishin'.—*Abe Martin.*

"I am going to start a garden," announced Mr. Subbubs. "A few months from now I won't be kicking about your prices." "No," said the grocer; "you'll be wondering how I can afford to sell vegetables so cheap."

GAS STOVE

A Georgia woman who moved to Philadelphia found she could not be contented without the colored mammy who had been her servant for many years. She sent for old mammy, and the servant arrived in due season. It so happened that the Georgia woman had to leave town the very day mammy arrived. Before departing she had just time to explain to mammy the modern conveniences with which her apartment was furnished. The gas stove was the contrivance which interested the colored woman most. After the mistress of the household had lighted the oven, the broiler, and the other burners and felt certain the old servant understood its operations, the mistress hurried for her train.

She was absent for two weeks and one of her first questions to mammy was how she had worried along.

"De fines' ever," was the reply. "And dat air gas stove—O my! Why do you know, Miss Flo'ence, dat fire aint gone out yit."

GENEROSITY

"This is a foine country, Bridget!" exclaimed Norah, who had but recently arrived in the United States. "Sure, it's

generous everybody is. I asked at the post-office about sindin'
money to me mither, and the young man tells me I can get
a money order for $10 for 10 cents. Think of that now!"

At one of these reunions of the Blue and the Gray so
happily common of late, a northern veteran, who had lost both
arms and both legs in the service, caused himself to be posted
in a conspicuous place to receive alms. The response to his
appeal was generous and his cup rapidly filled.

Nobody gave him more than a dime, however, except a
grizzled warrior of the lost cause, who plumped in a dollar.
And not content, he presently came that way again and plumped
in another dollar.

The cripple's gratitude did not quite extinguish his curiosity. "Why," he inquired, "do you, who fought on the other
side, give me so much more than any of those who were my
comrades in arms?"

The old rebel smiled grimly. "Because," he replied, "you're
the first Yank I ever saw trimmed up just to suit me."

At dinner one day, it was noticed that a small daughter
of the minister was putting aside all the choice pieces of chicken
and her father asked her why she did that. She explained that
she was saving them for her dog. Her father told her there
were plenty of bones the dog could have so she consented to
eat the dainty bits. Later she collected the bones and took
them to the dog saying, "I meant to give a free will offering
but it is only a collection."

A little newsboy with a cigarette in his mouth entered a
notion store and asked for a match.

"We only *sell* matches," said the storekeeper.

"How much are they?" asked the future citizen.

"Penny a box," was the answer.

"Gimme a box," said the boy.

He took one match, lit the cigarette, and handed the box
back over the counter, saying, "Here, take it and put it on
de shelf, and when anodder sport comes and asks for a match,
give him one on me."

Little Ralph belonged to a family of five. One morning he came into the house carrying five stones which he brought to his mother, saying:

"Look, mother, here are tombstones for each one of us."

The mother, counting them, said:

"Here is one for father, dear! Here is one for mother! Here is brother's! Here is the baby's; but there is none for Delia, the maid."

Ralph was lost in thought for a moment, then cheerfully cried:

"Oh, well, never mind, mother; Delia can have mine, and I'll live!"

She was making the usual female search for her purse when the conductor came to collect the fares.

Her companion meditated silently for a moment, then, addressing the other, said:

"Let us divide this Mabel; you fumble and I'll pay."

GENTLEMEN

"Sadie, what is a gentleman?"

"Please, ma'am," she answered, "a gentleman's a man you don't know very well."

Two characters in Jeffery Farnol's "Amateur Gentleman" give these definitions of a gentleman:

"A gentleman is a fellow who goes to a university, but doesn't have to learn anything; who goes out into the world, but doesn't have to work at anything; and who has never been black-balled at any of the clubs."

"A gentleman is (I take it) one born with the God-like capacity to think and feel for others, irrespective of their rank or condition. ... One who possesses an ideal so lofty, a mind so delicate, that it lifts him above all things ignoble and base, yet strengthens his hands to raise those who are fallen— no matter how low."

GERMANS

The poet Heine and Baron James Rothschild were close friends. At the dinner table of the latter the financier asked the poet why he was so silent, when usually so gay and full of witty remarks.

"Quite right," responded Heine, "but to-night I have exchanged views with my German friends and my head is fearfully empty."

GHOSTS

"I confess that the subject of psychical research makes no great appeal to me," Sir William Henry Perkin, the inventor of coal-tar dyes, told some friends in New York recently. "Personally, in the course of a fairly long career, I have heard at first hand but one ghost story. Its hero was a man whom I may as well call Snooks.

"Snooks, visiting at a country house, was put in the haunted chamber for the night. He said that he did not feel the slightest uneasiness, but nevertheless, just as a matter of precaution, he took to bed with him a revolver of the latest American pattern.

"He slept peacefully enough until the clock struck two, when he awoke with an unpleasant feeling of oppression. He raised his head and peered about him. The room was wanly illumined by the full moon, and in that weird, bluish light he thought he discerned a small, white hand clasping the rail at the foot of the bed.

" 'Who's there?' he asked tremulously.

"There was no reply. The small white hand did not move.

" 'Who's there?' he repeated. 'Answer me or I'll shoot.'

"Again there was no reply.

"Snooks cautiously raised himself, took careful aim and fired.

"From that night on he's limped. Shot off two of his own toes."

GIFTS

When Lawrence Barrett's daughter was married Stuart Robson sent a check for $5000 to the bridegroom. The come-

dian's daughter, Felicia Robson, who attended the wedding con-
veyed the gift.

"Felicia," said her father upon her return, "did you give
him the check?"

"Yes, Father," answered the daughter.

"What did he say?" asked Robson.

"He didn't say anything," replied Miss Felicia, "but he shed
tears."

"How long did he cry?"

"Why Father, I didn't time him. I should say, however,
that he wept fully a minute."

"Fully a minute," mused Robson. "Why, Daughter, I cried
an hour after I signed it."

A church house in a certain rural district was sadly in need
of repairs. The official board had called a meeting of the
parishioners to see what could be done toward raising the
necessary funds. One of the wealthiest and stingiest of the
adherents of that church arose and said that he would give
five dollars, and sat down.

Just then a bit of plastering fell from the ceiling and hit
him squarely upon the head. Whereupon he jumped up, looked
confused and said: "I—er—I meant I'll give fifty dollars!" then
again resumed his seat.

After a brief silence a voice was heard to say: "O Lord,
hit 'im again!"

He gives twice who gives quickly because the collectors
come around later on and hit him for another subscription.—
Puck.

"Presents," I often say, "endear Absents."—*Charles Lamb.*

In giving, man receives more than he gives, and the
more in proportion to the worth of the thing given.—*George
MacDonald.*

See also Christmas gifts.

GLUTTONY

A clergyman was quite ill as a result of eating many pieces of mince pie.

A brother minister visited him and asked him if he was afraid to die.

"No," the sick man replied, "But I should be ashamed to die from eating too much."

> There was a young person named Ned
> Who dined before going to bed,
>   On lobster and ham
>   And salad and jam,
> And when he awoke he was dead.

GOLF

Two Scotchmen met and exchanged the small talk appropriate to the hour. As they were parting to go supperward Sandy said to Jock:

"Jock, mon, I'll go ye a roond on the links in the morrn.'"

"The morrn'?" Jock repeated.

"Aye, mon, the morrn'," said Sandy. "I'll go ye a roond oh the links in the morrn.'"

"Aye, weel," said Jock, "I'll go ye. But I had intended to get marriet in the morrn'."

GOLFER (unsteadied by Christmas luncheon) to Opponent—"Sir, I wish you clearly to understand that I resent your unwarrant—your interference with my game, sir! Tilt the green once more, sir, and I chuck the match."

Doctor William S. Rainsford is an inveterate golf player. When he was rector of St. George's Church, in New York City, he was badly beaten on the links by one of his vestrymen. To console the clergyman the vestryman ventured to say: "Never mind, Doctor, you'll get satisfaction some day when I pass away. They you'll read the burial service over me."

"I don't see any satisfaction in that," answered the clergyman, "for you'll still be in the hole.'

SUNDAY SCHOOL TEACHER—"Willie, do you know what becomes of boys who use bad language when they're playing marbles?"

WILLIE—"Yes, miss. They grow up and play golf."

The game of golf, as every humorist knows, is conducive to profanity. It is also a terrible strain on veracity, every man being his own umpire.

Four men were playing golf on a course where the hazard on the ninth hole was a deep ravine.

They drove off. Three went into the ravine and one managed to get his ball over. The three who had dropped into the ravine walked up to have a look. Two of them decided not to try to play their balls out and gave up the hole. The third said he would go down and play out his ball. He disappeared into the deep crevasse. Presently his ball came bobbing out and after a time he climed up.

How many strokes?" asked one of his opponents.

"Three."

"But I heard six."

"Three of them were echoes!"

When Mark Twain came to Washington to try to get a decent copyright law passed, a representative took him out to Chevy Chase.

Mark Twain refused to play golf himself, but he consented to walk over the course and watch the representative's strokes. The representative was rather a duffer. Teeing off, he sent clouds of earth flying in all directions. Then, to hide his confusion he said to his guest: "What do you think of our links here, Mr. Clemens?"

"Best I ever tasted," said Mark Twain, as he wiped the dirt from his lips with his handkerchief.

GOOD FELLOWSHIP

A glass is good, a lass is good,
    And a pipe to smoke in cold weather,
The world is good and the people are good,
    And we're all good fellows together.

May good humor preside when good fellows meet,
And reason prescribe when 'tis time to retreat.

Here's to us that are here, to you that are there, and the
rest of us everywhere.

Here's to all the world,—
For fear some darn fool may take offence.

GOSSIP

A gossip is a person who syndicates his conversation.—*Dick
Dickinson.*

Gossips are the spies of life.

"However did you reconcile Adele and Mary?"
"I gave them a choice bit of gossip and asked them not to
repeat it to each other."

The seven-year-old daughter of a prominent suburban resident is, the neighbors say, a precocious youngster; at all events,
she knows the ways of the world.

Her mother had occasion to punish her one day last week
for a particularly mischievous prank, and after she had talked
it over very solemnly sent the little girl up to her room.

An hour later the mother went upstairs. The child was
sitting complacently on the window seat, looking out at the
other children.

"Well, little girl," the mother began, "did you tell God all
about how naughty you'd been?"

The youngster shook her head, emphatically. "Guess I
didn't," she gurgled; "why, it'd be all over heaven in no time."

Get a gossip wound up and she will run somebody down.
—*Life.*

"Papa, mamma says that one-half the world doesn't know
how the other half lives."
"Well, she shouldn't blame herself, dear, it isn't her fault."

It is only national history that "repeats itself." Your private history is repeated by the neighbors.

"You're a terrible scandal-monger, Linkum," said Jorrocks. "Why in thunder don't you make it a rule to tell only half what you hear?"

"That's what I do," said Linkum. "Only I tell the spicy half."

"What," asked the Sunday-school teacher, "is meant by bearing false witness against one's neighbor?"

"It's telling falsehoods about them," said the one small maid.

"Partly right and partly wrong," said the teacher.

"I know," said another little girl, holding her hand high in the air. "It's when nobody did anything and somebody went and told about it."—*H. R. Bennett.*

MAUD—"That story you told about Alice isn't worth repeating."

KATE—"It's young yet; give it time."

SON—"Why do people say 'Dame Gossip'?"

FATHER—"Because they are too polite to leave off the 'e.'"

> I cannot tell how the truth may be;
> I say the tale as 'twas said to me.

Never tell evil of a man, if you do not know it for a certainty, and if you do know it for a certainty, then ask yourself, "Why should I tell it?"—*Lavater.*

GOVERNMENT OWNERSHIP

"Don't you think the coal-mines ought to be controlled by the government?"

"I might if I didn't know who controlled the government."
—Life.

GOVERNORS

The governor of a western state was dining with the family of a Representative in Congress from that state, and opposite him at table sat the little girl of the family, aged ten. She gazed at the Governor solemnly throughout the repast.

Finally the youngster asked, "Are you really and truly a governor?"

"Yes," replied the great man laughingly; "I really and truly am."

"I've always wanted to see a governor," continued the child, "for I've heard Daddy speak of 'em."

"Well," rejoined the Governor, "now that you have seen one, are you satisfied?"

"No, sir," answered the youngster, without the slightest impertinence, but with an air of great conviction, "no, sir; I'm disappointed."

GRAFT

"What is meant by graft?" said the inquiring foreigner.

"Graft," said the resident of a great city, "is a system which ultimately results in compelling a large portion of the population to apologize constantly for not having money, and the remainder to explain how they got it."

LADY—"I guess you're gettin' a good thing out o' tending the rich Smith boy, ain't ye, doctor?"

DOCTOR—"Well, yes; I get a pretty good fee. Why?"

LADY—"Well, I hope you won't forget that my Willie threw the brick that hit 'im!"

Every man has his price, but some hold bargain sales.
—*Satire.*

The Democrats had a clear working majority in ——, Illionis, for a number of years. But when the Fifteenth Amendment went into effect it enfranchised so many of the "culled bredren" as to make it apparent to the party leaders that unless a good many black votes could be bought up, the Republicans would carry the city election. Accordingly advances were made to the Rev. Brother —— , whose influence it was thought desirable to secure, inasmuch as he was certain to control the votes of his entire church.

He was found "open to conviction," and arrangements progressed satisfactorily until it was asked how much money would be necessary to secure his vote and influence.

With an air of offended dignity, Brother ——replied:

"Now, gemmen, as a regular awdained minister ob de Baptist Church dis ting has gone jes as far as my conscience will 'low; but, gemmen, my son will call round to see you in de mornin'."

A well-known New York contractor went into the tailor's, donned his new suit, and left his old one for repairs. Then he sought a café and refreshed the inner man; but as he reached in his pocket for the money to settle his check, he realized that he had neglected to transfer both purse and watch when he left his suit. As he hesitated, somewhat embarrassed, he saw a bill on the floor at his feet. Seizing it thankfully, he stepped to the cashier's desk and presented both check and money.

"That was a two dollar bill," he explained when he counted his change.

"I know it," said the cashier, with a toss of her blond head. "I'm dividing with you. I saw it first."

GRATITUDE

After O'Connell had obtained the acquittal of a horse-stealer, the thief, in the ecstacy of his gratitude, cried out, "Och, counsellor, I've no way here to thank your honor; but I wish't I saw you knocked down in me own parish—wouldn't I bring a faction to the rescue?"

Some people are never satisfied. For example, the prisoner who complained of the literature that the prison angel gave him to read.

"Nutt'n but continued stories," he grumbled. "An' I'm to be hung next Tuesday."

It was a very hot day and a picnic had been arranged by the United Society of Lady Vegetarians.

They were comfortably seated, and waiting for the kettle to boil, when, horror of horrors! a savage bull appeared on the scene.

Immediately a wild rush was made for safety, while the raging creature pounded after one lady who, unfortunately, had a red parasol. By great good fortune she nipped over the stile before it could reach her. Then, regaining her breath, she turned around.

"Oh, you ungrateful creature!" she exclaimed. "Here have I been a vegetarian all my life. There's gratitude for you!"

Miss Passay—"You have saved my life, young man. How can I repay you? How can I show my gratitude? Are you married?"

Young Man—"Yes; come and be a cook for us."

GREAT BRITAIN

One of the stories told by Mr. Spencer Leigh Hughes in his speech in the House of Commons one night tickled everybody. It is the story of the small boy who was watching the Speaker's procession as it wended its way through the lobby. First came the Speaker, and then the Chaplain, and next the other officers.

"Who, father, is that gentleman?" said the small boy, pointing to the chaplain.

"That, my son," said the father, "is the chaplain of the House."

"Does he pray for the members?" asked the small boy.

The father thought a minute and then said: "No, my son; when he goes into the House he looks around and sees the members sitting there and then he prays for the country."

—*Cardiff Mail.*

There is a lad in Boston, the son of a well-know writer of history, who has evidently profited by such observations as he may have overheard his father utter touching certain phases of British empire-building. At any rate the boy showed a shrewd notion of the opinion not infrequently expressed in regard to the righteousness of "British occupation." It was he who handed in the following essay on the making of a British colony:

"Africa is a British colony. I will tell you how England does it. First she get a missionary; when the missionary has found a specially beautiful and fertile tract of country, he gets all his people round him and says: 'Let us pray,' and when all the eyes are shut, up goes the British flag."

GRIEF

Jim, who worked in a garage, had just declined Mr. Smith's invitation to ride in his new car.

"What's the matter, Jim?" asked Mr. Smith. "Are you sick?"

"No, sah," he replied. "Tain't that—I done los' $5, sah, an' I jes' nacherly got tuh sit an' grieve."

GUARANTEES

Traveler (on an English train)—"Shall I have time to get a drink?"

Guard—"Yes, sir."

Traveler—"Can you give me a guarantee that the train won't start?"

Guard—"Yes, I'll take one with you!"

GUESTS

"Look here, Dinah," said Binks, as he opened a questionable egg at breakfast, "is this the freshest egg you can find?"

"Naw, suh," replied Dinah. "We done got a haff dozen laid diss mornin', suh, but de bishop's comin' down hyar in August, suh, and we's savin' all de fresh aigs for him, suh."

> "Here's a health to thee and thine
> From the hearts of me and mine;
> And when thee and thine
> Come to see me and mine,

May me and mine make thee and thine
As welcome as thee and thine
Have ever made me and mine."

HABIT

Among the new class which came to the second-grade teacher, a young timid girl, was one Tommy, who for naughty deeds had been many times spanked by his first-grade teacher. "Send him to me any time when you want him spanked," suggested the latter; "I can manage him."

One morning, about a week after this conversation, Tommy appeared at the first-grade teacher's door. She dropped her work, seized him by the arm, dragged him to the dressing-room, turned him over her knee and did her duty.

When she had finished she said: "Well, Tommy, what have you to say?"

"Please, Miss, my teacher wants the scissors."

In reward of faithful political service an ambitious saloon keeper was appointed police magistrate.

"What's the charge ag'in this man?" he inquired when the first case was called.

"Drunk, yer honor," said the policeman.

The newly made magistrate frowned upon the trembling defendant.

"Guilty, or not guilty?" he demanded.

"Sure, sir," faltered the accused, "I never drink a drop."

"Have a cigar, then," urged his honor persuasively, as he absently polished the top of the judicial desk with his pocket handkerchief.

"We had a fine sunrise this morning," said one New Yorker to another. "Did you see it?"

"Sunrise?" said the second man. "Why, I'm always in bed before sunrise."

A traveling man who was a cigarette smoker reached town on an early train. He wanted a smoke, but none of the stores were open. Near the station he saw a newsboy smoking, and approached him with:

"Say, son, got another cigarette?"

"No, sir," said the boy, "but I've got the makings."

"All right," the traveling man said. "But I can't roll 'em very well. Will you fix one for me?"

The boy did.

"Don't believe I've got a match," said the man, after a search through his pockets.

The boy handed him a match. "Say, Captain," he said "you ain't got anything but the habit, have you?"

Habit with him was all the test of truth;
"It must be right: I've done it from my youth."

—*Crabbe.*

HADES

See Future life.

HAPPINESS

Lord Tankerville, in New York, said of the international school question:

"The subject of the American versus the English school has been too much discussed. The good got from a school depends, after all, on the schoolboy chiefly, and I'm afraid the average schoolboy is well reflected in that classic schoolboy letter home which said:

"'Dear parents—We are having a good time now at school. George Jones broke his leg coasting and is in bed. We went skating and the ice broke and all got wet. Willie Brown was drowned. Most of the boys here are down with influenza. The gardener fell into our cave and broke his rib, but he can work a little. The aviator man at the race course kicked us because we threw sand in his motor, and we are all black and blue. I broke my front tooth playing football. We are very happy."

Mankind are always happier for having been happy; so that if you make them happy now, you make them happy twenty years hence by the memory of it.—*Sydney Smith.*

HARNESSING

The story is told of two Trenton men who hired a horse and trap for a little outing not long ago. Upon reaching their destination, the horse was unharnessed and permitted peacefully to graze while the men fished for an hour or two.

When they were ready to go home, a difficulty at once presented itself, inasmuch as neither of the Trentonians knew how to reharness the horse. Every effort in this direction met with dire failure, and the worst problem was properly to adjust the bit. The horse himself seemed to resent the idea of going into harness again.

Finally one of the friends, in great disgust, sat down in the road. "There's only one thing we can do, Bill," said he.

"What's that?" asked Bill.

"Wait for the foolish beast to yawn!"

HARVARD UNIVERSITY

"Well, I'll tell you this," said the college man, "Wellesley is a match factory."

"That's quite true," assented the girl. "At Wellesley we make the heads, but we get the sticks from Harvard."—*C. Stratton.*

HASH

"George," said the Titian-haired school marm, "is there any connecting link between the animal kingdom and the vegetable kingdom?"

"Yeth, ma'am," answered George promptly. "Hash."

HASTE

The ferry-dock was crowded with weary home-goers when through the crowd rushed a man—hot, excited, laden to the chin with bundles of every shape and size. He sprinted down the pier, his eyes fixed on a ferryboat only two or three feet out from the pier. He paused but an instant on the string-piece, and then, cheered on by the amused crowd, he made a flying leap across the intervening stretch of water and landed safely on the deck. A fat man happened to be standing on the exact spot on which he struck, and they both went down with a resounding crash. When the arriving man had somewhat recovered his breath he apologized to the fat man. "I hope I didn't hurt you," he said. "I am sorry. But, anyway I caught the boat!"

"But you idiot," said the fat man, "the boat was coming in!"

HEALTH RESORTS

"Where've you been, Murray?"

"To a health resort. Finest place I ever struck. It was simply great."

"Then why did you come away?"

"Oh, I got sick and had to come home."

"Are you going back?"

"You bet. Just as soon as I get well enough."

HEARING

The Ladies' Aid ladies were talking about a conversation they had overheard before the meeting, between a man and his wife.

"They must have been to the Zoo," said Mrs. A., "because I heard her mention 'a trained deer.'"

"Goodness me!" laughed Mrs. B. "What queer hearing you must have! They were talking about going away, and she said, 'Find out about the train, dear.'"

"Well did anybody ever?" exclaimed Mrs. C. "I am sure they were talking about musicians, for she said 'a trained ear,' as distinctly as could be."

The discussion began to warm up, and in the midst of it the lady herself appeared. They carried their case to her promptly, and asked for a settlement.

"Well, well, you do beat all!" she exclaimed, after hearing each one. "I'd been out to the country overnight, and was asking my husband if it rained here last night."

After which the three disputants retired, abashed and in silence.—*W. J. Lampton.*

HEAVEN

"Tom," said an Indiana youngster who was digging in the yard, "don't you make that hole any deeper, or you'll come to gas."

"Well, what if I do? It won't hurt."

"Yes, 't will too. If it spouts out, we'll be blown clear up to heaven."

"Shucks, that would be fun! You an' me would be the only live ones up there."—*I. C. Curtis.*

See also Future life.

HEIRLOOMS

He (wondering if his rival has been accepted)—"Are both your rings heirlooms?"

She (concealing the hand)—"Oh, dear, yes. One has been in the family since the time of Alfred, but the other is newer" —(blushing)—"it only dates from the conquest."

"My grandfather was a captain of industry."

"Well?"

"He left no sword, but we still treasure the stubs of his check-books."

HELL

See Future life.

HEREDITY

"Papa, what does hereditary mean?"

"Something which descends from father to son."

"Is a spanking hereditary?"

William had just returned from college, resplendent in peg-top trousers, silk hosiery, a fancy waistcoat, and a necktie that spoke for itself. He entered the library where his father was reading. The old gentleman looked up and surveyed his son. The longer he looked, the more disgusted he became.

"Son," he finally blurted out, "you look like a d—— fool!"

Later, the old Major who lived next door came in and greeted the boy heartily. "William," he said with undisguised admiration, "you look exactly like your father did twenty-five years ago when he came back from school!"

"Yes," replied William, with a smile, "so Father was just telling me."

"There seems to be a strange affinity between a darky and a chicken. I wonder why?" said Jones.

"Naturally enough," replied Brown. "One is descended from Ham and the other from eggs."

"So you have adopted a baby to raise?" we ask of our friend. "Well, it may turn out all right, but don't you think you are taking chances?"

"Not a chance," he answers. "No matter how many bad habits the child may develop, my wife can't say he inherits any of them from my side of the house."

See also Ancestry.

HEROES

The Passer-by—"You took a great risk in rescuing that boy; you deserve a Carnegie medal. What prompted you to do it?"

The Hero—"He had my skates on!"—*Puck.*

Mr. Henpeck—"Are you the man who gave my wife a lot of impudence?"

Mr. Scraper—"I reckon I am."

Mr. Henpeck—"Shake! You're a hero."

Each man is a hero and an oracle to somebody.—*Emerson.*

HIGH COST OF LIVING

See Cost of living.

HINTING

Little James, while at a neighbor's, was given a piece of bread and butter, and politely said, "Thank you."

"That's right, James," said the lady. "I like to hear little boys say 'thank you.'"

"Well," rejoined James, "If you want to hear me say it again, you might put some jam on it."

HOME

Home is a place where you can take off your new shoes and put on your old manners.

> Who hath not met with home-made bread,
> A heavy compound of putty and lead—
> And home-made wines that rack the head,
> And home-made liquors and waters?
> Home-made pop that will not foam,
> And home-made dishes that drive one from home—
>
> * * * * * *
>
> Home-made by the homely daughters.
>
> —*Hood.*

HOMELINESS

See Beauty, Personal.

HOMESTEADS

"Malachi," said a prospective homesteader to a lawyer, "you know all about this law. Tell me what I am to do."

"Well," said the other, "I don't remember the exact wording of the law, but I can give you the meaning of it. It's this: The government is willin' to bet you one hundred and sixty acres of land against fourteen dollars that you can't live on it five years without starving to death."—*Fenimore Martin.*

HONESTY

"He's an honest young man" said the saloon keeper, with an approving smile. "He sold his vote to pay his whiskey bill."

VISITOR—"And you always did your daring robberies single-handed? Why didn't you have a pal?"

PRISONER—"Well, sir, I wuz afraid he might turn out to be dishonest."

Ex-District Attorney Jerome, at a dinner in New York, told a story about honesty. "There was a man," he said, "who applied for a position in a dry-goods house. His appearance wasn't prepossessing, and references were demanded. After some hesitation, he gave the name of a driver in the firm's employ. This driver, he thought, would vouch for him. A clerk sought out the driver, and asked him if the applicant was honest. "Honest?" the driver said. "Why, his honesty's been proved again and again. To my certain knowledge he's been arrested nine times for stealing and every time he was acquitted."

"How is it, Mr. Brown," said a miller to a farmer, "that when I came to measure those ten barrels of apples I bought from you, I found them nearly two barrels short?"

"Singular, very singular; for I sent them to you in ten of your own flour-barrels."

"Ahem! Did, eh?" said the miller. "Well, perhaps I made a mistake. Let's imbibe."

The stranger laid down four aces and scooped in the pot.

"This game ain't on the level," protested Sagebush Sam, at the same time producing a gun to lend force to his accusation. "That ain't the hand I dealt ye!"

A dumpy little woman with solemn eyes, holding by the hand two dumpy little boys, came to the box-office of a theater. Handing in a quarter, she asked meekly for the best seat she could get for that money.

"Those boys must have tickets if you take them in," said the clerk.

"Oh, no, mister," she said. "I never pay for them. I never can spare more than a quarter, and I just love a show. We won't cheat you any, mister, for they both go sound asleep just as soon as they get into a seat, and don't see a single bit of it."

The argument convinced the ticket man, and he allowed the two children to pass in.

Toward the end of the second act an usher came out of the auditorium and handed a twenty-five-cent piece to the ticket-seller.

"What's this?" demanded the latter.

"I don't know," said the usher. "A little chunk of a woman beckoned me clear across the house, and said one of her kids had waked up and was looking at the show, and that I should bring you that quarter."

HONOR

In the smoking compartment of a Pullman, there were six men smoking and reading. All of a sudden a door banged and the conductor's voice cried:

"All tickets, please!"

Then one of the men in the compartment leaped to his feet, scanned the faces of the others and said, slowly and impressively:

"Gentlemen, I trust to your honor."

And he dived under the seat and remained there in a small, silent knot till the conductor was safely gone.

> Titles of honour add not to his worth,
> Who is himself an honour to his titles.
> —*John Ford.*

HOPE

FRED—"My dear Dora, let this thought console you for your lover's death. Remember that other and better men than he have gone the same way."

BEREAVED ONE—"They haven't all gone, have they?"—*Puck.*

HORSES

A city man, visiting a small country town, boarded a stage with two dilapidated horses, and found that he had no other currency than a five-dollar bill. This he proffered to the driver. The latter took it, looked it over for a moment or so, and then asked:

"Which horse do you want?"

A traveler in Indiana noticed that a farmer was having trouble with his horse. It would start, go slowly for a short distance, and then stop again. Thereupon the farmer would have great difficulty in getting it started. Finally the traveler approached and asked, solicitously:

"Is your horse sick?"

"Not as I knows of."

"Is he balky?"

"No. But he is so danged 'fraid I'll say whoa and he won't hear me, that he stops every once in a while to listen."

A German farmer was in search of a horse.

"I've got just the horse for you," said the liveryman. "He's five years old, sound as a dollar and goes ten miles without stopping."

The German threw his hands skyward.

"Not for me," he said, "not for me. I live eight miles from town, und mit dot horse I haf to valk back two miles."

There's a grocer who is notorious for his wretched horse flesh.

The grocer's boy is rather a reckless driver. He drove one of his master's worst nags a little too hard one day, and the animal fell ill and died.

"You've killed my horse, curse you!" the grocer said to the boy the next morning.

"I'm sorry, boss," the lad faltered.

"Sorry be durned!" shouted the grocer. "Who's going to pay me for my horse?"

"I'll make it all right, boss," said the boy soothingly. "You can take it out of my next Saturday's wages."

Before Abraham Lincoln became President he was called out of town on important law business. As he had a long distance to travel he hired a horse from a livery stable. When a few days later he returned he took the horse back to the stable and asked the man who had given it to him: "Keep this horse for funerals?"

"No, indeed," answered the man indignantly.

"Glad to hear it," said Lincoln; "because if you did the corpse wouldn't get there in time for the resurrection."

HOSPITALITY

Night was approaching and it was raining hard. The traveler dismounted from his horse and rapped at the door of the one farmhouse he had struck in a five-mile stretch of traveling. No one came to the door.

As he stood on the doorstep the water from the eaves trickled down his collar. He rapped again. Still no answer. He could feel the stream of water coursing down his back. Another spell of pounding, and finally the red head of a lad of twelve was stuck out of the second story window.

"Watcher want?" it asked.

"I want to know if I can stay here over night," the traveler answered testily.

The red-headed lad watched the man for a minute or two before answering.

"Ye kin fer all of me," he finally answered, and then closed the window.

The old friends had had three days together.

"You have a pretty place here, John," remarked the guest on the morning of his departure. "But it looks a bit bare yet."

"Oh, that's because the trees are so young," answered the host comfortably. "I hope they'll have grown to a good size before you come again."

A youngster of three was enjoying a story his mother was reading aloud to him when a caller came. In a few minutes his mother was called to the telephone. The boy turned to the caller and said "Now you beat it home."

Ollie James, the famous Kentucky Congressman and raconteur, hails from a little town in the western part of the state, but his patriotism is state-wide, and when Louisville made a bid for his Democratic national convention she had no more enthusiastic supporter than James. A Denver supporter was protesting.

"Why, you know, Colonel," said he, "Louisville couldn't take care of the crowds. Even by putting cots in the halls, parlors, and the dining-rooms of the hotels there wouldn't be beds enough."

"Beds!" echoed the genial Congressman, "why, sir, Louisville would make her visitors have such a thundering good time that no gentleman would think of going to bed!"

HOSTS

I thank you for your welcome which was cordial,
And your cordial which was welcome.

Here's to the host and the hostess,
　We're honored to be here tonight;
May they both live long and prosper,
　May their star of hope ever be bright.

HOTELS

In a Montana hotel there is a notice which reads: "Boarders taken by the day, week or month. Those who do not pay promptly will be taken by the neck."—*Country Life.*

HUNGER

A man was telling about an exciting experience in Russia. His sleigh was pursued over the frozen wastes by a pack of at least a dozen famished wolves. He arose and shot the foremost one, and the others stopped to devour it. But they soon caught up with him, and he shot another, which was in turn devoured. This was repeated until the last famished wolf was almost upon him with yearning jaws, when——

"Say, partner," broke in one of the listeners, "according

to your reckoning that last famished wolf must have had the other 'leven inside of him."

"Well, come to think it over," said the story teller, "maybe he wasn't so darned famished after all."

HUNTING

A gentleman from London was invited to go for "a day's snipe-shooting" in the country. The invitation was accepted, and host and guest shouldered guns and sallied forth in quest of game.

After a time a solitary snipe rose, and promptly fell to the visitor's first barrel.

The host's face fell also.

"We may as well return," he remarked, gloomily, "for that was the only snipe in the neighborhood."

The bird had afforded excellent sport to all his friends for six weeks.

HURRY

See Haste.

HUSBANDS

"Is she making him a good wife?"

"Well, not exactly; but she's making him a good husband."

A husband and wife ran a freak show in a certain provincial town, but unfortunately they quarreled, and the exhibits were equally divided between them. The wife decided to continue business as an exhibitor at the old address, but the husband went on a tour.

After some years' wandering the prodigal returned, and a reconciliation took place, as the result of which they became business partners once more. A few mornings afterward the people of the neighborhood were sent into fits of laughter on reading the following notice in the papers:

"By the return of my husband my stock of freaks has been permanently increased."

An eminent German scientist who recently visited this country with a number of his colleagues was dining at an American house and telling how much he had enjoyed various phases of his visit.

"How did you like our railroad trains?" his host asked him.

"Ach, dhey are woonderful," the German gentleman replied; "so swift, so safe chenerally—und such luxury in all dhe furnishings und opp'indmends. All is excellent excebt one thing—our wives do not like dhe uper berths."

A couple of old grouches at the Metropolitan Club in Washington were one night speaking of an old friend who, upon his marriage, took up his residence in another city. One of the grouches had recently visited the old friend, and, naturally, the other grouch wanted news of the Benedict.

"It it true that he is henpecked?" asked the second grouch.

"I wouldn't say just that," grimly responded the first grouch, "but I'll tell you of a little incident in their household that came within my observation. The very first morning I spent with them, our old friend answered the letter carrier's whistle. As he returned to us, in the breakfast room, he carried a letter in his hand. Turning to his wife, he said:

"'A letter for me, dear. May I open it?'"

—*Edwin Tarrisse.*

"Your husband says he leads a dog's life," said one woman.

"Yes, it's very similar," answered the other. "He comes in with muddy feet, makes himself comfortable by the fire, and waits to be fed."

NEIGHBOR—"I s'pose your Bill's 'ittin' the 'arp with the hangels now?"

LONG-SUFFERING WIDOW—"Not 'im. 'Ittin' the hangels wiv the 'arp's nearer 'is mark!"

"You say you are your wife's third husband?" said one man to another during a talk.

"No, I am her fourth husband," was the reply.

"Heavens, man!" said the first man; "you are not a husband—you're a habit."

MR. HENPECK—"Is my wife going out, Jane?"

JANE—"Yessir."

MR. HENPECK—"Do you know if I am going with her?"

A happily married woman, who had enjoyed thirty-three years of wedlock, and who was the grandmother of four beautiful little children, had an amusing old colored woman for a cook.

One day when a box of especially beautiful flowers was left for the mistress, the cook happened to be present, and she said: "Yo' husband send you all the pretty flowers you gits, Missy?"

"Certainly, my husband, Mammy," proudly answered the lady.

"Glory!" exclaimed the cook, "he suttenly am holdin' out well."

An absent-minded man was interrupted as he was finishing a letter to his wife, in the office. As a result, the signature read:

Your loving husband,

HOPKINS BROS.

—*Winifred C. Bristol.*

Mrs. McKinley used to tell of a colored widow whose children she had helped educate. The widow, rather late in life, married again.

"How are you getting on?" Mrs. McKinley asked her a few months after her marriage.

"Fine, thank yo', ma'am," the bride answered.

"And is your husband a good provider?"

"'Deed he am a good providah, ma'am," was the enthusiastic reply. "Why, jes' dis las' week he got me five new places to wash at."

"I suffer so from insomnia I don't know what to do."

"Oh, my dear, if you could only talk to my husband awhile."

"Did Hardlucke bear his misfortune like a man?"

"Exactly like one. He blamed it all on his wife."—*Judge.*

A popular society woman announced a "White Elephant Party." Every guest was to bring something that she could not find any use for, and yet too good to throw away. The party would have been a great success but for the unlooked-for development which broke it up. Eleven of the nineteen women brought their husbands.

> A very man—not one of nature's clods—
> With human failings, whether saint or sinner:
> Endowed perhaps with genius from the gods
> But apt to take his temper from his dinner.
> —*J. G. Saxe.*

A woman mounted the steps of the elevated station carrying an umbrella like a reversed saber. An attendant warned her that she might put out the eye of the man behind her.

"Well, he's my husband!" she snapped.

OLD MONEY (dying)—"I'm afraid I've been a brute to you sometimes, dear."

YOUNG WIFE—"Oh, never mind that darling; I'll always remember how very kind you were when you left me."

An inveterate poker player, whose wife always complained of his late hours, stayed out even later than usual one night and tells in the following way of his attempt to get in unnoticed:

"I slipped off my shoes at the front steps, pulled off my clothes in the hall, slipped into the bedroom, and began to slip into bed with the ease of experience.

"My wife has a blamed fine dog that on cold night insists on jumping in the bed with us. So when I began to slide under the covers she stirred in her sleep and pushed me on the head.

" 'Get down, Fido, get down!' she said.

"And, gentlemen, I just did have presence of mind enough to lick her hand, and she dozed off again!"

Mr. Homebody—"I see you keep copies of all the letters you write to your wife. Do you do it to avoid repeating yourself?"
Mr. Faraway—"No. To avoid contradicting myself."

> There is gladness in his gladness, when he's glad,
> There is sadness in his sadness, when he's sad;
> But the gladness in his gladness,
> Nor the sadness in his sadness,
> Isn't a marker to his madness when he's mad.

See also Cowards; Domestic finance.

HYBRIDIZATION

We used to think that the smartest man ever born was the Connecticut Yankee who grafted white birch on red maples and grew barber poles. Now we rank that gentleman second. First place goes to an experimenter attached to the Berlin War Office, who has crossed carrier pigeons with parrots, so that Wilhelmstrasse can now get verbal messages through the enemy's lines.

—Warwick James Price.

HYPERBOLE

"Speakin' of fertile soil," said the Kansan, when the others had had their say, "I never saw a place where melons growed like they used to out in my part of the country. The first season I planted 'em I thought my fortune was sure made. However, I didn't harvest one."

He waited for queries, but his friends knew him, and he was forced to continue unurged:

"The vines growed so fast that they wore out the melons draggin' 'em 'round. However, the second year my two little boys made up their minds to get a taste of one anyhow, so they took turns, carryin' one along with the vine and——"

But his companions had already started toward the barroom door.

News comes from Southern Kansas that a boy climbed a cornstalk to see how the sky and clouds looked and now the stalk is growing faster than the boy can climb down. The boy is clear out of sight. Three men have taken the contract for cutting down the stalk with axes to save the boy a horrible death by starving, but the stalk grows so rapidly that they can't hit twice in the same place. The boy is living on green corn alone and has already thrown down over four bushels of cobs. Even if the corn holds out there is still danger that the boy will reach a height where he will be frozen to death. There is some talk of attempting his rescue with a balloon.—*Topeka Capital.*

HYPOCRISY

Hypocrisy is all right if we can pass it off as politeness.

TEACHER—"Now, Tommy, what is a hypocrite?"

TOMMY—"A boy that comes to school with a smile on his face."—*Graham Charteris.*

IDEALS

The fact that his two pet bantam hens laid very small eggs troubled little Johnny. At last he was seized with an inspiration. Johnny's father, upon going to the fowl-run one morning, was surprised at seeing an ostrich egg tied to one of the beams, with this injunction chalked above it:

"Keep your eye on this and do your best."

ILLUSIONS AND HALLUCINATIONS

A doctor came up to a patient in an insane asylum, slapped him on the back, and said: "Well, old man, you're all right. You can run along and write your folks that you'll be back home in two weeks as good as new."

The patient went off gayly to write his letter. He had it finished and sealed, but when he was licking the stamp it slipped through his fingers to the floor, lighted on the back of a cockroach that was passing, and stuck. The patient hadn't seen the

cockroach—what he did see was his escaped postage stamp zig-
zagging aimlessly across the floor to the baseboard, wavering up
over the baseboard, and following a crooked track up the wall
and across the ceiling. In depressed silence he tore up the letter
he had just written and dropped the pieces on the floor.

"Two weeks! Hell!" he said. "I won't be out of here in
three years."

IMAGINATION

One day a mother overheard her daughter arguing with a
little boy about their respective ages.

"I am older than you," he said, "'cause my birthday comes
first, in May, and yours don't come till September."

"Of course your birthday comes first," she sneeringly retorted, "but that is 'cause you came down first. I remember
looking at the angels when they were making you."

The mother instantly summoned her daughter. "It's breaking mother's heart to hear you tell such awful stories," she said.
"Don't you remember what happened to Ananias and Sapphira?"

"Oh, yes, mamma, I know; they were struck dead for lying.
I saw them carried into the corner drug store!"

IMITATION

Not long ago a company was rehearsing for an open-air performance of *As You Like It* near Boston. The garden wherein
they were to play was overlooked by a rising brick edifice.

One afternoon, during a pause in the rehearsal, a voice from
the building exclaimed with the utmost gravity:

"I prithee, malapert, pass me yon brick."

INFANTS

A wife after the divorce, said to her husband:

"I am willing to let you have the baby half the time."

"Good!" said he, rubbing his hands. "Splendid!"

"Yes," she resumed, "you may have him nights."

"Is the baby strong?"

"Well, rather! You know what a tremendous voice he has?"

"Yes."

"Well, he lifts that five or six times an hour!"

—*Comic Cuts.*

Recipe for a baby:

Clean and dress a wriggle, add a pint of nearly milk,
Smother with a pillow any sneeze;
Baste with talcum powder and mark upon its back—
"Don't forget that you were one of these."

—*Life.*

INQUISITIVENESS

See Wives.

INSANITY

See Editors; Love.

INSPIRATIONS

She was from Boston, and he was not.

He had spent a harrowing evening discussing authors of whom he knew nothing, and their books, of which he knew less.

Presently the maiden asked archly: "Of course, you've read 'Romeo and Juliet?'"

He floundered helplessly for a moment and then, having a brilliant thought, blurted out, happily:

"I've—I've read Romeo!"

INSTALMENT PLAN

Half the world doesn't know how many things the other half is paying instalments on.

INSTRUCTIONS

A lively looking porter stood on the rear platform of a sleeping-car in the Pennsylvania station when a fussy and choleric old man clambered up the steps. He stopped at the door, puffed for a moment, and then turned to the young man in uniform.

"Porter," he said. "I'm going to St. Louis, to the Fair. I want to be well taken care of. I pay for it. Do you understand?"

"Yes, sir, but——"

"Never mind any 'buts.' You listen to what I say. Keep the train boys away from me. Dust me off whenever I want you to. Give me an extra blanket, and if there is any one in the berth over me slide him into another. I want you to——"

"But, say, boss, I——"

"Young man, when I'm giving instructions I prefer to do the talking myself. You do as I say. Here is a two-dollar bill. I want to get the good of it. Not a word, sir."

The train was starting. The porter pocketed the bill with a grin and swung himself to the ground. "All right, boss!" he shouted. "You can do the talking if you want to. I'm powerful sorry you wouldn't let me tell you—but I ain't going out on that train."

INSURANCE, LIFE

A man went to an insurance office to have his life insured the other day.

'Do you cycle?" the insurance agent asked.

"No," said the man.

"Do you motor?"

"No."

"Do you, then, perhaps, fly?"

'No, no," said the applicant, laughing; "I have no dangerous——"

But the agent interrupted him curtly.

"Sorry, sir," he said, "but we no longer insure pedestrians."

INSURANCE BLANKS

See Irish bulls.

INSURGENTS

"And what," asked a visitor to the North Dakota State Fair, "do you call that kind of cucumber?"

"That," replied a Fargo politician, "is the Insurgent cucumber. It doesn't always agree with a party."

INTERVIEWS

"Haven't your opinions on this subject undergone a change?"

"No," replied Senator Soghum.

"But your views, as you expressed them some time ago?"

"Those were not my views. Those were my interviews."

INVITATIONS

"Recently," says a Richmond man, "I received an invitation to the marriage of a young colored couple formerly in my employ. I am quite sure that all persons similarly favored were left in little doubt as to the attitude of the couple. The invitation ran as follows:

"You are invited to the marriage of Mr. Henry Clay Barker and Miss Josephine Mortimer Dixon at the house of the bride's mother. All who cannot come may send."—*Howard Morse.*

One day a Chinese poor man met the head of his family in the street.

"Come and dine with us tonight," the mandarin said graciously.

"Thank you," said the poor relation. "But wouldn't tomorrow night do just as well?"

"Yes, certainly. But where are you dining tonight?" asked the mandarin curiously.

"At your house. You see, your estimable wife was good enough to give me tonight's invitation."

MARION (just from the telephone)—"He wanted to know if we would go to the theater with him, and I said we would."

MADELINE—"Who was speaking?"

MARION—"Oh, gracious! I forgot to ask."

Little Willie wanted a birthday party, to which his mother consented, provided he ask his little friend Tommy. The boys had had trouble, but, rather than not have the party, Willie promised his mother to invite Tommy.

On the evening of the party, when all the small guests had arrived except Tommy, the mother became suspicious and sought her son.

"Willie," she said, "did you invite Tommy to your party tonight?"

"Yes, Mother."

"And did he say he would not come?"

"No," explained Willie. "I invited him all right, but I dared him to come."

IRISH BULLS

Two Irishmen were among a class that was being drilled in marching tactics. One was new at the business, and, turning to his companion, asked him the meaning of the command "Halt!" "Why," said Mike, "when he says 'Halt,' you just bring the foot that's on the ground to the saide av the foot that's in the air, an' remain motionless."

"Dear teacher," wrote little Johnny's mother, "kindly excuse John's absence from school yesterday afternoon, as he fell in the mud. By doing the same you will greatly oblige his mother."

An Irishman once was mounted on a mule which was kicking its legs rather freely. The mule finally got its hoof caught in the stirrup, when the Irishman excitedly remarked: "Well, begorra, if you're goin' to git on I'll git off."

"The doctor says if 'e lasts till morning 'e'll 'ave some 'ope, but if 'e don't, the doctor says 'e give 'im up."

For rent—A room for a gentleman with all conveniences.

A servant of an English nobleman died and her relatives telegraphed him: "Jane died last night, and wishes to know if your lordship will pay her funeral expenses."

A pretty school teacher, noticing one of her little charges idle, said sharply: "John, the devil always finds something for idle hands to do. Come up here and let me give you some work."

A college professor, noted for strict discipline, entered the classroom one day and noticed a girl student sitting with her feet in the aisle and chewing gum.

"Mary," exclaimed the indignant professor, "take that gum out of your mouth and put your feet in."

MAGISTRATE—"You admit you stole the pig?"

PRISONER—"I 'ave to."

MAGISTRATE—"Very well, then. There has been a lot of pig-stealing going on lately, and I am going to make an example of you, or none of us will be safe."—*M. L. Hayward.*

"In choosing his men," said the Sabbath-school superintendent, "Gideon did not select those who laid aside their arms and threw themselves down to drink; but he took those who watched with one eye and drank with the other."—*Joe King.*

"If you want to put that song over you must sing louder."

"I'm singing as loud as I can. What more can I do?"

"Be more enthusiastic. Open your mouth and throw yourself into it."

A little old Irishman was trying to see the Hudson-Fulton procession from Grant's Tomb. He stood up on a bench, but was jerked down by a policeman. Then he tried the stone balustrade and being removed from that vantage point, climbed the railing of Li Hung Chang's gingko-tree. Pulled off that, he remarked: "Ye can't look at annything frum where ye can see it frum."

Mrs. Jenkins—"Mrs. Smith, we shall be neighbors now. I have bought a house next to you, with a water frontage."

Mrs. Smith—"So glad! I hope you will drop in some time."

In the hall of a Philharmonic society the following notice was posted:

"The seats in this hall are for the use of the ladies. Gentlemen are requested to make use of them only after the former are seated."

Sir Boyle Roche is credited with saying that "no man can be in two places at the same time, barring he is a bird."

A certain high-school professor, who at times is rather blunt in speech, remarked to his class of boys at the beginning of a lesson. "I don't know why it is—every time I get up to speak, some fool talks." Then he wondered why the boys burst out into a roar of laughter.—*Grub S. Arts.*

Once, at a criminal court, a young chap from Connemara was being tried for an agrarian murder. Needless to say, he had the gallery on his side, and the men and women began to express their admiration by stamping, not loudly, but like muffled drums. A big policeman came up to the gallery, scowled at the disturbers then, when that had no effect, called out in stage whisper:

"Wud ye howld yer tongues there! Howld yer tongues wid yer feet!"

The ways in which application forms for insurance are filled out are often more amusing than enlightening, as The British Medical Journal shows in the following excellent selection of examples:

Mother died in infancy.

Father went to bed feeling well, and the next morning woke up dead.

Grantmother died suddenly at the age of 103. Up to this time she bade fair to reach a ripe old age.

Applicant does not know anything about maternal posterity, except that they died at an advanced age.

Applicant does not know cause of mother's death, but states that she fully recovered from her last illness.

Applicant has never been fatally sick.

Applicant's brother who was an infant died when he was a mere child.

Mother's last illness was caused from chronic rheumatism, but she was cured before death.

IRISHMEN

A Peoria merchant deals in "Irish confetti." We take it that he runs a brick-yard.—*Chicago Tribune.*

Here are some words, concerning the Hibernian spoken by a New England preacher, Nathaniel Ward, in the sober year of sixteen hundred—a spark of humor struck from flint. "These Irish, anciently called 'Anthropophagi,' man-eaters, have a tradition among them that when the devil showed Our Savior all the kingdoms of the earth and their glory, he would not show Him Ireland, but reserved it for himself; it is probably true, for he hath kept it ever since for his own peculiar."

An Irishman once lined up his family of seven giant-like sons and invited his caller to take a look at them.

"Ain't they fine boys?" inquired the father.

"They are," agreed the visitor.

"The finest in the world!" exclaimed the father. "An' I nivver laid violent hands on any one of 'em except in silf-difince."—*Popular Magazine.*

See also Fighting; Irish bulls.

IRREVERENCE

There were three young women of Birmingham,
And I know a sad story concerning 'em:
    They stuck needles and pins
    In the reverend shins
Of the Bishop engaged in confirming 'em.
—*Gilbert K. Chesterton.*

JAMES, HENRY

A few years ago Henry James reviewed a new novel by Gertrude Atherton. After reading the review Mrs. Atherton wrote to Mr. James as follows:

"Dear Mr. James: I have read with much pleasure your review of my novel. Will you kindly let me know whether you liked it or not?   Sincerely,
          GERTRUDE ATHERTON."

JEWELS

The girl with the ruby lips we like,
  The lass with teeth of pearl,
The maid with the eyes like diamonds,
  The cheek-like-coral girl;
The girl with the alabaster brow,
  The lass from the Emerald Isle.
All these we like, but not the jade
  With the sardonyx smile.

JEWS

What is the difference between a banana and a Jew? You can skin the banana.

He was quite evidently from the country and he was also quite evidently a Yankee, and from behind his bowed spectacles he peered inquisitively at the little oily Jew who occupied the other half of the car seat with him.

The little Jew looked at him deprecatingly. "Nice day," he began politely.

"You're a Jew, ain't you?" queried the Yankee.

"Yes, sir, I'm a clothing salesman," handing him a card.

"But you're a Jew?"

"Yes, yes, I'm a Jew," came the answer.

"Well," continued the Yankee, "I'm a Yankee, and in the little village in Maine where I come from I'm proud to say there ain't a Jew."

"Dot's why it's a village," replied the little Jew quietly.

The men were arguing as to who was the greatest inventor. One said Stephenson, who invented the locomotive. Another declared it was the man who invented the compass. Another contended for Edison. Still another for the Wrights.

Finally one of them turned to a little man who had remained silent:

"Who do you think?"

"Vell," he said, with a hopeful smile, "the man who invented interest was no slouch."

Levinsky, despairing of his life, made an appointment with a famous specialist. He was surprised to find fifteen or twenty people in the waiting-room.

After a few minutes he leaned over to a gentleman near him and whispered, "Say, mine frient, this must be a pretty goot doctor, ain't he?"

"One of the best," the gentleman told him.

Levinsky seemed to be worrying over something.

"Vell, say," he whispered again, "he must be pretty exbensive, then, ain't he? Vat does he charge?"

The stranger was annoyed by Levinsky's questions and answered rather shortly: "Fifty dollars for the first consultation and twenty-five dollars for each visit thereafter."

"Mine Gott!" gasped Levinsky. "Fifty tollars the first time und twenty-five tollars each time afterwards!"

For several minutes he seemed undecided whether to go or to wait. "Und twenty-five tollars each time afterwards," he kept muttering. Finally, just as he was called into the office, he was seized with a brilliant inspiration. He rushed toward the doctor with outstretched hands.

"Hello, doctor," he said effusively. "Vell, here I am *again*."

The Jews are among the aristocracy of every land; if a literature is called rich in the possession of a few classic tragedies what shall we say to a national tragedy lasting for fifteen hundred years, in which the poets and the actors were also the heroes.—*George Eliot.*

See also Failures; Fires.

JOKES

A nut and a joke are alike in that they can both be cracked, and different in that the joke can be cracked again.—*William J. Burtscher.*

JOKELY—"I got a batch of aeroplane jokes ready and sent them out last week."

BOGGS—"What luck did you have with them?"

JOKELY—"Oh, they all came flying back."—*Will S. Gidley.*

> "I ne'er forget a joke I have
>   Once heard!" Augustus cried.
> "And neither do you let your friends
>   Forget it!" Jane replied.
>
> —*Childe Harold.*

A Negro bricklayer in Macon, Georgia, was lying down during the noon hour, sleeping in the hot sun. The clock struck one, the time to pick up his hod again. He rose, stretched, and grumbled: "I wish I wuz daid. 'Tain' nothin' but wuk, wuk from mawnin' tell night."

Another Negro, a story above, heard the complaint and dropped a brick on the grumbler's head.

Dazed he looked up and said:

"De Lawd can' stan' no jokes. He jes' takes ev'ything in yearnist."

The late H. C. Bunner, when editor of *Puck,* once received a letter accompanying a number of would-be jokes in which the writer asked: "What will you give me for these?"

"Ten yards start," was Bunner's generous offer, written beneath the query.

NEW CONGRESSMAN—"What can I do for you, sir?"

SALESMAN (of Statesmen's Anecdote Manufacturing Company)—"I shall be delighted if you'll place an order for a dozen of real, live, snappy, humorous anecdotes as told by yourself, sir."

Jokes were first imported to this country several hundred years ago from Egypt, Babylon and Assyria, and have since then grown and multiplied. They are in extensive use in all parts of the country and as an antidote for thought are indispensable at all dinner parties.

There were originally twenty-five jokes, but when this country was formed they added a constitution, which increased the number to twenty-six. These jokes have married and intermarried among themselves and their children travel from press to press.

Frequently in one week a joke will travel from New York to San Francisco.

The joke is no respecter of persons. Shameless and unconcerned, he tells the story of his life over and over again. Outside of the ballot-box he is the greatest repeater that we have.

Jokes are of three kinds—plain, illustrated and pointless. Frequently they are all three.

No joke is without honor, except in its own country. Jokes form one of our staples and employ an army of workers who toil night and day to turn out the often neatly finished product. The importation of jokes while considerable is not as great as it might be, as the flavor is lost in transit.

Jokes are used in the household as an antiseptic. As scene-breakers they have no equal.—*Life.*

Here's to the joke, the good old joke,
  The joke that our fathers told;
It is ready tonight and is jolly and bright
  As it was in the days of old.

When Adam was young it was on his tongue,
  And Noah got in the swim
By telling the jest as the brightest and best
  That ever happened to him.

So here's to the joke, the good old joke—
  We'll hear it again tonight.
It's health we will quaff; that will help us to laugh,
  And to treat it in manner polite.
                              —*Lew Dockstader.*

A jest's prosperity lies in the ear
Of him that hears it, never in the tongue
Of him that makes it.

—*Shakespeare.*

JOURNALISM

A Louisville journalist was excessively proud of his little boy. Turning to the old black nurse, "Aunty," said he, stroking the little pate, "this boy seems to have a journalistic head." "Oh," cried the untutored old aunty, soothingly, "never you mind 'bout dat; dat'll come right in time."

John R. McLean, owner of the Cincinnati *Enquirer* and the Washington *Post,* tells this story of the days when he was actively in charge of the Cincinnati newspaper: An *Enquirer* reporter was sent to a town in southwestern Ohio to get the story of a woman evangelist who had been greatly talked about. The reporter attended one of her meetings and occupied a front seat. When those who wished to be saved were asked to arise, he kept his seat and used his notebook. The evangelist approached, and, taking him by the hand, said, "Come to Jesus."

"Madam," said the newspaper man, "I'm here solely on business—to report your work."

"Brother," said she, "there is no business so important as God's."

"Well, may be not," said the reporter; "but you don't know John R. McLean."

A newspaper man named Fling
Could make "copy" from any old thing.
    But the copy he wrote
    Of a five dollar note
Was so good he is now in Sing Sing.

—*Columbia Jester.*

"Come in," called the magazine editor.

"Sir, I have called to see about that article of mine that you bought two years ago. My name is Pensnink—Percival

Perrhyn Pensnink. My composition was called 'The Behavior of Chipmunks in Thunderstorms,' and I should like to know how much longer I must watch and wait before I shall see it in print."

"I remember," the editor replied. "We are saving your little essay to use at the time of your death. When public attention is drawn to an author we like to have something of his on hand."

> Hear, land o' cakes, and brither Scots,
> Frae Maidenkirk to Johnny Groat's;
> If there's a hole in a' your coats,
> I rede you tent it:
> A chiel's amang you taking notes,
> And, faith, he'll prent it.
>
> —*Burns.*

See also Newspapers.

JUDGES

A judge once had a case in which the accused man understood only Irish. An interpreter was accordingly sworn. The prisoner said something to the interpreter.

"What does he say?" demanded his lordship.

"Nothing, my lord," was the reply.

"How dare you say that when we all heard him? Come on, sir, what was it?"

"My lord," said the interpreter beginning to tremble, "it had nothing to do with the case."

"If you don't answer I'll commit you, sir!" roared the judge. "Now, what did he say?"

"Well, my lord, you'll excuse me, but he said, "Who's that old woman with the red bed curtain round her, sitting up there?' "

At which the court roared.

"And what did you say?" asked the judge, looking a little uncomfortable.

"I said: 'Whist, ye spalpeen! That's the ould boy that's going to hang you.' "

A gentleman of color who was brought before a police judge, on a charge of stealing chickens, pleaded guilty. After sentencing him, the judge asked how he had managed to steal the chickens when the coop was so near the owner's house and there was a vicious dog in the yard.

"Hit wouldn't be of no use, Judge," answered the darky, "to try to 'splain dis yer thing to yo' 't all. Ef yo' was to try it, like as not yo' would get yer hide full o' shot, an' get no chicken, nuther. Ef yo' wants to engage in any rascality, Judge, yo' better stick to de bench whar yo' am familiar."—*Mrs. L. F. Clarke.*

Four things belong to a judge: to hear courteously, to answer wisely, to consider soberly, and to decide impartially.
—*Socrates.*

JUDGMENT

HUSBAND—"But you must admit that men have better judgment than women."

WIFE—"Oh, yes—you married me, and I you."—*Life.*

JURY

In the south of Ireland a judge heard his usher of the court say, "Gentlemen of the jury, take your proper places," and was convulsed with laughter at seeing seven of them walk into the dock.

There was recently haled into an Alabama court a little Irishman to whom the thing was a new experience. He was, however, unabashed, and wore an air of a man determined not to "get the worst of it."

"Prisoner at the bar," called out the clerk, "do you wish to challenge any of the jury?"

The Celt looked the men in the box over very carefully.

"Well, I tell ye," he finally replied, "Oi'm not exactly in trainin', but Oi think Oi could pull off a round or two with thot fat old boy in th' corner."

JUSTICE

There are two sides to every question—the wrong side and our side.

"What, Tommy, in the jam again, and you whipped for it only an hour ago!"

"Yes'm, but I heard you tell Auntie that you thought you whipped me too hard, so I thought I'd just even up."

> One man's word is no man's word,
> Justice is that both be heard.

He who decides a case without hearing the other side, though he decide justly cannot be considered just.—*Seneca.*

JUVENILE DELINQUENCY

A woman left her baby in its carriage at the door of a department-store. A policeman found it there, apparently abandoned, and wheeled it to the station. As he passed down the street a gamin yelled: "What's the kid done?"

KENTUCKY

Kentucky is the state where they have poor feud laws.

KINDNESS

Kindness goes a long ways lots o' times when it ought t' stay at home.—*Abe Martin.*

An old couple came in from the country, with a big basket of lunch, to see the circus. The lunch was heavy. The old wife was carrying it. As they crossed a street, the husband held out his hand and said, "Gimme that basket, Hannah."

The poor old woman surrendered the basket with a grateful look.

"That's real kind o' ye, Joshua," she quavered.

"Kind!" grunted the old man. "I wuz afeared ye'd git lost."

A fat woman entered a crowded street car and seizing a strap, stood directly in front of a man seated in the corner. As the car started she lunged against his newspaper and at the same time trod heavily on his toes.

As soon as he could extricate himself he rose and offered her his seat.

"You are very kind, sir," she said, panting for breath.

"Not at all, madam," he replied; "it's not kindness; it's simply self-defense."

KINGS AND RULERS

"I think," said the heir apparent, "that I will add music and dancing to my accomplishments."

"Aren't they rather light?"

"They may seem so to you, but they will be very handy if a revolution occurs and I have to go into vaudeville."

The late King George in his younger days visited Canada in company with the Duke of Clarence. One night at a ball in Quebec, given in honor of the two royalties, the younger Prince devoted his time exclusively to the young ladies, paying little or no attention to the elderly ones and chaperons.

His brother reprimanded him, pointing out to him his social position and his duty as well.

"That's all right," said the young Prince. "There are two of us. You go and sing God save your Grandmother, while I dance with the girls."

> And so we sing, "Long live the King;
> Long live the Queen and Jack;
> Long live the Ten-spot and the Ace,
> And also all the pack."
>
> —*Eugene Field.*

First European Society Lady—"Wouldn't you like to be presented to our sovereign?"

Second E. S. L.—"No. Simply because I have to be governed by a man is no reason why I should condescend to meet him socially."

One afternoon Kaiser Wilhelm caustically reproved old General Von Meerscheidt for some small lapses.

"If your Majesty thinks that I am too old for the service please permit me to resign," said the General.

"No; you are too young to resign," said the Kaiser.

In the evening of that same day, at a court ball, the Kaiser saw the old General talking to some young ladies, and he said:

"General, take a young wife, then your excitable temperament will vanish."

"Excuse me, your Majesty," replied the General. "It would kill me to have both a young wife and a young Emperor."

During the war of 1812, a dinner was given in Canada, at which both American and British officers were present. One of the latter offered the toast: "To President Madison, dead or alive!"

An American offered the response: "To the Prince Regent, drunk or sober!"—*Mrs. Gouverneur.*

A lady of Queen Victoria's court once asked her if she did not think that one of the satisfactions of the future life would be the meeting with the notable figures of the past, such as Abraham, Isaac and King David. After a moment's silence, with perfect dignity and decision the great Queen made answer: "I will *not* meet David!"

> Ten poor men sleep in peace on one straw heap,
>   as Saadi sings,
> But the immensest empire is too narrow for
>   two kings.
> —*William R. Alger.*

> Here lies our sovereign lord, the king,
>   Whose word no man relies on,
> Who never said a foolish thing,
>   And never did a wise one.

Said by a courtier of Charles II. To which the King replied, "That is very true, for my words are my own. My actions are my minister's."

KISSES

Here's to a kiss:
Give me a kiss, and to that kiss add a score,
Then to that twenty add a hundred more;
A thousand to that hundred, and so kiss on,
To make that thousand quite a million,
Treble that million, and when that is done
Let's kiss afresh as though we'd just begun.

"If I should kiss you I suppose you'd go and tell your mother."

"No; my lawyer."

"What is he so angry with you for?"

"I haven't the slightest idea. We met in the street, and we were talking just as friendly as could be, when all of a sudden he flared up and tried to kick me."

"And what were you talking about?"

"Oh, just ordinary small talk. I remember he said, 'I always kiss my wife three or four times every day.'"

"And what did you say?"

"I said, 'I know at least a dozen men who do the same,' and then he had a fit."

There was an old maiden from Fife,
Who had never been kissed in her life;
　　Along came a cat;
　　And she said, "I'll kiss that!"
But the cat answered, "Not on your life!"

Here's to the red of the holly berry,
　　And to its leaf so green;
And here's to the lips that are just as red,
　　And the fellow who's not so green.

There was a young sailor of Lyd,
Who loved a fair Japanese kid;
　　When it came to good-bye,
　　They were eager but shy,
So they put up a sunshade and—did.

There once was a maiden of Siam,
Who said to her lover, young Kiam,
  "If you kiss me, of course
  You will have to use force,
But God knows you're stronger than I am."

Lord! I wonder what fool it was that first invented kissing.—*Swift.*

See also Courtship; Servants.

KNOWLEDGE

A physician was driving through a village when he saw a man amusing a crowd with the antics of his trick dog. The doctor pulled up and said: "My dear man, how do you manage to train your dog that way? I can't teach mine a single trick."

The man glanced up with a simple rustic look and replied: "Well, you see, it's this way; you have to know more'n the dog or you can't learn him nothin'."

With knowledge and love the world is made.—*Anatole France.*

KULTUR

HERR HAMMERSCHLEGEL (winding up the argument)—"I think you iss a stupid fool!"

MONSIEUR—"And I sink you a polite gentleman; but possible, it is, we both mistaken."—*Life.*

LABOR AND LABORING CLASSES

A farmer in great need of extra hands at haying time finally asked Si Warren, who was accounted the town fool, if he could help him out.

"What'll ye pay?" asked Si.

"I'll pay you what you're worth," answered the farmer.

Si scratched his head a minute, then answered decisively: "I'll be *durned* if I'll work for that!"

LADIES

See Etiquet; Woman.

LANDLORDS

An English tourist was sightseeing in Ireland and the guide had pointed out the Devil's Gap, the Devil's Peak, and the Devil's Leap to him.

"Pat," he said, "the devil seems to have a great deal of property in this district!"

"He has, sir," replied the guide, "but, sure, he's like all the landlords—he lives in England!"

LANGUAGES

George Ade, with a fellow American, was traveling in the Orient, and his companion one day fell into a heated argument with an old Arab. Ade's friend complained to him afterward that although he had spent years in studying Arabic in preparation for this trip he could not understand a word that the native said.

"Never mind," replied Ade consolingly. "You see, the old duffer hasn't a tooth in his head, and he was only talking gum-Arabic."

Milton was one day asked by a friend whether he would instruct his daughters in the different languages.

"No, sir," he said; "one tongue is sufficient for any woman."

Prince Bismarck was once pressed by a certain American official to recommend his son for a diplomatic post. "He is a very remarkable fellow," said the proud father; "he speaks seven languages."

"Indeed!" said Bismarck, who did not hold a very high opinion of linguistic acquirements. "What a wonderful head-waiter he would make!"

LAUGHTER

TEACHER—"Freddie, you musn't laugh out loud in the school-room."

FREDDIE—"I didn't mean to do it. I was smiling, and the smile busted."

Laugh and the world laughs with you,
Weep, and the laugh's on you.

About the best and finest thing in this world is laughter.
—*Anna Alice Chapin.*

LAW

See Punishment.

LAWYERS

Ignorance of the law does not prevent the losing lawyer from collecting his bill.—*Puck.*

George Ade had finished his speech at a recent dinner-party, and on seating himself a well-know lawyer rose, shoved his hands deep into his trousers' pockets, as was his habit and laughingly inquired of those present:

"Doesn't it strike the company as a little unusual that a professional humorist should be funny?"

When the laugh had subsided, Ade drawled out:

"Doesn't it strike the company as a little unusual that a lawyer should have his hands in his own pockets?"

A man was charged with stealing a horse, and after a long trial the jury acquitted him. Later in the day the man came back and asked the judge for a warrant against the law-yer who had successfully defended him.

"What's the charge?" inquired the judge.

"Why, Your Honor," replied the man, "you see, I didn't have the money to pay him his fee, so he took the horse I stole."—*J. J. O'Connell.*

An elderly darky in Georgia, charged with the theft of some chickens, had the misfortune to be defended by a young and inexperienced attorney, although it is doubtful whether anyone could have secured his acquittal, the commission of the crime having been proved beyond all doubt.

The darky received a pretty severe sentence. "Thank you, sah," said he cheerfully, addressing the judge when the sentence had been pronounced. "Dat's mighty hard, sah, but it ain't anywhere what I 'spected. I thought, sah, dat between my character and dat speech of my lawyer dat you'd hang me, shore!"

"You have a pretty tough looking lot of customers to dispose of this morning, haven't you?" remarked the friend of a magistrate, who had dropped in at the police court.

"Huh!" rejoined the dispenser of justice, "you are looking at the wrong bunch. Those are the lawyers."

"Did youse git anyt'ing?" whispered the burglar on guard as his pal emerged from the window.

"Naw, de bloke wot lives here is a lawyer," replied the other in disgust.

"Dat's hard luck," said the first; "did youse lose anyt'ing?"

The dean of the Law Department was very busy and rather cross. The telephone rang.

"Well, what is it?" he snapped.

"Is that the city gas-works?" said a woman's soft voice.

"No, madam," roared the dean; "this is the University Law Department."

"Ah," she answered in the sweetest of tones, "I didn't miss it so far, after all, did I?"—*Carl Holliday.*

A lawyer cross-examining a witness, asked him where he was on a particular day; to which he replied that he had been in the company of two friends. "Friends!" exclaimed his tormentor; "two thieves, I suppose." "They may be so," replied the witness, dryly, "for they are both lawyers."

An impecunious young lawyer recently received the following letter from a tailor to whom he was indebted:

"Dear Sir: Kindly advise me by return mail when I may expect a remittance from you in settlement of my account.

Yours truly,

J. SNIPPEN."

The follower of Blackstone immediately replied:

"Dear Sir: I have your request for advice of a recent date, and beg leave to say that not having received any retainer from you I cannot act in the premises. Upon receipt of your check for $250 I shall be very glad to look the matter up for you and to acquaint you with the results of my investigations. I am, sir, with great respect, your most obedient servant,

"BARCLAY B. COKE."

A prisoner was brought before the bar in the criminal court, but was not represented by a lawyer.

"Where is your lawyer?" asked the judge who presided.

"I have none, sir," replied the prisoner.

"Why not?" queried the judge.

"Because I have no money to pay one."

"Do you want a lawyer?" asked the judge.

"Yes, sir."

"Well, there are Mr. Thomas W. Wilson, Mr. Henry Eddy, and Mr. George Rogers," said the judge, pointing to several young attorneys who were sitting in the room, waiting for something to turn up, "and Mr. Allen in out in the hall."

The prisoner looked at the attorneys, and, after critical survey, he turned to the judge and said:

"If I can take my choice, sir, I guess I'll take Mr. Allen."

—*A. S. Hitchcock.*

"What is that little boy crying about?" asked the benevolent old lady of the ragged boy.

"Dat other kid swiped his candy," was the response.

"But how is it that you have candy now?"

"Sure I got de candy now. I'm de little kid's lawyer."

A man walking along the street of a village stepped into a hole in the sidewalk and broke his leg. He engaged a famous lawyer, brought suit against the village for one thousand dollars and won the case. The city appealed to the Supreme Court, but again the great lawyer won.

After the claim was settled the lawyer sent for his client and handed him one dollar.

"What's this?" asked the man.

"That's your damages, after taking out my fee, the cost of appeal and other expenses," replied the counsel.

The man looked at the dollar, turned it over and carefully scanned the other side. Then looked up at the lawyer and said: "What's the matter with this dollar? Is it counterfeit?"

Deceive not thy Physician, Confessor nor Lawyer.

> A Sergeant of the Lawe, war and wys
> Ther was also, ful riche of excellence.
> Discreet he was, and of greet reverence:
> He seemed swich, his wordes weren so wyse.
>
> * * *
>
> No-wher so bisy a man as he ther nas,
> And yet he seemed bisier than he was.
>
> —*Chaucer.*

LAZINESS

A tourist in the mountains of Tennessee once had dinner with a querulous old mountaineer who yarned about hard times for fifteen minutes at a stretch.

"Why, man," said the tourist, "you ought to be able to make lots of money shipping green corn to the northern market."

"Yes, I oter," was the sullen reply.

"You have the land, I suppose, and can get the seed."

"Yes, I guess so."

"Then why don't you go into the speculation?"

"No use, stranger," sadly replied the cracker, "the old woman is too lazy to do the plowin' and plantin'."

While the train was waiting on a side track down in Georgia, one of the passengers walked over to a cabin near the track, in front of which sat a cracker dog, howling. The passenger asked a native why the dog was howling.

"Hookworm," said the native. "He's lazy."

"But," said the stranger, "I was not aware that the hookworm is painful."

" 'Taint," responded the garrulous native.

"Why, then," the stranger queried, "should the dog howl?"

"Lazy."

"But why does laziness make him howl?"

"Wal," said the Georgian, "that blame fool dawg is sittin' on a sand-bur, an' he's too tarnation lazy to get off, so he jes' sets thar an howls 'cause it hurts."

"How's times?" inquired a tourist.

"Oh, pretty tolerable," responded the old native who was sitting on a stump. "I had some trees to cut down, but a cyclone come along and saved me the trouble."

"Fine."

"Yes, and then the lightning set fire to the brush pile and saved me the trouble of burnin' it."

"Remarkable. But what are you going to do now?"

"Oh, nothin' much. Jest waitin' for an earthquake to come along and shake the potatoes out of the ground."

A tramp, after a day or two in the hustling, bustling town of Denver, shook the Denver dust from his boots with a snarl.

"They must be durn lazy people in this town. Everywhere you turn they offer you work to do."

An Atlanta man tells of an amusing experience he had in a mountainous region in a southwestern state, where the inhabitants are notoriously shiftless. Arriving at a dilapidated shanty at the noon hour, he inquired as to the prospects for getting dinner.

The head of the family, who had been "resting" on a fallen tree in front of his dwelling, made reply to the effect that he "guessed Ma'd hev suthin' on to the table putty soon."

With this encouragement, the traveler dismounted. To his chagrin, however, he soon discovered that the food set before him was such that he could not possibly "make a meal." He made such excuses as he could for his lack of appetite, and finally bethought himself of a kind of nourishment which he might venture to take, and which was sure to be found in any locality. He asked for some milk.

"Don't have milk no more," said the head of the place. "The dawg's dead."

"The dog!" cried the stranger, "What on earth has the dog to do with it?"

"Well," explained the host meditatively, "them cows don't seem to know 'nough to come up and be milked theirselves. The dog, he used to go for 'em an' fetch 'em up."

—*Edwin Tarrisse.*

Some temptations come to the industrious, but all temptations attack the idle.—*Spurgeon.*

LEAP YEAR

A girl looked calmly at a caller one evening and remarked: "George, as it is leap year——"

The caller turned pale.

"As it is leap year," she continued, "and you've been calling regularly now four nights a week for a long, long time, George, I propose——"

"I'm not in a position to marry on my salary Grace," George interrupted hurriedly.

'I know that, George," the girl pursued, "and so, as it is leap year, I thought I'd propose that you lay off and give some of the more eligible fellows a chance."—*L. F. Clarke.*

LEGISLATORS

Thomas B. Reed was one of the Legislative Committee sent to inspect an insane asylum. There was a dance on the night the committee spent in the investigation, and Mr. Reed took for a partner one of the fair unfortunates to whom he was introduced. "I don't remember having seen you here before," said she; "how long have you been in the asylum?" "Oh, I only came down yesterday," said the gentleman, "as one of the Legislative Committee." "Of course," returned the lady;

"how stupid I am! However, I knew you were an inmate or a member of the Legislature the moment I looked at you. But how was I to know? It is so difficult to know which."

LIARS

There are three kinds of liars:

1. The man whom others can't believe. He is harmless. Let him alone.

2. The man who can't believe others. He has probably made a careful study of human nature. If you don't put him in jail, he will find out that you are a hypocrite.

3. The man who can't believe himself. He is a cautious individual. Encourage him.

Two Irishmen were working on the roof of a building one day when one made a misstep and fell to the ground. The other leaned over and called:

"Are yez dead or alive, Mike?"

"Oi'm alive," said Mike feebly.

"Sure you're such a liar Oi don't know whether to belave yez or not."

"Well, then, Oi must be dead," said Mike, "for yez would never dare to call me a liar if Oi wor aloive."

FATHER (reprovingly)—"Do you know what happens to liars when they die?"

JOHNNY—"Yes, sir; they lie still."

A private, anxious to secure leave of absence, sought his captain with a most convincing tale about a sick wife breaking her heart for his absence. The officer, familiar with the soldier's ways, replied:

"I am afraid you are not telling the truth. I have just received a letter from your wife urging me not to let you come home because you get drunk, break the furniture, and mistreat her shamefully."

The private saluted and started to leave the room. He paused at the door, asking: "Sor, may I speak to you, not as an officer, but as mon to mon?"

"Yes; what is it?"

"Well, sor, what I'm after sayin' is this," approaching the captain and lowering his voice. "You and I are two of the most iligant liars the Lord ever made. I'm not married at all."

A conductor and a brakeman on a Montana railroad differ as to the proper pronunciation of the name Eurelia. Passengers are often startled upon arrival at his station to hear the conductor yell:

"You're a liar! You're a liar!"

And then from the brakeman at the other end of the car:

"You really are! You really are!"

MOTHER—"Oh, Bobby, I'm ashamed of you. I never told stories when I was a little girl."

BOBBY—"When did you begin, then, Mamma?"

—*Horace Zimmerman.*

The sages of the general store were discussing the veracity of old Si Perkins when Uncle Bill Abbott ambled in.

"What do you think about it, Uncle Bill?" they asked him. "Would you call Si Perkins a liar?"

'Well," answered Uncle Bill slowly, as he thoughtfully studied the ceiling, "I don't know as I'd go so far as to call him a liar exactly, but I do know this much: when feedin' time comes, in order to get any response from his hogs, he has to get somebody else to call 'em for him."

A lie is an abomination unto the Lord and an ever present help in time of trouble.

An Idaho guide whose services were retained by some wealthy young easterners desirous of hunting in the Northwest evidently took them to be the greenest of tenderfoots, since he undertook to chaff them with a recital something as follows:

"It was my first grizzly, so I was mighty proud to kill him in a hand-to-hand struggle. We started to fight about sunrise. When he finally gave up the ghost, the sun was going down."

At this point the guide paused to note the effect of his story. Not a word was said by the easterners, so the guide added very slowly, *"for the second time."*

"I gather, then," said one young gentleman, a dapper little Bostonian, "that it required a period of two days to enable you to dispose of that grizzly."

"Two days and a night," said the guide, with a grin. "That grizzly died mighty hard."

"Chocked to death?" asked the Bostonian.

"Yes, *sir,*" said the guide.

"Pardon me," continued the Hubbite, "but what did you try to get him to swallow?"

> When by night the frogs are croaking,
> Kindle but a torch's fire;
> Ha! how soon they all are silent;
> Thus Truth silences the liar.
> —*Friedrich von Logan.*

See also Epitaphs; Husbands; Politicians; Real Estate agents; Regrets.

LIBERTY

Liberty is being free from the things we don't like in order to be slaves of the things we do like.

> A day, an hour, of virtuous liberty
> Is worth a whole eternity in bondage.
> —*Addison.*

Where liberty dwells, there is my country.
> —*Benjamin Franklin.*

LIBRARIANS

A country newspaper printed the following announcement:
"The Public Library will close for two weeks, beginning August 3, for the annual cleaning and vacation of the librarians."

The modern librarian is a genius. All the proof needed is the statement that the requests for books with queer titles are filled with ones really wanted. The following are instances:

AS ASKED FOR	CORRECT TITLES
Indecent Orders	*In Deacon's Orders*
She Combeth Not Her Head	*She Cometh Not, She Said*
Trial of a Servant	*Trail of the Serpent*
Essays of a Liar	*Essays of Elia*
Soap and Tables	*Æsop's Fables*
Pocketbook's Hill	*Puck of Pook's Hill*
Dentist's Infirmary	*Dante's Inferno*
Holy Smoke	*Divine Fire*

One librarian has the following entries in a card catalog:
Lead Poisoning
Do, Kindly Light.

A distinguished librarian is a good follower of Chesterton. He says: "To my way of thinking, a great librarian must have a clear head, a strong hand and, above all, a great heart. Such shall be greatest among librarians; and when I look into the future, I am inclined to think that most of the men who will achieve this greatness will be women."

Many catalogers append notes to the main entries of their catalogs. Here are two:
An Ideal Husband:
Essentially a work of fiction,
and presumably written by a
woman (unmarried).
Aspects of Home Rule:
Political, not domestic.

In a branch library a reader asked for *The Girl He Married* (by James Grant.) This happened to be out, and the assistant was requested to select a similar book. Presumably he was a benedict, for he returned triumphantly with *His Better Half* (by George Griffith).

"Have you *A Joy Forever*?" inquired a lady borrower.

"No," replied the assistant librarian after referring to the stock.

"Dear me, how tiresome," said the lady; "have you Praed?"
"Yes, madam, but it isn't any good," was the prompt reply.

LIFE

Life's an aquatic meet—some swim, some dive, some back water, some float and the rest—sink.

> I count life just a stuff
> To try the soul's strength on.
> —*Robert Browning.*

> May you live as long as you like,
> And have what you like as long as you live.

> "Live, while you live," the epicure would say,
> "And seize the pleasures of the present day;"
> "Live, while you live," the sacred Preacher cries,
> "And give to God each moment as it flies."
> "Lord, in my views let both united be;
> I live in *pleasure,* when I live to *Thee.*"
> —*Philip Doddridge.*

> This world that we're a-livin' in
> Is mighty hard to beat,
> For you get a thorn with every rose—
> But ain't the roses sweet!

Dost thou love life? Then do not squander time, for that is the stuff life is made of.—*Benjamin Franklin.*

LISPING

"Have you lost another tooth, Bethesda?" asked auntie, who noticed an unusual lisp.

"Yes'm," replied the four-year-old, "and I limp now when I talk."

LOST AND FOUND

"I ain't losing any faith in human nature," said Uncle Eben, "but I kain't he'p noticin' dat dere's allus a heap mo' ahticles advertised 'Lost' den dar is 'Found.'"

"What were you in for?" asked the friend.

"I found a horse."

"Found a horse? Nonsense! They wouldn't jug you for finding a horse."

"Well, but you see I found him before the owner lost him."

"Party that lost purse containing twenty dollars need worry no longer—it has been found."—*Brooklyn Life.*

A lawyer having offices in a large office building recently lost a cuff-link, one of a pair that he greatly prized. Being absolutely certain that he had dropped the link somewhere in the building he posted this notice:

"Lost. A gold cuff-link. The owner, William Ward, will deeply appreciate its immediate return."

That afternoon, on passing the door whereon this notice was posted, what were the feelings of the lawyer to observe that appended thereto were these lines:

"The finder of the missing cuff-link would deem it a great favor if the owner would kindly lose the other link."

CHINAMAN—"You tellee me where railroad depot?"

CITIZEN—"What's the matter, John? Lost?"

CHINAMAN—"No! me here. Depot lost."

LOVE

Love is an insane desire on the part of a chump to pay a woman's board-bill for life.

MR. SLIMPURSE—"But why do you insist that our daughter should marry a man whom she does not like? You married for love, didn't you?"

MRS. SLIMPURSE—"Yes; but that is no reason why I should let our daughter make the same blunder."

MAUDE—"Jack is telling around that you are worth your weight in gold."

ETHEL—"The foolish boy. Who is he telling it to?"

MAUDE—"His creditors"

Rich Man—"Would you love my daughter just as much if she had no money?"

Suitor—"Why, certainly!"

Rich Man—"That's sufficient. I don't want any idiots in this family."

'Tis better to have lived and loved
Than never to have lived at all.

—*Judge.*

May we have those in our arms that we love in our hearts

Here's to love, the only fire against which there is no insurance.

Here's to those that I love;
Here's to those who love me;
Here's to those who love those that I love.
Here's to those who love those who love me.

It is best to love wisely, no doubt; but to love foolishly is better than not to be able to love at all.—*Thackeray.*

Mysterious love, uncertain treasure,
Hast thou more of pain or pleasure!
* * * * * * * *
Endless torments dwell about thee:
Yet who would live, and live without thee!

—*Addison.*

O, love, love, love!
    Love is like a dizziness;
It winna let a poor body
    Gang about his biziness!

—*Hogg.*

Let the man who does not wish to be idle, fall in love.
—*Ovid.*

LOYALTY

Jenkins, a newly wedded suburbanite, kissed his wife goodby the other morning, and, telling her he would be home at six o'clock that evening, got into his auto and started for town.

At six o'clock no hubby had appeared, and the little wife began to get nervous. When the hour of midnight arrived she could bear the suspense no longer, so she aroused her father and sent him off to the telegraph office with six telegrams to as many brother Elks living in town, asking each if her husband was stopping with him overnight.

Morning came, and the frantic wife had received no intelligence of the missing man. As dawn appeared, a farm wagon containing a farmer and the derelict husband drove up to the house, while behind the wagon trailed the broken-down auto. Almost simultaneously came a messenger boy with an answer to one of the telegrams, followed at intervals by five others. All of them read:

"Yes, John is spending the night with me."—*Bush Phillips.*

Boy—"Come quick, there's a man been fighting my father more'n half an hour."

Policeman—"Why didn't you tell me before?"

Boy—"'Cause father was getting the best of it till a few minutes ago."

LUCK

Some people are so fond of ill-luck that they run half-way to meet it.—*Douglas Jerrold.*

O, once in each man's life, at least,
　Good luck knocks at his door;
And wit to seize the flitting guest
　Need never hunger more.
But while the loitering idler waits
　Good luck beside his fire,
The bold heart storms at fortunes gates,
　And conquers its desire.

　　　　　　　　　　—Lewis J. Bates.

"Tommy," said his brother, "you're a regular little glutton. How can you eat so much?"

"Don't know; it's just good luck," replied the youngster.

A Negro who was having one misfortune after another said he was having as bad luck as the man with only a fork when it was raining soup.

See also Windfalls.

MAINE

The Governor of Maine was at the school and was telling the pupils what the people of different states were called.

"Now," he said, "the people from Indiana are called 'Hoosiers'; the people from North Carolina 'Tar Heels'; the people from Michigan we know as 'Michiganders.' Now, what little boy or girl can tell me what the people of Maine are called?"

"I know," said a little girl.

"Well, what are we called?" asked the Governor.

"Maniacs."

MAKING GOOD

"What's become ob dat little chameleon Mandy had?" inquired Rufus.

"Oh, de fool chile done lost him," replied Zeke. "She wuz playin' wif him one day, puttin' him on red to see him turn red, an' on blue to see him turn blue, an' on green to see him turn green, an' so on. Den de fool gal, not satisfied wif lettin' well enough alone, went an' put him on a plaid, an' de poor little thing went an' bust himself tryin' to make good."

See also Success.

MALARIA

The physician had taken his patient's pulse and temperature, and proceeded to ask the usual questions.

"It—er—seems," said he, regarding the unfortunate with scientific interest, "that the attacks of fever and the chills appear on alternate days. Do you think—is it your opinion—that they have, so to speak, decreased in violence, if I may use that word?"

The patient smiled feebly. "Doc," said he, "on fever days my head's so hot I can't think, and on ague days I shake so I can't hold an opinion."

MARKS(WO)MANSHIP

An Irishman who, with his wife, is employed on a truck-farm in New Jersey, recently found himself in a bad predicament, when, in attempting to evade the onslaughts of a savage dog, assistance came in the shape of his wife.

When the woman came up, the dog had fastened his teeth in the calf of her husband's leg and was holding on for dear life. Seizing a stone in the road, the Irishman's wife was about to hurl it, when the husband, with wonderful presence of mind, shouted:

"Mary! Mary! Don't throw the stone at the dog! throw it at me!"

Mary had a little lamb,
   It's fleece was gone in spots,
For Mary fired her father's gun,
   And lamby caught the shots!
         —*Columbia Jester.*

MARRIAGE

Mrs. Quackenness—"Am yo' daughter happily mar'd, Sistah Sagg?"

Mrs. Sagg—"She sho' is! Bless goodness she's done got a husband dat's skeered to death of her!"

"Where am I?" the invalid exclaimed, waking from the long delirium of fever and feeling the comfort that loving hands had supplied. "Where am I—in heaven?"

"No, dear," cooed his wife; "I am still with you."

Archbishop Ryan was visiting a small parish in a mining district one day for the purpose of administering confirmation, and asked one nervous little girl what matrimony is.

"It is a state of terrible torment which those who enter are compelled to undergo for a time to prepare them for a brighter and better world," she said.

"No, no," remonstrated her rector; "that isn't matrimony: that's the definition of purgatory."

"Leave her alone," said the Archbishop; "maybe she is right. What do you and I know about it?"

"Was Helen's marriage a success?"

"Goodness, yes. Why, she is going to marry a nobleman on the alimony."—*Judge.*

JENNIE—"What makes George such a pessimist?"

JACK—"Well, he's been married three times—once for love, once for money and the last time for a home."

Matrimony is the root of all evil.

One day Mary, the charwoman, reported for service with a black eye.

"Why Mary," said her sympathetic mistress, "what a bad eye you have!"

"Yes'm."

"Well, there's one consolation. It might have been worse."

"Yes'm."

"You might have had both of them hurt."

"Yes'm. Or worse'n that: I might not ha' been married at all."

A wife placed upon her husband's tombstone: "He had been married forty years and was prepared to die."

"I can take a hundred words a minute," said the stenographer.

"I often take more than that," said the prospective employer; "but then I have to, I'm married."

A man and his wife were airing their troubles on the side-walk one Saturday evening when a good Samaritan intervened.

"See here, my man," he protested, "this sort of thing won't do."

"What business is it of yours, I'd like to know," snarled the man, turning from his wife.

"It's only my business in so far as I can be of help in settling this dispute," answered the Samaritan mildly.

"This ain't no dispute," growled the man.

"No dispute! But, my dear friend——"

"I tell you it ain't no dispute," insisted the man. "She"—jerking his thumb toward the woman—"thinks she ain't goin to get my week's wages, and I know darn well she ain't. Where's the dispute in that?"

HIS BETTER HALF—"I think it's time we got Lizzie married and settled down, Alfred. She will be twenty-eight next week, you know."

HER LESSER HALF—"Oh, don't hurry, my dear. Better wait till the right sort of man comes along."

HIS BETTER HALF—"But why wait? I didn't!"

O'Flanagan came home one night with a deep band of black crape around his hat.

"Why, Mike!" exclaimed his wife. "What are ye wearin' thot mournful thing for?"

"I'm wearin' it for yer first husband," replied Mike firmly, "I'm sorry he's dead."

"What a strangely interesting face your friend the poet has," gurgled the maiden of forty. "It seems to possess all the ele-ments of happiness and sorrow, each struggling for supremacy."

"Yes, he looks to me like a man who was married and didn't know it," growled the Cynical Bachelor.

The not especially sweet-tempered young wife of a Kaslo, B. C., man one day approached her lord concerning the matter of one hundred dollars or so.

"I'd like to let you have it, my dear," began the husband,

"but the fact is I haven't that amount in the bank this morning—that is to say, I haven't that amount to spare, inasmuch as I must take up a note for two hundred dollars this afternoon."

"Oh, very well, James!" said the wife, with an ominous calmness, "If you think the man who holds the note can make things any hotter for you than I can—why, do as you say, James!"

A young lady entered a book store and inquired of the gentlemanly clerk—a married man, by-the-way—if he had a book suitable for an old gentleman who had been married fifty years.

Without the least hesitation the clerk reached for a copy of Parkman's "A Half Century of Conflict."

Smith and Jones were discussing the question of who should be head of the house—the man or the woman.

"I am the head of my establishment," said Jones. "I am the bread-winner. Why shouldn't I be?"

"Well," replied Smith, "before my wife and I were married we made an agreement that I should make the rulings in all major things, my wife in all the minor."

"How has it worked?" queried Jones.

Smith smiled. "So far," he replied, "no major matters have come up."

A poor lady the other day hastened to the nursery and said to her little daughter:

"Minnie, what do you mean by shouting and screaming? Play quietly, like Tommy. See, he doesn't make a sound."

"Of course he doesn't," said the little girl. That is our game. He is papa coming home late, and I am you."

The stranger advanced toward the door. Mrs. O'Toole stood in the doorway with a rough stick in her left hand and a frown on her brow.

"Good morning," said the stranger politely. "I'm looking for Mr. O'Toole."

"So'm I," said Mrs. O'Toole, shifting her club over to her other hand.

TIM—"Sarer Smith (you know 'er—Bill's missus), she throwed herself horf the end uv the wharf larst night."

TOM—"Poor Sarer!"

TIM—"An' a cop fished 'er out again."

TOM—"Poor Bill!"

The cooing stops with the honeymoon, but the billing goes on forever.

"Well, old man, how did you get along after I left you at midnight. Get home all right?"

"No; a confounded nosey policeman haled me to the station, where I spent the rest of the night."

"Lucky dog! I reached home."

STRANGER—"What's the fight about?"

NATIVE—"The feller on top is Hank Hill wot married the widder Strong, an' th' other's Joel Jenks, wot interdooced him to her."—*Life.*

A colored man had been arrested on a charge of beating and cruelly misusing his wife. After hearing the charge against the prisoner, the justice turned to the first witness.

"Madam," he said, "if this man were your husband and had given you a beating, would you call in the police?"

The woman addressed, a veritable Amazon in size and aggressiveness, turned a smiling countenance towards the justice and answered: "No, jedge. If he was mah husban,' and he treated me lak he did 'is wife, Ah wouldn't call no p'liceman. No, sah, Ah'd call de undertaker."

We admire the strict impartiality of the judge who recently fined his wife twenty-five dollars for contempt of court, but we would hate to have been in the judge's shoes when he got home that night.

"How many children have you?" asked the census-taker.

The man addressed removed the pipe from his mouth, scratched his head, thought it over a moment, and then replied:

"Five—four living and one married."

SHE—"How did they ever come to marry?"

HE—"Oh, it's the same old story. Started out to be good friends, you know, and later on changed their minds."—*Puck.*

Nat Goodwin and a friend were walking along Fifth Avenue one afternoon when they stopped to look into a florist's window, in which there was an artistic arrangement of exquisite roses.

"What wonderful American Beauties those are, Nat!" said the friend delightedly.

"They are, indeed," replied Nat.

"You see, I am very fond of that flower," continued the friend. "In fact, I might say it is my favorite. You know, Nat, I married an American beauty."

"Well," said Nat dryly, "you haven't got anything on me. I married a cluster."

"Are you quite sure that was a marriage license you gave me last month?"

"Of course! What's the matter?"

"Well, I thought there might be some mistake, seeing that I've lived a dog's life ever since."

Is not marriage an open question, when it is alleged, from the beginning of the world, that such as are in the institution wish to get out, and such as are out wish to get in.—*Emerson.*

HOUSEHOLDER—"Here, drop that coat and clear out!"

BURGLAR—"You be quiet, or I'll wake your wife and give her this letter I found in your pocket."

The reason why so few marriages are happy is because young ladies spend their time in making nets, not in making cages.—*Swift.*

See also Church discipline; Domestic finance; Trouble.

MARRIAGE FEES

A poor couple who went to the priest to be wedded were met with a demand for the marriage fee. It was not forthcoming. Both the consenting parties were rich in love and in their prospects, but destitute of financial resources. The father was obdurate. "No money, no marriage."

"Give me l'ave, your riverence," said the blushing bride, "to go and get the money."

It was given, and she sped forth on the delicate mission of raising a marriage fee out of pure nothing. After a short interval she returned with the sum of money, and the ceremony was completed to the satisfaction of all. When the parting was taking place the newly-made wife seemed a little uneasy.

"Anything on your mind, Catherine?" said the father.

"Well, your riverence, I would like to know if this marriage could not be spoiled now."

"Certainly not, Catherine. No man can put you asunder."

"Could you not do it yourself, father? Could you not spoil the marriage?"

"No, no, Catherine. You are past me now. I have nothing more to do with your marriage."

"That aises me mind," said Catherine, "and God bless your riverence. There's the ticket for your hat. I picked it up in the lobby and pawned it."

MANDY—"What foh yo' been goin' to de post-office so reg'lar? Are yo' corresponding wif some other female?"

RASTUS—"Nope; but since ah been a-readin' in de papers 'bout dese 'conscience funds' ah kind of thought ah might possibly git a lettah from dat ministah what married us."—*Life*.

> The knot was tied; the pair were wed,
> And then the smiling bridegroom said
> Unto the preacher, "Shall I pay
> To you the usual fee today.
> Or would you have me wait a year
> And give you then a hundred clear,
> If I should find the marriage state
> As happy as I estimate?"
> The preacher lost no time in thought,
> To his reply no study brought,
> There were no wrinkles on his brow:
> Said he, "I'll take three dollars now."

MATHEMATICS

See Arithmetic.

MATRIMONY

See Marriage.

MEASURING INSTRUMENTS

Golly, but I's tired!" exclaimed a tall and thin Negro, meeting a short and stout friend on Washington Street.

"What you been doin' to get tired?" demanded the other.

"Well," explained the thin one, drawing a deep breath, "over to Brother Smith's dey are measurin' de house for some new carpets. Dey haven't got no yawdstick, and I's just ezactly six feet tall. So to oblige Brother Smith, I's been a-layin' down and a-gettin' up all over deir house."

MEDICAL INSPECTION OF SCHOOLS

PASSER-BY—"What's the fuss in the schoolyard, boy?"

THE BOY—"Why, the doctor has just been around examinin' us an' one of the deficient boys is knockin' th' everlastin' stuffin's out of a perfect kid."

MEDICINE

The farmer's mule had just balked in the road when the country doctor came by. The farmer asked the physician if he could give him something to start the mule. The doctor said he could, and reaching down into his medicine case, gave the animal some powders. The mule switched his tail, tossed his head and started on a mad gallop down the road. The farmer looked first at the flying animal and then at the doctor.

"How much did that medicine cost, Doc?" he asked.

"Oh, about fifteen cents," said the physician.

"Well, give me a quarter's worth, quick!" And he swallowed it. "I've got to catch that mule."

"I hope you are following my instructions carefully, Sandy— the pills three times a day and a drop of whiskey at bedtime."

"Weel, sir, I may be a wee bit behind wi' the pills, but I'm about six weeks in front wi' the whusky."

Rarely has a double meaning turned with more deadly effect upon an innocent perpetrator than in an advertisement lately appearing in a western newspaper. He wrote: "Wanted— a gentleman to undertake the sale of a patent medicine. The advertiser guarantees it will be profitable to the undertaker."

I firmly believe that if the whole *materia medica* could be sunk to the bottom of the sea, it would be all the better for mankind and all the worse for the fishes.—*O. W. Holmes.*

A man's own observation, what he finds good of, and what he finds hurt of, is the best physic to preserve health.—*Bacon.*

MEEKNESS

One evening just before dinner a wife, who had been playing bridge all the afternoon, came in to find her husband and a strange man (afterward ascertained to be a lawyer) engaged in some mysterious business over the library table, upon which were spread several sheets of paper.

"What are you going to do with all that paper, Henry?" demanded the wife.

"I am making a wish," meekly responded the husband.

"A wish?"

"Yes, my dear. In your presence I shall not presume to call it a will."

MEMORIALS

Two Negroes were talking about a recent funeral of a member of their race, at which funeral there had been a profusion of floral tributes. Said the cook:

"Dat's all very well, Mandy; but when I dies I don't want no flowers on my grave. Jes' plant a good old watermelon-vine; an' when she gits ripe, you come dar, an' don't you eat it, but jes' bus' it on de grave, an' let de good old juice dribble down thro' de ground!"

"That's rather a handsome mantelpiece you have there, Mr. Binkston," said the visitor.

"Yes," replied Mr. Binkston, proudly. "That is a memorial to my wife."

"Why—I was not aware that Mrs. Binkston had passed away," said the visitor sympathetically.

"Oh no, indeed, she hasn't," smiled Mr. Binkston. "She is serving her thirtieth sojourn in jail. That mantelpiece is built of the bricks she was convicted of throwing."

MEMORY

"Uncle Mose," said a drummer, addressing an old colored man seated on a drygoods box in front of the village store, "they tell me that you remember seeing George Washington— am I mistaken?"

"No, sah," said Uncle Mose. "I uster 'member seein' him, but I done fo'got sence I jined de chu'ch."

A noted college president, attending a banquet in Boston, was surprised to see that the darky who took the hats at the door gave no checks in return.

"He has a most wonderful memory," a fellow diner explained. "He's been doing that for years and prides himself upon never having made a mistake."

As the college president was leaving, the darky passed him his hat.

"How do you know that this one is mine?"

"I don't know it, suh," admitted the darky.

"Then why do you give it to me?"

" 'Cause yo' gave it to me, suh."

"Tommy," said his mother reprovingly, "what did I say I'd do to you if I ever caught you stealing jam again?"

Tommy thoughtfully scratched his head with his sticky fingers.

"Why, that's funny, ma, that you should forget it, too. Hanged if I can remember."

Smith is a young New York lawyer, clever in many ways, but very forgetful. He was recently sent to St. Louis to interview an important client in regard to a case then pending in the Missouri courts. Later the head of his firm received this telegram from St. Louis:

"Have forgotten name of client. Please wire at once."

This was the reply sent from New York:

"Client's name Jenkins. Your name Smith."

> When time who steals our years away
>   Shall steal our pleasures too,
> The mem'ry of the past will stay
>   And half our joys renew.
>
> —*Moore.*

> The heart hath its own memory, like the mind,
>   And in it are enshrined
> The precious keepsakes, into which is wrought
>   The giver's loving thought.
>
> —*Longfellow.*

MEN

> Here's to the men! God bless them!
>   Worst of me sins, I confess them!
> In loving them all; be they great or small,
>   So here's to the boys! God bless them!

> May all single men be married,
> And all married men be happy.

"What is your ideal man?"

"One who is clever enough to make money and foolish enough to spend it!"

I have thought some of Nature's journeymen had made men and not made them well, they imitated humanity so abominably.—*Shakespeare.*

Men are four:
He who knows and knows not that he knows,—
   He is asleep—wake him;
He who knows not and knows not that he knows not,—
   He is a fool—shun him;
He who knows not and knows that he knows not,—
   He is a child—teach him;
He who knows and knows that he knows,—
   He is a king—follow him.

See also Dogs; Husbands.

MESSAGES

"Have you the rent ready?"

"No, sir; mother's gone out washing and forgot to put it out for you."

"Did she tell you she'd forgotten?"

"Yes, sir."

One of the passengers on a wreck was an exceedingly nervous man, who, while floating in the water, imagined how his friends would acquaint his wife of his fate. Saved at last, he rushed to the telegraph office and sent this message: "Dear Pat, I am saved. Break it gently to my wife."

METAPHOR

It was a Washington woman, angry because the authorities had closed the woman's rest-room in the Senate office building, who burst out:

"It is almost as of the Senate had hurled its glove into the teeth of the advancing wave that is sounding the clarion of equal rights."

A water consumer in Los Angeles, California, whose supply had been turned off because he wouldn't pay, wrote to the department as follows:

"In the matter of shutting off the water on unpaid bills, your company is fast becoming a regular crystallized Russian bureaucracy, running in a groove and deaf to the appeals of reform. There is no use of your trying to impugn the verity of this indictment by shaking your official heads in the teeth of your own deeds.

"If you will persist in this kind of thing, a widespread conflagration of the populace will be so imminent that it will require only a spark to let loose the dogs of war in our midst. Will you persist in hurling the corner stone of our personal liberty to your wolfish hounds of collectors, thirsting for its blood? If you persist, the first thing you know you will have the chariot of a justly indignant revolution rolling along in our midst and gnashing its teeth as it rolls.

"If your rascally collectors are permitted to continue coming to our doors with unblushing footsteps, with cloaks of hypocritical compunction in their mouths, and compel payment from your patrons, this policy will result in cutting the wool off the sheep that lays the golden egg, until you have pumped it dry—and then farewell, a long farewell, to our vaunted prosperity."

MICE

"What's the matter with Briggs?"

"He was getting shaved by a lady barber when a mouse ran across the floor."—*Life.*

MIDDLE CLASSES

Willie—"Paw, what is the middle class?"

Paw—"The middle class consists of people who are not poor enough to accept charity and not rich enough to donate anything."

MILITANTS

See Suffragettes.

MILITARY DISCIPLINE

Murphy was a new recruit in the cavalry. He could not ride at all, and by ill luck was given one of the most vicious horses in the troop.

"Remember," said the sergeant, "no one is allowed to dismount without orders."

Murphy was no sooner in the saddle than he was thrown to the ground.

"Murphy!" yelled the sergeant, when he discovered him lying breathless on the ground, "you dismounted!"

"I did."

"Did you have orders?"

"I did."

"From headquarters, I suppose?"

"No, sor; from hintquarters."

"How dare you come on parade," exclaimed an Irish sergeant to a recruit, "before a respictible man loike mysilf smothered from head to foot in graise an' poipe clay? Tell me now—answer me when I spake to yez!"

The recruit was about to excuse himself for his condition when the sergeant stopped him.

"Dare yez to answer me when I puts a question to yez?" he cried. "Hould yer lyin' tongue, and open your face at yer peril! Tell me now, what have ye been doin' wid yer uniform an' arms an' bilts? Not a word, or I'll clap yez in the guardroom. When I axes yez anything an' yez spakes I'll have yez tried for insolence to yer superior office, but if yez don't answer when I questions yez, I'll have yez punished for disobedience of orders! So, yez see, I have yez both ways!"

Mistake, error, is the discipline through which we advance.
—*Channing.*

MILLINERS

Recipe for a milliner:
    To a presence that's much more than queenly,
        Add a manner that's quite Vere de Vere;
    You feel like a worm in her sight when she says,
        "Only $300, my dear!"

—*Life.*

MILLIONAIRES

Recipe for a multi-millionaire:
>   Take a boy with bare feet as a starter
>   Add thrift and sobriety, mixed—
>   Flavor with quarts of religion,
>   And see that the tariff is fixed.

—Life.

MILLIONAIRE (to a beggar)—"Be off with you this minute!"

BEGGAR—"Look 'ere, mister; the only difference between you and me is that you are makin' your second million, while I am still workin' at my first."

"Now that you have made $50,000,000, I supose you are going to keep right on for the purpose of trying to get a hundred millions?"

"No, sir. You do me an injustice. I'm going to put in the rest of my time trying to get my conscience into a satisfactory condition.

"When I was a young man," said Mr. Cumrox, "I thought nothing of working twelve or fourteen hours a day."

"Father," replied the young man with sporty clothes, "I wish you wouldn't mention it. Those non-union sentiments are liable to make you unpopular."

No good man ever became suddenly rich.—*Syrus.*

>   And all to leave what with his toil he won,
>   To that unfeather'd two-legged thing, a son.

—Dryden.

See also Capitalists.

MINORITIES

Stepping out between the acts at the first production of one of his plays, Bernard Shaw said to the audience:

"What do you think of it?"

This startled everybody for the time being, but presently a man in the pit assembled his scattered wits and cried:

"Rotten!"

Shaw made a curtsey and melted the house with one of his Irish smiles.

"My friend," he said, shrugging his shoulders and indicating the crowd in front, "I quite agree with you, but what are we two against so many?"

MISERS

There was an old man of Nantucket
Who kept all his cash in a bucket;
    But his daughter, named Nan,
    Ran away with a man—
And as for the bucket, Nantucket.

A mere madness, to live like a wretch, and die rich.—*Robert Burton.*

MISSIONARIES

SHE—"Poor cousin Jack! And to be eaten by those wretched cannibals!"

HE—"Yes, my dear child; but he gave them their first taste in religion!"

At a meeting of the Women's Foreign Missionary Society in a large city church a discussion arose among the members present as to the race of people that inhabited a far-away land. Some insisted that they were not a man-eating people; others that they were known to be cannibals. However, the question was finally decided by a minister's widow, who said:

"I beg pardon for interrupting, Mrs. Chairman, but I can assure you that they are cannibals. My husband was a missionary there and they ate him."

MISSIONS

"What in the world are you up to, Hilda?" exclaimed Mrs. Bale, as she entered the nursery where her six-year-old daughter was stuffing broken toys, headless dolls, ragged clothes and general debris into an open box.

"Why, mother," cried Hilda, "can't you see? I'm packing a missionary box just the way the ladies do; and it's all right," she added reassuringly, "I haven't put in a single thing that's any good at all!"

MISTAKEN IDENTITY

There was a young fellow named Paul,
Who went to a fancy dress ball;
    They say, just for fun
    He dressed up like a bun,
And was "et" by a dog in the hall.

A Scottish woman, who was spending her holidays in London, entered a bric-a-brac shop, in search of something odd to take home to Scotland with her. After she had inspected several articles, but had found none to suit her, she noticed a quaint figure, the head and shoulders of which appeared above the counter.

"What is that Japanese idol over there worth?" she inquired of the salesman.

The salesman's reply was given in a subdued tone:

"About half a million, madam. That's the proprietor!"

The late James McNeil Whistler was standing bareheaded in a hat shop, the clerk having taken his hat to another part of the shop for comparison. A man rushed in with his hat in his hand, and, supposing Whistler to be a clerk angrily confronted him.

"See here," he said, "this hat doesn't fit."

Whistler eyed the stranger critically from head to foot, and then drawled out:

"Well, neither does your coat. What's more, if you'll pardon my saying so, I'll be hanged if I care much for the color of your trousers."

The steamer was on the point of leaving, and the passengers lounged on the deck and waited for the start. At length one of them espied a cyclist in the far distance, and it soon became evident that he was doing his level best to catch the boat.

Already the sailors' hands were on the gangways, and the cyclist's chance looked small indeed. Then a sportive passenger wagered a sovereign to a shilling that he would miss it. The offer was taken, and at once the deck became a scene of wild excitement.

"He'll miss it."

"No; he'll just do it."

"Come on!"

"He won't do it."

"Yes, he will. He's done it. Hurrah!"

In the very nick of time the cyclist arrived, sprang off his machine, and ran up the one gangway left.

"Cast off!" he cried.

It was the captain.

Much to the curious little girl's disgust, her elder sister and her girl friends had quickly closed the door of the back parlor, before she could wedge her small self in among them.

She waited uneasily for a little while, then she knocked. No response. She knocked again. Still no attention. Her curiosity could be controlled no longer. "Dodo!" she called in staccato tones as she knocked once again. "'Tain't me! It's Mamma!"

MOLLYCODDLES

'Tommy, why don't you play with Frank any more?" asked Tommy's mother, who noticed that he was cultivating the acquaintance of a new boy on the block. "I thought you were such good chums."

"We was," replied Tommy superciliously, "but he's a mollycoddle. He paid t' git into the ball-grounds."

MONEY

In some of the college settlements there are penny savings banks for children.

One Saturday a small boy arrived with an important air and withdrew 2 cents from his account. Monday morning he promptly returned the money.

"So you didn't spend your 2 cents?" observed the worker in charge.

"Oh, no," he replied, "but a fellow just likes to have a little cash on hand over Sunday."

See also Domestic finance.

MORAL EDUCATION

Two little boys, four and five years old respectively, were playing quietly, when the one of four years struck the other on his cheek. An interested bystander stepped up and asked him why he had hit the other who had done nothing.

"Well," replied the pugilistic one, "last Sunday our lesson in Sunday-school was about if a fellow hit you on the left cheek turn the other and get another crack, and I just wanted to see if Bobbie knew his lesson."

MOSQUITOES

Senator Gore, of Oklahoma, while addressing a convention in Oklahoma City recently, told this story, illustrating a point he made:

"A northern gentleman was being entertained by a southern colonel on a fishing-trip. It was his first visit to the South, and the mosquitoes were so bothersome that he was unable to sleep, while at the same time he could hear his friend snoring audibly.

"The next morning he approached the old darky who was doing the cooking.

"'Jim,' he said. 'how is it the colonel is able to sleep so soundly with so many mosquitoes around?'

"'I'll tell yo', boss,' the darky replied, 'de fust part of de night de kernel is too full to pay any 'tenshum to de skeeters, and de last part of de night de skeeters is too full to pay any 'tenshum to de kernel.'"

See also Applause; New Jersey.

MOTHERS

While reconnoitering in Westmoreland County, Virginia, one of General Washington's officers chanced upon a fine team of horses driven before a plow by a burly slave. Finer animals he had never seen. When his eyes had feasted on their beauty he cried to the driver: "Hello good fellow! I must have those horses. They are just such animals as I have been looking for."

The black man grinned, rolled up the whites of his eyes, put the lash to the horses' flanks and turned up another furrow in the rich soil.

The officer waited until he had finished the row; then throwing back his cavalier cloak the ensign of the rank dazzled the slave's eyes.

"Better see missus! Better see missus!" he cried waving his hand to the south, where above the cedar growth rose the towers of a fine old Virginia mansion.

The officer turned up the carriage road and soon was rapping the great brass knocker of the front door.

Quickly the door swung upon its ponderous hinges and a grave, majestic-looking woman confronted the visitor with an air of inquiry.

"Madam," said the officer doffing his cap and overcome by her dignity, "I have come to claim your horses in the name of the Government."

"My horses?" said she, bending upon him a pair of eyes born to command. "Sir, you cannot have them. My crops are out and I need my horses in the field."

"I am sorry," said the officer, "but I must have them, madam. Such are the orders of my chief."

"Your chief! Who is your chief, pray?" she demanded with restrained warmth.

"The commander of the American army, General George Washington," replied the other, squaring his shoulders and swelling his pride.

A smile of trumph softened the sternness of the woman's features. "You go and tell General George Washington for me," said she, "that his mother says he cannot have her horses."

The wagons of "the greatest show on earth" passed up the avenue at daybreak. Their incessant rumbling soon awakened ten-year-old Billie and five-year-old brother Robert. Their mother feigned sleep as the two white-robed figures crept past her bed into the hall, on the way to investigate. Robert struggled manfully with the unaccustomed task of putting on his clothes. "Wait for me, Billie," his mother heard him beg. "You'll get ahead of me."

"Get mother to help you," counseled Billie, who was having troubles of his own.

Mother started to the rescue, and then paused as she heard the voice of her younger, guarded but anxious and insistent.

"*You* ask her, Billie. You've known her longer than I have."

A little girl, being punished by her mother flew, white with rage, to her desk, wrote on a piece of paper, and then going out in the yard she dug a hole in the ground, put the paper in it and covered it over. The mother, being interested in her child's doings, went out after the little girl had gone away, dug up the paper and read:

Dear Devil:

Please come and take my mamma away.

One morning a little girl hung about the kitchen bothering the busy cook to death. The cook lost patience finally. "Clear out o' here, ye sassy little brat!" she shouted, thumping the table with a rolling-pin.

The little girl gave the cook a haughty look. "I never allow any one but my mother to speak to me like that," she said.

The public-spirited lady met the little boy on the street. Something about his appearance halted her. She stared at him in her near-sighted way.

THE LADY—"Little boy, haven't you any home?"

THE LITTLE BOY—"Oh, yes'm; I've got a home."

THE LADY—"And loving parents?"

THE LITTLE BOY—"Yes'm."

THE LADY—"I'm afraid you do not know what love really is. Do your parents look after your moral welfare?"

THE LITTLE BOY—"Yes'm."

THE LADY—"Are they bringing you up to be a good and helpful citizen?"

THE LITTLE BOY—"Yes'm."

THE LADY—"Will you ask your mother to come and hear me talk on 'When Does a Mother's Duty to Her Child Begin? next Saturday afternoon, at three o'clock, at Lyceum Hall?"

THE LITTLE BOY (explosively)—"What's th' matter with you ma! Don't you know me? I'm your little boy!"

Here's to the happiest hours of my life—
Spent in the arms of another man's wife:
My mother!

Happy he
With such a mother! faith in womankind
Beats with his blood, and trust in all things high
Comes easy to him, and though he trip and fall,
He shall not blind his soul with clay.
—*Tennyson.*

Women know
The way to rear up children (to be just);
They know a simple, merry, tender knack
Of tying sashes, fitting baby-shoes,
And stringing pretty words that make no sense,
And kissing full sense into empty words;
Which things are corals to cut life upon,
Although such trifles.
—*E. B. Browning.*

MOTHERS-IN-LAW

Justice David J. Brewer was asked not long ago by a man: "Will you please tell me, sir, what is the extreme penalty for bigamy?"

Justice Brewer smiled and answered:

"Two mothers-in-law."

SHE—"And so you are going to be my son-in-law?"

HE—"By Jove! I hadn't thought of that."

WAITER—"Have another glass, sir?"

HUSBAND (to his wife)—"Shall I have another glass, Henrietta?"

WIFE (to her mother)—"Shall he have another, mother?"

A blackmailer wrote the following to a wealthy business man: "Send me $5,000 or I will abduct your mother-in-law."

To which the business man replied: "Sorry I am short of funds, but your proposition interests me."

An undertaker telegraphed to a man that his mother-in-law had died and asked whether he should bury, embalm or cremate her. The man replied, "All three, take no chances."

MOTORCYCLES

The automobile was a thing unheard of to a mountaineer in one community, and he was very much astonished one day when he saw one go by without any visible means of locomotion. His eyes bulged, however, when a motocycle followed closely in its wake and disappeared like a flash around a bend in the road.

"Gee whiz!" he said, turning to his son, "who'd 'a' s'posed that thing had a colt?"

MOUNTAINS

Some real-estate dealers in British Columbia were accused of having victimized English and Scotch settlers by selling to them (at long range) fruit ranches which were situated on the tops of mountains. It is said that the captain of a steamboat on Kootenay Lake once heard a great splash in the water. Looking over the rail, he spied the head of a man who was swimming toward his boat. He hailed him. "Do you know," said the swimmer, "this is the third time to-day that I've fallen off that bally old ranch of mine?"

MOVING PICTURES

"Your soldiers look fat and happy. You must have a war chest." "Not exactly, but things are on a higher plane than they used to be. This revolution is being financed by a moving-picture concern."

MUCK-RAKING

The way of the transgressor is well written up.

MULES

Gen. O. O. Howard, as is well known, is a man of deep religious principles, and in the course of the war he divided his time pretty equally between fighting and evangelism. Howard's brigade was known all through the army as the Christian brigade, and he was very proud of it.

There was one hardened old sinner in the brigade, however, whose ears were deaf to all exhortation. General Howard was particularly anxious to convert this man, and one day he went down in the teamsters' part of the camp where the man was on duty. He talked with him long and earnestly about religion and finally said:

"I want to see you converted. Won't you come to the mourners' bench at the next service?"

The erring one rubbed his head thoughtfully for a moment and then replied:

"General, I'm plumb willin' to be converted, but if I am, seein' that everyone else has got religion, who in blue blazes is goin' to drive the mules?"

MUNICIPAL GOVERNMENT

"What's the trouble in Plunkville?"

"We've tried a mayor and we've tried a commission."

"Well?"

"Now we're thinking of offering the management of our city to some good magazine."

MUSEUMS

It had been anything but an easy afternoon for the teacher who took six of her pupils through the Museum of Natural

History, but their enthusiastic interest in the stuffed animals and their open-eyed wonder at the prehistoric fossils amply repaid her.

"Well, boys, where have you been all afternoon?" asked the father of two of the party that evening.

The answer came back with joyous promptness: "Oh, pop! Teacher took us to a dead circus."

Two Marylanders, who were visiting the National Museum at Washington, were seen standing in front of an Egyptian mummy, over which hung a placard bearing the inscription. "B. C. 1187."

Both visitors were much mystified thereby. Said one:

"What do you make of that, Bill?"

"Well," said Bill, "I dunno; but maybe it was the number of the motor-car that killed him."—*Edwin Tarrisse.*

MUSIC

The musical young woman who dropped her peekaboo waist in the piano player and turned out a Beethoven sonata, has her equal in the lady who stood in front of a five-bar fence and sang all the dots on her veil.

A thief broke into a Madison avenue mansion early the other morning and found himself in the music-room. Hearing footsteps approaching, he took refuge behind a screen.

From eight to nine o'clock the eldest daughter had a singing lesson.

From nine to ten o'clock the second daughter took a piano lesson.

From ten to eleven o'clock the eldest son had a violin lesson.

From eleven to twelve o'clock the other son had a lesson on the flute.

At twelve-fifteen all the brothers and sisters assembled and studied an ear-splitting piece for voice, piano, violin and flute.

The thief staggered out from behind the screen at twelve-forty-five, and falling at their feet, cried:

"For Heaven's sake, have me arrested!"

A lady told Swinburne that she would render on the piano a very ancient Florentine retornello which had just been discovered. She then played "Three blind mice" and Swinburne was enchanted. He found that it reflected to perfection the cruel beauty of the Medicis—which, perhaps, it does.—*Edmund Gosse.*

The accomplished and obliging pianist had rendered several selections, when one of the admiring group of listeners in the hotel parlor suggested Mozart's Twelfth Mass. Several people echoed the request, but one lady was particularly desirous of hearing the piece, explaining that her husband had belonged to that very regiment.

Dinner was a little late. A guest asked the hostess to play something. Seating herself at the piano, the good woman executed a Chopin nocturne with precision. She finished, and there was still an interval of waiting to be bridged. In the grim silence she turned to an old gentleman on her right and said:

"Would you like a sonata before going in to dinner?"

He gave a start of surprise and pleasure as he responded briskly:

Why, yes, thanks! I had a couple on my way here, but I could stand another."

Music is the universal language of mankind.—*Longfellow.*

I even think that, sentimentally, I am disposed to harmony. But organically I am incapable of a tune.—*Charles Lamb.*

> There's music in the sighing of a reed;
> There's music in the gushing of a rill;
> There's music in all things, if men had ears:
> Their earth is but an echo of the spheres.
> —*Byron.*

MUSICIANS

FATHER—"Well, sonny, did you take your dog to the 'vet' next door to your house, as I suggested?"

Boy—"Yes, sir."

FATHER—"And what did he say?"

Boy—"'E said Towser was suffering from nerves, so Sis had better give up playin' the pianner."

The "celebrated pianiste," Miss Sharpe, had concluded her recital. As the resultant applause was terminating, Mrs. Rochester observed Colonel Grayson wiping his eyes. The old gentleman noticed her look, and, thinking it one of inquiry, began to explain the cause of his sadness. "The girl's playing," he told the lady, "reminded me so much of the playing of her father. He used to be a chum of mine in the Army of the Potomac."

"Oh, indeed!" cooed Mrs. Rochester, with a conventional show of interest. "I never knew her father was a piano-player."

"He wasn't," replied the Colonel. "He was a drummer."

—G. T. Evans.

Recipe for an orchestra leader:
Four hundred and twenty-two movements—
Emanuel, Swedish and Swiss—
It's a wonder the band can keep playing,
You'd think they'd die laughing at this!

—Life.

'Tis God gives skill,
But not without men's hands: He could not make
Antonio Stradivari's violins
Without Antonio.

—George Eliot.

NAMES, PERSONAL

Israel Zangwill, the well-know writer, signs himself I. Zangwill. He was once approached at a reception by a fussy old lady, who demanded, "Oh, Mr. Zangwill, what is your Christian name?"

"Madame, I have none," he gravely assured her.—*John Pearson.*

FRIEND—"So your great Russian actor was a total failure?"

MANAGER—"Yes. It took all our profits to pay for running the electric light sign with his name on it."—*Puck.*

A somewhat unpatriotic little son of Italy, twelve years old, came to his teacher in the public school and asked if he could not have his name changed.

"Why do you wish to change your name?" the teacher asked.

"I want to be an American. I live in America now. I no longer want to be a Dago."

"What American name would you like to have?"

"I have it here," he said, handing the teacher a dirty scrap of paper on which was written—Patrick Dennis McCarty.

A shy young man once said to a young lady: "I wish dear, that we were on such terms of intimacy that you would not mind calling me by my first name."

"Oh," she replied, "your second name is good enough for me."

An American travelling in Europe engaged a courier. Arriving at an inn in Austria, the man asked his servant to enter his name in accordance with the police regulations of that country. Some time after, the man asked the servant if he had complied with his orders.

"Yes, sir," was the reply.

"How did you write my name?" asked the master.

"Well, sir I can't pronounce it," answered the servant, "but I copied it from your portmanteau, sir."

"Why, my name isn't there. Bring me the book." The register was brought, and, instead of the plain American name of two syllables, the following entry was revealed:

"Monsieur Warranted Solid Leather."

—*M. A. Hitchcock.*

The story is told of Helen Hunt, the famous author of "Ramona," that one morning after church service she found a purse full of money and told her pastor about it.

"Very well," he said, "you keep it, and at the evening service I will announce it," which he did in this wise:

"This morning there was found in this church a purse filled with money. If the owner is present he or she can go to Helen Hunt for it."

And the minister wondered why the congregation tittered!

A street-car "masher" tried in every way to attract the attention of the pretty young girl opposite him. Just as he had about given up, the girl, entirely unconscious of what had been going on, happened to glance in his direction. The "masher" immediately took fresh courage.

"It's cold out to-day, isn't it?" he ventured.

The girl smiled and nodded assent, but had nothing to say.

"My name is Specknoodle," he volunteered.

"Oh, I am so sorry," she said sympathetically, as she left the car.

The comedian came on with affected diffidence.

"At our last stand," quoth he, "I noticed a man laughing while I was doing my turn. Honest, now! My, how he laughed! He laughed until he split. Till he split, mind you. Thinks I to myself, I'll just find out about the man and so, when the show was over, I went up to him.

" 'My friend,' says I, 'I've heard that there's nothing in a name, but are you not one of the Wood family?'

" 'I am,' says he, 'and what's more, my grandfather was a Pine!'

"No Wood, you know, splits any easier than a Pine."—*Ramsey Benson.*

"But Eliza," said the mistress, "your little boy was christened George Washington. Why do you call him Izaak Walton? Walton, you know, was the famous fisherman."

"Yes'm," answered Eliza, "but dat chile's repetashun fo' telling de troof made dat change imper'tive."

The mother of the girl baby, herself named Rachel, frankly told her husband that she was tired of the good old names borne by most of the eminent members of the family, and she would like to give the little girl a name entirely different. Then she wrote on a slip of paper "Eugénie," and asked her husband if he didn't think that was a pretty name.

The father studied the name for a moment and then said: "Vell, cal her Yousheenie, but I don't see vat you gain by it."

There was a great swell in Japan,
Whose name on a Tuesday began;
　　It lasted through Sunday
　　Till twilight on Monday,
And sounded like stones in a can.

He was a young lawyer who had just started practicing in a small town and hung his sign outside of his office door. It read: "A. Swindler." A stranger who called to consult him saw the sign and said: "My goodness, man, look at that sign! Don't you see how it reads? Put in your first name—Alexander, Ambrose or whatever it is."

"Oh, yes I know," said the lawyer resignedly, "but I don't exactly like to do it."

"Why not?" asked the client. "It looks mighty bad as it is. What is your first name?"

"Adam."

Who hath not own'd, with rapture-smitten frame,
The power of grace, the magic of a name.

—*Campbell.*

NATIVES

FRIEND (admiring the prodigy)—"Seventh standard, is she? Plays the pianner an' talks French like a native, I'll bet."

FOND BUT "TOUCHY" PARENT—"I've no doubt that's meant to be very funny, Bill Smith; but as it 'appens you're only exposin' your ignorance; they ain't natives in France—they're as white as wot we are."—*Sketch.*

NATURE LOVERS

"Would you mind tooting your factory whistle a little?"

"What for?"

"For my father over yonder in the park. He's a trifle deaf and he hasn't heard a robin this summer."

NAVIGATION

The fog was dense and the boat had stopped when the old lady asked the Captain why he didn't go on.

"Can't see up the river, madam."

"But, Captain," she persisted, "I can see the stars overhead."

"Yes, ma'am," said the Captain, "but until the boilers bust we ain't goin' that way."

NEATNESS

The neatness of the New England housekeeper is a matter of common remark, and husbands in that part of the country are supposed to appreciate their advantages.

A bit of dialogue reported as follows shows that there may be another side to the matter.

"Martha, have you wiped the sink dry yet?" asked the farmer, as he made final preparations for the night.

"Yes, Josiah," she replied. "Why do you ask?"

"Well, I did want a drink, but I guess I can get along until morning."

NEGROES

A colored girl asked the drug clerk for "ten cents' wuth o' cou't-plaster."

"What color," he asked.

"Flesh cullah, suh."

Whereupon the clerk proffered a box of black court plaster.

The girl opened the box with a deliberation that was ominous, but her face was unruffled as she noted the color of the contents and said:

"I ast for flesh cullah, an' you done give me skin cullah."

A cart containing a number of Negro field hands was being drawn by a mule. The driver, a darky of about twenty, was endeavoring to induce the mule to increase its speed, when suddenly the animal let fly with its heels and dealt him such a kick on the head that he was stretched on the ground in a twinkling. He lay rubbing his woolly pate where the mule had kicked him.

"Is he hurt?" asked a stranger anxiously of an older Negro who had jumped from the conveyance and was standing over the prostrate driver.

"No, Boss," was the older man's reply; "dat mule will probably walk kind o' tendah for a day or two, but he ain't hurt."

In certain parts of the West Indies the Negroes speak English with a broad brogue. They are probably descended from the slaves of the Irish adventurers who accompanied the Spanish settlers.

A gentleman from Dublin upon arriving at a West Indian port was accosted by a burly Negro fruit vender with, "Th, top uv th' mornin' to ye, an' would ye be after wantin' to buy a bit o' fruit, sor?"

The Irishman stared at him in amazement.

"An' how long have ye been here?" he finally asked.

"Goin' on three months, yer Honor," said the vender, thinking of the time he had left his inland home.

"Three months, is it? Only three months an' as black as thot? Faith, I'll not land!"

Dinah, crying bitterly, was coming down the street with her feet bandaged.

"Why, what on earth's the matter?" she was asked. "How did you hurt your feet, Dinah?"

"Dat good fo' nothin' nigger [sniffle] done hit me on de haid wif a club while I was standin' on de hard stone pavement."

" 'Liza, what fo' yo' buy dat udder box of shoe-blacknin'?"

"Go on, Nigga', dat ain't shoe-blacknin', dat's ma massage cream!"

"Johnny," said the mother as she vigorously scrubbed the small boy's face with soap and water, "didn't I tell you never to blacken your face again? Here I've been scrubbing for half an hour and it won't come off."

"I-I—ouch!" sputtered the small boy; "I ain't your little boy. I—ouch! I'se Mose, de colored lady's little boy."

The day before she was to be married an old Negro servant came to her mistress and intrusted her savings to her keeping.

"Why should I keep your money for you? I thought you were going to be married?" said the mistress.

"So I is, Missus, but do you 'spose I'd keep all dis yer money in de house wid dat strange nigger?"

A southern colonel had a colored valet by the name of George. George received nearly all the colonel's cast-off clothing. He had his eyes on a certain pair of light trousers which were not wearing out fast enough to suit him, so he thought he would hasten matters somewhat by rubbing grease on one knee. When the colonel saw the spot, he called George and asked if he had noticed it. George said, "Yes, sah, Colonel, I noticed dat spot and tried mighty hard to get it out, but I couldn't."

"Have you tried gasoline?" the colonel asked.

"Yes, sah, Colonel, but it didn't do no good."

"Have you tried brown paper and a hot iron?"

"Yes, sah, Colonel, I'se done tried 'mos' everything I knows of, but dat spot wouldn't come out."

"Well, George, have you tried ammonia?" the colonel asked as a last resort.

"No, sah, Colonel, I ain't tried 'em on yet, but I knows dey'll fit."

A Negro went into a hardware shop and asked to be shown some razors, and after critically examining those submitted to him the would-be purchaser was asked why he did not try a "safety," to which he replied: "I ain' lookin' for that kind. I wants this for social purposes."

Before a house where a colored man had died, a small darkey was standing erect at one side of the door. It was about time for the services to begin, and the parson appeared from within and said to the darkey: "De services are about to begin. Aren't you a-gwine in?"

"I'se would if I'se could, parson," answered the little Negro, "but yo' see I'se de crape."

See also Chicken stealing.

NEIGHBORS

THE MAN AT THE DOOR—"Madame, I'm the piano-tuner."

THE WOMAN—"I didn't send for a piano-tuner."

THE MAN—"I know it, lady; the neighbors did."

NEW JERSEY

"You must have had a terrible experience with no food, and mosquitoes swarming around you," I said to the shipwrecked mariner who had been cast upon the Jersey sands.

"You just bet I had a terrible experience," he acknowledged. "My experience was worse than that of the man who wrote 'Water, water everywhere, but not a drop to drink.' With me it was bites, bites everywhere, but not a bite to eat."

NEW YORK CITY

At a convention of Methodist Bishops held in Washington, the Bishop of New York made a stirring address extolling the powers and possibilities of his state. Bishop Hamilton, of California, like all good Californians, is imbued with the conviction that it would be hard to equal a place he knows of on the Pacific, and following the Bishop of New York he gave a glowing picture of California, concluding:

"Not only is it the best place on earth to live in, but it has superior advantages, too, as a place to die in; for there we have at our threshold the beautiful Golden Gate, while in New York they only have—well, you know which gate it is over at New York!"

One night Dave Warfield was playing at David Belasco's new theatre, supported by one of Mr. Belasco's new companies. The performance ran with a smoothness of a Standard Oil lawyer explaining rebates to a Federal court. A worthy person of the farming classes, sitting in G 14, was plainly impressed. In an interval between the acts he turned to the metropolitan who had the seat next him.

"Where do all them troopers come from?" he inquired.

"I don't think I understand," said the city-dweller.

"I mean them actors up yonder on the stage," explained the man form afar. "Was they brought on specially for this show, or do they live here?"

"I believe most of them live here in town," said the New Yorker.

"Well, they do purty blamed well for home talent," said the stranger.

A traveler in Tennessee came across an aged Negro seated in front of his cabin door basking in the sunshine.

"He could have walked right on the stage for an Uncle Tom part without a line of makeup," says the traveler. "He must have been eighty years of age."

"Good morning, uncle," says the stranger.

"Mornin', sah! Mornin'," said the aged one. Then he added, "Be you the gentleman over yonder from New York?"

Being told that such was the case the old darky said; "Do you mind telling me something that has been botherin' my old haid? I have got a grandson—he runs on the Pullman cyars—and he done tell me that up thar in New York you-all burn up youah folks when they die. He is a poherful liar, and I don't believe him."

"Yes," replied the other, "that is the truth in some cases. We call it cremation."

"Well, you suttenly surprise me," said the Negro and then he paused as if in deep reflection. Finally he said; "You-all know I am a Baptist. I believe in the resurrection and the life everlastin' and the coming of the Angel Gabriel and the blowin' of that great horn, and Lawdy me, how am they evah goin' to find them folks on that great mawnin'?"

It was too great a task for an offhand answer, and the suggestion was made that the aged one consult his minister. Again the Negro fell into a brown study, and then he raised his head and his eyes twinkled merrily, and he said in a soft voice:

"Meanin' no offense, sah, but from what Ah have heard about New York I kinder calcerlate they is a lot of them New York people that doan' wanter be found on that mornin'."

NEWS

Soon after the installation of the telegraph in Fredericksburg, Virginia, a little darky, the son of my father's mammy, saw a piece of newspaper that had blown up on the telegraph wires and caught there. Running to my grandmother in a great state of excitement, he cried, "Miss Liza, come quick! Dem wires done buss and done let all the news out!"

—Sue M. M. Halsey.

"Our whole neighborhood has been stirred up," said the regular reader.

The editor of the country weekly seized his pen. "Tell me about it," he said. "What we want is news. What stirred it up?"

"Plowing," said the farmer.

There is nothing new except what is forgotten.

—Mademoiselle Bertin.

NEWSPAPERS

A kind old gentleman seeing a small boy who was carrying a lot of newspapers under his arm said: "Don't all those papers make you tired, my boy?"

"Naw, I don't read 'em," replied the lad.

Vox Populi—"Do you think you've boosted your circulation by giving a year's subscription for the biggest potato raised in the county?"

The Editor—"Mebbe not; but I got four barrels of samples."

Colonel Highflyer—"What are your rates per column?'
Editor of "Swell Society"—"For insertion or suppression?"

—*Life.*

Editor—"You wish a position as a proofreader?"
Applicant—"Yes, sir."
"Do you understand the requirements of that responsible position?"
"Perfectly, sir. Whenever you make any mistakes in the paper, just blame 'em on me, and I'll never say a word."

A prominent Montana newspaper man was making the round of the insane asylum of that state in an official capacity as an inspector. One of the inmates mistook him for a recent arrival.

"What made you go crazy?"

"I was trying to make money out of the newspaper business," replied the editor, to humor the demented one.

"Rats, you're not crazy; you're just a plain darn fool," was the lunatic's comment.

"Did you write this report on my lecture, 'The Curse of Whiskey'?"

"Yes, madam."

"Then kindly explain what you mean by saying, 'The lecturer was evidently full of her subject!'"

We clip the following for the benefit of those who doubt the power of the press:

"Owing to the overcrowded condition of our columns, a number of births and deaths are unavoidably postponed this week."

"Binks has sued us for libel," announced the assistant editor of the sensational paper.

The managing editor's face brightened.

"Tell him," he said, "that if he will put up a strong fight we'll cheerfully pay the damages and charge them up to the advertising account."

Booth Tarkington says that in no state have the newspapers more "journalistic enterprise" than in his native Indiana. While stopping at a little Hoosier hotel in the course of a hunting trip Mr. Tarkington lost one of his dogs.

"Have you a newspaper in town?" he asked of the landlord.

"Right across the way, there, back of the shoemaker's," the landlord told him. "The *Daily News*—best little paper of its size in the state."

The editor, the printer, and the printer's devil were all busy doing justice to Mr. Tarkington with an "in-our-midst" paragraph when the novelist arrived.

"I've just lost a dog," Tarkington explained after he had introduced himself, "and I'd like to have you insert this ad for me: 'Fifty dollars reward for the return of a pointer dog answering to the name of Rex. Disappeared from the yard of the Mansion House Monday night.'"

Why, we are just going to press, sir," the editor said, "but we'll be only too glad to hold the edition for your ad."

Mr. Tarkington returned to the hotel. After a few minutes he decided, however, that it might be well to add, "No questions asked" to his advertisement, and returned to the *Daily News* office.

The place was deserted, save for the skinny little freckle-faced devil, who sat perched on a high stool, gazing wistfully out of the window.

"Where is everybody?" Tarkington asked.

"Gawn to hunt for th' dawg," replied the boy.

"You are the greatest inventor in the world," exclaimed a newspaper man to Alexander Graham Bell.

"Oh, no, my friend, I'm not," said Professor Bell. "I've never been a reporter."

Not long ago a city editor in Ottumwa, Iowa, was told over the telephone that a prominent citizen had just died suddenly. He called a reporter and told him to rush out and get the "story." Twenty minutes later the reporter returned, sat down at his desk, and began to rattle off copy on his typewriter.

"Well, what about it?" asked the city editor.

"Oh, nothing much," replied the reporter, without looking

up. "He was walking along the street when he suddenly clasped his hands to his heart and said, 'I'm going to die!' Then he leaned up against a fence and made good."

Enraged over something the local newspaper had printed about him, a subscriber burst into the editor's office in search of the responsible reporter. "Who are you?" he demanded, glaring at the editor, who was also the main stockholder. "I'm the newspaper," was the calm reply. "And who are you?" he next inquired, turning his resentful gaze on the chocolate-colored office-devil clearing out the waste basket. "Me?" rejoined the darky, grinning from ear to ear. "Ah guess ah's de cul'ud supplement."

Four hostile newspapers are more to be feared than a thousand bayonets.—*Napoleon I.*

Newspapers always excite curiosity. No one ever lays one down without a feeling of disappointment.—*Charles Lamb.*

OBESITY

See Corpulence.

OBITUARIES

If you have frequent fainting spells, accompanied by chills, cramps, corns, bunions, chilblains, epilepsy and jaundice, it is a sign that you are not well, but liable to die any minute. Pay your subscription in advance and thus make yourself solid for a good obituary notice.—*Mountain Echo.*

See also Epitaphs.

OBSERVATION

In his daily half hour confidential talk with his boy an ambitious father tried to give some good advice.

"Be observing, my son," said the father on one occasion. "Cultivate the habit of seeing, and you will be a successful man. Study things and remember them. Don't go through the world blindly. Learn to use your eyes. Boys who are observing know a great deal more than those who are not."

Willie listened in silence.

Several days later when the entire family, consisting of his mother, aunt and uncle, were present, his father said:

"Well, Willie, have you kept using your eyes as I advised you to do?"

Willie nodded, and after a moment's hesitation said:

"I've seen a few things right around the house. Uncle Jim's got a bottle of hair dye hid under his trunk, Aunt Jennie's got an extra set of teeth in her dresser, Ma's got some curls in her hat, and Pa's got a deck of cards and a box of chips behind the books in the secretary."

OCCUPATIONS

Mrs. Hennessey, who was a late arrival in the neighborhood, was entertaining a neighbor one afternoon, when the latter inquired:

"An' what does your old man do, Mrs. Hennessey?"

"Sure, he's a di'mond-cutter."

"Ye don't mane it!"

Yis; he cuts th' grass off th' baseball grounds."

—*L. F. Clarke.*

All business men are apt to use the technical terms of their daily labors in situations outside of working hours. One time a railroad man was entertaining his pastor at dinner and his sons, who had to wait until their elders had finished got into mischief. At the end of the meal, their father excused himself for a moment saying he had to "switch some empties."

"Professor," said Miss Skylight, "I want you to suggest a course in life for me. I have thought of journalism——"

"What are your own inclinations?"

"Oh, my soul yearns and throbs and pulsates with an ambition to give the world a life-work that shall be marvelous in its scope, and weirdly entrancing in the vastness of its structural beauty!"

"Woman, you're born to be a milliner."

A woman, when asked her husband's occupation, said he was a mixologist. The city directory called him a bartender.

"A good turkey dinner and mince pie," said a well-known after-dinner orator, "always puts us in a lethargic mood—makes us feel, in fact, like the natives of Nola Chucky. In Nola Chucky one day I said to a man:

" 'What is the principal occupation of this town?'

" 'Wall, boss,' the man answered, yawning, 'in winter they mostly sets on the east side of the house and follers the sun around to the west, and in summer they sets on the west side and follers the shade around to the east.' "

JONES—"How'd this happen? The last time I was here you were running a fish-market, and now you've got a cheese-shop."

SMITH—"Yes. Well, you see the doctor said I needed a change of air."

The ugliest of trades have their moments of pleasure. Now, if I were a grave-digger, or even a hangman, there are some people I could work for with a great deal of enjoyment.

—*Douglas Jerrold.*

OCEAN

A resident of Nahant tells this one on a new servant his wife took down from Boston.

"Did you sleep well, Mary?" the girl was asked the following morning.

"Sure, I did not, ma'am," was the reply; "the snorin' of the ocean kept me awake all night."

Love the sea? I dote upon it—from the beach.

—*Douglas Jerrold.*

I never was on the dull, tame shore,
But I loved the great sea more and more.

—*Barry Cornwall.*

OFFICE BOYS

"Have you had any experience as an office-boy?"

"I should say I had, mister; why, I'm a dummy director in three mining-companies now."

OFFICE-SEEKERS

A gentleman, not at all wealthy, who had at one time represented in Congress, through a couple of terms a district not far from the national capitol, moved to California where in a year or so he rose to be sufficiently prominent to become a congressional subject, and he was visited by the central committee of his district to be talked to.

"We want you," said the spokesman, "to accept the nomination for Congress."

"I can't do it, gentlemen," he responded promptly.

"You must," the spokesman demanded.

"But I can't," he insisted. "I'm too poor."

"Oh, that will be all right; we've got plenty of money for the campaign."

"But that is nothing," contended the gentleman; "it's the expense in Washington. I've been there, and know all about it."

"Well you didn't lose by it, and it doesn't cost any more because you come from California."

The gentleman became very earnest.

"Doesn't it?" he exclaimed in a business-like tone. "Why my dear sirs, I used to have to send home every month about half a dozen busted office-seeker constituents, and the fare was only $3 apiece, and I could stand it, but it would cost me over $100 a head to send them out here, and I'm no millionaire; therefore, as much as I regret it, I must insist on declining."

"On a trip to Washington," said Col. W. F. Cody. "I had for a companion Sousa, the band leader. We had berths opposite each other. Early one monring as we approached the capital I thought I would have a little fun. I got a morning paper, and, after rustling it a few minutes, I said to Sousa:

" 'That's the greatest order Cleveland has just issued!'

" 'What's that?' came from the opposite berth.

" 'Why he's ordered all the office-seekers rounded up at the depot and sent home.'

"You should have seen the general consternation that ensued. From almost every berth on the car a head came out from between the curtains, and with one accord nearly every man shouted:

" 'What's that?' "

OLD AGE

See Age.

OLD MASTERS

See Paintings.

ONIONS

Can the Burbanks of the glorious West
  Either make or buy or sell
An onion with an onion's taste
  But with a violet's smell?

SHE—"They say that an apple a day will keep the doctor away."

HE—"Why stop there? An onion a day will keep everybody away."

OPERA

"Which do you consider the most melodious Wagnerian opera?" asked Mrs. Cumrox.

"There are several I haven't heard, aren't there?" rejoined her husband.

"Yes."

"Then I guess it's one of them."

OPPORTUNITY

Many a man creates his own lack of opportunities.—*Life.*

Who seeks, and will not take when once 'tis offer'd,
Shall never find it more.

—*Shakespeare.*

In life's small things be resolute and great
To keep thy muscles trained; know'st thou when fate
Thy measure takes? or when she'll say to thee,
"I find thee worthy, do this thing for me!"

—*Emerson.*

OPTIMISM

Optimism is Worry on a spree.—*Judge.*

An optimist is a man who doesn't care what happens just so it doesn't happen to him.

An optimist is the fellow who doesn't know what's coming to him.—*J. J. O'Connell.*

An optimist is a woman who thinks that everything is for the best, and that she is the best.—*Judge.*

A political optimist is a fellow who can make sweet, pink lemonade out of the bitter yellow fruit which his opponents hand him.

Mayor William S. Jordan, at a Democratic banquet in Jacksonville, said of optimism:

"Let us cultivate optimism and hopefulness. There is nothing like it. The optimistic man can see a bright side to everything —everything.

"A missionary in a slum once laid his hand on a man's shoulder and said:

"'Friend, do you hear the solemn ticking of that clock? Tick-tack; tick-tack. And oh, friend, do you know what day it inexorably and relentlessly brings nearer?'"

"'Yes—pay day,' the other, an honest, optimistic working-man, replied"

A Scotsman who has a keen appreciation of the strong characteristics of his countrymen delights in the story of a druggist known both for his thrift and his philosophy.

Once he was aroused from a deep sleep by the ringing of his night bell. He went down to his little shop and sold a dose of rather nauseous medicine to a distressed customer.

"What profit do you make out o' that?" grumbled his wife.

"A ha'penny," was the cheerful answer.

"And for that bit of money you'll lie awake maybe an hour," she said impatiently.

"Never grumble o'er that, woman," was his placid answer. "The dose will keep him awake all night. We must thank heaven we ha' the profit and none o' the pain o' this transaction."

A German shoemaker left the gas turned on in his shop one night and upon arriving in the morning struck a match to light it.

There was a terrific explosion, and the shoemaker was blown out through the door almost to the middle of the street.

A passer-by rushed to his assistance, and, after helping him to rise, inquired if he was injured.

The little German gazed at his place of business, which was now burning quite briskly, and said:

"No, I ain't hurt. But I got out shust in time, eh?"

> My own hope is, a sun will pierce
> The thickest cloud earth ever stretched;
> That, after Last, returns the First,
> Tho' a wide compass round be fetched;
> That what began best, can't prove worst,
> Nor what God blessed once, prove accursed.
>
> —*Browning.*

ORATORS

It is narrated that Colonel Breckenridge, meeting Majah Buffo'd on the streets of Lexington one day asked: "What's the meaning, suh, of the conco's befor' the co't house?"

To which the majah replied:

"General Buckneh is making a speech. General Buckneh, suh, is a bo'n oratah."

"What do you mean by bo'n oratah?"

"If you or I, suh, were asked how much two and two make, we would reply 'foh.' When this is asked of a bo'n oratah, he replies: 'When in the co'se of human events it becomes necessary to take an integah of the second denomination and add it, suh, to an integah of the same denomination, the result, suh——and I have the science of mathematics to back me up in my judgment—the result, suh, and I say it without feah of successful contradiction, suh—the result is fo'.' That's a bo'n oratah."

When Demosthenes was asked what was the first part of Oratory, he answered, "Action," and which was the second, he replied, "Action," and which was the third, he still answered "Action."—*Plutarch.*

OUTDOOR LIFE

One day, in the spring of '74, Cap Smith's freight outfit pulled into Helena, Montana. After unloading the freight, the "mule-skinners," to a man, repaired to the Combination Gambling House and proceeded to load themselves. Late in the afternoon, Zeb White, Smith's oldest skinner, having exchanged all of his hard coin for liquid refreshment, zigzagged into the corral, crawled under a wagon, and went to sleep. After supper, Smith, making his nightly rounds, happened on the sleeping Zeb.

"Kinder chilly, ain't it?" he asked, after earnestly prodding Zeb with a convenient stick.

"I reckon 'tis," Zeb drowsily mumbled.

"Ain't yer 'fraid ye'll freeze?"

"'Tis cold, ain't it? Say, Cap, jest throw on another wagon, will yer?"

PAINTING

See Art.

PAINTINGS

She had engaged a maid recently from the country, and was now employed in showing her newly acquired treasure over the house and enlightening her in regard to various duties, etc. At last they reached the best room. "These," said the mistress of the house, pausing before an extensive row of masculine portraits, "are very valuable, and you must be very careful when dusting. They are old masters." Mary's jaw dropped, and a look of intense wonder overspread her rubicund face.

"Lor', mum," she gasped, gazing with bulging eyes on the face of her new employer, "lor', mum, who'd ever 'ave thought you'd been married all these times!"

A picture is a poem without words.—*Cornificus.*

PANICS

One night at a theatre some scenery took fire, and a very perceptible odor of burning alarmed the spectators. A panic seemed to be imminent, when an actor appeared on the stage.

"Ladies and gentlemen," he said, "compose yourselves. There is no danger."

The audience did not seem reassured.

"Ladies and gentlemen," continued the comedian, rising to the necessity of the occasion, "confound it all—do you think if there was any danger I'd be here?"

The panic collapsed.

PARENTS

William, aged five, had been reprimanded by his father for interrupting while his father was telling his mother about the new telephone for their house. He sulked awhile, then went to his mother, and, patting her on the cheeks, said, "Mother dear, I love you."

"Don't you love me too?" asked his father.

Without glancing at him, William said disdainfully, "The wire's busy."

"What does your mother say when you tell her those dreadful lies?"

"She says I take after father."

"A little lad was desperately ill, but refused to take the medicine the doctor had left. At last his mother gave him up.

"Oh, my boy will die; my boy will die," she sobbed.

But a voice spoke from the bed, "Don't cry, mother. Father'll be home soon and he'll make me take it."

Mrs. White was undoubtedly the disciplinarian of the family. The master of the house, a professor, and consequently a very busy man, was regarded by the children as one of themselves, subject to the laws of "Mother."

Mrs. White had been ill for some weeks and although the father felt that the children were showing evidence of running wild, he seemed powerless to correct the fault. One evening at dinner, however, he felt obliged to reprimand Marion severely.

"Marion," he said, sternly, "stop that at once, or I shall take you from the table and punish you soundly."

He experienced a feeling of profound satisfaction in being able to thus reprove when it was necessary and glanced across the table expecting to see a very demure little miss. Instead, Marion and her little brother exchanged glances and then simultaneously a grin overspread their faces, while Marion said in a mirthful tone:

"Oh, Francis, hear father trying to talk like mother!"

Robert has lately acquired a stepmother. Hoping to win his affection this new parent has been very lenient with him, while his father, feeling his responsibility, has been unusually strict. The boys of the neighborhood, who had taken pains to warn Robert of the terrible character of stepmothers in general, recently waited for him in a body, and the following conversation was overheard:

"How do you like your stepmother, Bob?"

"Like her! Why fellers, I just love her. All I wish is I had a stepfather, too."

"Well, Bobby, what do you want to be when you grow up?"

Bobby (remembering private seance in the wood-shed)— "A orphan."

Little Eleanor's mother was an American, while her father was a German.

One day, after Eleanor had been subjected to rather severe disciplinary measures at the hands of her father, she called her mother into another room, closed the door significantly, and said: "Mother, I don't want to meddle in your business, but I wish you'd send that husband of yours back to Germany."

The lawyer was sitting at his desk absorbed in the preparation of a brief. So bent was he on his work that he did not hear the door as it was pushed gently open, nor see the curly head that was thrust into his office. A little sob attracted his notice, and, turning he saw a face that was streaked with tears and told plainly that feelings had been hurt.

"Well, my little man, did you want to see me?"

"Are you a lawyer?"

"Yes. What do you want?"

"I want"—and there was resolute ring in his voice—"I want a divorce from my papa and mama."

PARROTS

Pat had but a limited knowledge of the bird kingdom. One day, walking down the street, he noticed a green bird in a cage, talking and singing. Thinking to pet it he stroked its head. The bird turned quickly, screaming, "Hello! What do you want?" Pat shied off like a frightened horse, lifting his hat and bowing politely as he stuttered out: "Ex-excuse me s-sir, I thought you was a burrd!"

PARTNERSHIP

A West Virginia darky, a blacksmith, recently announced a change in his business as follows: "Notice—De co-pardnership heretofore resisting between me and Mose Skinner is hereby resolved. Dem what owe de firm will settle wid me, and dem what de firm owes will settle wid Mose."

PASSWORDS

"I want to change my password," said the man who had for two years rented a safety-deposit box.

"Very well," replied the man in charge. "What is the old one?"

"Gladys."

"And what do you wish the new one to be?"

"Mabel. Gladys has gone to Reno."

Senator Tillman not long ago piloted a plain farmer-constituent around the Capitol for a while, and then, having some work to do on the floor, conducted him to the Senate gallery.

After an hour or so the visitor approached a gallery door-keeper and said: "My name is Swate. I am a friend of Senator Tillman. He brought me here and I want to go out and look around a bit. I thought I would tell you so I can get back in."

"That's all right," said the doorkeeper, "but I may not be here when you return. In order to prevent any mistake I will give you the password so you can get your seat again."

Swate's eyes rather popped out at this. "What's the word?" he asked.

"Idiosyncrasy."

"What?"

"Idiosyncrasy."

"I guess I'll stay in," said Swate.

PATIENCE

"Your husband seems to be very impatient lately."

"Yes, he is, very."

"What is the matter with him?"

"He is getting tired waiting for a chance to get out where he can sit patiently hour after hour waiting for a fish to nibble at his bait."

PATRIOTISM

General Gordon, the Confederate commander, used to tell the following story: He was sitting by the roadside one blazing hot day when a dilapidated soldier, his clothing in rags, a shoe lacking, his head bandaged, and his arm in a sling, passed him. He was soliloquizing in this manner:

"I love my country. I'd fight for my country. I'd starve and go thirsty for my country. I'd die for my country. But if ever this damn war is over I'll never love another country!"

A snobbish young Englishman visiting Washington's home at Mount Vernon was so patronizing as to arouse the wrath of guards and caretakers; but it remained for "Shep" Wright, an aged gardener and one of the first scouts of the Confederate army, to settle the gentleman. Approaching "Shep," the Englishman said:

"Ah—er—my man, the hedge! Yes, I see, George got this hedge from dear old England."

"Reckon he did," replied "Shep." "He got this whole blooming country from England."

Speaking of the policy of the Government of the United States with respect to its troublesome neighbors in Central and South America, "Uncle Joe" Cannon told of a Missouri congressman who is decidedly opposed to any interference in this regard by our country. It seems that this spring the Missourian met an Englishman at Washington with whom he conversed touching affairs in the localities mentioned. The westerner asserted his usual views with considerable forcefulness, winding up with this observation:

"The whole trouble is that we Americans need a — good licking!"

"You do, indeed!" promptly asserted the Britisher, as if pleased by the admission. But his exultation was of brief duration, for the Missouri man immediately concluded with:

"But there ain't nobody can do it!"

A number of Confederate prisoners, during the Civil War, were detained at one of the western military posts under conditions much less unpleasant than those to be found in the ordinary military prison. Most of them appreciated their comparatively good fortune. One young fellow, though, could not be reconciled to association with Yankees under any circumstances, and took advantage of every opportunity to express his feelings. He was continually rubbing it in about the battle of Chickamauga, which had just been fought with such disastrous results for the Union forces.

"Maybe we didn't eat you up at Chickamauga!" was the way he generally greeted a bluecoat.

The Union men, when they could stand it no longer, reported the matter to General Grant. Grant summoned the prisoner.

"See here," said Grant, "I understand that you are continually insulting the men here with reference to the battle of Chickamauga. They have borne with you long enough, and I'm going to give you your choice of two things. You will either take the oath of allegiance to the United States, or be sent to a Northern prison. Choose."

The prisoner was silent for some time. "Well," he said at last, in a resigned tone, "I reckon, General, I'll take the oath."

The oath was duly administered. Turning to Grant, the fellow then asked, very penitently, if he might speak.

"Yes," said the general indifferently. "What is it?"

"Why, I was just thinkin', General," he drawled, "they certainly did give us hell at Chickamauga."

Historical controversies are creeping into the schools. In a New York public institution attended by many races, during an examination in history the teacher asked a little chap who discovered America.

He was evidently thrown into a panic and hesitated, much to the teacher's surprise, to make any reply.

"Oh, please, ma'am," he finally stammered, "ask me somethin' else."

"Something else, Jimmy? Why should I do that?"

"The fellers was talkin' 'bout it yesterday," replied Jimmy. "Pat McGee said it was discovered by an Irish saint. Olaf, he said it was a sailor from Norway, and Giovanni said it was Columbus, an' if you'd a-seen what happened you wouldn't ask a little feller like me."

Our country! When right to be kept right; when wrong to be put right!—*Carl Schurz.*

Our country! In her intercourse with foreign nations, may she always be in the right; but our country, right or wrong.
—*Stephen Decatur.*

There are no points of the compass on the chart of true patriotism.—*Robert C. Winthrop.*

Patriotic exercises and flag worship will avail nothing unless the states give to their people of the kind of government that arouses patriotism.—*Franklin Pierce II.*

PENSIONS

WILLIS—"I wonder if there will ever be universal peace."

GILLIS—"Sure. All they've got to do is to get the nations to agree that in case of war the winner pays the pensions."
—*Puck.*

"Why was it you never married again, Aunt Sallie?" inquired Mrs. McClane of an old colored woman in West Virginia.

"'Deed, Miss Ellie," replied the old woman earnestly, "dat daid nigger's wuth moah to me dan a live one. I gits a pension."—*Edith Howell Armor.*

If England had a system of pensions like ours, we should see that "all that was left of the Noble Six Hundred" was six thousand pensioners.

PESSIMISM

A pessimist is a man who lives with an optimist.—*Frances Wilson.*

How happy are the Pessimists!
A bliss without alloy
Is theirs when they have proved to us
There's no such thing as joy!
—*Harold Susman.*

A pessimist is one who, of two evils, chooses them both.

"I had a mighty queer surprise this morning," remarked a local stock broker. "I put on my last summer's thin suit on account of this extraordinary hot weather, and in one of the trousers pockets I found a big roll of bills which I had entirely forgotten."

"Were any of them receipted?" asked a pessimist.

To tell men that they cannot help themselves is to fling them into recklessness and despair.—*Froude.*

> With earth's first clay they did the last man knead,
> And there of the last harvest sowed the seed:
> And the first morning of creation wrote
> What the last dawn of reckoning shall read.

> Yesterday this day's madness did prepare;
> Tomorrow's silence, triumph, or despair.
> Drink! For you know not whence you came, nor why;
> Drink! For you know not why you go, nor where.
> > —*Omar Khayyam.*

PHILADELPHIA

A Staten Island man, when the mosquitoes began to get busy in the borough across the bay, has been in the habit every summer of transplanting his family to the Delaware Water Gap for a few weeks. They were discussing their plans the other day, when the oldest boy, aged eight, looked up from his geography and said:

"Pop, Philadelphia is on the Delaware River, isn't it?"

Pop replied that such was the case.

"I wonder if that's what makes the Delaware Water Gap?" insinuated the youngster.—*S. S. Stinson.*

Among the guests at an informal dinner in New York was a bright Philadelphia girl.

"These are snails," said a gentleman next to her, when the dainty was served. "I suppose Philadelphia people don't eat them for fear of cannibalism."

"Oh, no," was her instant reply; "it isn't that. We couldn't catch them."

PHILANTHROPISTS

Little grains of short weight,
Little crooked twists,
Fill the land with magnates
And philanthropists.

See also Charity.

PHILOSOPHY

Philosophy is finding out how many things there are in the world which you can't have if you want them, and don't want if you can have them.—*Puck*.

PHYSICIANS AND SURGEONS

The eight-year-old son of a Baltimore physician, together with a friend, was playing in his father's office, during the absence of the doctor, when suddenly the first lad threw open a closet door and disclosed to the terrified gaze of his little friend an articulated skeleton.

When the visitor had sufficiently recovered from his shock to stand the announcement the doctor's son explained that his father was extremely proud of that skeleton.

"Is he?" asked the other. "Why?"

"I don't know," was the answer; "maybe it was his first patient."

The doctor stood by the bedside, and looked gravely down at the sick man.

"I can not hide from you the fact that you are very ill," he said. "Is there any one you would like to see?"

"Yes," said the sufferer faintly.

"Who is it?"

"Another doctor."—*Judge*.

"Doctor, I want you to look after my office while I'm on my vacation."

"But I've just graduated, doctor. Have had no experience."

"That's all right, my boy. My practice is strictly fashionable. Tell the men to play golf and ship the lady patients off to Europe."

An old darky once lay seriously ill of fever and was treated for a long time by one doctor, and then another doctor, for some reason, came and took the first one's place. The second physician made a thorough examination of the patient. At the end he said, "Did the other doctor take your temperature?"

"Ah dunno, sah," the patient answered. "Ah hain't missed nuthin' so far but mah watch."

There had been an epidemic of colds in the town, and one physician who had had scarcely any sleep for two days called upon a patient—an Irishman—who was suffering from pneumonia, and as he leaned over to hear the patient's respiration he called upon Pat to count.

The doctor was so fatigued that he fell asleep, with his ear on the sick man's chest. It seemed but a minute when he suddenly awoke to hear Pat still counting: "Tin thousand an' sivinty-six, tin thousand an' sivinty-sivin—"

First Doctor—"I operated on him for appendicitis."

Second Doctor—"What was the matter with him?"—*Life.*

Fussy Lady Patient—"I was suffering so much, doctor, that I wanted to die."

Doctor—"You did right to call me in, dear lady."

Medical Student—"What did you operate on that man for?"

Eminent Surgeon—"Two hundred dollars."

Medical Student—"I mean what did he have?"

Eminent Surgeon—"Two hundred dollars."

The three degrees in medical treatment—Positive, ill; comparative, pill; superlative, bill.

"What caused the coolness between you and that young doctor? I thought you were engaged."

"His writing is rather illegible. He sent me a note calling for 10,000 kisses."

"Well?"

"I thought it was a prescription, and took it to the druggist to be filled."

A tourist while traveling in the north of Scotland, far away from anywhere, exclaimed to one of the natives: "Why, what do you do when any of you are ill? You can never get a doctor."

"Nae, sir," replied Sandy. "We've jist to dee a naitural death."

When the physician gives you medicine and tells you to take it, you take it. "Yours not to reason why; yours but to do and die."

Physicians, of all men, are most happy: whatever good success soever they have, the world proclaimeth; and what faults they commit, the earth covereth.—*Quarles.*

> This is the way that physicians mend or end us,
> Secundum artem: but although we sneer
> In health—when ill, we call them to attend us,
> Without the least propensity to jeer.
>
> —*Byron.*

See also Bills.

PICKPOCKETS

See Thieves; Wives.

PINS

"Oh, dear!" sighed the wife as she was dressing for a dinner-party, "I can't find a pin anywhere. I wonder where all the pins go to, anyway?"

"That's a difficult question to answer," replied her husband, "because they are always pointed in one direction and headed in another."

PITTSBURGH

"How about that airship?"

"It went up in smoke."

"Burned, eh?"

"Oh, no. Made an ascension at Pittsburgh."

SKYBOUGH—"Why have you put the vacuum cleaner in front of your airship?"

KLOUDLEIGH—"To clear a path. I have an engagement to sail over Pittsburgh."

A man just back from South America was describing a volcanic disturbance.

"I was smoking a cigar before the door of my hotel," said he, "when I was startled by a rather violent earthquake. The next instant the sun was obscured and darkness settled over the city. Looking in the direction of the distant volcano, I saw heavy clouds of smoke rolling from it, with an occasional tongue of flame flashing against the dark sky.

"Some of the natives about me were on their knees praying; others darted aimlessly about, crazed with terror and shouting for mercy. The landlord of the hotel rushed out and seized me by the arm.

"'To the harbor!' he cried in my ear.

"Together we hurried down the narrow street. As we panted along, the dark smoke whirled in our faces, and a dangerous shower of red-hot cinders sizzled about us. Do you know, I don't believe I was ever so homesick in all my life!"

"Homesick?" gasped the listener. "Homesick at a time like that?"

"Sure. I live in Pittsburgh, you know."

PLAY

The mother heard a great commotion, as of cyclones mixed up with battering-rams, and she hurried upstairs to discover what was the matter. There she found Tommie sitting in the middle of the floor with a broad smile on his face.

"Oh, Mama," said he delightedly, "I've locked Grandpa and Uncle George in the cupboard, and when they get a little angrier I am going to play Daniel in the lion's den."

PLEASURE

BILLY—"Huh! I bet you didn't have a good time at your birthday party yesterday."

WILLIE—"I bet I did."

BILLY—"Then why ain't you sick today?"

Winnie had been very naghty, and her mamma said: "Don't you know you will never go to Heaven if you are so naughty?"

After thinking a moment she said: "Oh, well, I have been to the circus once and 'Uncle Tom's Cabin' twice. I can't expect to go everywhere."

In Concord, New Hampshire, they tell of an old chap who made his wife keep a cash account. Each week he would go over it, growling and grumbling. On one such occasion he delivered himself of the following:

"Look here, Sarah, mustard-plasters, fifty cents; three teeth extracted, two dollars! There's two dollars and a half in one week spent for your own private pleasure. Do you think I am made of money?"

Here's to beauty, wit and wine and to a full stomach, a full purse and a light heart.

> A dinner, coffee and cigars,
> Of friends, a half a score.
> Each favorite vintage in its turn,—
> What man could wish for more?

The roses of pleasure seldom last long enough to adorn the brow of him who plucks them; for they are the only roses which do not retain their sweetness after they have lost their beauty.—*Hannah More.*

See also Amusements.

POETRY

Poetry is a gift we are told, but most editors won't take it even at that.

POETS

EDITOR—"Have you submitted this poem anywhere else?"
JOKESMITH—"No, sir."
EDITOR—"Then where did you get that black eye?"—*Satire.*

"Why is it," asked the persistent poetess, "that you always insist that we write on one side of the paper only? Why not on both?"
In that moment the editor experienced an access of courage—courage to protest against the accumulated wrongs of his kind.
"One side of the paper, madame," he made answer, "is in the nature of a compromise."
"A compromise?"
"A compromise. What we really desire, if we could have our way, is not one, or both, but neither."

Sir Lewis Morris was complaining to Oscar Wilde about the neglect of his poems by the press. "It is a complete conspiracy of silence against me, a conspiracy of silence. What ought I to do, Oscar?" "Join it," replied Wilde.

God's prophets of the Beautiful,
These Poets were.
—*E. B. Browning.*

We call those poets who are first to mark
Through earth's dull mist the coming of the dawn,—
Who see in twilight's gloom the first pale spark,
While others only note that day is gone.

                                        —*O. W. Holmes.*

POLICE

A man who was "wanted" in Russia had been photographed in six different positions, and the pictures duly circulated among the police department. A few days later the chief of police wrote to headquaters: "Sir, I have duly received the portraits of the six miscreants. I have arrested five of them, and the sixth will be secured shortly."

"I had a message from the Black Hand," said the resident of Graftburg. "They told me to leave $2,000 in a vacant house in a certain street."

"Did you tell the police?"

"Right away."

"What did they do?"

"They said that while I was about it I might leave them a couple of thousand in the same place."

Recipe for a policeman:

To a quart of boiling temper add a pint of Irish stew
   Together with cracked nuts, long beats and slugs;
Serve hot with mangled citizens who ask the time of day—
   The receipt is much the same for making thugs.

                                        —*Life.*

See also Servants.

POLITENESS

See Courtesy; Etiquet.

POLITICAL PARTIES

Zoo Superintendent—"What was all the rumpus out there this morning?"

ATTENDANT—"The bull moose and the elephant were fighting over their feed."

"What happened?"

"The donkey ate it."—*Life.*

POLITICIANS

Politicians always belong to the opposite party.

The man who goes into politics as a business has no business to go into politics.—*Life.*

A political orator, evidently better acquainted with western geography than with the language of the Greeks, recently exclaimed with fervor that his principles should prevail "from Alpha to Omaha."

POLITICIAN—"Congratulate me, my dear, I've won the nomination."

HIS WIFE (in surprise)—"Honestly?"

POLITICIAN—"Now what in thunder did you want to bring up that point for?"

"What makes you think the baby is going to be a great politician?" asked the young mother, anxiously.

"I'll tell you," answered the young father, confidently; "he can say more things that sound well and mean nothing at all than any kid I ever saw."

"The mere proposal to set the politician to watch the capitalist has been disturbed by the rather disconcerting discovery that they are both the same man. We are past the point where being a capitalist is the only way of becoming a politician, and we are dangerously near the point where being a politician is much the quickest way of becoming a capitalist."—*G. K. Chesterton.*

At a political meeting the speakers and the audience were much annoyed and disturbed by a man who constantly called out: "Mr. Henry! Henry, Henry, Henry! I call for Mr.

Henry!" After several interruptions of this kind during each speech, a young man ascended the platform, and began an eloquent and impassioned speech in which he handled the issues of the day with easy familiarity. He was in the midst of a glowing period when suddenly the old cry echoed thru the hall: "Mr. Henry! Henry, Henry, Henry! I call for Mr. Henry!" With a word to the speaker, the chairman stepped to the front of the platform and remarked that it would oblige the audience very much if the gentleman in the rear of the hall would refrain from any further calls for Mr. Henry, as that gentleman was then addressing the meeting.

"Mr. Henry? Is that Mr. Henry?" came in astonished tones from the rear. "Thunder! that can't be him. Why, that's the young man that asked me to call for Mr. Henry."

A political speaker, while making a speech, paused in the midst of it and exclaimed: "Now gentlemen, what do you think?"

A man rose in the assembly, and with one eye partially closed, replied modestly, with a strong Scotch brogue: "I think, sir, I do, indeed, sir—I think if you and I were to stump the country together we could tell more lies than any other two men in the country, sir, and I'd not say a word myself during the whole time, sir."

The Rev. Dr. Biddell tells a lively story about a Presbyterian minister who had a young son, a lad about ten years of age. He was endeavoring to bring him up in the way he should go, and was one day asked by a friend what he intended to make of him. In reply he said:

"I am watching the indications. I have a plan which I propose trying with the boy. It is this: I am going to place in my parlor a Bible, an apple and a silver dollar. Then I am going to leave the room and call in the boy. I am going to watch him from some convenient place without letting him know that he is seen. Then, if he chooses the Bible, I shall make a preacher of him; if he takes the apple, a farmer he shall be; but if he chooses the dollar, I will make him a business man."

The plan was carried out. The arrangements were made and the boy called in from his play. After a little while the preacher and his wife softly entered the room. There was the youngster. He was seated on the Bible, in one hand was the apple, from which he was just taking a bite, and in the other he clasped the silver dollar. The good man turned to his consort. "Wife," he said, "the boy is a hog. I shall make a politician of him."

Senator Mark Hanna was walking through his mill one day when he heard a boy say:

"I wish I had Hanna's money and he was in the poorhouse."

When he returned to the office the senator sent for the lad, who was plainly mystified by the summons.

"So you wish you had my money and I was in the poorhouse," said the great man grimly. "Now supposing you had your wish, what would you do?"

"Well," said the boy quickly, his droll grin showing his appreciation of the situation, "I guess I'd get you out of the poorhouse the first thing."

Mr. Hanna roared with laughter and dismissed the youth.

"You might as well push that boy along," he said to one of his assistants; "he's too good a politician to be kept down."

See also Candidates; Public Speakers.

POLITICS

Politics consists of two sides and a fence.

If I were asked to define politics in relation to the British public, I should define it as a spasm of pain recurring once in every four or five years.—*A. E. W. Mason.*

Little Clarence (who has an inquiring mind)—"Papa, the Forty Thieves——"

Mr. Callipers—"Now, my son, you are too young to talk politics."—*Puck.*

"Many a man," remarked the milk toast philosopher, "has gone into politics with a fine future, and come out with a terrible past."

Lord Dufferin delivered an address before the Greek class of the McGill University about which a reporter wrote:

"His lordship spoke to the class in the purest ancient Greek, without mispronouncing a word or making the slightest grammatical solecism."

"Good heavens!" remarked Sir Hector Langevin to the late Sir John A. Macdonald, "how did the reporter know that!"

"I told him," was the Conservative statesman's answer.

"But you don't know Greek."

"True; but I know a little about politics."

Little Millie's father and grandfather were Republicans; and, as election drew near, they spoke of their opponents with increasing warmth, never heeding Millie's attentive ears and wondering eyes.

One night, however, as the little maid was preparing for bed, she whispered in a frightened voice: "Oh, mamma, I don't dare to go upstairs. I'm afraid there's a Democrat under the bed."

"The shortest after-dinner speech I ever heard," said Cy Warman, the poet, "was at a dinner in Providence."

"A man was assigned to the topic, 'The Christian in Politics.' When he was called upon he arose, bowed and said: 'Mr. Chairman, ladies and gentlemen: The Christian in Politics— he ain't.'"

Politics is but the common pulse-beat of which revolution is the fever spasm.—*Wendell Phillips.*

POVERTY

Poverty is no disgrace, but that's about all that can be said in its favor.

A traveler passing through the Broad Top Mountain district in northern Bedford County, Pennsylvania, last summer, came across a lad of sixteen cultivating a patch of miserable potatoes. He remarked upon their unpromising appearance and expressed pity for anyone who had to dig a living out of such soil.

"I don't need no pity," said the boy resentfully.

The traveler hastened to soothe his wounded pride. But in the offended tone of one who has been misjudged the boy added: "I ain't as poor as you think. I'm only *workin'* here. I don't *own* this place."

One day an inspector of a New York tenement-house found four families living in one room, chalk lines being drawn across in such manner as to mark out a quarter for each family.

"How do you get along here?" inquired the inspector.

"Very well," was the reply. "Only the man in the farthest corner keeps boarders."

There is no man so poor but that he can afford to keep one dog, and I hev seen them so poor that they could afford to keep three.—*Josh Billings.*

May poverty be always a day's march behind us.

Not he who has little, but he who wishes for more, is poor.
—*Seneca.*

PRAISE

WIFE (complainingly)—"You never praise me up to any one."

HUB—"I don't, eh! You should hear me describe you at the intelligence office when I'm trying to hire a cook."

"What sort of a man is he?"

"Well, he's just what I've been looking for—a generous soul, with a limousine body."—*Life.*

PRAYER MEETINGS

A foreigner who attended a prayer meeting in Indiana was asked what the assistants did. "Not very much," he said, "only they sin and bray."

PRAYERS

During the winter the village preacher was taken sick, and several of his children were also afflicted with the mumps. One day a number of the devout church members called to pray for the family. While they were about it a boy, the son of a member living in the country, knocked at the preacher's door. He had his arms full of things. "What have you there?" a deacon asked him.

"Pa's prayers for a happy Thanksgiving," the boy answered, as he proceeded to unload potatoes, bacon, flour and other provisions for the afflicted family.

A little girl in Washington surprised her mother the other day by closing her evening prayers in these words: "Amen, good bye; ring off."

TEACHER—"Now, Tommy, suppose a man gave you $100 to keep for him and then died, what would you do? Would you pray for him?"

TOMMY—"No, sir; I would pray for another like him."

A well-known revivalist whose work has been principally among the Negroes of a certain section of the South remembers one service conducted by him that was not entirely successful. He had had very poor attendance, and spent much time in questioning the darkies as to their reason for not attending.

"Why were you not at our revival?" he asked one old man, whom he encountered on the road.

"Oh, I dunno," said the backward one.

"Don't you ever pray?" demanded the preacher.

The old man shook his head. "No," said he; "I carries a rabbit's foot."—*Taylor Edwards.*

A little girl attending an Episcopal church for the first time, was amazed to see all kneel suddenly. She asked her mother what they were going to do. Her mother replied, "Hush, they're going to say their prayers."

"What with all their clothes on?"

The new minister in a Georgia church was delivering his first sermon. The darky janitor was a critical listener from a back corner of the church. The minister's sermon was eloquent, and his prayers seemed to cover the whole category of human wants.

After the services one of the deacons asked the old darky what he thought of the new minister. "Don't you think he offers up a good prayer, Joe?"

"Ah mos' suhtainly does, boss. Why, dat man axed de good Lord fo' things dat de odder preacher didn't even know He had!"

Hilma was always glad to say her prayers, but she wanted to be sure that she was heard in the heavens above as well as on the earth beneath.

One night, after the usual "Amen," she dropped her head upon her pillow and closed her eyes. After a moment she lifted her hand and, waving it aloft, said, "Oh, Lord! this prayer comes from 203 Selden Avenue."

Willie's mother had told him that if he went to the river to play he should go to bed. One day she was away, and on coming home about two o'clock in the afternoon found Willie in bed.

"What are you in bed for?" asked his mother.

"I went to the river to play, and I knew you would put me in bed, so I didn't wait for you to come."

"Did you say your prayers before you went to bed?" asked his mother.

"No," said Willie. "You don't suppose God would be loafing around here this time of day, do you? He's at the office."

Little Polly, coming in from her walk one morning, informed her mother that she had seen a lion in the park. No amount of persuasion or reasoning could make her vary her statement one hairbreadth. That night, when she slipped down on her knees to say her prayers, her mother said, "Polly, ask God to forgive you for that fib."

Polly hid her face for a moment. Then she looked straight

into her mother's eyes, her own eyes shining like stars, and said, "I did ask him, mamma, dearest, and he said, 'Don't mention it, Miss Polly; that big yellow dog has often fooled me.'"

Prayer is the spirit speaking truth to Truth.—*Bailey.*

> Pray to be perfect, though material leaven
> Forbid the spirit so on earth to be;
> But if for any wish thou darest not pray,
> Then pray to God to cast that wish away.
> —*Hartley Coleridge.*

See also Courage.

PREACHING

The services in the chapel of a certain western university are from time to time conducted by eminent clergymen of many denominations and from many cities.

On one occasion, when one of these visiting divines asked the president how long he should speak, that witty officer replied:

"There is no limit, Doctor, upon the time you may preach; but I may tell you that there is a tradition here that the most souls are saved during the first twenty-five minutes."

One Sunday morning a certain young pastor in his first charge announced nervously:

"I will take for my text the words, 'And they fed five men with five thousand loaves of bread and two thousand fishes.'"

At this misquotation an old parishioner from his seat in the amen corner said audibly:

"That's no miracle—I could do it myself."

The young preacher said nothing at the time, but the next Sunday he announced the same text again. This time he got it right:

"And they fed five thousand men on five loaves of bread and two fishes."

He waited a moment, and then, leaning over the pulpit and looking at the amen corner, he said:

"And could you do that, too, Mr. Smith?"

"Of course I could," Mr. Smith replied.

"And how would you do it?" said the preacher.

"With what was left over from last Sunday," said Mr. Smith.

The late Bishop Foss once visited a Philadelphia physician for some trifling ailment. "Do you, sir," the doctor asked, in the course of his examination, "talk in your sleep?"

"No sir," answered the bishop. "I talk in other people's. Aren't you aware that I am a divine?"

"Yes, sir," said the irate man, "I got even with that clergyman. I slurred him. Why, I hired one hundred people to attend his church and go to sleep before he had preached five minutes."

A noted eastern Judge when visiting in the west went to church on Sunday; which isn't so remarkable as the fact that he knew beforehand that the preacher was exceedingly tedious and long winded to the last degree. After the service the preacher met the Judge in the vestibule and said:

"Well, your Honor, how did you like the sermon?"

"Oh, most wonderfully," replied the Judge. "It was like the peace of God; for it passed all understanding, and, like His mercy, I thought it would have endured forever."

The preacher's evening discourse was dry and long, and the congregation gradually melted away. The sexton tiptoed up to the pulpit and slipped a note under one corner of the Bible. It read:

"When you are through, will you please turn off the lights, lock the door, and put the key under the mat?"

The new minister's first sermon was very touching and created much favorable comment among the members of the church. One morning, a few days later, his nine-year-old son happened to be alone in the pastor's study and with childish curiosity started to read through some papers on the desk. They happened to be this identical sermon, but he was most interested in the marginal notes. In one place in the margin were written the words, "Cry a little." Further on in the discourse appeared another marginal remark, "Cry a little more." On the next to the last sheet the boy found his good father had penned another remark, "Cry like thunder."

A young preacher, who was staying at a clergy-house, was in the habit of retiring to his room for an hour or more each day to practice pulpit oratory. At such times he filled the house with sounds of fervor and pathos, and emptied it of almost everything else. Phillips Brooks chanced to be visiting a friend in this house one day when the budding orator was holding forth.

"Gracious me!" exclaimed the Bishop, starting up in assumed terror, "pray, what might that be?"

"Sit down, Bishop," his friend replied. "That's only young D—— practising what he preaches."

A distinguished theologian was invited to make an address before a Sunday-school. The divine spoke for over an hour and his remarks were of too deep a character for the average juvenile mind to comprehend. At the conclusion, the superintendent, according to custom, requested some one in the school to name an appropriate hymn to be sung.

"Sing 'Revive Us Again,'" shouted a boy in the rear of the room.

A clergyman was once sent for in the middle of the night by one of his woman parishioners.

"Well, my good woman," said he, "so you are ill and require the consolations of religion? What can I do for you?"

"No," replied the old lady, "I am only nervous and can't sleep!"

"But how can I help that?" said the parson.

"Oh, sir, you always put me to sleep so nicely when I go to church that I thought if you would only preach a little for me!"

I never see my rector's eyes,
He hides their light divine;
For when he prays, he shuts his own,
And when he preaches, mine.

A stranger entered the church in the middle of the sermon and seated himself in the back pew. After a while he began to fidget. Leaning over to the white-haired man at his side, evidently an old member of the congregation, he whispered:

"How long has he been preaching?"

"Thirty or forty years, I think," the old man answered.

"I'll stay then," decided the stranger. "He must be nearly done."

Once upon a time there was an Indian named Big Smoke, employed as a missionary to his fellow Smokes.

A white man encountering Big Smoke, asked him what he did for a living.

"Umph!" said Big Smoke, "me preach."

"That so? What do you get for preaching?"

"Me get ten dollars a year."

"Well," said the white man, "that's damn poor pay."

"Umph!" said Big Smoke, "me damn poor preacher."

See also Clergy.

PRESCRIPTIONS

After a month's work in intensely warm weather a gardener in the suburbs became ill, and the anxious little wife sent for a doctor, who wrote a prescription after examining the patient. The doctor, upon departing, said: "Just let your husband take that and you'll find he will be all right in a short time."

Next day the doctor called again, and the wife opened the door, her face beaming with smiles. "Sure, that was a wonderful wee bit of paper you left yesterday," she exclaimed. "William is better to-day."

"I'm glad to hear that," said the much-pleased medical man

"Not but what I hadn't a big job to get him to swallow it,"

she continued, "but, sure, I just wrapped up the wee bit of paper quite small and put it in a spoonful of jam and William swallowed it unbeknownst. By night he was entirely better."

PRESENCE OF MIND

"What did you do when you met the train-robber face to face?"

"I explained that I had been interviewed by the ticket-seller, the luggage-carriers, the dining-car waiters, and the sleeping-car porters and borrowed a dollar from him."

PRINTERS

The master of all trades: He beats the farmer with his fast "hoe," the carpenter with his "rule," and the mason in "setting up tall columns"; and he surpasses the lawyer and the doctor in attending to the "cases," and beats the parson in the management of the devil.

PRISONS

A man arrested for stealing chickens was brought to trial. The case was given to the jury, who brought him in guilty, and the judge sentenced him to three months' imprisonment. The jailer was a jovial man, fond of a smile, and feeling particularly good on that particular day, considered himself insulted when the prisoner looking around the cell told him it was dirty, and not fit for a hog to be put in. One word brought on another, till finally the jailer told the prisoner if he did not behave himself he would put him out. To which the prisoner replied: "I will give you to understand, sir, I have as good a right here as you have!"

SHERIFF—"That fellow who just left jail is going to be arrested again soon."

"How do you know?"

SHERIFF—"He chopped my wood, carried the water, and mended my socks. I can't get along without him."

PRODIGALS

"Why did the father of the prodigal son fall on his neck and weep?"

"Cos he had ter kill the fatted calf, an' de son wasn't wort' it."

PROFANITY

THE RECTOR—"It's terrible for a man like you to make every other word an oath."

THE MAN—"Oh, well, I swear a good deal and you pray a good deal, but we don't neither of us mean nuthin' by it."

FIRST DEAF MUTE—"He wasn't so very angry, was he?"

SECOND DEAF MUTE—"He was so wild that the words he used almost blistered his fingers."

The little daughter of a clergyman stubbed her toe and said, "Darn!"

"I'll give you ten cents," said father, "if you'll never say that word again."

A few days afterward she came to him and said: "Papa, I've got a word worth half a dollar."

Very frequently the winter highways of the Yukon valley are mere trails, traversed only by dog-sledges. One of the bishops in Alaska, who was very fond of that mode of travel, encountered a miner coming out with his dog-team, and stopped to ask him what kind of a road he had come over.

The miner responded with a stream of forcible and picturesque profanity, winding up with:

"And what kind o' trail did you have?"

"Same as yours," replied the bishop feelingly.—*Elgin Burroughs.*

> A scrupulous priest of Kildare,
> Used to pay a rude peasant to swear,
> Who would paint the air blue,
> For an hour or two,
> While his reverence wrestled in prayer.

Donald and Jeanie were putting down a carpet. Donald slammed the end of his thumb with the hammer and began to pour forth his soul in language befitting the occasion.

"Donald, Donald!" shrieked Jeanie, horrified. "Dinna swear that way!"

"Wummun!" vociferated Donald; "gin ye know ony better way, now is the time to let me know it!"

"It is not always necessary to make a direct accusation," said the lawyer who was asking damages because insinuations had been made against his client's good name. "You may have heard of the woman who called to the hired girl, 'Mary, Mary, come here and take the parrot downstairs—the master has dropped his collar button!'"

Little Bartholomew's mother overheard him swearing like a mule-driver. He displayed a fluency that overwhelmed her. She took him to task, explaining the wickedness of profanity as well as its vulgarity. She asked where he had learned all those dreadful words. Bartholomew announced that Cavert, one of his playmates, had taught him.

Cavert's mother was straightway informed and Cavert was brought to book. He vigorously denied having instructed Bartholomew, and neither threats nor tears could make him confess. At last he burst out:

"I didn't tell Bartholomew any cuss words. Why should I know how to cuss any better than he does? Hasn't his father got an automobile, too?"

They were in Italy together.

"If you would let me curse them black and blue," said the groom, "we shouldn't have to wait so long for the trunks."

"But, darling, please don't. It would distress me so," murmured the bride.

The groom went off, but quickly returned with the porters before him trundling the trunks at a double quick.

"Oh, dearest, how did you do it? You didn't——?"

"Not at all. I thought of something that did quite as well. I said, 'S-s-s-susquehanna, R-r-r-rappahannock!'"—*Cornelia C. Ward.*

A school girl was required to write an essay of two hundred and fifty words about a motorcar. She submitted the following:

"My uncle bought a motorcar. He was riding in the country when it busted up a hill. I guess this is about fifty words. The other two hundred are what my uncle said when he was walking back to town, but they are not fit for publication."

The ashman was raising a can of ashes above his head to dump the contents into his cart, when the bottom of the can came out. Ethel saw it and ran in and told her mother.

"I hope you didn't listen to what he said," the mother remarked.

"He didn't say a word to me," replied the little girl; "he just walked right off by the side of his cart, talking to God."

A young man entered the jeweler's store and bought a ring, which he ordered engraved. The jeweler asked what name.

"George Osborne to Harriet Lewis, but I prefer only the initials, G. O. to H. L."

For it comes to pass oft that a terrible oath, with a swaggering accent sharply twanged off, gives manhood more approbation than ever proof itself would have earned him.—*Shakespeare.*

PROHIBITION

"Talking about dry towns, have you ever been in Leavenworth, Kansas?" asked the commercial traveler in the smoking-car. "No? Well, that's a dry-town for you, all right."

"They can't sell liquor at all there?" asked one of the men.

"Only if you had been bitten by a snake," said the drummer. "They have only one snake in town, and when I got to it the other day after standing in line for nearly half a day it was too tired to bite."

It was prohibition country. As soon as the train pulled up, a seedy little man with a covered basket on his arm hurried to the open windows of the smoker and exhibited a quart bottle filled with rich, dark fluid.

"Want to buy some nice cold tea?" he asked, with just the suspicion of a wink.

Two thirsty-looking cattlemen brightened visibly, and each paid a dollar for a bottle.

"Wait until you get outer the station before you take a drink," the little man cautioned them. "I don't wanter get in trouble."

He found three other customers before the train pulled out, in each case repeating his warning.

"You seem to be doing a pretty good business," remarked a man who had watched it all. "But I don't see why you'd run any more risk of getting in trouble if they took a drink before the train started."

"Ye don't, hey? Well, what them bottles had in 'em, pardner, was real cold tea."

PROMOTING

Mr. Harcourt, the Secretary of State for the Colonies, at the British North Borneo dinner, said that a City friend of his was approached with a view to floating a rubber company. His friend was quite ready. "How many trees have you?" he asked. "We have not got any trees," was the answer. "How much land have you?" "We have no land." What then have you got?" "I have a bag of seeds!"

There are many tales about the caution of Russell Sage and the cleverness with which he outwitted those who sought to get some of his money from him. Two brilliant promoters went to him one time and presented a scheme. The financier listened for an hour, and when they departed they were told that Mr. Sage's decision would be mailed to them in a few days.

"I think we have got Uncle Russell," said one of the promoters. "I really believe we have won his confidence."

"I fear not," observed the other doubtfully. "He is too suspicious."

"Suspicious? I didn't observe any sign of it."

"Didn't you notice that he counted his fingers after I had shaken hands with him and we were coming away?"

PROMOTION

Promotion cometh neither from the east nor the west, but from the cemetery.—*Edward Sanford Martin.*

PROMPTNESS

"Are you first in anything at school, Earlie?"
"First out of the building when the bell rings."

The head of a large business house bought a number of those "Do it now" signs and hung them up around his offices. When, after the first few days of those signs, the business man counted up the results, he found that the cashier had skipped out with $20,000, the head bookkeeper had eloped with the stenographer, three clerks had asked for a raise in salary, and the office boy had lit out for the west to become a highwayman.

"Are you waiting for me, dear?" she said, coming downstairs at last, after spending half an hour fixing her hat.
"Waiting," exclaimed the impatient man. "Oh no, not waiting—sojourning."

PRONUNCIATION

A tale is told of a Kansas minister, a great precisionist in the use of words, whose exactness sometimes destroyed the force of what he was saying. On one occasion, in the course of an eloquent prayer, he pleaded:

"O Lord! waken thy cause in the hearts of this congregation and give them new eyes to see and new impulse to do. Send down Thy lev-er or lee-ver, according to Webster's or Worcester's dictionary, whichever Thou usest, and pry them into activity."

"I'm at the head of my class, pa," said Willie.
"Dear me, son, how did that happen?" cried his father.
"Why, the teacher asked us this morning how to pronounce C-h-i-h-u-a-h-u-a, and nobody knew," said Willie, "but when she got down to me I sneezed and she said that was right."

See also Liars.

PROPORTION

A middle-aged colored woman in a Georgia village, hearing a commotion in a neighbor's cabin, looked in at the door. On the floor lay a small boy writhing in great distress while his bother bent solicitously over him.

"What-all's de matter wif de chile?" asked the visitor sympathetically.

"I spec's hit's too much watermillion," responded the mother.

"Ho! go 'long wif you," protested the visitor scornfully. "Dey cyan't never be too much watermillion. Hit mus' be dat dere ain't enough boy."

PROPOSALS

A love-smitten youth who was studying the approved method of proposal asked one of his bachelor friends if he thought that a young man should propose to a girl on his knees.

"If he doesn't," replied his friend, "the girl should get off."

A gentleman who had been in Chicago only three days, but who had been paying attention to a prominent Chicago belle, wanted to propose, but was afraid he would be thought too hasty. He delicately broached the subject as follows: 'If I were to speak to you of marriage, after having only made your acquaintance three days ago, what would you say of it?"

"Well, I should say, never put off till tomorrow that which should have been done the day before yesterday."

There was a young man from the West,
Who proposed to the girl he loved best,
  But so closely he pressed her
  To make her say, yes, sir,
That he broke two cigars in his vest.
The Tobacconist.

They were dining on fowl in a restaurant. "You see," he explained, as he showed her the wishbone, "you take hold here.

Then we must both make a wish and pull, and when it breaks the one who has the bigger part of it will have his or her wish granted." "But I don't know what to wish for," she protested. "Oh! you can think of something," he said. "No, I can't," she replied; "I can't think of anything I want very much." "Well, I'll wish for you," he explained. "Will you, really?" she asked. "Yes." "Well, then there's no use fooling with the old wishbone," she interrupted with a glad smile, "you can have me."

"Dear May," wrote the young man, "pardon me, but I'm getting so forgetful. I proposed to you last night, but really forget whether you said yes or no."

"Dear Will," she replied by note, "so glad to hear from you. I know I said 'no' to some one last night, but I had forgotten just who it was."

The four Gerton girls were all good-looking; indeed, the three younger ones were beautiful; while Annie, the oldest, easily made up in capability and horse sense what she lacked in looks.

A young chap, very eligible, called on the girls frequently, but seemed unable to decide which to marry. So Annie put on her thinking cap, and, one evening when the young chap called, she appeared with her pretty arms bare to the elbow and her hands white with flour.

"Oh, you must excuse my appearance," she said. "I have been working in the kitchen all day. I baked bread and pies and cake this morning, and afterward, as the cook was ill, I prepared dinner."

"Miss Annie, is that so?" said the young man. He looked at her, deeply impressed. Then, after a moment's thought, he said:

"Miss Annie, there is a question I wish to ask you, and on your answer will depend much of my life's happiness."

"Yes?" she said, with a blush, and she drew a little nearer. "Yes? What is it?"

"Miss Annie," said the young man, in deep earnest tones, "I am thinking of proposing to your sister Kate—will you make your home with us?"

It was at Christmas, and he had been calling on her twice a week for six months, but had not proposed.

"Ethel," he said, 'I—er—am going to ask you an important question."

"Oh, George," she exclaimed, "this is so sudden! Why, I——"

"No, excuse me," he interrupted; "what I want to ask is this: What date have you and your mother decided upon for our wedding?"

A Scotch beadle led the maiden of his choice to a church-yard and, pointing to the various headstones, said:

"My folks are all buried there, Jennie. Wad ye like to be buried there too?"

IMPECUNIOUS LOVER—"Be mine, Amanda, and you will be treated like an angel."

WEALTHY MAIDEN—"Yes, I suppose so. Nothing to eat, and less to wear. No, thank you."

The surest way to hit a woman's heart is to take aim kneeling.—*Douglas Jerrold.*

PROPRIETY

There was a young lady of Wilts,
Who walked up to Scotland on stilts;
　　When they said it was shocking
　　To show so much stocking,
She answered: "Then what about kilts?"
　　　　　　　　　　—*Gilbert K. Chesterton.*

PROSPERITY

May bad fortune follow you all your days
And never catch up with you.

PROTESTANT EPISCOPAL CHURCH

One of our popular New England lecturers tells this amusing story.

A street boy of diminutive stature was trying to sell some very young kittens to passers-by. One day he accosted the late Reverend Phillips Brooks, asking him to purchase, and recommending them as good Episcopal kittens. Dr. Brooks laughingly refused, thinking them too small to be taken from their mother. A few days later a Presbyterian minister who had witnessed this episode was asked by the same boy to buy the same kittens. This time the lad announced that they were faithful Presbyterians.

"Didn't you tell Dr. Brooks last week that they were Episcopal kittens?" the minister asked sternly.

"Yes sir," replied the boy quickly, "but they's had their eyes opened since then, sir."

An Episcopal clergyman who was passing his vacation in a remote country district met an old farmer who declared that he was a " 'Piscopal."

"To what parish do you belong?" asked the clergyman.

"Don't know nawthin' 'bout enny parish," was the answer.

"Who confirmed you, then?" was the next question.

"Nobody," answered the farmer.

"Then how are you an Episcopalian?" asked the clergyman.

"Well," was the reply, "you see it's this way: Last winter I went to church, an' it was called 'Piscopal, an' I heerd them say that they left undone the things what they'd oughter done and they'd done some things what they oughtenter done, and I says to myself says I: 'That's my fix exac'ly,' and ever sence then I've been a 'Piscopalian."

PROTESTANTS

A Protestant mission meeting had been held in an Irish town and this was the gardener's contribution to the controversy that ensued: "Pratestants!" he said with lofty scorn, " 'Twas mighty little St. Paul thought of the Pratestants. You've all heard tell of the 'pistle he wrote to the Romans, but I'd ax ye this, did any of yez iver hear of his writing a 'pistle to the Pratestants?"

PROVIDENCE

"Why did papa have appendicitis and have to pay the doctor a thousand dollars, Mama?"

"It was God's will, dear."

"And was it because God was mad at papa or pleased with the doctor?"—*Life*.

There's a certain minister whose duties sometimes call him out of the city. He has always arranged for some one of his parishioners to keep company with his wife and little daughter during these absences. Recently, however, he was called away so suddenly that he had no opportunity of providing a guardian.

The wife was very brave during the early evening, but after dark had fallen her courage began to fail. She stayed up with her little girl till there was no excuse for staying any longer and then took her upstairs to bed.

"Now go to sleep, Dearie," she said. "Don't be afraid. God will protect you."

"Yes, Mother," answered the little girl, "that'll be all right tonight, but next time let's make better arrangements."

PROVINCIALISM

Some time ago an English friend of Colonel W. J. Lampton's living in New York and having never visited the South, went to Virginia to spend a month with friends. After a fortnight of it, he wrote back:

"Oh, I say, old top, you never told me that the South was anything like I have found it, and so different to the North. Why, man, it's God's country."

The Colonel, who gets his title from Kentucky, answered promptly by postal.

"Of course it is," he wrote. "You didn't suppose God was a Yankee, did you?"

A southerner, with the intense love for his own district, attended a banquet. The next day a friend asked him who was present. With a reminiscent smile he replied: "An elegant gentleman from Virginia, a gentleman from Kentucky, a man from Ohio, a bounder from Chicago, a fellow from New York, and a galoot from Maine."

They had driven fourteen miles to the lake, and then rowed six miles across the lake to get to the railroad station, when the Chicago man asked:

"How in the world do you get your mail and newspapers here in the winter when the storms are on?"

"Wa-al, we don't sometimes. I've seen this lake thick up so that it was three weeks before we got a Chicago paper," answered the man from "nowhere."

"Well, you were cut off," said the Chicago man.

"Ya-as, we were so," was the reply. "Still, the Chicago folks were just as badly off."

"How so?"

"Wa-al," drawled the man, "we didn't know what was going on in Chicago, of course. But then, neither did Chicago folks know what was going on down here."

PUBLIC SERVICE CORPORATIONS

The attorney demanded to know how many secret societies the witness belonged to, whereupon the witness objected and appealed to the court.

"The court sees no harm in the question," answered the judge. "You may answer."

"Well, I belong to three."

"What are they?"

"The Knights of Pythias, the Odd Fellows, and the gas company."

"Yes, he had some rare trouble with his eyes," said the celebrated oculist. "Every time he went to read he would read double."

"Poor fellow," remarked the sympathetic person. "I suppose that interfered with his holding a good position?"

"Not at all. The gas company gobbled him up and gave him a lucrative job reading gas-meters."

PUBLIC SPEAKERS

ORATOR—"I thought your paper was friendly to me?"

EDITOR—"So it is. What's the matter?"

ORATOR—"I made a speech at the dinner last night, and you didn't print a line of it."

EDITOR—"Well, what further proof do you want?"

TRAVELING LECTURER FOR SOCIETY (to the remaining listener)—"I should like to thank you, sir, for so attentively hearing me to the end of a rather too long speech."

LOCAL MEMBER OF SOCIETY—"Not at all, sir. I'm the second speaker."

Ex-senator Spooner of Wisconsin says the best speech of introduction he ever heard was delivered by the German mayor of a small town in Wisconsin, where Spooner had been engaged to speak.

The mayor said:

"Ladies und shentlemens, I haf been asked to indrotoose you to the Honorable Senator Spooner, who vill make to you a speech, yes. I haf now done so; he vill now do so."

"When I arose to speak," related a martyred statesman, "some one hurled a base, cowardly egg at me and it struck me in the chest."

"And what kind of an egg might that be?" asked a fresh young man.

"A base, cowardly egg," explained the statesman, "is one that hits you and then runs."

"Uncle Joe" Cannon has a way of speaking his mind that is sometimes embarrassing to others. On one occasion an inexperienced young fellow was called upon to make a speech at a banquet at which ex-speaker Cannon was also present.

"Gentlemen," began the young fellow, "my opinion is that the generality of mankind in general is disposed to take advantage of the generality of——"

"Sit down, son," interrupted "Uncle Joe." "You are coming out of the same hole you went in at."

A South African tribe has an effective method of dealing with bores, which might be adopted by Western peoples. This simple tribe considers long speeches injurious to the orator and his hearers; so to protect both there is an unwritten law that every public orator must stand on only one leg when he is addressing an audience. As soon as he has to place the other leg on the ground his oration is brought to a close, by main force, if necessary.

A rather turgid orator, noted for his verbosity and heaviness, was once assigned to do some campaigning in a mining camp in the mountains. There were about fifty miners present when he began; but when, at the end of a couple of hours, he gave no sign of finishing, his listeners dropped away.

Some went back to work, but the majority sought places to quench their thirst, which had been aggravated by the dryness of the discourse.

Finally there was only one auditor left, a dilapidated, weary-looking old fellow. Fixing his gaze on him, the orator pulled out a large six-shooter and laid it on the table. The old fellow rose slowly and drawled out:

"Be you going to shoot if I go?"

"You bet I am," replied the speaker. "I'm bound to finish my speech, even if I have to shoot to keep an audience."

The old fellow sighed in a tired manner, and edged slowly away, saying as he did so:

"Well, shoot if you want to. I may jest as well be shot as talked to death."

The self-made millionaire who had endowed the school had been invited to make the opening speech at the commencement exercises. He had not often had a chance of speaking before the public and he was resolved to make the most of it. He dragged his address out most tiresomely, repeating the same thought over and over. Unable to stand it any longer a couple of the boys in the rear of the room slipped out. A coachman who was waiting outside asked them if the millionaire had finished his speech.

"Gee, yes!" replied the boys, "but he won't stop."

Mark Twain once told this story:

"Some years ago in Hartford, we all went to church one hot, sweltering night to hear the annual report of Mr. Hawley, a city missionary who went around finding people who needed help and didn't want to ask for it. He told of the life in cellars, where poverty resided; he gave instances of the heroism and devotion of the poor. When a man with millions gives, he said, we make a great deal of noise. It's a noise in the wrong place, for it's the widow's mite that counts. Well, Hawley worked me up to a great pitch. I could hardly wait for him to get through. I had $400 in my pocket. I wanted to give that and borrow more to give. You could see greenbacks in every eye. But instead of passing the plate then, he kept on talking and talking and talking, and as he talked it grew hotter and hotter and hotter, and we grew sleepier and sleepier and sleepier. My enthusiasm went down, down, down, down— $100 at a clip—until finally, when the plate did come around, I stole ten cents out of it. It all goes to show how a little thing like this can lead to crime."

See also After dinner speeches; Candidates; Politicians.

PUNISHMENT

A parent who evidently disapproved of corporal punishment wrote the teacher:

"Dear Miss: Don't hit our Johnnie. We never do it at home except in self-defense."

"No, sirree!" ejaculated Bunkerton. "There wasn't any of that nonsense in my family. My father never thrashed me in all his life."

"Too bad, too bad," sighed Hickenlooper. "Another wreck due to a misplaced switch."

James the Second, when Duke of York, made a visit to Milton, the poet, and asked him among other things, if he did not think the loss of his sight a *judgment* upon him for what he had written againnt his father, Charles the First. Milton answered: "If your Highness think my loss of sight a *judgment* upon me, what do you think of your father's losing his head."—*Life*.

A white man during reconstruction times was arraigned before a colored justice of the peace for killing a man and stealing his mule. It was in Arkansas, near the Texas border, and there was some rivalry between the states, but the colored justice tried to preserve an impartial frame of mind.

"We's got two kinds ob law in dis yer co't," he said: "Texas law an' Arkansas law. Which will you hab?"

The prisoner thought a minute and then guessed that he would take the Arkansas law.

"Den I discharge you fo' stealin' de mule, an' hang you fo' killin' de man."

"Hold on a minute, Judge," said the prisoner. "Better make that Texas law."

'All right. Den I fin' you fo' killin' de man, an' hang you fo' stealin' de mule."

A lawyer was defending a man accused of housebreaking, and said to the court:

"Your Honor, I submit that my client did not break into the house at all. He found the parlor window open and merely inserted his right arm and removed a few trifling articles. Now, my client's arm is not himself, and I fail to see how you can punish the whole individual for an offense committed by only one of his limbs."

"That argument," said the judge, "is very well put. Following it logically, I sentence the defendant's arm to one year's imprisonment. He can accompany it or not, as he chooses."

The defendant smiled, and with his lawyer's assistance unscrewed his cork arm, and, leaving it in the dock, walked out.

Muriel, a five-year-old subject of King George, has been thought by her parents too young to feel the weight of the rod, and has been ruled by moral suasion alone. But when, the other day, she achieved disobedience three times in five minutes, more vigorous measures were called for, and her mother took an ivory paper-knife from the table and struck her smartly across her little bare legs. Muriel looked astounded. Her mother explained the reason for the blow. Muriel thought deeply for a moment. Then, turning toward the door with a grave and disapproving countenance, she announced in her clear little English voice:

"I'm going up-stairs to tell God about that paper-knife. And then I shall tell Jesus. And if *that* doesn't do, I shall put flannel on my legs!"

During the reconstruction days of Virginia, a negro was convicted of murdering his wife and sentenced to be hanged. On the morning of the execution he mounted the scaffold with reasonable calmness. Just before the noose was to be placed around his neck the sheriff asked him if he had anything to say. He studied a moment and said:

"No, suh, boss, thankee, suh, 'ceptin' dis is sho gwine to be a lesson to me."

"What punishment did that defaulting banker get?"
"I understand his lawyer charged him $40,000."

An Indian in Washington County once sized up Maine's game laws thus: "Kill cow moose, pay $100; kill man, too bad!"

TEACHER—"Willie, did your father cane you for what you did in school yesterday?"
PUPIL—"No, ma'am; he said the licking would hurt him more than it would me."
TEACHER—"What rot! Your father is too sympathetic."
PUPIL—"No, ma'am; but he's got the rheumatism in both arms."

"Boohoo! Boohoo!" wailed little Johnny.
"Why, what's the matter, dear?" his mother asked comfortingly.
'Boohoo—er—p-picture fell on papa's toes."
"Well, dear, that's too bad, but you mustn't cry about it, you know."
"I d-d-didn't. I laughed. Boohoo! Boohoo!"

The fact that corporal punishment is discouraged in the public schools of Chicago is what led Bobby's teacher to address this note to the boy's mother:

DEAR MADAM:—I regret very much to have to tell you that your son, Robert, idles away his time, is disobedient, quarrelsome, and disturbs the pupils who are trying to study their lessons. He needs a good whipping and I strongly recommend that you give him one.

Yours truly,
MISS BLANK.

To this Bobby's mother responded as follows:

DEAR MISS BLANK—Lick him yourself. I ain't mad at him.
Yours truly,
MRS. DASH.

A little fellow who was being subjected to a whipping pinched his father under the knee. "Willie, you bad boy! How dare you do that?" asked the parent wrathfully.

A pause. Then Willie answered between sobs: "Well, Father, who started this war, anyway?"

A little girl about three years old was sent upstairs and told to sit on a certain chair that was in the corner of her room, as a punishment for something she had done but a few minutes before.

Soon the silence was broken by the little one's question: "Mother, may I come down now?"

"No, you sit right where you are."

"All right, 'cause I'm sittin' on your best hat."

It is less to suffer punishment than to deserve it.—*Ovid*.

If Jupiter hurled his thunderbolt as often as men sinned, he would soon be out of thunderbolts.—*Ovid*.

See also Church discipline; Future life; Marriage.

PUNS

A father once said to his son,
"The next time you make up a pun,
Go out in the yard
And kick yourself hard,
And I will begin when you've done."

PURE FOOD

Into a general store of a town in Arkansas there recently came a darky complaining that a ham which he had purchased there was not good.

"The ham is all right, Zeph," insisted the storekeeper.

"No, it aint, boss," insisted the negro. "Dat ham's shore bad."

"How can that be," continued the storekeeper, "when it was cured only a week?"

The darky scratched his head reflectively, and finally suggested:

"Den, mebbe it's had a relapse."

On a recent trip to Germany, Doctor Harvey Wiley, the pure-food expert, heard an allegory with reference to the subject of food adulteration which, he contends, should cause Americans to congratulate themselves that things are so well ordered in this respect in the United States.

The German allegory was substantially as fellows:

Four flies, which had made their way into a certain pantry, determined to have a feast.

One flew to the sugar and ate heartily; but soon died, for the sugar was full of white lead.

The second chose the flour as his diet, but he fared no better, for the flour was loaded with plaster of Paris.

The third sampled the syrup, but his six legs were presently raised in the air, for the syrup was colored with aniline dyes.

The fourth fly, seeing all his friends dead, determined to end his life also, and drank deeply of the fly-poison which he found in a convenient saucer.

He is still alive and in good health. That, too, was adulterated.

QUARRELS

"But why did you leave your last place?" the lady asked of the would-be cook.

"To tell the truth, mum, I just couldn't stand the way the master an' the missus used to quarrel, mum."

"Dear me! Do you mean to say that they actually used to quarrel?"

"Yis, mum, all the time. When it wasn't me an' him, it was me an' her."

"I hear ye had words with Casey."

"We had no words."

"Then nothing passed between ye?"

"Nothing but one brick."

"There had been a wordy falling-out between Mrs. Halloran and Mrs. Donohue; there had been words; nay, more, there had been language. Mrs. Halloran had gone to church early in the morning, had fulfilled the duties of her religion, and was returning primly home, when Mrs. Donohue spied her, and, still smouldering with volcanic fire, sent a broadside of lava at Mrs. Halloran. The latter heard, flushed, opened her lips—and then suddenly checked herself. After a moment she spoke: "Mrs. Donohue, I've just been to church, and I'm in a state of grace. But, plaze Hivin, the next time I meet yez, I won't be, and thin I'll till yez what I think of yez!"

A quarrel is quickly settled when deserted by one party: there is no battle unless there be two.—*Seneca.*

See also Marriage; Servants

QUESTIONS

The more questions a woman asks the fewer answers she remembers.—*Wasp.*

It was a very hot day and the fat drummer who wanted the twelve-twenty train got through the gate at just twelve-twenty-one. The ensuing handicap was watched with absorbed interest both from the train and the station platform. At its conclusion the breathless and perspiring knight of the road wearily took the back trail, and a vacant-faced "red-cap" came out to relieve him of his grip.

"Mister," he inquired, "was you tryin' to ketch that Pennsylvania train?"

"No, my son," replied the patient man. "No; I was merely chasing it out of the yard."

A party of young men were camping, and to avert annoying questions they made it a rule that the one who asked a question that he could not answer himself had to do the cooking.

One evening, while sitting around the fire, one of the boys asked: "Why is it that a ground-squirrel never leaves any dirt at the mouth of its burrow?"

They all guessed and missed. So he was asked to answer it himself.

"Why," he said, "because it always begins to dig at the other end of the hole."

"But," one asked, "how does it get to the other end of the hole?"

"Well," was the reply, "that's your question."

A browbeating lawyer was demanding that a witness answer a certain question either in the negative or affirmative.

"I cannot do it," said the witness. "There are some questions that cannot be answered by a 'yes' or a 'no,' as any one knows."

"I defy you to give an example to the court," thundered the lawyer.

The retort came like a flash: "Are you still beating your wife?"

Officers have a right to ask questions in the performance of their duty, but there are occasions when it seems as if they might curtail or forego the privilege. Not long ago an Irishman whose hand had been badly mangled in an accident entered the Boston City Hospital relief station in a great hurry. He stepped up to the man in charge and inquired:

"Is this the relief station, sor?"

"Yes. What is your name?"

"Patrick O'Connor, sor."

"Are you married?" questioned the officer.

"Yis, sor, but is this the relief station?" He was nursing his hand in agony.

"Of course it is. How many children have you?"

"Eight, sor. But sure, this is the relief station?"

"Yes, it is," replied the officer, a little angry at the man's persistence.

"Well," said Patrick, "sure, an' I was beginning to think that it might be the pumping station."

> The sages say, Dame Truth delights to dwell
> (Strange Mansion!) in the bottom of a well:
> Questions are then the Windlass and the rope
> That pull the grave old Gentlewoman up.
>
> —*John Wolcott.*

See also Curiosity.

QUOTATIONS

Stanley Jordan, the well-known Episcopal minister, having cause to be anxious about his son's college examinations, told him to telegraph the result. The boy sent the following message to his parent: "Hymn 342, fifth verse, last two lines."

Looking it up the father found the words: "Sorrow vanquished, labor ended, Jordan passed."

RACE PREJUDICES

A Negro preacher in a southern town was edified on one occasion by the recital of a dream had by a member of the church.

"I was a-dreamin' all dis time," said the narrator, "dat I was in ole Satan's dominions. I tell you, pahson, dat was shore a bad dream!"

"Was dere any white men dere?" asked the dusky divine.

"Shore dere was—plenty of 'em," the other hastened to assure his minister.

"What was dey a-doin'?"

"Ebery one of 'em," was the answer, "was a-holdin' a cullud pusson between him an' de fire!"

RACE PRIDE

Sam Jones, the evangelist, was leading a revival meeting in Huntsville, Teaxs, a number of years ago, and at the close of one of the services an old negro woman pushed her way up through the crowd to the edge of the pulpit platform. Sam took the perspiring black hand that was held out to him, and heard the old woman say: "Brudder Jones, you sho' is a fine preacher! Yes, suh; de Lord bless you. You's des everybody's preacher. You's de white folk's preacher, and de niggers' preacher, and everybody's preacher. Brudder Jones, yo' skin's white, but, thank de Lord, yo' heart's des as black as any nigger's!"

An Irishman and a Jew were discussing the great men who had belonged to each race and, as may be expected, got into a heated argument. Finally the Irishman said:

"Ikey, listen. For ivery great Jew ye can name ye may pull out one of me whiskers, an' for ivery great Irishman I can name I'll pull one of yours. Is it a go?"

They consented, and Pat reached over, got hold of a whisker, said, "Robert Emmet," and pulled.

"Moses!" said the Jew, and pulled one of Pat's tenderest.

"Dan O'Connell," said Pat and took another.

"Abraham," said Ikey, helping himself again.

"Patrick Henry," returned Pat with a vicious yank.

"The Twelve Apostles," said the Jew, taking a handful of whiskers.

Pat emitted a roar of pain, grasped the Jew's beard with both hands, and yelled, "The ancient Order of Hibernians."

RACE   SUICIDE

"Prisoner, why did you assault this landlord?"

"Your Honor, because I have several children he refused to rent me a flat."

"Well, that is his privilege."

"But, your Honor, he calls his apartment house 'The Roosevelt.'"

RACES

In answer to the question, "What are the five great races of mankind?" a Chinese student replied, "The 100 yards, the hurdles, the quartermile, the mile, and the three miles."

"Now, Thomas," said the foreman of the construction gang to a green hand who had just been put on the job, "keep your eyes open. When you see a train coming throw down your tools and jump off the track. Run like blazes."

"Sure!" said Thomas, and began to swing his pick. In a few moments the Empire State Express came whirling along. Thomas threw down his pick and started up the track ahead of the train as fast as he could run. The train overtook him and tossed him into a ditch. Badly shaken up he was taken to the hospital, where the foreman visited him.

"You blithering idiot," said the foreman, "didn't I tell you to get out of the road? Didn't I tell you to take care and get out of the way? Why didn't you run up the side of the hill?"

"Up the soide of the hill is it, sor?" said Thomas through the bandages on his face. "Up the soide of the hill? Be the powers, I couldn't bate it on the level, let alone runnin' up-hill!"

RAILROADS

"Talk 'bout railroads bein' a blessin'," said Brother Dickey, "des look at de loads an' loads er watermelons deys haulin' out de state, ter dem folks 'way up North what never done nuthin' ter deserve sich a dispensation!"

On one of the southern railroads there is a station-building that is commonly known by travelers as the smallest railroad station in America. It is of this station that the story is told that an old farmer was expecting a chicken-house to arrive there, and he sent one of his hands, a new-comer, to fetch it. Arriving there the man saw the house, loaded it on to his wagon and started for home. On the way he met a man in uniform with the words "Station Agent" on his cap.

"Say, hold on. What have you got on that wagon?" he asked.

"My chicken-house, of course," was the reply.

"Chicken-house be jiggered!" exploded the official. "That's the station!"

"I read of the terrible vengeance inflicted upon one of their members by a band of robbers in Mississippi last week."

"What did they do? Shoot him?"

"No; they tied him upon the railroad tracks."

"Awful! And he was ground to pieces, I suppose?"

"Nothing like it. The poor fellow starved to death waiting for the next train."—*W. Dayton Wegefarth.*

The reporter who had accompanied the special train to the scene of the wreck, hurried down the embankment and found a man who had one arm in a sling, a bandage over one eye, his front teeth gone, and his nose knocked four points to starboard, sitting on a piece of the locomotive and surveying the horrible ruin all about him.

"Can you give me some particulars of this accident?" asked the reporter, taking out his notebook.

"I haven't heard of any accident, young man," replied the disfigured party stiffly.

He was one of the directors of the railroad.

The Hon. John Sharp Williams had an engagement to speak in a small southern town. The train he was traveling on was not of the swiftest, and he lost no opportunity of keeping the conductor informed as to his opinions of that particular road.

"Well, if yer don't like it," the conductor finally blurted out, "why in thunder don't yer git out an' walk?"

"I would," Mr. Williams blandly replied, "but you see the committee doesn't expect me until this train gets in."

"We were bounding along," said a recent traveler on a local South African single-line railway, "at the rate of about seven miles an hour, and the whole train was shaking terribly. I epexcted every moment to see my bones protruding through my skin. Passengers were rolling from one end of the car to the other. I held on firmly to the arms of the seat. Presently we settled down a bit quieter; at least, I could keep my hat on, and my teeth didn't chatter.

"There was a quiet looking man opposite me. I looked up with a ghastly smile, wishing to appear cheerful, and said:

" 'We are going a bit smoother, I see.'

" 'Yes,' he said, 'we're off the track now.' "

Three men were talking in rather a large way as to the excellent train service each had in his special locality: one was from the west, one from New England, and the other from New York. The former two had told of marvelous doings of trains, and it is distinctly "up" to the man from New York.

"Now in New York," he said, "we not only run our trains fast, but we also start them fast. I remember the case of a friend of mine whose wife went to see him off for the west on the Pennsylvania at Jersey City. As the train was about to start my friend said his final good-by to his wife, and leaned down from the car platform to kiss her. The train started, and, would you belief it, my friend found himself kissing a strange woman on the platform at Trenton!"

And the other men gave it up.

"Say, young man," asked an old lady at the ticket-office, "what time does the next train pull in here and how long does it stay?"

"From two to two to two-two," was the curt reply.

"Well, I declare! Be you the whistle?"

An express on the Long Island Railroad was tearing away at a wild and awe-inspiring rate of six miles an hour, when all of a sudden it stopped altogether. Most of the passengers did not notice the difference; but one of them happened to be somewhat anxious to reach his destination before old age claimed him for its own. He put his head through the window to find that the cause of the stop was a cow on the track. After a while they continued the journey for half an hour or so, and then—another stop.

"What's wrong now?" asked the impatient passenger of the conductor.

"A cow on the track."

"But I thought you drove it off."

"So we did," said the conductor, "but we caught up with it again."

The president of one great southern railway pulled into a southern city in his private car. It was also the terminal of a competing road, and the private car of the president of the other line was on a side track. There was great rivalry between these two lines, which extended from the president of each down to the most humble employe. In the evening the colored cook from one of the cars wandered over to pass the time of day with the cook on the other car.

One of these roads had recently had an appaling list of accidents, and the death-toll was exceptionally high. The cook from this road sauntered up to the back platform of the private car, and after an interchange of courtesies said:

"Well, how am youh ole jerkwatah railroad these days? Am you habbing prosper's times?"

"Man," said the other, "we-all am so prosperous that if we was any moah prosperous we just naturally couldn't stand hit.'

"Hough!" said the other, "we-all am moah prosperous than you-all."

"Man," said the other, "we dun carry moah'n a million passengers last month."

"Foah de Lord's sake!" ejaculated the first negro. "You-all carried moah'n a million passengers? Go on with you, nigger; we dun kill moah passengers than you carry."

It was on a little branch railway in a southern state that the New England woman ventured to refer to the high rates.

"It seems to me five cents a mile is extortion," she said, with frankness, to her southern cousin.

"It's a big lot of money to pay if you think of it by the mile," said the southerner, in her soft drawl; "but you just think how cheap it is by the hour, Cousin Annie—only about thirty-five cents."—*Youth's Companion*

RAPID TRANSIT

One cold, wintry morning a man of tall and angular build was walking down a steep hill at a quick pace. A treacherous piece of ice under the snow caused him to lose control of his feet; he began to slide and was unable to stop.

At a cross-street half-way down the decline he encountered a large heavy woman, with her arms full of bundles. The meeting was sudden, and before either realized it a collision ensued and both were sliding down hill, a grand ensemble—the thin man underneath, the fat woman and bundles on top. When the bottom was reached and the woman was trying in vain to recover her breath and her feet, these faint words were borne to her ear:

"Pardon me, madam, but you will have to get off here. This is as far as I go."

READING

See Books and Reading.

REAL ESTATE AGENTS

Little Nelly told little Anita what she termed a "little fib."

ANITA—"A fib is the same as a story, and a story is the same as a lie."

NELLY—"No, it is not."

ANITA—"Yes, it is, because my father said so, and my father is a professor at the university."

NELLY—"I don't care if he is. My father is a real estate man, and he knows more about lying than your father does."

REALISM

The storekeeper at Yount, Idaho, tells the following tale of Ole Olson, who later became the little town's mayor.

"One night, just before closin' up time, Ole, hatless, coatless, and breathless, come rushin' into the store, an' droppin' on his knees yelled, 'Yon, Yon, hide me, hide me! Ye sheriff's after me!'

"'I've no place to hide you here, Ole,' said I.

"'You moost, you moost!' screamed Ole.

"'Crawl into that gunny-sack then,' said I.

"He'd no more'n gotten hid when in runs the sheriff.

"'Seen Ole?' said he.

"'Don't see him here,' said I, without lyin'.

"Then the sheriff went a-nosin' round an' pretty soon he spotted the gunny-sack over in the corner.

"'What's in here?' said he.

"'Oh, just some old harness and sleigh-bells,' said I.

"With that he gives it an awful boot.

"'Yingle, yingle, yingle!' moaned Ole."

MOTHER—"Tommy, if you're pretending to be an automobile, I wish you'd run over to the store and get me some butter."

TOMMY—"I'm awful sorry, Mother, but I'm all out of gasoline."—*Judge*

"Children," said the teacher, instructing the class in composition, "you should not attempt any flights of fancy; simply be yourselves and write what is in you. Do not imitate any other person's writings or draw inspiration from outside sources."

As a result of this advice Tommy Wise turned out the following composition: "We should not attempt any flights of fancy, but write what is in us. In me there is my stummick, lungs, hart, liver, two apples, one piece of pie, one stick of lemon candy and my dinner."

"A great deal of fun has been poked at the realistic school of art," says a New York artist, "and it must be confessed that some ground has been given to the enemy. Why, there recently came to my notice a picture of an Assyrian bath, done by a Chicago man, and so careful was he of all the details that the towels hanging up were all marked 'Nebuchadnezzar' in the corner, in cuneiform characters."

RECALL

SUNDAY SCHOOL TEACHER—"Johnny, what is the text from Judges?"

JOHNNY—"I don't believe in recalling the judiciary, mum."

"Senator, why don't you unpack your trunk? You'll be in Washington for six years."

"I don't know about that. My state has the recall."

RECOMMENDATIONS

A firm of shady outside London brokers was prosecuted for swindling. In acquitting them the court, with great severity, said:

"There is not sufficient evidence to convict you, but if anyone wishes to know my opinion of you I hope that they will refer to me."

Next day the firm's advertisement appeared in every available medium with the following, well displayed: "Reference as to probity, by special permission, the Lord Chief Justice of England."

MISTRESS—"Have you a reference?"

BRIDGET—"Foine; Oi held the poker over her till Oi got it"

There is a story of a Scotch gentleman who had to dismiss his gardener for dishonesty. For the sake of the man's wife and family, however, he gave him a "character," and framed it in this way: "I hereby certify that A. B. has been my gardener for over two years, and that during that time he got more out of the garden than any man I ever employed."

The buxom maid had been hinting that she did not think much of working out, and this in conjunction with the nightly appearance of a rather sheepish young man caused her mistress much apprehension.

"Martha, is it possible that you are thinking of getting married?"

"Yes'm," admitted Martha, blushing.

"Not that young fellow who has been calling on you lately?"

"Yes'm he's the one."

"But you have only known him a few days."

"Three weeks come Thursday," corrected Martha

"Do you think that is long enough to know a man before taking such an important step?"

"Well," answered Martha with spirit, "tain't 's if he was some new feller. He's well recommended; a perfectly lovely girl I know was engaged to him for a long while."

An Englishman and an Irishman went to the captain of a ship bound for America and asked permission to work their passage over. The captain consented, but asked the Irishman for references and let the Englishman go on without them. This made the Irishman angry and he planned to get even.

One day when they were washing off the deck, the Englishman leaned far over the rail, dropped the bucket, and was just about to haul it up when a huge wave came and pulled him overboard. The Irishman stopped scrubbing, went over to the rail and, seeing the Englishman had disappeared, went to the Captain and said: "Perhaps yez remember whin I shipped aboard this vessel ye asked me for riferences and let the Englishman come on widout thim?"

The Captain said: "Yes, I remember."

"Well, ye've been decaved," said the Irishman; "he's gone off wid yer pail!"

RECONCILIATIONS

"Yes, I quarreled with my wife about nothing."

"Why don't you make up?"

"I'm going to. All I'm worried about now is the indemnity."

REFORMERS

LOUISE—"The man that Edith married is a reformer."

JULIA—"How did he lose his money?"—*Judge.*

He was earnestly but prosily orating at the audience. "I want land reform," he wound up, 'I want housing reform, I want educational reform, I want—"

And said a bored voice in the audience: "Chloroform."

The young woman sat before her glass and gazed long and earnestly at the reflection there. She screwed up her face in many ways. She fluffed her hair and then smoothed it down again; she raised her eyes and lowered them; she showed her teeth and she pressed her lips tightly together. At last she got up, with a weary sigh and said:

"It's no use. I'll be some kind of reformer."

REGRETS

A Newport man who was invited to a house party at Bar Harbor, telegraphed to the hostess: "Regret I can't come. Lie follows by post."

After the death of Lord Houghton, there was found in his correspondence the following reply to a dinner invitation: "Mrs. — presents her compliments to Lord Houghton. Her husband died on Tuesday, otherwise he would have been delighted to dine with Lord Houghton on Thursday next."

A young woman prominent in the social set of an Ohio town tells of a young man there who had not familiarized himself with the forms of polite correspondence to the fullest extent. When, on one occasion, he found it necessary to decline an invitation, he did so in the following terms:

"Mr. Henry Blank declines with pleasure Mrs. Wood's invitation for the nineteenth, and thanks her extremely for having given him the opportunity of doing so."

REHEARSALS

The funeral procession was moving along the village street when Uncle Abe stepped out of a store. He hadn't heard the news.

"Sho," said Uncle Abe, "who they buryin' today?"

"Pore old Tite Harrison," said the storekeeper.

"Sho," said Uncle Abe. "Tite Harrison, hey? Is Tite dead?"

"You don't think we're rehearsin' with him, do you?" snapped the storekeeper.

RELATIVES

"It is hard, indeed," said the melancholy gentleman, "to lose one's relatives."

"Hard?" snorted the gentleman of wealth. "Hard? It is impossible!"

RELIGIONS

When Bishop Phillips Brooks sailed from America on his last trip to Europe, a friend jokingly remarked that while abroad he might discover some new religion to bring home with him. "But be careful of it, Bishop Brooks," remarked a listening friend; "it may be difficult to get your new religion through the Custom House."

"I guess not," replied the Bishop, laughingly, "for we may take it for granted that any new religion popular enough to import will have no duties attached to it."

At a recent conference of Baptists, Methodists, and English Friends, in the city of Chengtu, China, two Chinamen were heard discussing the three denominations. One of them said to the other:

"They say these denominations have different beliefs. Just what is the difference between them?"

"Oh," said the other, "Not much! Big washee, little washee, no washee, that is all."

A recent book on Russia relates the story of the anger of the Apostle John because a certain peasant burned no tapers to his ikon, but honored, instead, the ikon of Apostle Peter in St. John's own church. The two apostles talked it over as they walked the fields near Kieff, and Apostle John decided to send a terrible storm to destroy the just ripe corn of the peasant. His decision was carried out, and the next day he met Apostle Peter and boasted of his punishing wrath.

And Apostle Peter only laughed. "Ai yi, yi, Apostle John," he said, "what a mess you've made of it. I stepped around, saw my friend, and told him what you were going to do, so he sold his corn to the priest of your church."

The priest of a New York parish met one of his parishioners, who had long been out of work, and asked him whether he had found anything to do. The man grinned with infinite satisfaction, and replied:

"Yiss indade, yer Riverince, an' a foine job too! Oi'm gettin' three dollars a day fur pullin' down a Prodesant church!"

A man addicted to walking in his sleep went to bed all right one night, but when he awoke he found himself on the street in the grasp of a policeman. "Hold on," he cried, "you mustn't arrest me. I'm a somnambulist." To which the policeman replied: "I don't care what your religion is—yer can't walk the streets in yer nightshirt."

The friendship existing between Father Kelly and Rabbi Levi is proof against differences in race and religion. Each distinguished for his learning, his eloquence and his wit; and they delight in chaffing each other. They were seated apposite each other at a banquet where some delicious roast ham was served and Father Kelly made comments upon its flavor. Presently be leaned forward and in a voice that carried far, he addressed his friend:

"Rabbi Levi, when are you going to become liberal enough to eat ham?"

"At your wedding, Father Kelly," retorted the rabbi.

The broad-minded see the truth in different religions; the narrow-minded see only their differences.—*Chinese proverb.*

REMEDIES

Mistress—"Did the mustard plaster do you any good, Bridget?"

Maid—"Yes; but, begorry, mum, it do bite the tongue!"

Sufferer—"I have a terrible toothache and want something to cure it."

Friend—"Now, you don't need any medicine. I had a toothache yesterday and I went home and my loving wife kissed me and so consoled me that the pain soon passed away. Why don't you try the same?"

Sufferer—"I think I will. Is your wife at home now?"

> For every ill beneath the sun
> There is some remedy or none;
> If there be one, resolve to find it;
> If not, submit, and never mind it.

REMINDERS

The wife of an overworked promoter said at breakfast:
"Will you post this letter for me, dear? It's to the furrier, countermanding my order for that $900 sable and ermine stole. You'll be sure to remember?"

The tired eyes of the harassed, shabby promoter lit up with joy. He seized a skipping rope that lay with a heap of dolls and toys in a corner, and going to his wife he said:

Here, tie my right hand to my left foot so I won't forget!"

REPARTEE

Repartee is saying on the instant what you didn't say until the next morning.

Among the members of a working gang on a certain railroad was an Irishman who claimed to be very good at figures. The boss, thinking that he would get ahead of Pat, said: "Say, Pat, how many shirts can you get of a yard?"

"That depends," answered Pat, "on whose yard you get into."

A middle-aged farmer accosted a serious-faced youth outside the Grand Central Station in New York the other day.

"Young man," he said, plucking his sleeve, "I wanter go to Central Park."

The youth seemed lost in consideration for a moment.

"Well," he said finally, "you may just this once. But I don't want you ever, *ever* to ask me again."

SEEDY VISITOR—"Do you have many wrecks about here, boatman?"

BOATMAN—"Not very many, sir. You're the first I've seen this season."

HER DAD—"No, sir; I won't have my daughter tied for life to a stupid fool."

HER SUITOR—"Then don't you think you'd better let me take her off your hands?"

Wendell Phillips was traveling through Ohio once when he fell in with a car full of ministers returning from a convention. One of the ministers, a southerner from Kentucky, was naturally not very cordial to the opinions of the great abolitionist and set out to embarrass Mr. Phillips. So, before the group of ministers, he said:

"You are Wendell Phillips, are you not?"

"Yes," answered the great abolitionist.

"And you are trying to free the niggers, aren't you?"

"Yes, sir; I am."

"Well, why do you preach your doctrines up here? Why don't you go over into Kentucky?"

"Excuse me, are you a preacher?"

"I am, sir."

"Are you trying to save souls from hell?"

"Yes, sir; that is my business."

"Well, why don't you go there then?" asked Mr. Phillips.

SOLEMN SENIOR—"So your efforts to get on the team were fruitless, were they?"

FOOLISH FRESHMAN—"Oh, no! Not at all. They gave me a lemon."—*Harvard Lampoon.*

A benevolent person watched a workman laboriously wind-lassing rock from a shaft while the broiling sun was beating down on his bare head.

"My dear man," observed the onlooker, "are you not afraid that your brain will be affected in the hot sun?"

The laborer contemplated him for a moment and then replied:

"Do you think a man with any brains would be working at this kind of a job?"

Winston Churchill, the young English statesman, recently began to raise a mustache, and while it was still in the budding stage he was asked at a dinner party to take in to dinner an English girl who had decided opposing political views.

"I am sorry," said Mr. Churchill, "we cannot agree on politics."

"No, we can't," rejoined the girl, "for to be frank with you I like your politics about as little as I do your mustache."

"Well," replied Mr. Churchill, "remember that you are not likely to come into contact with either."

Strickland Gillilan, the lecturer and the man who pole-vaulted into fame by his "Off Ag'in, On Ag'in, Finnigin" verses, was about to deliver a lecture in a small Missouri town. He asked the chairman of the committee whether he might have a small pitcher of ice-water on the platform table.

"To drink?" queried the committeeman.

"No," answered Gillilan. "I do a high-diving act."

TRAVELER—"Say, boy, your corn looks kind of yellow."

BOY—"Yes, sir. That's the kind we planted."

TRAVELER—"Looks as though you will only have half a crop."

BOY—"Don't expect any more. The landlord gets the other **half.**"

TRAVELER (after a moment's thought)—"Say, there is not much difference between you and a fool."

BOY—"No, sir. Only the fence."

President Lincoln was busily engaged in his office when an attendant, a young man of sixteen, unceremoniously entered and gave him a card. Without rising, the President glanced at the card. "Pshaw. She here again? I told her last week that I could not interfere in her case. I cannot see her," he said impatiently. "Get rid of her any way you can. Tell her I am asleep, or anything you like."

Quickly returning to the lady in an adjacent room, this exceedingly bright boy said to her, "The President told me to tell you that he is asleep."

The lady's eyes sparkled as she responded, "Ah, he says he is asleep, eh? Well, will you be kind enough to return and ask him when he intends to wake up?"

The garrulous old lady in the stern of the boat had pestered the guide with her comments and questions ever since they had started. Her meek little husband, who was hunched toadlike in the bow, fished in silence. The old lady had seemingly exhausted every possible point in fish and animal life, woodcraft, and personal history when she suddenly espied one of those curious paths of oily, unbroken water frequently seen on small lakes which are ruffled by a light breeze.

"Oh, guide, guide," she exclaimed, "what makes that funny streak in the water— No, there— Right over there!"

The guide was busy re-baiting the old gentleman's hook and merely mumbled "U-m-mm."

"Guide," repeated the old lady in tones that were not to be denied, "look right over there where I'm pointing and tell me what makes that funny streak in the water."

The guide looked up from his baiting with a sigh.

"That? Oh, that's where the road went across the ice last winter."

Nothing more clearly expresses the sentiments of Harvard men in seasons of athletic rivalry than the time-honored "To hell with Yale!"

Once when Dean Briggs, of Harvard, and Edward Everett Hale were on their way to a game at Soldiers' Field a friend asked:

"Where are you going, Dean?"

"To yell with Hale," answered Briggs with a meaning smile.

John Kendrick Bangs one day called up his wife on the telephone. The maid at the other end did not recognize her "master's voice," and after Bangs had told her whom he wanted the maid asked:

"Do you wish to speak with Mrs. Bangs?"

"No, indeed," replied the humorist; "I want to kiss her."

A boy took a position in an office where two different telephones were installed.

"Your wife would like to speak to you on the 'phone, sir," he said to his employer.

"Which one?" inquired the boss, starting toward the two booths.

"Please, sir, she didn't say, and I didn't know that you had more than one."

An Englishman was being shown the sights along the Potomac. "Here," remarked the American, "is where George Washington threw a dollar across the river."

"Well," replied the Englishman, "that is not very remarkable, for a dollar went much further in those days than it does now."

The American would not be worsted, so after a short pause, he said: "But Washington accomplished a greater feat than that. He once chucked a sovereign across the Atlantic."

Pat was busy on a road working with his coat off. There were two Englishmen laboring on the same road, so they decided to have a joke with the Irishman. They painted a donkey's head on the back of Pat's coat, and watched to see him put it on. Pat, of course, saw the donkey's head on his coat, and, turning to the Englishmen, said:

"Which of yez wiped your face on me coat?"

A district leader went to Sea Girt, in 1912, to see the Democratic candidate for President. In the course of an animated conversation, the leader, noticing that Governor Wilson's eyeglasses were perched perilously near the tip of his nose remarked: "Your glasses, Governor, are almost on your mouth."

"That's all right," was the quick response. "I want to see what I'm talking about."

According to the London *Globe* two Germans were halted at the French frontier by the customs officers. "We have each to declare three bottles of red wine," said one of the Germans to the *douaniers*. "How much to pay?"

"Where are the bottles?" asked the customs man.

"They are within!" laughed the Teuton making a gesture.

The French *douanier*, unruffled, took down his tariff book and read, or pretended to read: "Wines imported in bottles pay so much, wines imported in barrels pay so much, and wines *en peaux d'âne* pay no duty. You can pass, gentlemen."

A small boy was hoeing corn in a sterile field by the roadside, when a passer-by stopped and said:

"'Pears to me your corn is rather small."

"Certainly," said the boy; "it's dwarf corn."

"But it looks yaller."

"Certainly; we planted the yaller kind."

"But it looks as if you wouldn't get more than half a crop."

"Of course not; we planted it on halves."

REPORTING

See Journalism; Newspapers.

REPUBLICAN PARTY

The morning after a banquet, during the Democratic convention in Baltimore, a prominent Republican thus greeted an equally well-know Democrat:

"I understand there were some Republicans at the banquet last night."

"Oh, yes," said the Democrate genially, "one waited on me."

REPUTATION

Popularity is when people like you; and reputation is when they ought to, but really can't.—*Frank Richardson.*

RESEMBLANCES

Senator Blackburn is a thorough Kentuckian, and has all the local pride of one born in the blue-grass section of his

State. He also has the prejudice against being taken for an Indianian which seems inherent in all native-born Kentuckians. While coming to Congress, several sessions ago, he was approached in the Pullman coach by a New Yorker, who, after bowing politely to him, said:

"Is not this Senator Blackburn of Indiana?"

The Kentuckian sprang from his seat, and glaring at his interlocutor exclaimed angrily:

"No, sir, by ——. The reason I look so bad is I have been sick!"

"Every time the baby looks into my face he smiles," said Mr. Meekins.

"Well," answered his wife, "it may not be exactly polite, but it shows he has a sense of humor."

Mark Twain constantly received letters and photographs from men who had been told that they looked like him. One was from Florida, and the likeness, as shown by the man's picture, was really remarkable—so remarkable, indeed, that Mr. Clemens sent the following acknowledgment:

"My Dear Sir: I thank you very much for your letter and the photograph. In my opinion you are certainly more like me than any other of my doubles. In fact, I am sure that if you stood before me in a mirrorless frame I could shave by you."

NEIGHBOR—"Johnny, I think in looks you favor your mother a great deal."

JOHNNY—"Well, I may look like her, but do you tink dat's a favor?"

RESIGNATION

"Then you don't think I practice what I preach, eh?" queried the minister in talking with one of the deacons at a meeting.

"No, sir, I don't," replied the deacon. "You've been preacin' on the subject of resignation for two years an' ye haven't resigned yet."

RESPECTABILITY

"Is he respectable?"

"Eminently so. He's never been indicted for anything less than stealing a railroad."—*Wasp.*

REST CURE

A weather-beaten damsel somewhat over six feet in height and with a pair of shoulders proportionately broad appeared at a back door in Wyoming and asked for light housework. She said that her name was Lizzie, and explained that she had been ill with typhoid and was convalescing.

"Where did you come from, Lizzie?" inquired the woman of the house. "Where have you been?"

"I've been workin' out on Howell's ranch," replied Lizzie, "diggin' post-holes while I was gittin' my strength back."

RETALIATION

You know that fellow, Jim McGroiarty, the lad that's always comin' up and thumpin ye on the chest and yellin', 'How are ye?'"

"I know him."

"I'll bet he's smashed twinty cigars for me—some of them clear Havanny—but I'll get even with him now."

"How will you do it?"

"I'll tell ye. Jim always hits me over the vest pocket where I carry my cigars. He'll hit me just once more. There's no cigar in me vest pocket this mornin'. Instead of it, there's a stick of dynamite, d'ye mind!"

Once when Henry Ward Beecher was in the midst of an eloquent political speech some wag in the audience crowed like a cock. It was done to perfection and the audience was convulsed with laughter. The great orator's friends felt uneasy as to his reception of the interruption.

But Mr. Beecher stood perfectly calm. He stopped speaking, listened till the crowing ceased, and while the audience was laughing he pulled out his watch. Then he said: "That's strange. My watch says it is only ten o'clock. But there can't be any mistake about it. Is must be morning for the instincts of the lower animals are absolutely infallible."

An Episcopal clergyman, rector of a fashionable church in one of Boston's most exclusive suburbs, so as not to be bothered with the innumerable telephone calls that fall to one in his profession, had his name left out of the telephone book. A prominent merchant of the same name, living in the same suburb, was continually annoyed by requests to officiate at funerals and baptisms. He went to the rector, told his troubles in a kindly way, and asked the parson to have his name put in the directory. But without success.

The merchant then determined to complain to the telephone company. As he was writing the letter, one Saturday evening, the telephone rang and the timid voice of a young man asked if the Rev. Mr. Blank would marry him at once. A happy thought came to the merchant: "No, I'm too damn busy writing my sermon," he replied.

REVOLUTIONS

Haiti was in the midst of a revolution.

As a phase of it two armed bodes were approaching each other so that a third was about to be caught between them.

The commander of the third party saw the predicament. On the right government troops, on the left insurgents.

"General, why do you not give the order to fire?" asked an aide, dashing up on a lame mule.

"I would like to," responded the general, "but, Great Scott! I can't remember which side we're fighting for."

REWARDS

Said a great Congregational preacher
To a hen, "You're a beautiful creature."
  And the hen, just for that,
  Laid an egg is his hat,
And thus did the Hen reward Beecher.

RHEUMATISM

FARMER BARNES—"I've bought a barometer, Hannah, to tell when it's going to rain, ye know."

MRS. BARNES—"To tell when it's goin' to rain! Why, I never heard o' such extravagance. What do ye s'pose th' Lord has given ye th' rheumatis for?"—*Tit-Bits.*

ROADS

A Yankee just returning to the states was dining with an Englishman, and the latter complained of the mud in America.

"Yes," said the American, "but it's nothing to the mud over here."

"Nonsense!" said the Englishman.

"Fact," the American replied. "Why, this afternoon I had a remarkable adventure—came near getting into trouble with an old gentleman—all through your confounded mud."

"Some of the streets are a little greasy at this season, I admit," said the Englishman. "What was your adventure, though?"

"Well," said the American, "as I was walking along I noticed that the mud was very thick, and presently I saw a high hat afloat on a large puddle of very rich ooze. Thinking to do some one a kindness, I gave the hat a poke with my stick, when an old gentleman looked up from beneath, surprised and frowning. 'Hello!' I said. 'Your're in pretty deep!' 'Deeper than you think,' he said. 'I'm on the top of an omnibus!'"

ROASTS

As William Faversham was having his luncheon in a Birmingham hotel he was much annoyed by another visitor, who, during the whole of the meal, stood with his back to the fire warming himself and watching Faversham eat. At length, unable to endure it any longer, Mr. Faversham rang the bell and said:

"Waiter, kindly turn that gentleman around. I think he is done on that side."

ROOSEVELT, THEODORE

A delegation from Kansas visited Theodore Roosevelt at Oyster Bay some years ago, while he was president. The host met them with coat and collar off, mopping his brow.

"Ah, gentlemen," he said, "dee-lighted to see you. Dee-lighted. But I'm very busy putting in my hay just now. Come down to the barn with me and we'll talk things over while I work."

Down to the barn hustled President and delegation.

Mr. Roosevelt seized a pitchfork and—but where was the hay?

"John!" shouted the President. "John! where's all the hay?"

"Sorry, sir," came John's voice from the loft, "but I ain't had time to throw it back since you threw it up for yesterday's delegation."

SALARIES

A country school-teacher was cashing her monthly check at the bank. The teller apologized for the filthy condition of the bills, saying, "I hope you're not afraid of microbes."

"Not a bit of it," the schoolma'am replied. "I'm sure no microbe could live on my salary!"—*Frances Kirkland.*

SALESMEN AND SALESMANSHIP

A dark fruit-dealer in Georgia has a sign above his wares that reads:

Watermelons

Our choice .... 25 cents.
Your choice .... 35 cents.
—*Elgin Burroughs.*

The quick wit of a traveling salesman who has since become a well-known merchant was severely tested one day. He sent in his card by the office-boy to the manager of a large concern, whose inner office was separated from the waiting-room by a ground-glass partition. When the boy handed his card to the manager the salesman saw him impatiently tear it in half and throw it in the waste-basket; the boy came out and told the caller that he could not see the chief. The salesman told the boy to go back and get him his card; the boy brought out five cents, with the message that his card was torn up. Then the salesman took out another card and sent the boy back, saying: "Tell your boss I sell two cards for five cents."

He got his interview and sold a large bill of goods.

A young man entered a hat store and asked to see the latest styles in derbies. He was evidently hard to please, for soon the counter was covered with hats that he had tried on and found wanting. At last the salesman picked up a brown derby, brushed it off on his sleeve, and extended it admiringly.

"These are being very much worn this season, sir," he said. "Won't you try it on?"

The customer put the hat on and surveyed himself critically in the mirror. "You're sure it's in style?"

"The most fashionable thing we have in the shop, sir. And it suits you to perfection—if the fit's right."

"Yes, it fits very well. So you think I had better have it?"

"I don't think you could do better."

"No, I don't think I could. So I guess I won't buy a new one after all."

The salesman had been boosting the customer's old hat, which had become mixed among the many new ones.

VISITOR—"Can I see that motorist who was brought here an hour ago?"

NURSE—"He hasn't come to his senses yet."

VISITOR—"Oh, that's all right. I only want to sell him another car."—*Judge*.

"That fellow is too slick for me. Sold me a lot that was two feet under water. I went around to demand my money back."

"Get it?"

"Get nothing! Then he sold me a second-hand gasoline launch and a copy of 'Venetian Life,' by W. D. Howells."

In a small South Carolina town that was "finished" before the war, two men were playing checkers in the back of a store. A traveling man who was making his first trip to the town was watching the game, and, not being acquainted with the business methods of the citizens, he called the attention of the owner of the store to some customers who had just entered the front door.

"Sh! Sh!" answered the storekeeper, making another move on the checkerboard. "Keep perfectly quiet and they'll go out."

> He who finds he has something to sell,
> And goes and whispers it down a well,
> Is not so apt to collar the dollars,
> As he who climbs a tree and hollers.
>
> —*The Advertiser.*

SALOONS

"Where can I get a drink in this town?" asked a traveling man who landed at a little town in the oil region of Oklahoma, of the 'bus driver.

"See that millinery shop over there?" asked the driver, pointing to a building near the depot.

"You don't mean to say that they sell whiskey in a millinery store?" exclaimed the drummer.

"No, I mean that's the only place here they don't sell it," said the 'bus man.

SALVATION

WILLIS—"Some of these rich fellows seem to think that they can buy their way into heaven by leaving a million dollars to a church when they die."

GILLIS—"I don't know but that they stand as much chance as some of these other rich fellows who are trying to get in on the instalment plan of ten cents a Sunday while they're living."—*Lauren S. Hamilton.*

An Italian noble at church one day gave a priest who begged for the souls in purgatory, a piece of gold.

"Ah, my lord," said the good father, "you have now delivered a soul."

The count threw another piece upon the plate.

"Here is another soul delivered," said the priest.

"Are you positive of it?" replied the count.

"Yes, my lord," replied the priest; "I am certain they are now in heaven."

"Then," said the count, "I'll take back my money, for it signifies nothing to you now, seeing the souls have already got to heaven."

An Episcopal missionary in Wyoming visited one of the outlying districts in his territory for the purpose of conducting prayer in the home of a large family not conspicuous for its piety. He made known his intentions to the woman of the house, and she murmured vaguely that "she'd go out and see." She was long in returning, and after a tiresome wait the missionary went to the door and called with some impatience:

"Aren't you coming in? Don't you care anything about your souls?"

"Souls?" yelled the head of the family from the orchard. "We haven't got time to fool with our souls when the bees are swarmin.' "

Edith was light-hearted and merry over everything. Nothing appealed to her seriously. So, one day, her mother decided to invite a very serious young parson to dinner, and he was placed next the light-hearted girl. Everything went well until she asked him:

"You speak of everybody having a mission. What is yours?"

"My mission," said the parson, "is to save young men."

"Good," replied the girl, "I'm glad to meet you. I wish you'd save one for me."

SAVING

Take care of the pennies and the dollars will be blown in by your heirs.—*Puck.*

"Do you save up money for a rainy day, dear?"

"Oh, no! I never shop when it rains."

JOHNNY—"Papa, would you be glad if I saved a dollar for you?"

PAPA—"Certainly, my son."

JOHNNY—"Well, I saved it for you, all right. You said if I brought a first-class report from my teacher this week you would give me a dollar, and I didn't bring it."

According to the following story, economy has its pains as well as its pleasures, even after the saving is done.

One spring, for some reason, old Eli was going round town with the face of dissatisfaction, and, when questioned, poured forth his voluble tale of woe thus:

Marse Geo'ge, he come to me last fall an' he say, 'Eli, dis gwine ter be a hard winter, so yo' be keerful, an' save yo' wages fas' an' tight.'

"An' I b'lieve Marse Geo'ge, yas, sah, I b'lieve him, an' I save an' I save, an' when de winter come it ain't got no hardship, an' dere was I wid all dat money jes' frown on mah hands!"

"Robert dear," said the coy little maiden to her sweetheart, "I'm sure you love me; but give me some proof of it, darling. We can't marry on fifteen dollars a week, you know."

"Well, what do you want me to do?" said he, with a grieved air.

"Why, save up a thousand dollars, and have it safe in the bank, and then I'll marry you."

About two months later she cuddled up close to him on the sofa one evening, and said:

"Robert dear, have you saved up that thousand yet?"

"Why, no, my love," he replied; "not all of it."

"How much have you saved, darling?"

"Just two dollars and thirty-five cents, dear."

"Oh, well," said the sweet young thing as she snuggled a little closer, "don't let's wait any longer, darling. I guess that'll do."—*R. M. Winans.*

See also Economy; Thrift.

SCANDAL

An ill wind that blows nobody good.

SCHOLARSHIP

There is in Washington an old "grouch" whose son was graduated from Yale. When the young man came home at the end of the first term, he exulted in the fact that he stood next to the head of his class. But the old gentleman was not satisfied.

"*Next* to the head!" he exclaimed. "What do you mean? I'd like to know what you think I'm sending you to college for? *Next* to the head! Why aren't you at the head, where you ought to be?"

At this the son was much crestfallen; but upon his return, he went about his work with such ambition that at the end of the term he found himself in the coveted place. When he went home that year he felt very proud. It would be great news for the old man.

When the announcement was made, the father contemplated his son for a few minutes in silence; then, with a shrug, he remarked:

"At the head of the class, eh? Well, that's a fine commentary on Yale University!"—*Howard Morse.*

"Well, there were only three boys in school to-day who could answer one question that the teacher asked us," said a proud boy of eight.

"And I hope my boy was one of the three," said the proud mother.

"Well, I was," answered Young Hopeful, "and Sam Harris and Harry Stone were the other two."

"I am very glad you proved yourself so good a scholar, my son; it makes your mother proud of you. What question did the teacher ask, Johnnie?"

"'Who broke the glass in the back window?'"

Sammy's mother was greatly distressed because he had such poor marks in his school work. She scolded, coaxed, even promised him a dime if he would do better. The next day he came running home.

"Oh, mother," he shouted, "I got a hundred!"

"And what did you get a hundred in?"

"In two things," replied Sammy without hesitation. "I got forty in readin' and sixty in spellin'."

Who ceases to be a student has never been one.—*George Iles.*

See also College students.

SCHOOLS

"Mamma," complained little Elsie, "I don't feel very well."

"That's too bad, dear," said mother sympathetically. "Where do you feel worst?"

"In school, mamma."

SCIENTIFIC MANAGEMENT

The late Sylvanus Miller, civil engineer, who was engaged in railroad enterprise in Central America, was seeking local support for a road and attempted to give the matter point. He asked a native:

"How long does it take you to carry your goods to market by muleback?"

"Three days," was the reply.

"There's the point," said Miller. "With our road in operation you could take your goods to market and be back home in one day."

Very good, señor," answered the native. "But what would we do with the other two days?"

A visitor from New York to the suburbs said to his host during the afternoon:

"By the way, your front gate needs repairing. It was all I could do to get it open. You ought to have it trimmed or greased or something."

"Oh, no," replied the owner—"Oh, no, that's all right."

"Why is it?" asked the visitor.

"Because," was the reply, "every one who comes through that gate pumps two buckets of water into the tank on the roof."

THE SCOTCH

A Scotsman is one who prays on his knees on Sunday and preys on his neighbors on week days.

It being the southerner's turn, he told about a county in Missouri so divided in sentiment that year after year the vote of a single man prohibits the sale of liquor there. "And what," he asked, "do you suppose is the name of the chap who keeps a whole county dry?"

Nobody had an idea.

"Mackintosh, as I'm alive!" declared the southerner.

Everybody laughed except the Englishman. "It's just like a Scotsman to be so obstinate!" he sniffed, and was much astonished when the rest of the party laughed more than ever.

A Scottish minister, taking his walk early in the morning, found one of his parishioners recumbent in a ditch.

"Where hae you been the nicht, Andrew?" asked the minister.

"Weel, I dinna richtly ken," answered the prostrate one, "whether it was a wedding or a funeral, but whichever it was it was a most extraordinary success."

See also Thrift.

SEASICKNESS

A Philadelphian, on his way to Europe, was experiencing seasickness for the first time. Calling his wife to his bedside, he said in a weak voice: "Jennie, my will is in the Commercial Trust Company's care. Everything is left to you, dear. My various stocks you will find in my safe-deposit box." Then he said fervently: "And, Jenny, bury me on the other side. I can't stand this trip again, alive or dead."—*Joe King.*

Motto for the dining saloon of an ocean steamship: "Man wants but little here below, nor wants that little long."

On the steamer the little bride was very much concerned about her husband, who was troubled with dyspepsia.

"My husband is peculiarly liable to seasickness, Captain," remarked the bride. "Could you tell him what to do in case of an attack?"

"That won't be necessary, Madam," replied the Captain; "he'll do it."

A clergyman who was holding a children's service at a Continental winter resort had occasion to catechize his hearers on the parable of the unjust steward. "What is a steward?" he asked.

A little boy who had arrived from England a few days before held up his hand. "He is a man, sir," he replied, with a reminiscent look on his face, "who brings you a basin."

"The first day out was perfectly lovely," said the young lady just back from abroad. "The water was as smooth as glass, and it was simply gorgeous. But the second day was rough and—er—decidedly disgorgeous."

The great liner rolled and pitched.

"Henry," faltered the young bride, "do you still love me?"

"More than ever, darling!" was Henry's fervent answer.

Then there was an eloquent silence.

"Henry," she gasped, turning her pale, ghastly face away, "I thought that would make me feel better, but it doesn't!"

There was a young man from Ostend,
Who vowed he'd hold out to the end;
 But when half way over
 From Calais to Dover,
He did what he didn't intend.

SEASONS

There was a young fellow named Hall,
Who fell in the spring in the fall;
 'Twould have been a sad thing
 If he'd died in the spring,
But he didn't—he died in the fall.

SENATORS

A Senator is very often a man who has risen from obscurity to something worse.

"You have been conspicuous in the halls of legislation, have you not?" said the young woman who asks all sorts of questions.

"Yes, miss," answered Senator Sorghum, blandly; "I think I have participated in some of the richest hauls that legislation ever made."

An aviator alighted on a field and said to a rather well-dressed individual: "Here, mind my machine a minute, will you?"

"What," the well-dressed individual snarled. "Me mind your machine? Why, I'm a United States Senator!"

"Well, what of it?" said the aviator. "I'll trust you."

SENSE OF HUMOR

"What of his sense of humor?"

"Well, he has to see a joke twice before he sees it once."

—*Richard Kirk.*

"A sense of humor is a help and a blessing through life," says Rear Admiral Buhler. "But even a sense of humor may exist in excess. I have in mind the case of a British soldier who was sentenced to be flogged. During the flogging he laughed continually. The harder the lash was laid on, the harder the soldier laughed.

"'Wot's so funny about bein' flogged?' demanded the sergeant.

"'Why,' the soldier chuckled, 'I'm the wrong man.'"

Mark Twain once approached a friend, a business man, and confided to him that he needed the assistance of a stenographer.

"I can send you one, a fine young fellow," the friend said. "He came to my office yesterday in search of a position, but I didn't have an opening."

"Has he a sense of humor?" Mark asked cautiously.

"A sense of humor? He has—in fact, he got off one or two pretty witty things himself yesterday," the friend hastened to assure him.

"Sorry, but he won't do, then," Mark said.

"Won't do? Why?"

"No," said Mark. "I had one once before with a sense of humor, and it interfered too much with the work. I cannot afford to pay a man two dollars a day for laughing."

The perception of the ludicrous is a pledge of sanity.—*Emerson.*

SENTRIES

See Armies.

SERMONS

See Preaching.

SERVANTS

Tommy—"Pop, what is it that the Bible says is here to-day and gone tomorrow?"

Pop—"Probably the cook, my son."

As usual, they began discussing the play after the theater. "Well, how did you like the piece, my dear?" asked the fond husband who had always found his wife a good critic.

"Very much. There's only one improbable thing in it: the second act takes place two years after the first, and they have the same servant."

Smith—'We are certainly in luck with our new cook—soup, meat, vegetables and dessert, everything perfect!"

Mrs. S.—"Yes, but the dessert was made by her successor."

The New Girl—"An' may me intended visit me every Sunday afternoon, ma'am?"

Mistress—"Who is your intended, Delia?"

The New Girl—"I don't know yet, ma'am. I'm a stranger in town."

"And do you have to be called in the morning?" asked the lady who was about to engage a new girl.

"I don't has to be, mum," replied the applicant, "unless you happens to need me."

A maid dropped and broke a beautiful platter at a dinner recently. The host did not permit a trifle like this to ruffle him in the least.

"These little accidents happen 'most every day," he said apologetically. "You see, she isn't a trained waitress. She was a dairymaid originally, but she had to abandon that occupation on account of her inability to handle the cows without breaking their horns."

Young housewives obliged to practice strict economy will sympathize with the sad experience of a Washington woman.

When her husband returned home one evening he found her dissolved in tears, and careful questioning elicited the reason for her grief.

"Dan," said she, "every day this week I have stopped to look at a perfect love of a hat in Mme. Louise's window. Such a hat, Dan, such a beautiful hat! But the price—well, I wanted it the worst way, but just couldn't afford to buy it."

"Well, dear," began the husband recklessly, "we might manage to——"

"Thank you, Dan," interrupted the wife, "but there isn't any 'might' about it. I paid the cook this noon, and what do you think? She marched right down herself and bought that hat!"—*Edwin Tarrisse.*

It is probable that many queens of the kitchen share the sentiment good-naturedly expressed by a Scandinavian servant, recently taken into the service of a young matron of Chicago.

The youthful assumer of household cares was disposed to be a trifle patronizing.

"Now, Lena," she asked earnestly, "are you a *good* cook?"

"Ya-as, 'm, I tank so," said the girl, with perfect naiveté, "if you vill not try to help me."—*Elgin Burroughs.*

"Have you a good cook now?"

"I don't know. I haven't been home since breakfast!"

Mrs. Littletown—"This magazine looks rather the worse for wear."

Mrs. Neartown—"Yes, it's the one I sometimes lend to the servant on Sundays."

Mrs. Littletown—"Doesn't she get tired of always reading the same one?"

Mr. Neartown—"Oh, no. You see, it's the same book, but it's always a different servant."—*Suburban Life.*

Mrs. Housen Hohm—"What is your name?"

Applicant for Cookship—"Miss Arlington."

Mrs. Housen Hohm—"Do you expect to be called Miss Arlington?"

Applicant—"No, ma'am; not if you have an alarm clock in my room."

Mistress—"Nora, I saw a policeman in the park to-day kiss a baby. I hope you will remember my objection to such things."

Nora—"Sure, ma'am, no policeman would ever think iv kissin' yer baby whin I'm around."

See also Gratitude; Recommendations.

SHOPPING

Clerk—"Can you let me off to-morrow afternoon? My wife wants me to go shopping with her."

Employer—"Certainly not. We are much too busy."

Clerk—"Thank you very much, sir. You are very kind!"

SHYNESS

The late "Ian Maclaren" (Dr. John Watson) once told this story on himself to some friends:

"I was coming over on the steamer to America, when one day I went into the library to do some literary work. I was very busy and looked so, I suppose. I had no sooner started to write than a diffident-looking young man plumped into the chair opposite me, began twirling his cap and stared at me. I let him sit there. An hour or more passed, and he was still there, returning my occasional and discouraging glances at him with a foolish, ingratiating smile. I was inclined to be annoyed. I had a suspicion that he was a reader of my books, perhaps an admirer—or an autograph-hunter. He could wait. But at last he rose, and still twirling his cap, he spoke:

"'Excuse me, Doctor Watson; I'm getting deathly sick in here and I'm real sorry to disturb you, but I thought you'd like to know that just as soon as you left her Mrs. Watson fell down the companionway stairs, and I guess she hurt herself pretty badly.'"

SIGNS

When the late Senator Wolcott first went to Colorado he and his brother opened a law office at Idaho Springs under the firm name of "Ed. Wolcott & Bro." Later the partnership was dissolved. The future senator packed his few assets, including the sign that had hung outside of his office, upon a burro and started for Georgetown, a mining town farther up in the hills. Upon his arrival he was greeted by a crowd of miners who critically surveyed him and his outfit. One of them, looking first at the sign that hung over the pack, then at Wolcott, and finally at the donkey, ventured:

"Say, stranger, which of you is Ed?"

"Buck" Kilgore, of Texas, who once kicked open the door of the House of Representatives when Speaker Reed had all doors locked to prevent the minority from leaving the floor and thus escaping a vote, was noted for his indifference to forms and rules. Speaker Reed, annoyed by members bringing lighted cigars upon the floor of the House just before opening time, had signs conspicuously posted as follows: "No smoking on the floor of the House." One day just before convening the House his eagle eye detected Kilgore nonchalantly puffing away at a fat cigar. Calling a page, he told him to give his compliments to the gentleman from Texas and ask him if he had not seen the signs. After a while the page returned and seated himself without reporting to the Speaker, and Mr. Reed was irritated to see the gentleman from Texas continue his smoke. With a frown he summoned the page and asked:

"Did you tell the gentleman from Texas what I said?"

"I did," replied the page.

"What did he say?" asked Reed.

"Well—er," stammered the page, "he said to give his compliments to you and tell you he did not believe in signs."

SILENCE

A conversation with an Englishman.—*Heine.*

Ball—"What is silence?"

Hall—"The college yell of the school of experience."

The other day upon the links a distinguished clergyman was playing a closely contested game of golf. He carefully teed up his ball and addressed it with the most approved grace; he raised his driver and hit the ball a tremendous clip, but instead of soaring into the azure it perversely went about twelve feet to the right and then buzzed around in a circle. The clerical gentleman frowned, scowled, pursed up his mouth and bit his lips, but said nothing, and a friend who stood by him said: "Doctor, that is the most profane silence I ever witnessed."

SIN

Man-like is it to fall into sin,
Fiend-like is it to dwell therein,
Christ-like is it for sin to grieve,
God-like is it all sin to leave.

—*Friedrich von Logan.*

"Now," said the clergyman to the Sunday-school class, "can any of you tell me what are sins of omission?"

"Yes, sir," said the small boy. "They are the sins we ought to have done and haven't."

SINGERS

As the celebrated soprano began to sing, little Johnnie became greatly exercised over the gesticulations of the orchestra conductor.

"What's that man shaking his stick at her for?" he demanded indignantly.

"Sh-h! He's not shaking his stick at her."

But Johnny was not convinced.

"Then what in thunder's she hollering for?"

A visiting clergyman was occupying a pulpit in St. Louis one Sunday when it was the turn of the bass to sing a solo, which he did very badly, to the annoyance of the preacher, a lover of music. When the singer fell back in his seat, red of face and exhausted, the clergyman arose, placed his hands on the unopened Bible, deliberately surveyed the faces of the congregation, and announced the text:

"And the wind ceased and there was a great calm."

It wasn't the text he had chosen, but it fitted his sermon as well as the occasion.

One cold, wet, and windy night he came upon a Negro shivering in the doorway of an Atlanta store. Wondering what the darky could be doing, standing on a cold, wet night in such a draughty position, the proprietor of the shop said:

"Jim, what are you doing here?"

"'Scuse me, sir," said Jim, "but I'm gwine to sing bass tomorrow mornin' at church, an' I am tryin' to ketch a cold."

—*Howard Morse*

"The man who sings all day at work is a happy man."

"Yes, but how about the man who works and has to listen to him?"

Miss Jeanette Gilder was one of the ardent enthusiasts at the début of Tetrazzini. After the first act she rushed to the back of the house to greet one of her friends. "Don't you think she is a wonder?" she asked excitedly.

"She is a great singer unquestionably," responded her more phlegmatic friend, "but the registers of her voice are not so even as, for instance, Melba's."

"Oh, bother Melba," said Miss Gilder. "Tetrazzini gives infinitely more heat from her registers."

At a certain Scottish dinner it was found that every one had contributed to the evening's entertainment but a certain Doctor MacDonald.

"Come, come, Doctor MacDonald," said the chairman, "we cannot let you escape."

The doctor protested that he could not sing.

"My voice is altogether unmusical, and resembles the sound caused by the act of rubbing a brick along the panels of a door."

The company attributed this to the doctor's modesty. Good singers, he was reminded, always needed a lot of pressing.

"Very well," said the doctor, "if you can stand it I will sing."

Long before he had finished his audience was uneasy.

There was a painful silence as the doctor sat down, broken at length by the voice of a braw Scot at the end of the table.

"Mon," he exclaimed, "your singin's no up to much, but your veracity's just awful. You're richt aboot that brick."

She smiles, my darling smiles, and all
   The world is filled with light;
She laughs—'tis like the bird's sweet call,
   In meadows fair and bright.
She weeps—the world is cold and gray,
   Rain-clouds shut out the view;
She sings—I softly steal away
   And wait till she gets through.

God sent his singers upon earth
With songs of sadness and of mirth,
That they might touch the hearts of men,
And bring them back to heaven again.

—Longfellow.

SKATING

A young lady entered a crowded car with a pair of skates slung over her arm. An elderly gentleman arose to give her his seat.

"Thank you very much, sir," she said, "but I've been skating all afternoon, and I'm tired of sitting down."

SKY-SCRAPERS

See Buildings.

SLEEP

Recently a friend who had heard that I sometimes suffer from insomnia told me of a sure cure. "Eat a pint of peanuts and drink two or three glasses of milk before going to bed," said he, "and I'll warrant you'll be asleep within half an hour." I did as he suggested, and now for the benefit of others who may be afflicted with insomnia, I feel it my duty to report what happened, so far as I am able to recall the details.

First, let me say my friend was right. I did go to sleep very soon after my retirement. Then a friend with his head under his arm came along and asked me if I wanted to buy his feet. I was negotiating with him, when the dragon on which I was riding slipped out of his skin and left me floating in mid-air. While I was considering how I should get down, a bull with two heads peered over the edge of the wall and said he would haul me up if I would first climb up and rig a windlass for him. So as I was sliding down the mountainside the brakeman came in, and I asked him when the train would reach my station.

"We passed your station four hundred years ago," he said, calmly folding the train up and slipping it into his vest pocket.

At this juncture the clown bounded into the ring and pulled the center-pole out of the ground, lifting the tent and all the people in it up, up, while I stood on the earth below watching myself go out of sight among the clouds above. Then I awoke, and found I had been asleep almost ten minutes.—*The Good Health Clinic.*

SMILES

There was a young lady of Niger,
Who went for a ride on a tiger;
   They returned from the ride
   With the lady inside,
And a smile on the face of the tiger.

—*Gilbert K. Chesterton.*

SMOKING

A woman is only a woman, but a good cigar is a smoke.

—*Rudyard Kipling.*

AUNT MARY—(horrified)—"Good gracious. Harold, what would your mother say if she saw you smoking cigarets?"

HAROLD (calmly)—"She'd have a fit. They're her cigarets."

An Irish soldier on sentry duty had orders to allow no one to smoke near his post. An officer with a lighted cigar approached whereupon Pat boldly challenged him and ordered him to put it out at once.

The officer with a gesture of disgust threw away his cigar, but no sooner was his back turned than Pat picked it up and quietly retired to the sentry box.

The officer happening to look around, observed a beautiful cloud of smoke issuing from the box. He at once challenged Pat for smoking on duty.

"Smoking, is it, sor? Bedad, and I'm only keeping it lit to show the corporal when he comes as evidence agin you."

SNEEZING

While campaigning in Iowa Speaker Cannon was once inveigled into visiting the public schools of a town where he was billed to speak. In one of the lower grades an ambitious teacher called upon a youthful Demosthenes to entertain the distinguished visitor with an exhibition of amateur oratory. The selection attempted was Byron's "Battle of Waterloo," and just as the boy reached the end of the first paragraph, Speaker Cannon gave vent to a violent sneeze. "But, hush! hark!" declaimed the youngster; "a deep sound strikes like a rising knell! Did ye not hear it?"

The visitors smiled and a moment later the second sneeze—which the Speaker was vainly trying to hold back—came with increased violence.

"But, hark!" bawled the boy, "that heavy sound breaks in once more, and nearer, clearer, deadlier than before! Arm! arm! it is—it is—the cannon's opening roar!"

This was too much, and the laugh that broke from the party swelled to a roar when "Uncle Joe" chuckled: "Put up your weapons, children; I won't shoot any more."

SNOBBERY

Snobbery is the pride of those who are not sure of their position.

SNORING

Snore—An unfavorable report from headquarters.—*Foolish Dictionary.*

SOCIALISTS

Among the stories told of the late Baron de Rothschild is one which details how a "change of heart" once came to his valet —an excellent fellow, albeit a violent "red."

Alphonse was as good a servant as one would wish to employ, and as his socialism never got further than attending a weekly meeting, the baron never objected to his political faith. After a few months of these permissions to absent himself from duty, his employer noticed one week that he did not ask to go. The baron thought Alphonse might have forgotten the night, but when the next week he stayed at home, he inquired what was up.

"Sir," said the valet, with the utmost dignity, "some of my former colleagues have worked out a calculation that if all the wealth in France were divided equally per capita, each individual would be the possessor of two thousand francs."

Then he stopped as if that told the whole story, so said the baron, "What of that?"

"Sir," came back from the enlightened Alphonse, "I have five thousand francs now."—*Warwick James Price.*

SOCIETY

Smart Society is made up of the worldly, the fleshy, and the devilish.—*Harold Melbourne.*

"What are her days at home?"

"Oh, a society leader has no days at home anymore. Nowadays she has her telephone hours."

Society consists of two classes, the upper and the lower. The latter cultivates the dignity of labor, the former the labor of dignity.—*Punch.*

> There was a young person called Smarty,
> Who sent out his cards for a party;
>   So exclusive and few
>   Were the friends that he knew
> That no one was present but Smarty.

SOLECISMS

A New York firm recently hung the following sign at the entrance of a large building: "Wanted: Sixty girls to sew buttons on the sixth floor."

Reporters are obliged to write their descriptions of accidents hastily and often from meager data, and in the attempt to make them vivid they sometimes make them ridiculous; for example, a New York City paper a few days ago, in describing a collision between a train and a motor bus, said: "The train, too, was filled with passengers. Their shrieks mingled with the *cries of the dead* and the dying of the bus!"

SONS

"I thought your father looked very handsome with his gray hairs."

"Yes, dear old chap. I gave him those."

SOUVENIRS

"A friend of mine, traveling in Ireland, stopped for a drink of milk at a white cottage with a thatched roof, and, as he sipped his refreshment, he noted, on a center table under a glass dome, a brick with a faded rose upon the top of it.

" 'Why do you cherish in this way,' my friend said to his host, 'that common brick and that dead rose?'

" 'Shure, sir,' was the reply, 'there's certain memories attachin' to them. Do you see this big dent in my head? Well, it was made by that brick.'

" 'But the rose?' said my friend.

"His host smiled quietly.

" 'The rose,' he explained, 'is off the grave of the man that threw the brick.' "

SPECULATION

There are two times in a man's life when he should not speculate: when he can't afford it, and when he can.—*Mark Twain.*

SPEED

"I always said old Cornelius Husk was slow," said one Quag man to another.

"Why, what's he been doin' now?" the other asked.

"Got himself run over by a hearse!"

"So you heard the bullet whiz past you?" asked the lawyer of the darky.

"Yes, sah, heard it twict."

"How's that?"

"Heard it whiz when it passed me, and heard it again when I passed it."

A near race riot happened in a southern town. The Negroes gathered in one crowd and the whites in another. The whites fired their revolvers into the air, and the Negroes took to their heels. Next day a plantation owner said to one of his men: "Sam, were you in that crowd that gathered last night?" "Yassir." "Did you run like the wind, Sam?" "No, sir. I didn't run like the wind, 'deed I didn't. But I passed two niggers that was running like the wind."

A guest in a Cincinnati hotel was shot and killed. The Negro porter who heard the shooting was a witness at the trial.

"How many shots did you hear?" asked the lawyer.

"Two shots, sah," he replied.

"How far apart were they?"

"'Bout like dis way," explained the Negro, clapping his hands with an interval of about a second between claps.

"Where were you when the first shot was fired?"

"Shinin' a gemman's shoe in the basement of de hotel."

"Where were you when the second shot was fired?"

"Ah was passin' de Big Fo' depot."

SPINSTERS

"Is there anyone present who wishes the prayers of the congregation for a relative or friend?" asks the minister.

"I do," says the angular lady arising from the rear pew. "I want the congregation to pray for my husband."

"Why, sister Abigail!" replies the minister. "You have no husband as yet."

"Yes, but I want you all to pitch in an' pray for one for me!"

Some time ago the wife of an assistant state officer gave a party to a lot of old maids of her town. She asked each one to bring a photograph of the man who had tried to woo and wed her. Each of the old maids brought a photograph and they were all pictures of the same man, the hostess's husband.

Maude Adams was one day discussing with her old Negro "mammy" the approaching marriage of a friend.

"When is you gwine to git married, Miss Maudie?" asked the mammy, who took a deep interest in her talented young mistress.

"I don't know, mammy," answered the star. "I don't think I'll ever get married."

"Well," sighed mammy, in an attempt to be philosophical, "they do say ole maids is the happies' kind after they quits strugglin'."

Here's to the Bachelor, so lonely and gay,
For it's not his fault, he was born that way;
And here's to the Spinster, so lonely and good;
For it's not her fault, she hath done what she could.

An old maid on the wintry side of fifty, hearing of the marriage of a pretty young lady, her friend, observed with a deep and sentimental sigh: "Well, I suppose it is what we must all come to."

A famous spinster, known throughout the country for her charities, was entertaining a number of little girls from a charitable institution. After the luncheon, the children were shown through the place, in order that they might enjoy the many beautiful things it contained.

"This," said the spinster, indicating a statue, "is Minerva."

"Was Minerva married?" asked one of the little girls.

"No, my child," said the spinster, with a smile; "Minerva was the Goddess of Wisdom."—*E. T.*

There once was a lonesome, lorn spinster,
And luck had for years been ag'inst her;
 When a man came to burgle
 She shrieked, with a gurgle,
"Stop thief, while I call in a min'ster!"

SPITE

Think twice before you speak, and then you may be able to say something more aggravating than if you spoke right out at once.

A man had for years employed a steady German workman. One day Jake came to him and asked to be excused from work the next day.

"Certainly, Jake," beamed the employer. "What are you going to do?"

"Vall," said Jake slowly. 'I tink I must go by mein wife's funeral. She dies yesterday."

After the lapse of a few weeks Jake again approached his boss for a day off.

"All right, Jake, but what are you going to do this time?"

"Aber," said Jake, "I go to make me, mit mein fräulein, a wedding."

"What? So soon? Why, it's only been three weeks since you buried your wife."

"Ach!" replied Jake, "I don't hold spite long."

SPRING

In the spring the housemaid's fancy
 Lightly turns from pot and pan
To the greater necromancy
 Of a young unmarried man.
You can hold her through the winter,
 And she'll work around and sing,
But it's just as good as certain
 She will marry in the spring.

It is easy enough to look pleasant,
When the spring comes along with a rush;
  But the fellow worth-while
  Is the one who can smile
When he slips and sits down in the slush.

                —Leslie Van Every.

STAMMERING

One of the ushers approached a man who appeared to be annoying those about him.

"Don't you like the show?"

"Yes, indeed!"

"Then why do you persist in hissing the performers?"

"Why, m-man alive, I w-was-n't h-hissing! I w-was s-simply s-s-s-saying to S-s-s-sammie that the s-s-s-singing is s-s-s-superb."

A man who stuttered badly went to a specialist and after ten difficult lessons learned to say quite distinctly, "Peter Piper picked a peck of pickled peppers." His friends congratulated him upon this splendid achievement.

"Yes," said the man doubtfully, "but it's s-s-such a d-d-deucedly d-d-d-difficult rem-mark to w-w-work into an ordin-n-nary c-c-convers-s-sa-tion, y' know."

STATESMEN

A statesman is a dead politician.—*Mr. Dooley.*

A statesman is a man who finds out which way the crowd is going, then jumps in front and yells like blazes.

STATISTICS

An earnest preacher in Georgia, who has a custom of telling the Lord all the news in his prayers, recently began a petition for help against the progress of wickedness in his town, with the statement:

"Oh, Thou great Jehovah, crime is on the increase. It is becoming more prevalent daily. I can prove it to you by statistics."

PATIENT—"Tell me candidly, Doc, do you think I'll pull through?"

DOCTOR—"Oh, you're bound to get well—you can't help yourself. *The Medical Record* shows that out of one hundred cases like yours, one per cent invariably recovers. I've treated ninety-nine cases, and every one of them died. Why, man alive, you can't die if you try! There's no humbug in statistics."

STEAK

"Can I get a steak here and catch the one o'clock train?"

"It depends on your teeth, sir."

STEAM

"Can you tell what steam is?" asked the examiner.

"Why, sure, sir," replied Patrick confidently. "Steam is—Why—er—it's wather thos's gone crazy wid the heat."

STEAMSHIPS AND STEAMBOATS

"That new steamer they're building is a whopper," says the man with the shoe-button nose.

"Yes," agrees the man with the recalcitrant hair, "but my uncle is going to build one so long that when a passenger gets seasick in one end of it he can go to the other end and be clear away from the storm."

STENOGRAPHERS

A beautiful statuesque blond had left New York to act as stenographer to a dignified Philadelphian of Quaker descent. On the morning of her first appearance she went straight to the desk of her employer.

"I presume," she remarked, "that you begin the day over here the same as they do in New York?"

"Oh, yes," replied the employer, without glancing up from a letter he was reading.

"Well, hurry up and kiss me, then," was the startling rejoinder, "I want to get to work."

STOCK BROKERS

A grain broker in New Boston, Maine,
Said, "That market gives me a pain;
  I can hardly bear it,
  To bull—I don't dare it,
For it's going against the grain."

          —Minnesota Minne-Ha-Ha.

STRATEGY

A bird dog belonging to a man in Mulvane disappeared last week. The owner put this "ad" in the paper and insisted that it be printed exactly as he wrote it:

LOST OR RUN AWAY—One livver culered burd dog called Jim. Will show signs of hyderfobby in about three days.

The dog came home the following day.

"Boy, take these flowers to Miss Bertie Bohoo, Room 12."

"My, sir, you're the fourth gentleman wot's sent her flowers to-day."

"What's that? What the deuce? W-who sent the others?"

"Oh, they didn't send any names. They all said, 'She'll know where they come from.'"

"Well, here, take my card, and tell her these are from the same one who sent the other three boxes."

The little girl was having a great deal of trouble pronouncing some of the words she met with. "Vinegar" had given her the most trouble, and she was duly grieved to know that the village was being entertained by her efforts in this direction.

She was sent one day to the store with the vinegar-jug, to get it filled, and had no intention of amusing the people who were gathered in the store. So she handed the jug to the clerk with:

"Smell the mouth of it and give me a quart."

A young couple had been courting for several years, and the young man seemed to be in no hurry to marry. Finally, one day, he said:

"Sall, I canna marry thee."

"How's that?" asked she.

"I've changed my mind," said he.

"Well, I'll tell thee what we'll do," said she. "If folks know that it's thee as has given me up I shanna be able to get another chap; but if they think I've given thee up then I can get all I want. So we'll have banns published and when the wedding day comes the parson will say to thee, 'Wilt thou have this woman to be thy wedded wife?' and thou must say, 'I will.' And when he says to me, 'Wilt thou have this man to be thy wedded husband?' I shall say, 'I winna.'"

The day came, and when the minister asked the important question the man answered:

"I will."

Then the parson said to the woman:

"Wilt thou have this man to be thy wedded husband?" and she said:

"I will."

"Why," said the young man furiously, "you said you would say 'I winna.'"

"I know that," said the young woman, "but I've changed my mind since."

Charles Stuart, formerly senator from Michigan, was traveling by stage through his own state. The weather was bitter cold, the snow deep, and the roads practically unbroken. The stage was nearly an hour late at the dinner station and everybody was cross and hungry.

In spite of the warning, "Ten minutes only for refreshmenents," Senator Stuart sat down to dinner with his usual deliberation. When he had finished his first cup of coffee the other passengers were leaving the table. By the time his second cup arrived the stage was at the door. "All aboard!" shouted the driver. The senator lingered and called for a third cup of coffee.

While the household, as was the custom, assembled at the door to see the stage off, the senator calmly continued his meal. Suddenly, just as the stage was starting, he pounded violently on the dining-room table. The landlord hurried in. The senator wanted a dish of rice-pudding. When it came he called for a spoon. There wasn't a spoon to be found.

"That shock-headed fellow took 'em!" exclaimed the landlady. "I knew him for a thief the minute I laid eyes on him."

The landlord jumped to the same conclusion.

"Hustle after that stage!" he shouted to the sheriff, who was untying his horse from the rail in front of the tavern. "Bring 'em all back. They've taken the silver!"

A few minutes later the stage, in charge of the sheriff, swung around in front of the house. The driver was in a fury.

"Search them passengers!" insisted the landlord.

But before the officer could move, the senator opened the stage door, stepped inside, then leaned out, touched the sheriff's arm and whispered:

"Tell the landlord he'll find his spoons in the coffee-pot."

SUBWAYS

Any one who has ever traveled on the New York subway in rush hours can easily appreciate the following:

A little man, wedged into the middle of a car, suddenly thought of pickpockets, and quite as suddenly remembered that he had some money in his overcoat. He plunged his hand into his pocket and was somewhat shocked upon encountering the fist of a fat fellow-passenger.

"Aha!" snorted the latter. "I caught you that time!"

"Leggo!" snarled the little man. "Leggo my hand!"

"Pickpocket!" hissed the fat man.

"Soundrel!" retorted the little one.

Just then a tall man in their vicinity glanced up from his paper.

"I'd like to get off here," he drawled, "if you fellows don't mind taking your hands out of my pocket."

SUCCESS

Nothing succeeds like excess.—*Life*

Nothing succeeds like looking successful.—*Henriette Cork-land.*

Success in life often consists in knowing just when to disagree with one's employer.

A New Orleans lawyer was asked to address the boys of a business school. He commenced:

"My young friends, as I approached the entrance to this room I noticed on the panel of the door a word eminently appropriate to an institution of this kind. It expresses the one thing most useful to the average man when he steps into the arena of life. It was——"

"Pull," shouted the boys, in a roar of laughter, and the lawyer felt that he had taken his text from the wrong side of the door.

> I'd rather be a Could Be
>   If I could not be an Are;
> For a Could Be is a May Be,
>   With a chance of touching par.
> I'd rather be a Has Been
>   Than a Might Have Been, by far;
> For a Might Have Been has never been,
>   But a Has was once an Are.

> 'Tis not in mortals to command success,
> But we'll do more, Sempronius,—
> We'll deserve it.
>   —*Addison.*

There are two ways of rising in the world: either by one's own industry or profiting by the foolishness of others.—*La Bruyère.*

Success is counted sweetest
By those who ne'er succeed.
—*Emily Dickinson.*

See also Making good.

SUFFRAGETTES

When a married woman goes out to look after her rights, her husband is usually left at home to look after his wrongs.
—*Child Harold.*

"'Ullo, Bill, 'ow's things with yer?"
"Lookin' up, Tom, lookin' up."
"'Igh cost o' livin' not 'ittin' yer, Bill?"
"Not so 'ard, Tom—not so 'ard. The missus 'as went 'orf on a hnnger stroike and me butcher's bill is cut in arf!"

I'd hate t' be married t' a suffragette an' have t' eat Battle Creek breakfasts.—*Abe Martin.*

FIRST ENGLISHMAN—"Why do you allow your wife to be a militant suffragette?"
SECOND ENGLISHMAN—"When she's busy wrecking things outside we have comparative peace at home."—*Life.*

Recipe for a suffragette:
To the power that already lies in her hands
You add equal rights with gents;
You'll find votes that used to bring two or three plunks,
Marked down to ninety-eights cents.

When Mrs. Pankhurst, the English suffragette, was in America she met and became very much attached to Mrs. Lee Preston, a New York woman of singular cleverness of mind and personal attraction. After the acquaintance had ripened somewhat Mrs. Pankhurst ventured to say:
"I do hope, Mrs. Preston, that you are a suffragette."
"Oh, dear no!" replied Mrs. Preston; "you know, Mrs. Pankhurst, I am happily married."

BILL—"Jake said he as going to break up the suffragette meeting the other night. Were his plans carried out?"
DILL—"No, Jake was."—*Life*

SLASHER—"Been in a fight?"
MASHER—"No. I tried to flirt with a pretty suffragette."
—*Judge.*

"What sort of a ticket does your suffragette club favor?"
"Well," replied young Mrs. Torkins, "if we owned right up, I think most of us would prefer matinée tickets."

See also Woman suffrage

SUICIDE

The Chinese Consul at San Francisco, at a recent dinner, discussed his country's customs.

"There is one custom," said a young girl, "that I can't understand—and that is the Chinese custom of committing suicide by eating gold-leaf. I can't understand how gold-leaf can kill."

"The partaker, no doubt," smiled the Consul, "succumbs from a consciousness of inward gilt."

SUMMER RESORTS

GABE—"What are you going back to that place for this summer? Why, last year it was all mosquitoes and no fishing."

STEVE—"The owner tells me that he has crossed the mosquitoes with the fish, and guarantees a bite every second."

"I suppose," said the city man, "there are some queer characters around an old village like this."

"You'll find a good many," admitted the native, "when the hotels fill up."

SUNDAY

Albert was a solemn-eyed, spiritual-looking child.

"Nurse," he said one day, leaving his blocks and laying his hand on her knee, "nurse, is this God's day?"

"No, dear," said the nurse, "this is not Sunday; it is Thursday."

"I'm so sorry," he said, sadly, and went back to his blocks.

The next day and the next in his serious manner he asked the same question, and the nurse tearfully said to the cook:

"That child is too good for this world."

On Sunday the question was repeated, and the nurse with a sob in her voice, said: "Yes, lambie, this is God's day."

"Then where is the funny paper?" he demanded.

TEACHER—"Good little boys do not skate on Sunday, Corky. Don't you think that is very nice of them?"

CORKY—"Sure t'ing!"

TEACHER—"And why is it nice of them, Corky?"

CORKY—"Aw, it leaves more room on de ice! See?"

> Of all the days that's in the week,
>   I dearly love but one day,
> And that's the day that comes betwixt
>   A Saturday and Monday.
>
> —*Henry Carey.*

> O day of rest! How beautiful, how fair,
> How welcome to the weary and the old!
> Day of the Lord! and truce to earthly care!
> Day of the Lord, as all our days should be!
>
> —*Longfellow.*

SUNDAY SCHOOLS

"Now, Willie," said the superintendent's little boy, addressing the blacksmith's little boy, who had come over for a frolic, "we'll play 'Sabbath School.' You give me a nickel every Sunday for six months, and then at Christmas I'll give you a ten-cent bag of candy."

When Lottie returned from her first visit to Sunday-school, she was asked what she had learned.

"God made the world in six days and was arrested on the seventh day," was her version of the lesson imparted.

The teacher asked: "When did Moses live?"

After the silence had become painful she ordered: "Open your Old Testaments. What does it say there?"

A boy answered: "Moses, 4000."

"Now," said the teacher. "why didn't you know when Moses lived?"

"Well," replied the boy, "I thought it was his telephone number."—*Suburban Life.*

"How many of you boys," asked the Sunday-school superintendent, "can bring two other boys next Sunday?"

There was no response until a new recruit raised his hand hesitatingly.

"Well, William?"

"I can't bring two, but there's one little feller I can lick, and I'll do my damnedest to bring him."

SUPERSTITION

Superstition is a premature explanation overstaying its time.
—*George Iles.*

SURPRISE

"Where are you goin', ma?" asked the youngest of five children.

"I'm going to a surprise party, my dear," answered the mother.

"Are we goin', too?"

"No, dear. You weren't invited."

After a few moments' deep thought:

"Say, ma, then don't you think they'd be lots more surprised if you did take us all?"

SWIMMERS

Two Negro roustabouts at New Orleans were continually bragging about their ability as long distance swimmers and a steamboat man got up a match. The man who swam the longest distance was to receive $5. The Alabama Whale immediately stripped on the dock, but the Human Steamboat said he had some business and would return in a few minutes. The Whale swam the river four or five times for exercise and by that time the Human Steamboat returned. He wore a pair of swimming trunks and had a sheet iron cook stove strapped on his back. Tied around his neck were a dozen packages containing bread, flour, bacon and other eatables. The Whale gazed at his opponent in amazement.

"Whar yo' vittles?" demanded the Human Steamboat.

"Vittles fo'what?" asked the Whale.

"Don't you ask me fo' nothin' on the way ovah," warned the Steamboat. "Mah fust stop is New York an' mah next stop is London."

SYMPATHY

A sympathizer is a fellow that's for you as long as it doesn't cost anything.

Dwight L. Moody was riding in a car one day when it was hailed by a man much the worse for liquor, who presently staggered along the car between two rows of well-dressed people, regardless of tender feet.

Murmurs and complaints arose on all sides and demands were heard that the offender should be ejected at once.

But amid the storm of abuse one friendly voice was raised Mr. Moody rose from his seat, saying:

"No, no, friends! Let the man sit down and be quiet."

The drunken one turned, and, seizing the famous evangelist by the hand, exclaimed:

"Thank ye, sir—thank ye! I see you know what it is to be drunk."

The man rushed excitedly into the smoking car. "A lady has fainted in the next car! Has anybody got any whiskey?" he asked.

Instantly a half-dozen flasks were thrust out to him. Taking the nearest one, he turned the bottle up and took a big drink, then, handing the flask back, said, "Thank you. It always did make me feel sick to see a lady faint."

A tramp went to a farmhouse, and sitting down in the front yard began to eat the grass.

The housewife's heart went out to him: "Poor man, you must indeed be hungry. Come around to the back."

The tramp beamed and winked at the hired man.

"There," said the housewife, when the tramp hove in sight, pointing to a circle of green grass, "try that: you will find that grass so much longer."

Strengthen me by sympathizing with my strength, not my weakness.—*Amos Bronson Alcott.*

SYNONYMS

"I don't believe any two words in the English language are synonymous."

"Oh, I don't know. What's the mattter with 'raise' and 'lift'?"

"There's a big difference. I 'raise' chickens and have a neighbor who has been known to 'lift' them."

TABLE MANNERS

See Dining

TACT

It was at the private theatricals, and the young man wished to compliment his hostess, saying:

"Madam, you played your part splendidly. It fits you to perfection."

"I'm afraid not. A young and pretty woman is needed for that part," said the smiling hostess.

"But, madam, you have positively proved the contrary."

TAFT, WILLIAM HOWARD

When Mr. Taft was on his campaigning tour in the west, before he had been elected President, he stopped at the home of an old friend. It was a small house, not well built, and as he walked about in his room the unsubstantial little house fairly shook with his tread. When he got into bed that receptacle, unused to so much weight, gave way, precipitating Taft on the floor.

His friend hurried to his door.

"What's the matter, Bill?"

"Oh, I'm all right, I guess," Taft called out to his friend good-naturedly; "but say, Joe, if you don't find me here in the morning look in the cellar."

One morning a few summers ago President Taft, wearing the largest bathing suit known to modern times, threw his substantial form into the cooling waves of Beverly Bay. Shortly afterward one neighbor said to another: "Let's go bathing."

How can we?" was the response. "The President is using the ocean."

TALENT

See Actors and actresses.

TALKERS

Some years ago, Mark Twain was a guest of honor at an opera box-party given by a prominent member of New York society. The hostess had been particularly talkative all during the performance—to Mr. Clemens's increasing irritation.

Toward the end of the opera, she turned to him and said gushingly:

"Oh, my dear Mr. Clemens, I do so want you to be with us next Friday evening. I'm certain you will like it—the opera will be 'Tosca.'"

"Charmed, I'm sure," replied Clemens. "I've never heard you in that."

It was a beautiful evening and Ole, who had screwed up courage to take Mary for a ride, was carried away by the magic of the night.

"Mary," he asked, "will you marry me?"

"Yes, Ole," she answered softly.

Ole lapsed into a silence that at last became painful to his fiancée.

"Ole," she said desperately, "why don't you say something?"

"Ay tank," Ole replied, "they bane too much said already."

"Sir," said the sleek-looking agent, approaching the desk of the meek, meaching-looking man and opening one of those folding thingumjigs showing styles of binding, "I believe I can interest you in this massive set of books containing the speeches of the world's greatest orators. Seventy volumes, one dollar down and one dollar a month until the price, six hundred and eighty dollars has been paid. This set of books gives you the most celebrated speeches of the greatest talkers the world has ever known and——"

"Let me see the index," said the meek man.

The agent handled it to him and he looked through it carefully and methodically, running his finger along the list of names.

Reaching the end he handed the index back to the agent and said: "It isn't what you claim it is. I happen to know the greatest talker in the world, and you haven't her in the index."

A guest was expected for dinner and Bobby had received five cents as the price of his silence during the meal. He was as quiet as a mouse until, discovering that his favorite dessert was being served, he could no longer curb his enthusiasm. He drew the coin from his pocket, and rolling it across the table, exclaimed: "Here's your nickel, Mamma. I'd rather talk."

A belated voyager in search of hilarity stumbled home after one o'clock and found his wife waiting for him. The curtain lecture that followed was of unusual virulence, and in the midst of it he fell asleep. Awakening a few hours later he found his wife still pouring forth a regular cascade of denunciation. Eyeing her sleepily he said curiously,

"Say, are you talking yet or again?"

"You must not talk all the time, Ethel," said the mother who had been interrupted.

"When will I be old enough to, Mama?" asked the little girl.

While the late Justice Brewer was judge in a minor court he was presiding at the trial of a wife's suit for separation and alimony. The defendant acknowledged that he hadn't spoken to his wife in five years, and Judge Brewer put in a question.

"What explanation have you," he asked severely, "for not speaking to your wife in five years?"

"Your Honor," replied the husband, "I didn't like to interrupt the lady."

She was in an imaginative mood.

"Henry dear," she said after talking two hours without a recess, "I sometimes wish I were a mermaid."

"It would be fatal," snapped her weary hubby.

"Fatal! In what way?"

"Why, you couldn't keep your mouth closed long enough to keep from drowning."

And after that, Henry did not get any supper.

"Here comes Blinkers. He's got a new baby, and he'll talk us to death."

"Well, here comes a neighbor of mine who has a new settter dog. Let's introduce them and leave them to their fate."—*Life*.

A street-car was getting under way when two women, rushing from opposite sides of the street to greet each other, met right in the middle of the car-track and in front of the car. There the two stopped and began to talk. The car stopped, too, but the women did not appear to realize that it was there. Certain of the passengers, whose heads were immediately thrust out of the windows to ascertain what the trouble was, began to make sarcastic remarks, but the two women heeded them not.

Finally the motorman showed that he had a saving sense of humor. Leaning over the dash-board, he inquired, in the gentlest of tones:

"Pardon me, ladies, but shall I get you a couple of chairs?"

A—"I used a word in speaking to my wife which offended her sorely a week ago. She has not spoken a syllable to me since."

B—"Would you mind telling me what it was?"

> In general those who have nothing to say
> Contrive to spend the longest time in doing it.
> —*Lowell.*

See also Wives.

TARDINESS

"You'll be late for supper, sonny," said the merchant, in passing a small boy who was carrying a package.

"No, I won't, was the reply. "I've dot de meat."—*Mabel Lang.*

"How does it happen that you are five minutes late at school this morning?" the teacher asked severely.

"Please, ma'am," said Ethel, "I must have overwashed myself."

TARIFF

Why not have an illuminated sign on the statue of Liberty saying, "America expects every man to pay his duty?"—*Kent Packard.*

TASTE

"It isn't wise for a painter to be too frank in his criticisms," said Robert Henri at a luncheon. "I know a very outspoken painter whose little daughter called at a friend's house and said:

"'Show me your new parlor rug, won't you, please?'

"So, with great pride, the hostess led the little girl into the drawing-room, and raised all the blinds, so that the light might stream in abundantly upon the gorgeous colors of an expensive Kirmanshah.

"The little girl stared down at the rug in silence. Then, as she turned away, she said in a rather disappointed voice:

"'It doesn't make *me* sick!'"

TEACHERS

A rural school has a pretty girl as its teacher, but she was much troubled because many of her pupils were late every morning. At last she made the announcement that she would kiss the first pupil to arrive at the schoolhouse the next morning. At sunrise the largest three boys of her class were sitting on the doorstep of the schoolhouse, and by six o'clock every boy in the school and four of the directors were waiting for her to arrive.

"Why did you break your engagement with that school teacher?"

"If I failed to show up at her house every evening, she expected me to bring a written excuse signed by my mother."

Among the youngsters belonging to a college settlement in a New England city was one little girl who returned to her humble home with glowing accounts of the new teacher.

"She's a perfect lady," exclaimed the enthusiastic youngster.

The child's mother gave her a doubtful look. "How do *you* know?" she said. "You've only known her two days."

"It's easy enough tellin'," continued the child. "I know she's a perfect lady, because she makes you feel polite all the time."

MOTHER—"The teacher complains you have not had a correct lesson for a month; why is it?"

SON—"She always kisses me when I get them right."

There was a meeting of the new teachers and the old. It was a sort of love feast, reception or whatever you call it. Anyhow all the teachers got together and pretended they didn't have a care in the world. After the eats were et the symposiarch proposed a toast:

"Long Live Our Teachers!"

It was drunk enthusiastically. One of the new teachers was called on to respond. He modestly accepted. His answer was: "What On?"

TEACHER—"Now, Willie, where did you get that chewing gum? I want the truth."

WILLIE—"You don't want the truth, teacher, an' I'd ruther not tell a lie."

TEACHER—"How dare you say I don't want the truth! Tell me at once where you got that chewing-gum."

WILLIE—"Under your desk."

Grave is the Master's look; his forehead wears
Thick rows of wrinkles, prints of worrying cares:
Uneasy lie the heads of all that rule,
His worst of all whose kingdom is a school
—*O. W. Holmes.*

TEARS

Two Irishmen who had just landed were eating their dinner in a hotel, when Pat spied a bottle of horseradish. Not knowing what it was he partook of a big mouthful, which brought tears to his eyes.

Mike, seeing Pat crying exclaimed: "Phat be ye cryin' fer?"

Pat, wishing to have Mike fooled also, exclaimed: "I'm crying fer me poor ould mother, who's dead way over in Ireland."

By and by Mike took some of the radish, whereupon tears filled *his* eyes. Pat, seeing them, asked his friend what *he* was crying for.

Mike replied: "Because ye didn't die at the same time yer poor ould mother did."

TEETH

There was an old man of Tarentum,
Who gnashed his false teeth till he bent 'em:
    And when asked for the cost
    Of what he had lost,
Said, "I really can't tell for I rent 'em!"
—Gilbert K. Chesterton.

Pat came to the office with his jaw very much swollen from a tooth he desired to have pulled. But when the suffering son of Erin got into the dentist's chair and saw the gleaming pair of forceps approaching his face, he positively refused to open his mouth.

The dentist quietly told his office boy to prick his patient with a pin, and when Pat opened his mouth to yell the dentist seized the tooth, and out it came.

"It didn't hurt as much as you expected it would, did it?" the dentist asked smiling.

"Well, no," replied Pat hesitatingly, as if doubting the truthfulness of his admission. "But," he added, placing his hand on the spot where the boy jabbed him with the pin, "begorra, little did I think the roots would reach down like that."

An Irishman with one side of his face badly swollen stepped into Dr. Wicten's office and iquired if the dentist was in.

"I am the dentist," said the doctor.

"Well, then, I want ye to see what's the matter wid me tooth."

The doctor examined the offending molar, and explained:

"The nerve is dead; that's what's the matter."

"Thin, be the powers," the Irishman exclaimed, "the other teeth must be houldin' a wake over it!"

For there was never yet philosopher
That could endure the toothache patiently.
—Shakespeare.

TELEPHONE

Two girls were talking over the wire. Both were discussing what they should wear to the Christmas party. In the midst of this important conversation a masculine voice interrupted, asking humbly for a number. One of the girls became indignant and scornfully asked:

"What line do you think you are on, anyhow?"

"Well," said the man, "I am not sure, but, judging from what I have heard, I should say I was on the clothesline."

When Grover Cleveland's little girl was quite young her father once telephoned to the White House from Chicago and asked Mrs. Cleveland to bring the child to the 'phone. Lifting the little one up to the instrument, Mrs. Cleveland watched her expression change from bewilderment to wonder and then to fear. It was surely her father's voice—yet she looked at the telephone incredulously. After examining the tiny opening in the receiver the little girl burst into tears. "Oh, Mamma!" she sobbed. "How can we ever get Papa out of that little hole?"

New York Elks are having a lot of fun with a member of their lodge, a Fifteenth Street jeweler. The other day his wife was in the jewelry store when the 'phone rang. She answered it.

"I want to speak to Mr. H——," said a woman's voice.

"Who is this?" demanded the jeweler's wife.

"Elizabeth."

"Well, Elizabeth, this is his wife. Now, madam, what do you want?"

"I want to talk to Mr. H——."

"You'll talk to me."

"Please let me speak to Mr. H——."

The jeweler's wife grew angry. "Look here, young lady," she said, "who are you that calls my husband and insists on talking to him?"

"I'm the telephone operator at Elizabeth, N. J.," came the reply.

And now the Elks take turns calling the jeweler up and telling him it's Elizabeth.

OPERATOR—"Number, please."

SUBSCRIBER—"I vas talking mit my husband und now I don't hear him any more. You must of pushed him off de vire."

A German woman called up Central and instructed her as follows:

"Ist dis de mittle? Vell dis is Lena. Hang my hustband on dis line. I vant to speak mit him."

In China when the subscriber rings up exchange the operator may be expected to ask:

"What number does the honorable son of the moon and stars desire?"

"Hohi, two-three."

Silence. Then the exchange resumes.

"Will the honorable person graciously forgive the inadequacy of the insignificant service and permit this humbled slave of the wire to inform him that the never-to-be-sufficiently censured line is busy?"

Recipe for a telephone operator:
   To a fearful and wonderful rolling of r's,"
      And a voice cold as thirty below,
   Add a dash of red pepper, some ginger and sass
      If you leave out the "o" in "hello"!

TEMPER

Hearing the crash of china Dinah's mistress arrived in time to see her favorite coffee-set in pieces. The sight was too much for her mercurial temper. "Dinah," she said, "I cannot stand it any longer. I want you to go. I want you to go soon, I want you to go right now."

"Lawzee," replied Dinah, "this surely am a co-instence. I was this very minute cogitatin' that same thought in my own mind—I want to go, I thank the good Lawd I kin go, and I pity your husband, ma'am, that he can't go."

TEMPERANCE

A Boston deacon who was a zealous advocate for the cause of temperance employed a carpenter to make some alterations in his home. In repairing a corner near the firepleace, it was found necessary to remove the wainscot, when some things were brought to light which greatly astonished the workman. A brace of decanters, sundry bottles containing "something to take," a pitcher, and tumblers were cosily reposing in their snug quarters. The joiner ran to the proprietor with the intelligence.

"Well, I declare!" exclaimed the deacon. "That is curious, sure enough. It must be old Captain Bunce that left those things there when he occupied the premises thirty years since."

"Perhaps he did, returned the discoverer, but, Deacon, that ice in the pitcher must have been well frozen to remain solid."—*Abbie C. Dixon*

> Here's to a temperance supper
> With water in glasses tall,
> And coffee and tea to end with—
> And me not there at all.

The best prohibition story of the season comes from Kansas where, it is said, a local candidate stored a lot of printed prohibition literature in his barn, but accidently left the door open and a herd of milch cows came in and ate all the pamphlets. As a result every cow in the herd went dry.

—*Adrian Times.*

A Michigan citizen recently received a letter from a Kentucky whisky house, requesting him to send them the names of a dozen or more persons who would like to get some fine whisky shipped to them at a very low price. The letter wound up by saying:

"We will give you a commission on all the orders sent in by parties whose names you send us."

The Michigan man belonged to a practical joke class, and filled in the names of some of his prohibition friends on the blank spaces left for that purpose.

He had forgotten all about his supposed practical joke when Monday he received another letter from the same house. He supposed it was a request for some more names, and was just about to throw the communication in the waste basket when it occurred to him to send the name of another old friend to the whisky house. He accordingly tore open the envelope, and came near collapsing when he found a check for $4.80, representing his commission on the sale of whisky to the parties whose names he had sent in about three weeks before.

Abstinence is as easy to me as temperance would be difficult.—*Samuel Johnson.*

TEXAS

The bigness of Texas is evident from a cursory examination of the map. But its effect upon the people of that state is not generally known. It is about six hundred miles from Brownsville, at the bottom of the map, to Dallas, which is several hundreds of miles from the top of the map. Hence the following conversation in Brownsville recently between two of the old-time residents:

"Where have you been lately, Bob? I ain't seen much of you."

"Been on a trip north."

"Where'd you go?"

"Went to Dallas."

"Have a good time?"

"Naw; I never did like them damn Yankees, anyway."

TEXTS

In the Tennessee mountains a mountaineer preacher, who had declared colleges "the works of the devil," was preaching without previous meditation an inspirational sermon from the text," "The voice of the turtle shall be heard in the land." Not noting that the margin read "turtle-dove," he proceeded in this manner:

"This text, my hearers, strikes me as one of the most peculiar texts in the whole book, because we all know that a turtle ain't got no voice. But by the inward enlightenment I begin to see the meaning and will expose it to you. Down in the hollers by the streams and ponds you have gone in the springtime, my brethren, and observed the little turtles, a-sleeping on the logs. But at the sound of the approach of a human being, they went *kerflop-kerplunk,* down into the water. This I say, then, is the meaning of the prophet: he, speaking figgeratively, referred to the *kerflop* of the turtle as the *voice* of the turtle, and hence we see that in those early times the prophet, looking down at the ages to come, clearly taught and prophesied the doctrine I have always preached to this congregation—*that immersion is the only form of baptism."*

John D. Rockefeller, Jr., once asked a clergyman to give him an appropriate Bible verse on which to base an address which he was to make at the latter's church.

"I was thinking," said young Rockefeller, "that I would take the verse from the Twenty-third Psalm: 'The Lord is my shepherd.' Would that seem appropriate?"

"Quite," said the clergyman; "but do you really want an appropriate verse?"

"I certainly do," was the reply.

"Well, then," said the clergyman, with a twinkle in his eye, "I would select the verse in the same Psalm: 'Thou anointest my head with oil; my cup runneth over.'"

THEATER

"Say, old man," chattered the press-agent, who had cornered a producer of motion-picture plays, "I've got a grand idea for a film-drama. Listen to the impromptu scenario: Scene one, exterior of a Broadway theater, with the ticket-speculators getting the coin in handfuls, and——"

"You're out!" interrupted the producer. "Why, don't you know that the law don't permit us to show an actual robbery on the screen?"—*P. H. Carey.*

"Why don't women have the same sense of humor that men possess?" asked Mr. Torkins.

"Perhaps," answered his wife gently, "it's because we don't attend the same theaters."

It appears that at the rehearsal of a play, a wonderful climax had been reached, which was to be heightened by the effective use of the usual thunder and lightning. The stage-carpenter was given the order. The words were spoken, and instantly a noise which resembled a succession of pistol-shots was heard off the wings.

"What on earth are you doing, man?" shouted the manager, rushing behind the scenes. "Do you call that thunder? It's not a bit like it."

"Awfully sorry, sir," responded the carpenter; "but the fact is, sir, I couldn't hear you because of the storm. That was real thunder, sir!"

Everybody has his own theater, in which he is manager, actor, prompter, playwright, sceneshifter, boxkeeper, doorkeeper, all in one, and audience into the bargain.

—*J. C. and A. W. Hare.*

THIEVES

GEORGIA LAWYER (to a colored prisoner)—"Well, Ras, so you want me to defend you. Have you any money?"

RASTUS—"No; but I'se got a mule, and a few chickens, and a hog or two."

LAWYER—"Those will do very nicely. Now, let's see; what do they accuse you of stealing?"

RASTUS—"Oh, a mule, and a few chickens, and a hog or two."

At a dinner given by the prime minister of a little kingdom on the Balkan Peninsula, a distinguished diplomat complained to his host that the minister of justice, who had been sitting on his left, had stolen his watch.

"Ah, he shouldn't have done that," said the prime minister, in tones of annoyance. "I will get it back for you."

Sure enough, toward the end of the evening the watch was returned to its owner.

"And what did he say?" asked the diplomat.

"Sh-h," cautioned the host, glancing anxiously about him "He doesn't know that I have got it back."

Senator "Bob" Taylor, of Tennessee, tells a story of how, when he was "Fiddling Bob," governor of that state, an old Negrees came to him and said:

"Massa Gov'na, we's mighty po' this winter, and Ah wish you would pardon mah old man. He is a fiddler same as you is, and he's in the pen'tentry."

"What was he put in for?" asked the governor.

"Stead of workin' fo' it that good-fo'-nothin' nigger done stole some bacon."

"If he is good for nothing what do you want him back for?"

"Well, yo' see, we's all out of bacon ag'in," said the old Negress innocently.

"Did ye see as Jim got ten years' penal for stealing that 'oss?"

"Serve 'im right, too. Why didn't 'e buy the 'oss and not pay for 'im like any other gentleman?"

Some time ago a crowd of Bowery sports went over to Philadelphia to see a prize fight. One "wise guy," who, among other things, is something of a pickpocket, was so sure of the result that he was willing to bet on it.

"The Kid's goin' t' win. It's a pipe," he told a friend.

The friend expressed doubts.

"Sure he'll win," the pickpocket persisted. "I'll bet you a gold watch he wins."

Still the friend doubted.

"Why," exclaimed the pickpocket, "I'm willin' to bet you a good gold watch he wins! Y' know what I'll do? Come through the train with me now, an' y' can pick out any old watch y' like."

> In vain we call old notions fudge
>   And bend our conscience to our dealing.
> The Ten Commandments will not budge
>   And stealing will continue stealing.
>   —*Motto of American Copyright League.*

Suspicion always haunts the guilty mind;
The thief doth fear each bush an officer.

—Shakespeare.

See also Chicken stealing; Lawyers; Lost and found.

THIN PEOPLE

There was an old fellow named Green,
Who grew so abnormally lean,
    And flat, and compressed,
    That his back touched his chest,
And sideways he couldn't be seen.

There was a young lady of Lynn,
Who was so excessively thin,
    That when she essayed
    To drink lemonade
She slipped through the straw and fell in.

THRIFT

It was said of a certain village "innocent" or fool in Scotland that if he were offered a silver sixpence or copper penny he would invariably choose the larger coin of smaller value. One day a stranger asked him:

"Why do you always take the penny? Don't you know the difference in value?

"Aye," answered the fool, "I ken the difference in value. But if I took the saxpence they would never try me again."

    The Mrs. never misses
        Any bargain sale,
    For the female of the species
        Is more thrifty than the male.

McAndrews (the chemist, at two A. M.)—"Two penn'orth of bicarbonate of soda for indigestion at this time o' night, when a glass of hot water does just as well!"

Sandy (hastily)—"Well, well! Thanks for the advice, I'll not bother ye, after all. Gude nicht!"

The foreman and his crew of bridgemen were striving hard to make an impression on the select board provided by Mrs. Rooney at her Arkansas eating establishment.

"The old man sure made a funny deal down at Piney yesterday," observed the foreman, with a wink at the man to his right.

"What'd he do?" asked the new man at the other end of the table.

"Well, a year or so ago there used to be a water tank there, but they took down the tub and brought it up to Cabin Creek. The well went dry and they covered it over. It was four or five feet round, ninety feet deep, and plumb in the right of way. Didn't know what to do with it until along comes an old lollypop yesterday and gives the Old Man five dollars for it."

"Five dollars for what?" asked the new man.

"Well," continued the foreman, ignoring the interruption, "that old lollypop borrowed two jacks from the trackmen and jacked her up out of there and carried her home on wheels."

"What'd he do with it?" persisted the new man.

"Say that old lollypop must've been a Yank. Nobody else could have figured it out. The ground on his place is hard and he needed some more fence. So he calc'lated 'twould be easier and cheaper to saw that old well up into post-holes than 'twould be to dig 'em."

A certain workman, notorious for his sponging proclivities, met a friend one morning, and opened the conversation by saying:

"Can ye len' us a match, John?"

John having supplied him with the match, the first speaker began to feel his pockets ostentatiously, and then remarked dolefully, "Man, I seem to have left my tobacco pouch at hame."

John, however, was equal to the occasion, and holding out his hand, remarked:

"Aweel, ye'll no be needin' that match then."

A Highlander was summoned to the bedside of his dying father. When he arrived the old man was fast nearing his end. For a while he remained unconscious of his son's presence. Then at last the old man's eyes opened, and he began to murmur. The son bent eagerly to listen.

"Dugald," whispered the parent, "Luckie Simpson owes me five shilling."

"Ay, man, ay," said the son eagerly.

"An' Dugal More owes me seven shillins."

"Ay," assented the son.

"An' Hamish McGraw owes me ten shillins."

"Sensible tae the last," muttered the delighted heir. "Sensible tae the last."

Once more the voice from the bed took up the tale.

"An', Dugald, I owe Calum Beg two pounds."

Dugald shook his head sadly.

"Wanderin' again, wanderin' again," he sighed. "It's a peety."

The canny Scot wandered into the pharmacy.

"I'm wanting threepenn'orth o' laudanum," he announced.

"What for?" asked the chemist suspiciously.

"For twopence," responded the Scot at once.

A Scotsman wishing to know his fate at once, telegraphed a proposal of marriage to the lady of his choice. After spending the entire day at the telegraph office he was finally rewarded late in the evening by an affirmative answer.

"If I were you," suggested the operator when he delivered the message, "I'd think twice before I'd marry a girl that kept me waiting all day for my answer."

"Na, na," retorted the Scot. "The lass who waits for the night rates is the lass for me."

"Well, yes," said Old Uncle Lazzenberry, who was intimately acquainted with most of the happenstances of the village. "Almira Stang has broken off her engagement with Charles Henry Tootwiler. They'd be goin' together for about eight years, durin' which time she had been inculcatin' into him, as you might call it, the beauties of economy; but when she discovered, just lately, that he had learnt his lesson so well that he had saved up two hundred and seventeen pairs of socks for her to darn immediately after the wedding, she 'peared to conclude that he had taken her advice a little too literally, and broke off the match."—*Puck.*

They sat each at an extreme end of the horsehair sofa. They had been courting now for something like two years, but the wide gap between had always been respectfully preserved.

"A penny for your thochts, Sandy," murmured Maggie, after a silence of an hour and a half.

"Weel," replied Sandy slowly, with surprising boldness, "tae tell ye the truth, I was jist thinkin' how fine it wad be if ye were tae gie me a wee bit kissie."

"I've nae objection," simpered Maggie, slithering over, and kissed him plumply on the tip of his left ear.

Sandy relapsed into a brown study once more, and the clock ticked twenty-seven minutes.

"An' what are ye thinkin' about noo—anither, eh?"

"Nae, nae, lassie; it's mair serious the noo."

"It is, laddie?" asked Maggie softly. Her heart was going pit-a-pat with expectation. "An' what micht it be?"

"I was jist thinkin'," answered Sandy, "that it was aboot time ye were paying me that penny!"

The coward calls himself cautious, the miser thrifty.

—*Syrus.*

There are but two ways of paying debt: increase of industry in raising income, increase of thrift in laying out.—*Carlyle.*

See also Economy; Saving.

TIDES

A Kansan sat on the beach at Atlantic City watching a fair and very fat bather disporting herself in the surf. He knew nothing of tides, and he did not notice that each succeeding wave came a little closer to his feet. At last an extra big wave washed over his shoe tops.

"Hey, there!" he yelled at the fair, fat bather. "Quit yer jumpin' up and down! D'ye want to drown me?"

At a recent Confederate reunion in Charleston, S. C., two Kentuckians were viewing the Atlantic Ocean for the first time.

"Say, cap'n," said one of them, "what ought I to carry home to the children for a souvenir?"

"Why, colonel, it strikes me that some of this here ocean water would be right interestin'."

"Just the thing!" exclaimed the colonel delightedly. From a rear pocket he produced a flask, and, with the aid of the captain, soon emptied it. Then, picking his way down to the water's edge, he filled it to the neck and replaced the cork.

"Hi, there! Don't do that!" cried the captain in great alarm. "Pour out about a third of that water. If you don't, when the tide rises she'll bust sure."

Nae man can tether time or tide.—*Burns.*

TIME

Mrs. Hooligan was suffering from the common complaint of having more to do than there was time to do it in. She looked up at the clock and then slapped the iron she had lifted from the stove back on the lid with a clatter. "Talk about toime and toide waitin' fer no man," she muttered as she hurried into the pantry; "there's toimes they waits, an' toimes they don't. Yistherday at this blessed minit 'twas but tin o'clock an' to-day it's a quarther to twilve."

Mrs. Murphy—"Oi hear yer brother-in-law, Pat Keegan, is pretty bad off."

Mrs. Casey—"Shure, he's good for a year yit."

Mrs. Murphy—"As long as thot?"

Mrs. Casey—"Yis; he's had four different doctors, and each one av thim give him three months to live."—*Puck.*

A long-winded attorney was arguing a technical case before one of the judges of the superior court in a western state. He had rambled on in such a desultory way that it became very difficult to follow his line of thought, and the judge had just yawned very suggestively.

With just a trace of sarcasm in his voice, the tiresome attorney ventured to observe: "I sincerely trust that I am not unduly trespassing on the time of this court."

"My friend," returned his honor, "there is a considerable difference between trespassing on time and encroaching upon eternity."—*Edwin Tarrisse.*

A traveler, finding that he had a couple of hours in Dublin, called a cab and told the driver to drive him around for two hours. At first all went well, but soon the driver began to whip up his horse so that they narrowly escaped several collisions.

"What's the matter?" demanded the passenger. "Why are you driving so recklessly? I'm in no hurry."

"Ah, g'wan wid yez," retorted the cabby. "D'ye think thot I'm goin' to put in me whole day drivin' ye around for two hours? Gitap!"

Frank comes into the house in a sorry plight.

"Mercy on us!" exclaims his father. "How you look! You are soaked."

"Please, papa, I fell into the canal."

"What! with your new trousers on?"

"Yes, papa, I didn't have time to take them off."

A well-known Bishop, while visiting at a bride's new home for the first time, was awakened quite early by the soft tones of a soprano voice singing "Nearer, My God, to Thee." As the Bishop lay in bed he meditated upon the piety which his young hostess must possess to enable her to begin her day's work in such a beautiful frame of mind.

At breakfast he spoke to her about it, and told her how pleased he was.

"Oh," she replied, "that's the hymn I boil the eggs by; three verses for soft and five for hard."

There was a young woman named Sue,
Who wanted to catch the 2:02;
   Said the trainman, "Don't hurry
   Or flurry or worry;
It's a minute or two to 2:02."

FATHER—"Mildred, if you disobey again I will surely spank you."

On father's return home that evening, Mildred once more acknowledged that she had again disobeyed.

FATHER (firmly)—"You are going to be spanked. You may choose your own time. When shall it be?"

MILDRED (five years old, thoughtfully)—"Yesterday."

A northerner passing a rundown looking place in the South, stopped to chat with the farmer. He noticed the hogs running wild and explained that in the North the farmers fattened their hogs much faster by shutting them in and feeding them well.

"Hell!" replied the southerner. "What's time to a hog."

Dost thou love life? Then waste not time; for time is the stuff that life is made of.—*Benjamin Franklin.*

Time fleeth on,
Youth soon is gone,
   Naught earthly may abide;
Life seemeth fast,
But may not last—
   It runs as runs the tide.

                              —*Leland.*

See also Scientific management.

TIPS

American travelers in Europe experience a great deal of trouble from the omnipresent need of tipping those from whom they expect any service, however slight. They are very apt to carry it much too far, or else attempt to resist it altogether. There is a story told of a wealthy and ostentatious American in a Parisian restaurant. As the waiter placed the order before him he said in a loud voice:

"Waiter, what is the largest tip you ever received?"

"One thousand francs, monsieur."

"*Eh bien!* But I will give you two thousand," answered the upholder of American honor; and then in a moment he added: "May I ask who gave you the thousand francs?"

"It was yourself, monsieur," said the obsequious waiter.

Of quite an opposite mode of thought was another American visiting London for the first time. Goaded to desperation by the incessant necessity for tips, he finally entered the washroom of his hotel, only to be faced with a large sign which read: "Please tip the basin after using." "I'm hanged if I will!" said the Yankee, turning on his heel, "I'll go dirty first!"

Grant Allen relates that he was sitting one day under the shade of the Sphinx, turning for some petty point of detail to his Baedeker.

A sheik looked at him sadly, and shook his head. "Murray good," he said in a solmn voice of warning; "Baedeker no good. What for you see Baedeker?"

"No, no; Baedeker is best," answered Mr. Allen. "Why do you object to Baedeker?"

The sheik crossed his hands, and looked down at him with the pitying eyes of Islam. "Baedeker bad book," he repeated; "Murray very, very good. Murray say, 'Give the sheik half a crown'; Baedeker say, 'Give the sheik a shilling.'"

"What do you consider the most important event in the History of Paris?"

"Well," replied the tourist, who had grown weary of distributing tips, "so far as financial prosperity is concerned, I should say the discovery of America was the making of this town."

In telling this one, Miss Glaser always states that she does not want it understood that she considers the Scotch people at all stingy; but they are a very careful and thrifty race.

An intimate friend of hers was very anxious to have a well known Scotchman meet Miss Glaser, and gave her a letter of introduction to him. Miss Glaser, wishing to show him all the attention possible, invited him to a dinner which she was giving in London and after rather an elaborate repast the bill was paid, the waiter returning five shillings. She let it lie, intending, of course, to give it to the waiter. The Scotchman glanced at the money very frequently, and finally he said, his natural thrift getting the best of him:

"Are you going to give all that to the waiter?"

In an inimitable way, Miss Glaser quietly replied:

"No, take some."

"A tip is a small sum of money you give to somebody because you're afraid he won't like not being paid for something you haven't asked him to do."—*The Bailie, Glasgow.*

TITLES OF HONOR AND NOBILITY

An English lord was traveling through this country with a small party of friends. At a farmhouse the owner invited the party in to supper. The good housewife, while preparing the table, discovering she was entertaining nobility, was nearly overcome with surprise and elation.

While seated at the table scarcely a moment's peace did she grant her distinguished guest in her endeavor to serve and please him. It was "My Lord, will you have some of this?" and "My Lord, do try that," "Take a piece of this, my Lord," until the meal was nearly finished.

The little four-year-old son of the family, heretofore unnoticed, during a moment of supreme quiet saw his lordship trying to reach the pickle-dish, which was just out of his reach, and turning to his mother said:

"Say, Ma, God wants a pickle."

Dean Stanley was once visiting a friend who gave one of the pages strict orders that in the morning he was to go and knock at the Dean's door, and when the Dean inquired who was knocking he was to say: "The boy, my Lord." According to directions he knocked and the Dean asked: "Who is there?" Embarrassed by the voice of the great man the page answered: "The Lord, my boy."

"How did he get his title of colonel?"

"He got it to distinguish him from his wife's first husband, who was a captain, and his wife's second husband, who was a major."

For titles do not reflect honor on men, but rather men on their titles.—*Machiavelli.*

I hope I shall always possess firmness and virtue enough to maintain what I consider the most enviable of all titles, the character of an "Honest Man."—*George Washington.*

TOASTS

See Drinking; Good fellowship; Woman.

TOBACCO

"Tobaccy wanst saved my life," said Paddy Blake, an inveterate smoker. "How was that?" inquired his companion.

"Ye see, I was diggin' a well, and came up for a good smoke, and while I was up the well caved in."

See also Smoking.

TOURISTS

See Liars; Travelers.

TRADE UNIONS

CHAIRMAN OF THE COMMITTEE—"Is this the place where you are happy all the time?"

ST. PETER (proudly)—"It is, sir."

"Well, I represent the union, and if we come in we can only agree to be happy eight hours a day.

TRAMPS

LADY—"Can't you find work?"

TRAMP—"Yessum; but everyone wants a reference from my last employer."

LADY—"And can't you get one?"

TRAMP—"No, mum. Yer see, he's been dead twenty-eight years."

TRANSMUTATION

Fred Stone, of Montgomery and Stone fame, and Eugene Wood, whose stories and essays are well known, met on Broadway recently. They stopped for a moment to exchange a few cheerful views, when a woman in a particularly noticeable sheath-gown passed. Simultaneously, Wood turned to Stone; Stone turned to Wood; then both turned to rubber.

TRAVELERS

An American tourist, who was stopping in Tokio had visited every point of interest and had seen everything to be seen except a Shinto funeral. Finally she appealed to the Japanese clerk of the hotel, asking him to instruct her guide to take her to one. The clerk was politeness itself. He bowed gravely and replied: "I am very sorry, Madam, but this is not the season for funerals."

A gentleman whose travel-talks are known throughout the world tells the following on himself:

"I was booked for a lecture one night at a little place in Scotland four miles from a railway station.

"The 'chairman' of the occasion, after introducing me as 'the mon wha's coom here tae broaden oor intellects,' said that he felt a wee bit of prayer would not be out of place.

"'O Lord,' he continued, 'put it intae the heart of this mon tae speak the truth, the hale truth, and naething but the truth, and gie us grace tae understan' him.'

"Then, with a glance at me, the chairman said, 'I've been a traveler meself!'"—*Fenimore Martin.*

Two young Americans touring Italy for the first time stopped off one night at Pisa, where they fell in with a convivial party at a café. Going hilariously home one pushed the other against a building and held him there.

"Great heavens!" cried the man next the wall, suddenly glancing up at the structure above him. "See what we're doing!" Both roisterers fled.

They left town on an early morning train, not thinking it safe to stay over and see the famous leaning tower.

Mr. Hiram Jones had just returned from a personally conducted tour of Europe.

"I suppose," commented a friend, "that when you were in England you did as the English do and dropped your H's."

"No," moodily responded the returned traveller; "I didn't. I did as the Americans do. I dropped my V's and X's."

Then he slowly meandered down to the bank to see if he couldn't get the mortgage extended.—*W. Hanny.*

A number of tourists were recently looking down the crater of Vesuvius. An American gentleman said to his companion: "That looks a good deal like the infernal regions."

An English lady, overhearing the remark, said to another: "Good gracious! How these Americans do travel."

An American tourist hailing from the west was out sightseeing in London. They took him aboard the old battle-ship *Victory,* which was Lord Nelson's flagship in several of his most famous naval triumphs. An English sailor escorted the American over the vessel, and coming to a raised brass tablet on the deck he said, as he reverently removed his hat:

" 'Ere, sir, is the spot where Lord Nelson fell."

"Oh, is it?" replied the American, blankly. "Well, that ain't nothin'. I nearly tripped on the blame thing myself."

On one of the famous scenic routes of the west there is a brakeman who has lost the forefinger of his right hand.

His present assignment as rear-end brakeman on a passenger train places him in the observation car, where he is the target for an almost unceasing fusillade of questions from tourists who insist upon having the name, and, if possible, the history, of all the mountain cañons and points of interest along the route.

One especially enthusiastic lady tourist had kept up her Gattling fire of questions until she had thoroughly mastered the geography of the country. Then she ventured to ask the brakeman how he had lost his finger:

"Cut off in making a coupling between cars, I suppose?"

"No, madam; I wore that finger off pointing out scenery to tourists."

Know most of the rooms of thy native country before thou goest over the threshold thereof.—*Fuller.*

When I was at home, I was in a better place; but travelers must be content.—*Shakespeare.*

As the Spanish proverb says, "He who would bring home the wealth of the Indies must carry the wealth of the Indies with him." So it is in traveling: a man must carry knowledge with him, if he would bring home knowledge.—*Samuel Johnson.*

TREASON

It was during the Parnell agitation in Ireland that an anti-Parnellite, criticising the ways of tenants in treating absentee landlords, exclaimed to Archbishop Ryan of Philadelphia: "Why, it looks very much like treason."

Instantly came the answer in the Archbishop's best brogue: "Sure, treason is reason when there's an absent 't'."

Treason doth never prosper: what's the reason?
Why if it prosper, none dare call it treason.

TREES

CURIOUS CHARLEY—"Do nuts grow on trees, father?"
FATHER—"They do, my son."

CURIOUS CHARLEY—"Then what tree does the doughnut grov on?"

FATHER—"The pantry, my son."

TRIGONOMETRY

A prisoner was brought before a police magistrate. He looked around and discovered that his clerk was absent. "Here, officer," he said, "what's this man charged with?"

"Bigotry, your Honor," replied the policeman. "He's got three wives."

The magistrate looked at the officer as though astounded at such ignorance. "Why, officer," he said, "that's not bigotry—that's trigonometry."

TROUBLE

"What is the trouble, wifey?"

"Nothing."

"Yes, there is. What are you crying about, something that happened at home or something that happened in a novel?"

It was married men's night at the revival meeting.

"Let all you husbands who have troubles on your minds stand up!" shouted the preacher at the height of his spasm.

Instantly every man in the church arose except one.

"Ah!" exclaimed the preacher, peering out at this lone individual, who occupied a chair near the door. "You are one in a million."

"It ain't that," piped back this one helplessly as the rest of the congregation gazed suspiciously at him: "I can't get up—I'm paralyzed!"

JUDGE—"Your innocence is proved. You are acquitted."

PRISONER (to the jury)—"Very sorry, indeed, gentlemen, to have given you all this trouble for nothing."

A friend of mine, returning to his home in Virginia after several years' absence, met one of the old Negroes, a former servant of his family. "Uncle Moses," he said, "I hear you got married."

"Yes, Marse Tom, I is, and I's having a moughty troublesome time, Marse Tom, moughty troublesome."

"What's the trouble?" said my friend.

"Why, dat yaller woman, Marse Tom. She all de time axin' me for money. She don't give me no peace."

"How long have you been married, Uncle Moses?"

"Nigh on ter two years, come dis spring."

"And how much money have you given her?"

"Well, I ain't done gin her none yit."—*Sue M. M. Halsey.*

If you want to forget all your other troubles, wear tight shoes.

Never bear more than one kind of trouble at a time. Some people bear three—all they have had, all they have now, and all they expect to have.—*Edward Everett Hale.*

TRUSTS

A trust is known by the companies it keeps.—*Ellis O. Jones.*

TOMPKINS—"Ventley has received a million dollars for his patent egg dating machine. You know it is absolutely interference-proof, and dates correctly and indelibly as the egg is being laid."

DEWLEY—"Is the machine on the market yet?"

TOMPKINS—"Oh, my no! and it won't be on the market. The patent was bought by the Cold Storage Trust."

TRUTH

There was a young lady named Ruth,
Who had a great passion for truth.
   She said she would die
   Before she would lie,
And she died in the prime of her youth.

Women do not really like to deceive their husbands, but they are too tender-hearted to make them unhappy by telling them the truth.

Nature . . . has buried truth deep in the bottom of the sea.
                                                    —*Democritus.*

'Tis strange—but true; for truth is always strange,
Stranger than fiction.
                                                    —*Byron.*

TURKEYS

"Ah," says the Christmas guest. "How I wish I could sit down to a Christmas dinner with one of those turkeys we raised on the farm, when I was a boy, as the central figure!"

"Well," says the host, "you never can tell. This may be one of them."—*Life.*

TUTORS

A tutor who tooted a flute
Tried to teach two young tooters to toot.
    Said the two to the tutor,
    "Is it harder to toot, or
To tutor two tutors to toot?"
                                                    —*Carolyn Wells.*

TWINS

"Faith, Mrs. O'Hara, how d' ye till thim twins aparrt?"

"Aw, 't is aisy—I sticks me finger in Dinnis's mouth, an' if he bites I know it's Moike."—*Harvard Lampoon.*

UMBRELLAS

A man left his umbrella in the stand in a hotel recently, with a card bearing the following inscription attached to it. "This umbrella belong to a man who can deal a blow of 250 pounds weight. I shall be back in ten minutes." On returning to seek his property he found in its place a card thus inscribed: "This card was left here by a man who can run twelve miles an hour. I shall not be back."

A reputable citizen had left four umbrellas to be repaired. At noon he had luncheon in a restaurant, and as he was departing he absent-mindedly started to take an umbrella from a hook near his hat.

"That's mine, sir," said a woman at the next table.

He apologized and went out. When he was going home in a street car with his four repaired umbrellas, the woman he had seen in the restaurant got in. She glanced from him to his umbrellas and said:

"I see you had a good day."

"That's a swell umbrella you carry."

"Isn't it?"

"Did you come by it honestly?"

"I haven't quite figured out. It started to rain the other day and I stepped into a doorway to wait till it stopped. Then I saw a young fellow coming along with a nice large umbrella, and I thought if he was going as far as my house I would be the shelter of his umbershoot. So I stepped out and asked: 'Where are you going with that umbrella, young fellow?' and he dropped the umbrella and ran."

One day a man exhibited a handsome umbrella. "It's wonderful how I make things last," he exclaimed. "Look at this umbrella, now. I bought it eleven years ago. Since then I had it recovered twice. I had new ribs put in in 1910, and last month I exchanged it for a new one in a restaurant. And here it is—as good as new."

VALUE

"The trouble with father," said the gilded youth, "is that he has no idea of the value of money."

"You don't mean to imply that he is a spendthrift?"

"Not at all. But he puts his money away and doesn't appear to have any appreciation of all the things he might buy with it."

VANITY

McGorry—"I'll buy yez no new hat, d' yez moind thot? Ye are vain enough ahlriddy."

Mrs. McGorry—"Me vain? Oi'm not! Shure, Oi don't t'ink mesilf half as good lookin' as Oi am."

"Of course," said a suffragette lecturer, "I admit that women are vain and men are not. There are a thousand proofs that this is so. Why, the necktie of the handsomest man in the room is even now up the back of his collar." There were six men present and each of them put his hand gently behind his neck.

A New York woman of great beauty called one day upon a friend, bringing with her her eleven-year-old daughter, who gives promise of becoming as great a beauty as her mother.

It chanced that the callers were shown into a room where the friend had been receiving a milliner, and there were several beautiful hats lying about. During the conversation the little girl amused herself by examining the milliner's creations. Of the number that she tried on, she seemed particularly pleased with a large black affair which set off her light hair charmingly. Turning to her mother, the little girl said:

"I look just like you now, Mother, don't I?"

"'Sh!" cautioned the mother, with uplifted finger. "Don't be vain, dear."

That which makes the vanity of others unbearable to us is that which wounds our own.—*La Rochefoucauld.*

VERSATILITY

A clergyman who advertised for an organist received this reply:

"*Dear Sir*:

"I notice you have a vacancy for an organist and music teacher, either lady or gentleman. Having been both for several years I beg to apply for the position."

VOICE

A lanky country youth entered the crossroads general store to order some groceries. He was seventeen years old and was passing through that stage of adolescence during which a boy seems all hands and feet, and his vocal organs, rapidly developing, are wont to cause his voice to undergo sudden and involuntary changes from high treble to low bass.

In an authoritative rumbling bass voice he demanded of the busy clerk, "Give me a can of corn" (then, his voice suddenly changing to a shrill falsetto, he continued) "and a sack of flour."

"Well, don't be in a hurry. I can't wait on both of you at once," snapped the clerk.

Aspiring Vocalist—"Professor, do you think I will ever be able to do anything with my voice?"

Perspiring Teacher—"Well it might come in handy in case of fire or shipwreck."—*Cornell Widow.*

The devil hath not, in all his quiver's choice,
An arrow for the heart like a sweet voice.

—*Byron.*

WAGES

"Me gotta da good job," said Pietro, as he gave the monkey a little more line after grinding out on his organ a selection from "Santa Lucia." "Getta forty dollar da month and eata myself; thirty da month if da boss eata me."

Commenting on the comparatively small salaries allowed by Congress for services rendered in the executive branch of the Government and the more liberal pay of some of the officials, a man in public life said:

"It reminds me of the way a gang of laborers used to be paid down my way. The money was thrown at a ladder, and what stuck to the rungs went to the workers, while that which fell through went to the bosses."

A certain prominent lawyer of Toronto is in the habit of lecturing his office staff from the junior partner down, and Tommy, the office boy, comes in for his full share of the admonition. That his words were appreciated was made evident to the lawyer by a conversation between Tommy and another office boy on the same floor which he recently overheard.

"Wotcher wages?" asked the other boy.

"Ten thousand a year," replied Tommy.

"Aw, g'wan!"

"Sure," insisted Tommy, unabashed. "Four dollars a week in cash, an' de rest in legal advice."

While an Irishman was gazing in the window of a Washington bookstore the following sign caught his eye:

DICKENS' WORKS

ALL THIS WEEK FOR

ONLY $4.00

"The divvle he does!" exclaimed Pat in disgust. "The dirty scab!"

The difference between wages and salary is—when you receive wages you save two dollars a month, when you receive salary you borrow two dollars a month.

He is well paid that is well satisfied.—*Shakespeare.*

The ideal social state is not that in which each gets an equal amount of wealth, but in which each gets in proportion to his contribution to the general stock.—*Henry George.*

WAITERS

Recipe for a waiter:

Stuff a hired dress-suit case with an effort to please,
  Add a half-dozen stumbles and trips;
Remove his right thumb from the cranberry sauce,
  Roll in crumbs, melted butter and tips.

—Life.

WAR

"Flag of truce, Excellency."

"Well, what do the revolutionists want?"

"They would like to exchange a couple of Generals for a can of condensed milk."

If you favor war, dig a trench in your backyard, fill it half full of water, crawl into it, and stay there for a day or two without anything to eat, get a lunatic to shoot at you with a brace of revolvers and a machine gun, and you will have something just as good, and you will save your country a great deal of expense.

"Who are those people who are cheering?" asked the recruit as the soldiers marched to the train.

"Those," replied the veteran, "are the people who are not going."—*Puck*.

> He who did well in war, just earns the right
> To begin doing well in peace.
> —*Robert Browning.*

A great and lasting war can never be supported on this principle [patriotism] alone. It must be aided by a prospect of interest, or some reward.—*George Washington.*

See also Arbitration, International; European War.

WARNINGS

Pietro had drifted down to Florida and was working with a gang at railroad construction. He had been told to beware of rattlesnakes, but assured that they would always give the warning rattle before striking.

One hot day he was eating his noon luncheon on a pine log when he saw a big rattler coiled a few feet in front of him. He eyed the serpent and began to lift his legs over the log. He had barely got them out of the way when the snake's fangs hit the bark beneath him.

"Son of a guna!" yelled Pietro. "Why you no ringa da bell?"

WASHINGTON, GEORGE

A Barnegat schoolma'am had been telling her pupils something about George Washington, and finally she asked:

"Can any one now tell me which Washington was—a great general or a great admiral"

The small son of a fisherman raised his hand, and she signaled him to speak.

"He was a great general," said the boy. "I seen a picture of him crossing the Delaware, and no great admiral would put out from shore standing up in a skiff."

A Scotsman visiting America stood gazing at a fine statue of George Washington, when an American approached.

"That was a great and good man, Sandy," said the American; "a lie never passed his lips."

"Weel," said the Scot, "I praysume he talked through his nose like the rest of ye."

WASPS

The wasp cannot speak, but when he says "Drop it," in his own inimitable way, neither boy nor man shows any remarkable desire to hold on.

WASTE

The automobile rushed down the road—huge, gigantic, sublime. Over the fence hung the woman who works hard and long—her husband is at the cafe and she has thirteen little ones. (An unlucky number.) Suddenly upon the thirteenth came the auto, unseeing, slew him, and hummed on, unknowing. The woman who works hard and long rushed forward with hands, hands made rough by toil, upraised. She paused and stood inarticulate—a goddess, a giantess. Then she hurled forth these words of derision, of despair: "Mon Dieu! And I'd just washed him!"—*Literally translated from Le Sport of Paris.*

A Boston physician tells of the case of a ten-year-old boy who, by reason of an attack of fever, became deaf. The physician could afford the lad little relief, so the boy applied himself to the task of learning the deaf-and-dumb alphabet. The other members of his family, too, acquired a working knowledge of the alphabet, in order that they might converse with the unfortunate youngster.

During the course of the next few months, however, Tommy's hearing suddenly returned to him, assisted no doubt by a slight operation performed by the physician.

Every one was, of course, delighted, particularly the boy's mother, who one day exclaimed:

"Oh, Tommy, isn't it delightful to talk to and hear us again?"

"Yes," assented Tommy, but with a degree of hesitation: "but here we've all learned the sign language, and we can't find any more use for it!"

WEALTH

If you want to make a living you have to work for it, while if you want to get rich you must go about it in some other way.

The traditional fool and his money are lucky ever to have got together in the first place.—*Puck.*

He that is proud of riches is a fool. For if he be exalted above his neighbors because he hath more gold, how much inferior is he to a gold mine!—*Jeremy Taylor.*

WEATHER

"How did you find the weather in London?" asked the friend of the returned traveler.

"You don't have to find the weather in London," replied the traveler. "It bumps into you at every corner."

An American and a Scotsman were discussing the cold experienced in winter in the North of Scotland.

"Why, it's nothing at all compared to the cold we have in the States," said the American. "I can recollect one winter when a sheep, jumping from a hillock into a field, became suddenly frozen on the way, and stuck in the air like a mass of ice."

"But, man," exclaimed the Scotsman, "the law of gravity wouldn't allow that."

"I know that," replied the tale-pitcher. "But the law of gravity was frozen, too!"

Two commercial travelers, one from London and one from New York, were discussing the weather in their respective countries.

The Englishman said that English weather had one great fault—its sudden changes.

"A person may take a walk one day," he said, "attired in a light summer suit, and still feel quite warm. Next day he needs an overcoat."

"That's nothing," said the American. "My two friends, Johnson and Jones, were once having an argument. There were eight or nine inches of snow on the ground. The argument got heated, and Johnson picked up a snowball and threw it at Jones from a distance of not more than five yards. During the transit of that snowball, belive me or not, as you like, the weather changed and became hot and summer like, and Jones, instead of being hit with a snowball, was—er—scalded with hot water!"

Ex-President Taft on one of his trips was playing golf on a western links when he noticed that he had a particularly good caddie, an old man of some sixty years, as they have on the Scottish links.

"And what do you do in winter?" asked the President.

"Such odd jobs as I can pick up, sir," replied the man.

"Not much chance for caddying then, I suppose?" asked the President.

"No, sir, there is not," replied the man with a great deal of warmth. "When theres' no frost there's sure to be snow, and when there's no snow there's frost, and when there's neither there's sure to be rain. And the few days when it's fine they're always Sundays."

On the way to the office of his publishers one crisp fall morning, James Whitcomb Riley met an unusually large number of acquaintances who commented conventionally upon the fine weather. This unremitting applause amused him. When greeted at the office with "Nice day, Mr. Riley," he smiled broadly.

"Yes," he agreed. "Yes, I've heard it very highly spoken of."

The darky in question had simmered in the heat of St. Augustine all his life, and was decoyed by the report that colored men could make as much as $4 a day in Duluth.

He headed North in a seersucker suit and into a hard winter. At Chicago, while waiting for a train, he shivered in an engine room, and on the way to Duluth sped by miles of snow fields.

On arriving he found the mercury at 18 below and promptly lost the use of his hands. Then his feet stiffened and he lost all sensation.

They picked him up and took him to a crematory for unknown dead. After he had been in the oven for awhile somebody opened the door for inspection. Rastus came to and shouted:

"Shut dat do' and close dat draff!"

There was a small boy in Quebec,
Who was buried in snow to his neck;
  When they said, "Are you friz?"
  He replied, "Yes, I is—
But we don't call this cold in Quebec."
                              —*Rudyard Kipling.*

Sunshine is delicious, rain is refreshing, wind braces up, snow is exhilarating; there is really no such thing as bad weather, only different kinds of good weather.—*Ruskin.*

WEDDING ANNIVERSARIES

Uncle Ephraim had put on a clean collar and his best coat, and was walking majestically up and down the street.

"Are you working to-day, Uncle?" asked somebody.

"No, suh. I'se celebratin' mah golden weddin' suh."

"You were married fifty years ago to-day, then!"

"Yes, suh."

"Well, why isn't your wife helping you to celebrate?"

"Mah present wife, suh," replied Uncle Ephraim with dignity, "ain't got nothin' to do with it."

WEDDING PRESENTS

Among the presents lately showered upon a dusky bride in a rural section of Virginia, was one that was a gift of an old woman with whom both bride and groom were great favorites.

Some time ago, it appears, the old woman accumulated a supply of cardboard mottoes, which she worked and had framed as occasion arose.

So it happened that in a neat combination of blues and reds, suspended by a cord of orange, there hung over the table whereon the other presents were displayed for the delectation of the wedding guests, this motto:

FIGHT ON; FIGHT EVER.

WEDDINGS

An actor who was married recently for the third time, and whose bride had been married once before, wrote across the bottom of the wedding invitations: "Be sure and come; this is no amateur performance."

A wealthy young woman from the west was recently wedded to a member of the nobility of England, and the ceremony occurred in the most fashionable of London churches—St. George's.

Among the guests was a cousin of the bride, as sturdy an American as can be imagined. He gave an interesting summary of the wedding when asked by a girl friend whether the marriage was a happy one.

"Happy? I should say it was," said the cousin. "The bride was happy, her mother was overjoyed, Lord Stickleigh, the groom, was in ecstasies, and his creditors, I understand, were in a state of absolute bliss."—*Edwin Tarrisse.*

The best man noticed that one of the wedding guests, a gloomy-looking young man, did not seem to be enjoying himself. He was wandering about as though he had lost his last friend. The best man took it upon himself to cheer ·him up.

"Er—have you kissed the bride?" he asked by way of introduction.

"Not lately," replied the gloomy one with a far-away expression.

The curate of a large and fashionable church was endeavoring to teach the significance of white to a Sunday-school class.

"Why," said he, "does a bride invariably desire to be clothed in white at her marriage?"

As no one answered, he explained. "White," said he, "stands for joy, and the wedding-day is the most joyous occasion of a woman's life."

A small boy queried, "Why do the men all wear black?"—*M. J. Moor.*

Lilly May came to her mistress. "Ah would like a week's vacation, Miss Annie," she said, in her soft Negro accent; "Ah wants to be married."

Lillie had been a good girl, so her mistress gave her the week's vacation, a white dress, a veil and a plum-cake.

Promptly at the end of the week Lillie returned, radiant. "Oh, Miss Annie!" she exclaimed, "Ah was the mos' lovely bride! Ma dress was perfec', ma veil mos' lovely, the cake mos' good! An' oh, the dancin' an' the eatin'!"

"Well, Lillie, this sounds delightful," said her mistress, "but you have left out the point of your story—I hope you have a good husband."

Lillie's tone changed to indignation: "Now, Miss Annie, what yo' think? Tha' darn nigger nebber turn up!"

There is living in Illinois a solemn man who is often funny without meaning to be. At the time of his wedding, he lived in a town some distance from the home of the bride. The wedding was to be at her house. On the eventful day the solemn man started for the station, but on the way met the village grocer, who talked so entertainingly that the bridegroom missed his train.

Naturally he was in a "state." Something must be done, and done quickly. So he sent the following telegram:

Don't marry till I come.—HENRY.

—*Howard Morse.*

In all the wedding cake, hope is the sweetest of the plums.

—*Douglas Jerrold.*

WEIGHTS AND MEASURES

"Didn't I tell ye to feed that cat a pound of meat every day until ye had her fat?" demanded an Irish shopkeeper, nodding toward a sickly, emaciated cat that was slinking through the store.

"Ye did thot," replied the assistant, "an' I've just been after feedin' her a pound of meat this very minute."

"Faith, an' I don't believe ye. Bring me the scales."

The poor cat was lifted into the scales. They balanced at exactly one pound.

"There!" exclaimed the assistant triumphantly. "Didn't I tell ye she'd had her pound of meat?"

"That's right," admitted the boss, scratching his head. "That's yer pound of meat all right. But"—suddenly looking up—"where the divvil is the cat?"

WELCOMES

When Ex-President Taft was on his transcontinental tour, American flags and Taft pictures were in evidence everywhere. Usually the Taft pictures contained a word of welcome under them. Those who heard the President's laugh ring out will not soon forget the western city which, directly under the barred window of the city lockup, displayed a Taft picture with the legend "Welcome" on it.—*Hugh Morist.*

Come in the evening, or come in the morning,
Come when you're looked for, or come without warning,
Kisses and welcome you'll find here before you,
And the oftener you come here the more I'll adore you.
—*Thomas O. Davis.*

WEST, THE

EASTERN LADY (traveling in Montana)—"The idea of calling this the 'Wild-West'! Why, I never saw such politeness anywhere."

COWBOY—"We're allers perlite to ladies, ma'am."

EASTERN LADY—"Oh, as for that, there is plenty of politeness everywhere. But I refer to the men. Why, in New York the men behave horribly towards one another, but here they treat one another as delicately as gentlemen in a drawing-room."

COWBOY—"Yes, ma'am; it's safer."—*Abbie C. Dixon.*

WHISKY

This is from an Irish priest's sermon, as quoted in Samuel M. Hussey's "Reminiscences of an Irish Land Agent": "'It's whisky makes you bate your wives; it's whisky makes your homes desolate; it's whisky makes you shoot your landlords, and'—with emphasis, as he thumped the pulpit—'it's whisky makes you miss them.'"

In a recent trial of a "bootlegger" in western Kentucky a witness testified that he had purchased some "squirrel" whisky from the defendant.

"Squirrel whisky?" questioned the court.

"Yes, you know: the kind that makes you talk nutty and want to climb trees."

General Carter, who went to Texas in command of the regulars sent south for maneuvers along the Mexican border, tells this story of an old Irish soldier: The march had been a long and tiresome one, and as the bivouac was being made for the night, the captain noticed that Pat was looking very much fatigued. Thinking that a small drop of whisky might do him good, the captain called Pat aside and said, "Pat, will you have a wee drink of whisky?" Pat made no answer, but folded his arms in a reverential manner and gazed upward. The captain repeated the question several times, but no answer from Pat, who stood silent and motionless, gazing devoutly into the sky. Finally the captain, taking him by the shoulder and giving him a vigorous shake said: "Pat, why don't you answer? I said, 'Pat, will you have a drink of whisky?'" After looking around in considerable astonishment Pat replied: "And is it yez, captain? Begorrah and I thought it was an angel spakin' to me."

See also Drinking.

WHISKY BREATH

See Breath.

WIDOWS

During the course of conversation between two ladies in a hotel parlor one said to the other: "Are you married?"

"No, I am not," replied the other. "Are you?"

"No," was the reply, "I, too, am on the single list," adding: "Strange that two such estimable women as ourselves should have been overlooked in the great matrimonial market! Now that lady," pointing to another who was passing, "has been widowed four times, two of her husbands having been cremated. The woman," she continued, "is plain and uninteresting, and yet she has them to burn."

WIND

VISITOR—"What became of that other windmill that was here last year?"

NATIVE—"There was only enough wind for one, so we took it down."

Whichever way the wind doth blow
Some heart is glad to have it so;
Then blow it east, or blow it west,
The wind that blows, that wind is best.
—*Caroline A. Mason.*

WINDFALLS

A Nebraska man was carried forty miles by a cyclone and dropped in a widow's front yard. He married the widow and returned home worth about $30,000 more than when he started.

WINE

When our thirsty souls we steep,
Every sorrow's lull'd to sleep.
Talk of monarchs! we are then
Richest, happiest, first of men.

When I drink, my heart refines
And rises as the cup declines;
Rises in the genial flow,
That none but social spirits know.

To-day we'll haste to quaff our wine,
As if to-morrow ne'er should shine;
But if to-morrow comes, why then—
We'll haste to quaff our wine again.

Let me, oh, my budding vine,
Spill no other blood than thine.
Yonder brimming goblet see,
That alone shall vanquish me.

I pray thee, by the gods above,
Give me the mighty bowl I love,
And let me sing, in wild delight,
"I will—I will be mad to-night!"

When Father Time swings round his scythe,
Intomb me 'neath the bounteous vine,
So that its juices red and blythe,
May cheer these thirsty bones of mine.

—*Eugene Field.*

See also Drinking.

WISHES

George Washington drew a long sigh and said: "Ah wish Ah had a hundred watermillions."

Dixie's eyes lighted. "Hum! Dat would suttenly be fine! An' if yo' had a hundred watermillions would yo' gib me fifty?"

"No, Ah wouldn't."

"Wouldn't yo' give me twenty-five?"

No, Ah wouldn't gib yo' no twenty-five."

Dixie gazed with reproachful eyes at his close-fisted friend. "Seems to me, you's powahful stingy, George Washington," he said, and then continued in a heartbroken voice. "Wouldn't yo' gib me one?"

"No, Ah wouldn't gib yo' one. Look a' hear, nigger! Are yo' so good for nuffen lazy dat yo' cahn't wish fo' yo' own watermillions?"

"Man wants but little here below
  Nor wants that little long,"
'Tis not with me exactly so;
  But 'tis so in the song.
My wants are many, and, if told,
  Would muster many a score;
And were each a mint of gold,
  I still should long for more.

—*John Quincy Adams.*

WITNESSES

"The trouble is," said Wilkins as he talked the matter over with his counsel, "that in the excitement of the moment I admitted that I had been going too fast, and wasn't paying any attention to the road just before the collision. I'm afraid that admission is going to prove costly."

"Don't worry about that," said his lawyer. "I'll bring seven witnesses to testify that they wouldn't belive you under oath."

On his eighty-fourth birthday, Paul Smith, the veteran Adirondack hotel-keeper, who started life as a guide and died owning a million dollars' worth of forest land, was talking about boundary disputes with an old friend.

"Didn't you hear of the lawsuit over a title that I had with Jones down in Malone last summer?" asked Paul. The friend had not heard.

"Well," said Paul, "it was this way. I sat in the court room before the case opened with my witnesses around me. Jones busted in, stopped, looked my witnesses over carefully, and said: 'Paul, are those your witnesses?' 'They are,' said I. 'Then you win,' said he. 'I've had them witnesses twice myself.' "

WIVES

"Father," said a little boy, "had Solomon seven hundred wives?"

"I believe so, my son," said the father.

"Well, father, was he the man who said, 'Give me liberty or give me death?' "—*Town Topics.*

A charitable lady was reading the Old Testament to an aged woman who lived at the home for old people, and chanced upon the passage concerning Solomon's household.

"Had Solomon really seven hundred wives?" inquired the old woman, after reflection.

"Oh, yes, Mary! It is so stated in the Bible."

"Lor', mum!" was the comment. "What privileges them early Christians had!"

CASEY—"Now, phwat wu'u'd ye do in a case loike thot?"
CLANCY—"Loike phwat?"
CASEY—"Th' walkin' diligate tils me to stroike, an' me ould woman orders me to ke-ape on wurrkin'."

Governor Vardaman, of Mississippi, was taken to task because he had made a certain appointment, a friend maintaining that another man should have received the place. The governor listened quietly and then said:

"Did I ever tell you about Mose Williams? One day Mose sought his employer, an acquaintance of mine, and inquired:

" 'Say, boss; is yo' gwine to town t'morrer?"

" 'I think so. Why?'

" 'Well, hit's dishaway. Me an' Easter Johnson's gwine to git mahred, an' Ah 'lowed to ax yo' ter get a pair of licenses fo' me.'

" 'I shall be delighted to oblige you, Mose, and I hope you will be very happy.'

"The next day when the gentleman rode up to his house the old man was waiting for him.

" 'Did you git 'em, boss?' he inquired eagerly.

" 'Yes, here they are.'

"Mose looked at them ruefully, shaking his head. 'Ah'm po'ful sorry yo' got 'em, boss!'

" 'What's the matter? Has Easter gone back on you?'

" 'It ain't dat, boss. Ah done changed mah min'. Ah'm gwine to mahry Sophie Coleman, dat freckled-faced yaller girl what works up to Mis' Mason's, for she sholy can cook!'

" 'Well, I'll try and have the name changed for you, but it will cost you fifty cents more.'

"Mose assented, somewhat dubiously, and the gentleman had the change made. Again he found Mose waiting for him.

" 'Wouldn't change hit, boss, would he?'

" 'Certainly he changed it. I simply had to pay him the fifty cents.'

" 'Ah was hopin' he wouldn't do it. Mah min's made up to mahry Easter Johnson after all.'

" 'You crazy nigger, you don't know what you do want. What made you change your mind again?'

" 'Well, boss, Ah been thinkin' it over an' Ah jes' 'lowed dar wasn't fifty cents wuth ob diff'runce in dem two niggers.' "

A wife is a woman who is expected to purchase without means, and sew on buttons before they come off.

"What are you cutting out of the paper?"

"About a California man securing a divorce because his wife went through his pockets."

"What are you going to do about it?"

"Put it in my pocket."

A woman missionary in China was taking tea with a mandarin's eight wives. The Chinese ladies examined her clothing, her hair, her teeth, and so on, but her feet especially amazed them.

"Why," cried one, "you can walk or run as well as a man!"

"Yes, to be sure," said the missionary.

"Can you ride a horse and swim, too?"

"Yes."

"Then you must be as strong as a man!"

"I am."

"And you wouldn't let a man beat you—not even if he was your husband—would you?"

"Indeed I wouldn't," the missionary said.

The mandarin's eight wives looked at one another, nodding their heads. Then the oldest said softly:

"Now I understand why the foreign devil never has more than one wife. He is afraid!"—*Western Christian Advocate.*

PAT—"I hear your woife is sick, Moike."

MIKE—"She is thot."

PAT—"Is it dangerous she is?"

MIKE—"Divil a bit. She's too weak to be dangerous any more!"

SON—"Say, mama, father broke this vase before he went out."

MOTHER—"My beautiful majolica vase! Wait till he comes back, that's all."

SON—"May I stay up till he does?"

"Because a fellow has six talking machines," said the boarder who wants to be an end man, "it doesn't follow that he is a Mormon."

It was a wizened little man who appeared before the judge and charged his wife with cruel and abusive treatment. His better half was a big, square-jawed woman with a determined eye.

"In the first place, where did you meet this woman who, according to your story, has treated you so dreadfully?" asked the judge.

"Well," replied the little man, making a brave attempt to glare defiantly at his wife, "I never did meet her. She just kind of overtook me."

"Harry, love," exclaimed Mrs. Knowall to her husband, on his return one evening from the office, "I have b-been d-dreadfully insulted!"

"Insulted?" exclaimed Harry, love. "By whom?"

"B-by your m-mother," answered the young wife, bursting into tears.

"My mother, Flora? Nonsense! She's miles away!"

Flora dried her tears.

"I'll tell you all about it, Harry, love," she said. "A letter came to you this morning, addressed in your mother's writing, so, of course, I—I opened it."

"Of course," repeated Harry, love, dryly.

"It—it was written to you all the way through. Do you understand?"

"I understand. But where does the insult to you come in?"

"It—it came in the p-p-postscript," cried the wife, bursting into fresh floods of briny. "It s-said: 'P-P-P. S.—D-dear Flora, d-don't f-fail to give this l-letter to Harry. I w-want him to have it.'"

"By jove, I left my purse under the pillow!"

"Oh, well, your servent is honest, isn't she?"

"That's just it. She'll take it to my wife."

There swims no goose so gray, but soon or late
She finds some honest gander for her mate.

—*Pope.*

A clerk showed forty patterns of ginghams to a man whose wife had sent him to buy some for her for Christmas, and at every pattern the man said: "My wife said she didn't want anything like that."

The clerk put the last piece back on the shelf. "Sir," he said, "you don't want gingham. What you want is a divorce."

Maids are May when they are maids, but the sky changes when they are wives.—*Shakespeare.*

> In the election of a wife, as in
> A project of war, to err but once is
> To be undone forever.
> —*Thomas Middleton.*

> Of earthly goods, the best is a good wife;
> A bad, the bitterest curse of human life.
> —*Simonides.*

See also Domestic finance; Suffragettes; Talkers; Temper; Woman suffrage.

WOMAN

Woman—the only sex which attaches more importance to what's on its head than to what's in it.

"How very few statues there are of real women."
"Yes! it's hard to get them to look right."
"How so?"
"A woman remaining still and saying nothing doesn't seem true to life."

> "Oh, woman! in our hours of ease
> Uncertain, coy, and hard to please"—
> So wrote Sir Walter long ago.
> But how, pray, could he really know?
> If woman fair he strove to please,
> Where did he get his "hours of ease"?
> —*George B. Morewood.*

Miss Scribble—"The heroine of my next story is to be one of those modern advanced girls who have ideas of their own and don't want to get married."

The Colonel (politely)—"Ah, indeed, I don't think I ever met that type."—*Life*.

> You are a dear, sweet girl,
> God bless you and keep you—
> Wish I could afford to do so.

Here's to man—he can afford anything he can get. Here's to woman—she can afford anything that she can get a man to get for her.—*George Ade*.

> Here's to the soldier and his arms,
> Fall in, men, fall in;
> Here's to woman and her arms,
> Fall in, men, fall in!

Most Southerners are gallant. An exception is the Georgian who gave his son this advice:

"My boy, never run after a woman or a street car—there will be another one along in a minute or two."

> Here's to the maid of bashful fifteen;
> Here's to the widow of fifty;
> Here's to the flaunting, extravagant queen;
> And here's to the housewife that's thrifty.
>   Chorus:
>   Let the toast pass,—
>   Drink to the lass,
> I'll warrant she'll prove an excuse for the glass.
>   —*Sheridan*.

> Here's to the ladies, the good, young ladies;
> But not too good, for the good die young,
> And we want no dead ones.
> And here's to the good old ladies,
> But not too old, for we want no dyed ones.

When a woman repulses, beware. When a woman beckons, bewarer.—*Henriette Corkland.*

The young woman had spent a busy day.

She had browbeaten fourteen salespeople, bullyragged a floor-walker, argued victoriously with a milliner, laid down the law to a modiste, nipped in the bud a taxi chauffeur's attempt to overcharge her, made a street car conductor stop the car in the middle of a block for her, discharged her maid and engaged another, and otherwise refused to allow herself to be imposed upon.

Yet she did not smile that evening when a young man begged:

"Let me be your protector through life!"

I am very fond of the company of ladies. I like their beauty, I like their delicacy, I like their vivacity, and I like their silence.—*Samuel Johnson.*

> Auld Nature swears, the lovely dears
> Her noblest work she classes, O:
> Her 'prentice hand she tried on man,
> An' then she made the lasses, O.
>
> —*Burns.*

> Not from his head was woman took,
> As made her husband to o'erlook;
> Not from his feet, as one designed
> The footstool of the stronger kind;
> But fashioned for himself, a bride;
> An equal, taken from his side.
>
> —*Charles Wesley.*

See also Mice; Mothers; Smoking; Suffragettes; Wives; Woman suffrage.

WOMAN SUFFRAGE

Woman Voter—"Now, I may as well be frank with you. I absolutely refuse to vote the same ticket as that horrid Jones woman."

Kate Douglas Wiggin was asked how she stood on the vote for women question. She replied she didn't "stand at all," and told a story about a New England farmer's wife who had no very romantic ideas about the opposite sex, and who, hurrying from churn to sink, from sink to shed, and back to the kitchen stove, was asked if she wanted to vote. "No, I certainly don't! I say if there's one little thing that the men folks can do alone, for goodness sakes let 'em do it!" she replied.

Mr. E. N. Quire—"What are those women mauling that man for?"

Mrs. Henballot—"He insulted us by saying that the suffrage movement destroyed our naturally timid sweetness and robbed us of all our gentleness."

"Did you cast your vote, Aunty?"

"Oh, yes! Isn't it grand? A real nice gentleman with a beautiful moustache and yellow spats marked my ballot for me. I know I should have marked it myself, but it seemed to please him greatly."

"Does your wife want to vote?"

"No. She wants a larger town house, a villa on the sea coast and a new limousine car every six months. I'd be pleased most to death if she could fix her attention on a smaller matter like the vote."

"What you want, I suppose, is to vote, just like the men do."

"Certainly not," replied Mrs. Baring-Banners. "If we couldn't do any better than that there would be no use of our voting."

"There's only one thing I can think of to head off this suffrage movement," said the mere man.

"What is that?" asked his wife.

"Make the legal age for voting thirty-five instead of twenty-one."—*Catholic Universe.*

MAMIE—"I believe in woman's rights."

GERTIE—"Then you think every woman should have a vote?"

MAMIE—"No; but I think every woman should have a voter."—*The Woman's Journal.*

During the Presidential campaign the question of woman suffrage was much discussed among women pro and con, and at an afternoon tea the conversation turned that way between the women guests.

"Are you a woman suffragist?" asked the one who was most interested.

"Indeed, I am not," replied the other most emphatically.

"Oh, that's too bad, but just supposing you were, whom would you support in the present campaign?"

"The same man I've always supported, of course," was the apt reply—"my husband."

See also Suffragettes.

WOMEN'S CLUBS

See Clubs.

WORDS

See Authors.

WORK

All work and no play
Makes Jack surreptitiously gay.

"Wot cheer, Alf? Yer lookin' sick; wot is it?"

"Work! nuffink but work, work, work, from mornin' till night!"

" 'Ow long 'ave yer been at it?"

"Start tomorrow."—*Punch.*

Several men were discussing the relative importance and difficulty of mental and physical work, and one of them told the following experience:

"Several years ago, a tramp, one of the finest specimens of physical manhood that I have ever seen, dropped into my yard and asked me for work. The first day I put him to work helping to move some heavy rocks, and he easily did as much work as any two other men, and yet was as fresh as could be at the end of the day.

"The next morning, having no further use for him, I told him he could go; but he begged so hard to remain that I let him go into the cellar and empty some apple barrels, putting the good apples into one barrel and throwing away the rotten ones—about a half hour's work.

"At the end of two hours he was still in the cellar, and I went down to see what the trouble was. I found him only half through, but almost exhausted, beads of perspiration on his brow.

" 'What's the matter?' I asked. 'Surely that work isn't hard.' "

" 'No not hard,' he replied. 'But the strain on the judgment is *awful.*' "

See also Rest cure.

WORMS

A country girl was home from college for the Christmas holidays and the old folks were having a reception in her honor. During the event she brought out some of her new gowns to show to the guests. Picking up a beautiful silk creation she held it up before the admiring crowd.

"Isn't this perfectly gorgeous!" she exclaimed. "Just think, it came from a poor little insignificant worm!"

Her hard-working father looked a moment, then he turned and said: "Yes, darn it, an' I'm that worm!"

YALE UNIVERSITY

The new cook, who had come into the household during the holidays, asked her mistress:

"Where ban your son? I not seeing him round no more."

"My son," replied the mistress pridefully. "Oh, he has gone

back to Yale. He could only get away long enough to stay until New Year's day, you see. I miss him dreadfully, tho."

"Yas, I knowing yoost how you feel. My broder, he ban in yail sax times since Thanksgiving."

YONKERS

An American took an Englishman to a theater. An actor in the farce, about to die, exclaimed: "Please, dear wife, don't bury me in Yonkers!"

The Englishman turned to his friend and said: "I say, old chap, what *are* yonkers?"

"YOU"

Here's to the world, the merry old world,
To its days both bright and blue;
Here's to our future, be it what it may,
And here's to my best—that's you!

ZONES

TEACHER—"How many zones has the earth?"
PUPIL—"Five."
TEACHER—"Correct. Name them."
PUPIL—"Temperate zone, intemperate, canal, horrid, and o."

—Life.